Progress in IS

More information about this series at http://www.springer.com/series/10440

Bernd Blöbaum

Editor

Trust and Communication in a Digitized World

Models and Concepts of Trust Research

Springer

Editor
Bernd Blöbaum
University of Münster
Münster, Germany

ISSN 2196-8705   ISSN 2196-8713   (electronic)
Progress in IS
ISBN 978-3-319-80263-3   ISBN 978-3-319-28059-2   (eBook)
DOI 10.1007/978-3-319-28059-2

Springer Cham Heidelberg New York Dordrecht London
© Springer International Publishing Switzerland 2016
Softcover reprint of the hardcover 1st edition 2016

Printed on acid-free paper

Springer International Publishing AG Switzerland is part of Springer Science+Business Media (www.springer.com)

Preface

"Trust dies but mistrust blossoms." (Sophocles)

Often, not until times of crisis do we realize how fragile trust relations are. Normally, we experience a state of intimacy or familiarity with partners and friends, but also vis-à-vis organizations and institutions. We do not realize, however, that the banking and financial system are fraught with risk. As regards science, we do not expect scientific misconduct. Moreover, before the revelations by Edward Snowden, it seemed impossible that intelligence services would spy on the phone and mail traffic of private people and politicians. Finally and most recently, a respectable German automobile manufacturer has been caught manipulating emission tests, thereby destroying its customers' trust. While living and acting within an environment of trustworthiness vis-à-vis people, organizations, and institutions, only crises reveal the risks entailed. That is when intimacy and familiarity—conditions that neglect risk—turn into trust, and risk is perceived as a central element to this relation. Thus, trust constitutes a relationship shaped by risk, in which the person who trusts makes him- or herself dependent on the person he or she trusts.

Without trust, societies, organizations, and individuals cannot act. Trust functions as a social glue. It creates options for decision making and actions. In previous years, academia has given more attention to trust as a scientific category. It has been a focus of research in management studies, psychology, and sociology, as well as in communication and media studies, sports sciences, law, political studies, history, religious studies, and information science. Depending on the perspective, trust is conceptualized as a quality inherent to relationships, a state, or an individual disposition.

The influence of digitization on personal relationships, on the actions of organizations, and on society as a whole is unparalleled in recent years. The Internet has transformed work processes within the economic system along with the relation between media and their audience and the notions of privacy in our network society—to name just a few examples.

Digitization transforms the conditions for creating and maintaining trust. Manipulations within the financial sector, the surveillance of data traffic, or revelations of plagiarism and forgery in science are closely related to digitization. On the one hand, the Internet provides new opportunities for manipulation, enhancing breaches of trust. On the other hand, it facilitates access to knowledge and experience. Drawing on the evaluations and comments of others—be they laypeople or experts—reduces the amount of risk inherent in trust-based social actions.

The contributions to this book examine how trust is built and maintained under the conditions of digitization. The chapters revolve around media, sports, science, and the economy as four prototypical fields of research, accompanied by the aspect of social relations. The contributors focus less on presenting empirical findings from trust research in the abovementioned areas. Rather, the authors draw upon models and concepts derived from their analyses of trust in their fields of interest. Digitization challenges trust research to reconsider its conceptualizations of trust, trustworthiness, and trust relations. This book presents insights into this.

Although numerous trust crises illustrate that trust relations have become more fragile in a digitized world, several contributions give evidence that the Internet provides options for enhancing trust. What is more, the Internet has developed equivalent means that have the potential to replace trust. Thus, when it comes to trust relationships, digitization involves not only the question of risk but also of opportunities. Further, the chapters provide insights into the role of antecedents and moderating influences when people evaluate trustworthiness. They reveal which factors influence trust building in personal relationships, within organizations, and within social systems.

Bernd Blöbaum's contribution systematizes—by no means exhaustively—factors on behalf of both trustor and trustee that influence their trust relationship. He distinguishes between various trust objects and factors that have an impact on the evaluation of trustworthiness. Mostly through the example of mass media, the author further reflects upon how digitization is transforming trust relationships and the elements affected by this process. *Anil Kunnel* and *Thorsten Quandt* elaborate on the concepts of relational trust and distrust. Whereas relational trust encourages interactions and helps build relationships, the function of relational distrust is to prevent hazardous relationships. Kunnel and Quandt's model of relational trust and distrust in social relations discloses those elements that contribute to a shared identity and strength of ties—especially under the conditions of network technology.

The chapter by *Katherine Grosser, Valerie Hase*, and *Bernd Blöbaum* focuses on online journalism as a specific field of interest. The authors present a model that takes into account changes with regard to both journalism and recipients. They underline how, as a result of digitization, new elements related to journalistic research and presentation become more important for the recipients' evaluation of journalism's trustworthiness. In general, though, online journalism struggles to prove its trustworthiness. The contribution by *Florian Wintterlin* and *Bernd Blöbaum* is also located within the field of journalism research. The scholars

examine how newsrooms and journalists check the trustworthiness of digital
sources. To present valid information, media rely on credible sources. By means
of digitization, many sources have not just become more easily accessible; newsrooms also receive vast amounts of information whose origin remains unclear. The
authors present a model that systematizes journalism's trust in (digital) sources and
its antecedences. Taking a sociological approach, *Christian Wiencierz* and *Ulrike
Röttger* analyze trust in organizations. With the example of political parties and
nongovernmental organizations, they demonstrate which factors influence the
trustworthiness of organizations, as well as the implications of these results for
organizations' day-to-day business. *Sarah Westphal* and *Bernd Blöbaum* conceptualize trust as a form of social action that only comes into effect under specific
circumstances. According to their argumentation, trust in online information
sources is not an omnipresent phenomenon, but is rather a special type of relationship limited to one individual source and, overall, a rare occurrence in this context.

Doping represents a major challenge for the development of trust within the field
of sports. *Dennis Dreiskämper, Katharina Pöppel, Daniel Westmattelmann,
Gerhard Schewe*, and *Bernd Strauss* disclose that doping constitutes a serious
problem for trust relations with regard to sports—for athletes and sports associations as well as for their audiences and supporters. The contributors present a model
including both the antecedents of trust in high-performance sports and a description
of the particular risks for athletes, associations, and audiences. Special emphasis is
placed on discussing the effects of digitization and mediatization on the process of
trust building.

As with other areas of society, science depends on trust. This includes both trust
in science and trust within the system of science. *Friederike Hendriks, Dorothe
Kienhues*, and *Rainer Bromme* introduce the concept of epistemic trust as a means
to overcome uncertainty. Referring to the digitized knowledge society, they discuss
antecedents of trust in the relationship between experts and laypersons.

How does digitization change trust relationships with regard to the economic
sphere? In their contribution, *Philipp Romeike, Christina Wohlers, Guido Hertel*,
and *Gerhard Schewe* analyze how trust building is transformed within work processes based on digital communication. They disclose how in order to overcome
temporal and spatial distances, electronic performance monitoring—if enacted properly—may supplement and support mutual trust between supervisors and employees.
In that regard, what matters is the employees' subjective perception that such control
is appropriate or legitimate. The authors outline a clear agenda for supervisors in
modern workplaces to work upon maximizing such perceptions on the side of their
employees. Analyzing only those factors relevant for trust relations between superiors and employees, the authors define implications for trust-enhancing leadership in
working relations. *Jens Mazei* and *Guido Hertel* refer to a different context in which
trust is relevant. They take into consideration the increasing use of digital communication in negotiation processes, thereby focusing on both the antecedents and the
consequences of trust in electronic negotiations. The scholars illustrate which

psychological negotiation strategies result in an increase of trust and also illustrate potential benefits of digital as compared to face-to-face negotiation. The question which skills promote trust in working relations takes center stage in *Jens Kanthak* and *Guido Hertel's* contribution. Their research revolves around virtual teams working in different time zones at separate locations and getting in touch with each other only via digital means of communication. Bearing in mind the asynchronicity of this communication, Kanthak and Hertel's model reveals those factors that are fundamental in creating trust within virtual teams. *Ayten Öksüz, Nicolai Walter, Bettina Distel, Michael Räckers,* and *Jörg Becker's* chapter focuses on modern information technologies and discusses their usage within the discipline of information systems. The authors disclose an openness toward the question of trust within this field of research. Rather than concentrating merely on the aspect of trust in technology, the discipline further analyzes which factors contribute to building trust by means of information technology, particularly when dealing with issues of risk.

Social media in particular are responsible for transforming communication between individuals and within groups. There remain numerous challenges regarding trust building and the relationship between privacy and the public sphere. *Regina Jucks, Gesa Linnemann, Franziska Thon,* and *Maria Zimmermann* examine how people build and perceive trust through language, e.g., the specific words used in the digital environment. While some expressions are related to self-disclosure and empathy, others, e.g., technical jargon, point to competence of the speaker. *Ricarda Moll* and *Stephanie Pieschl* refer to the term "collective privacy" in order to describe a central trust phenomenon of communication within online social networks. The contributors argue that social media users may be willing to reveal private information because they assume that against the backdrop of collective privacy their disclosures will be hardly acknowledged by other users.

The numerous contributions are the result of an intensive, interdisciplinary cooperation stretching over several years—a cooperation that still remains a rare phenomenon within academia. Scholars of various disciplines from the University of Münster such as communication and media studies, psychology, economics, sport science, and information science examined the effects of digitization on trust building in more than 20 research projects. The findings presented in this volume represent merely a segment of our joint research (for further publications, see www.uni-muenster.de/GK-Vertrauen-Kommunikation/publikationen/publikationenindex.html.) The studies are part of the Research Training Group "Trust and Communication in a Digitized World," financed by the German Research Foundation (DFG), a cooperation of doctoral students, postdoctoral researchers, and professors from five disciplines. Each doctoral thesis is supervised by a team of supervisors from two academic fields and, usually, further supported by international mentors. With this volume, the authors hope to contribute to a more thorough understanding of trust in the age of the Internet. However, at the same time, the chapters uncover major research gaps and show the need for further research.

  The publication of this volume was possible only due to the great support of many. Alongside the contributing authors, I would like to thank in particular Franziska Rohde and Stephan Völlmicke from the Research Training Group, who were deeply involved in the management of the publication. Also, a very special thanks to the Alfried Krupp Wissenschaftskolleg Greifswald for providing the editor with a trusting environment in which to prepare this publication.

Münster, Germany   Bernd Blöbaum

Contents

Part I
Trust, Communication, Digitalization as Field of Research

Key Factors in the Process of Trust. On the Analysis of Trust under Digital Conditions

Bernd Blöbaum

Abstract In academic debate, trust is modeled either as a state or as a relation between trustee and trustor. This chapter systematizes a number of key features that influence the process of trust in order to make visible the tasks of future research. It discusses the differentiation of objects of trust (system, organization, role holders, and performance or product). The various factors pertaining to the trustee that influence the trustee's trustworthiness are presented. With reference to knowledge and experiences, personality features, situational features, and the differentiation of various communication situations, the chapter describes which elements pertaining to the trustor influence trust. Trust only becomes risky when it manifests itself in the form of an action. Only a person who acts risks something and makes himself or herself vulnerable and dependent on the trustee. The chapter explains what effects digitalization has on the development of trust. On the one hand, digital possibilities for developing equivalents of trust are opening up; on the other hand, trustees have to find new forms of presenting their trustworthiness.

Keywords Trust • Trustworthiness • Act of trust • Risk • Digitalization • Journalism

1 Introduction

Public discourse on trust is predominantly conducted in terms of negative scenarios. Problems of trust, losses of trust, and mistrust—illustrated by such cases as the financial crisis, the relationship between citizens and politicians, and the surveillance and analysis of emails and telephone calls—are being identified everywhere. The fact that trust and the erosion of trust are frequently addressed themes attests to the major significance that trust has for social life. As with the matters of climate and security, trust only attracts public attention when it is jeopardized. Lament about loss of trust is not a new phenomenon. Even Sophocles once complained, "Trust dies but mistrust blossoms."

B. Blöbaum (✉)
University of Münster, Münster, Germany
e-mail: bernd.bloebaum@uni-muenster.de

© Springer International Publishing Switzerland 2016
B. Blöbaum (ed.), *Trust and Communication in a Digitized World*, Progress in IS,
DOI 10.1007/978-3-319-28059-2_1

Social entities, such as societies, families, teams, and companies, require trust in order to function. The complexity of modern societies is accompanied by a growing need for trust as an "effective form of complexity reduction" (Luhmann 1968, p. 6, author's translation from the German). Because individuals are obliged to make choices in light of the many unclear possibilities that lie beyond the realm of their own experiences, trust provides a social mechanism for reducing the diversity and for managing the risk associated with decisions with an eye to an uncertain future (Luhmann 1968, p. 13). On the basis of an analysis of encyclopedia articles, the historian Frevert described how trust was primarily rooted in small-scale social relations, such as those associated with family, friendships, and doctor-patient relationships, in the nineteenth century and then broke free of this domain of personal interactions to be "injected [into] objective relations and abstract organizations, such as the economy, society, and politics" (2013, p. 39, author's translation from the German). Today, trust is not just a factor among individuals; it supports the operations of companies and institutions as well as the functioning of major social subsystems, such as politics, health care, the economy, sport, science, and the media.

The Internet has resulted in the development of a technical communication platform that is bringing about lasting changes in relations between individuals, relations with organizations, and relations with social institutions. Digitalization is leading to profound changes in working and living environments. Social media, big data, e-government, industry 4.0, and self-measurement are among the keywords that apply to this development. How can trust be established and maintained under digital conditions? Are there digital equivalents of trust? The models and concepts that have been developed within the scope of trust research predominantly take interpersonal trust in face-to-face situations as their starting point and occasionally also include organizations as objects of trust. Even in the digital world, trust is still trust—however, a number of components of the process of trust change.

The present text systematizes a number of elements that influence trust—yet, in so doing, it does not provide hypotheses about dependencies, directions, or strengths of influences. Instead, the aim is to make visible, for the sake of future research, those factors that ought to be taken into account in models and for the purpose of empirical analyses, without claiming to be exhaustive.

The next two sections address aspects pertaining to the trustee. In these sections, various objects of trust are differentiated, and factors that are important for evaluating trustworthiness are presented. This is followed by a section that summarizes a number of features pertaining to the trustor. The chapter also provides a reflection on how digitalization influences individual elements of the trust relationship.

2 Trust and Objects of Trust

Trust exists, but it is difficult to describe. In everyday understanding, trust is often linked to positive expectations to the effect that something will never happen or that something will go the way one wishes. The disappointment of expectations is interpreted as a crisis of trust. The fact that trust is a very delicate commodity in our society is demonstrated by the ways in which it is protected: The seal of confession at church, the protection of sources in journalism, legal privilege, and medical confidentiality protect special trust relationships between trustors and people who are the recipients of trust. In the social sciences, there are numerous definitions of trust. As a scientific construct, trust is not located within one particular discipline; however, most contributions can be attributed to the subjects of management, psychology, and sociology. The analyses undertaken from a communication science perspective are situated at the intersection between sociology and psychology, two subjects whose theoretical and methodological inventories have considerably benefited communication science since the 1960s. Whereas psychology conceptualizes trust primarily as the state of an individual, the sociologically oriented literature tends to focus on the social significance of trust and describes trust as a relation between trustor and trustee. The studies by Simmel (1908) and Luhmann (1968) are fundamental to the view of trust as a social component within the context of society. Because individuals do not know everything about their counterparts and cannot read their thoughts, trust is necessary in order for them to be able to interact socially at all (Simmel 1908). For Simmel, trust is a mechanism for bridging knowledge gaps, "an intermediate state between knowledge and ignorance. (...) Someone who knows all need not trust, someone who knows nothing cannot reasonably trust at all" [1908, p. 346, author's translation from the German based on the translation by Blasi et al. (2009)]. The sociologists Luhmann and Giddens also linked their observations about trust to social development. Because social interactions are breaking free of spatial and temporal limits, trust provides a method of maintaining individuals' ability to act (Giddens 1997). Since actors in modern society constantly can and must choose between various options to establish shared expectations and to make decisions, trust develops as a mechanism for reducing complexity (Luhmann 1968). Trust thereby becomes a resource that permits individuals to remain able to act in light of the limited nature of their knowledge (Luhmann 2001). In the act of trust, a particular future is anticipated and access is opened up to information and events outside the realm of one's own experience (Blöbaum 2014, p. 17f.). Trust, therefore, is not only a prerequisite for action by individuals where their knowledge is insufficient in a complex environment, but it is also linked to social relations.

Twenty years ago, Mayer et al. (1995, p. 709) noted "confusion between trust and its antecedents and outcomes." To date, little has changed with regard to this finding. Nevertheless, a number of key features of trust can be distilled from the overviews of trust research (Bachmann and Zaheer 2013; Corritore et al. 2003;

Lewicki et al. 2006; Fulmer and Gelfand 2012; Schoorman et al. 2015; Nienaber et al. 2015). Trust

- arises between two units, the trustor and the trustee
- is based on a free decision
- is oriented toward the future
- is founded on perceptions and experiences
- entails a risk in the sense of the potential damage being greater than the benefit
- bears reference (to a situation, an object, a performance, a problem to be solved)
- is constituted in an act of trust in which the trustor makes himself or herself vulnerable to the trustee
- is easier to destroy than to build.

Psychologically oriented research focuses on trust as a state of willingness to make oneself vulnerable (Mayer et al. 1995; Schoorman et al. 2015; Rousseau et al. 1998). "Trust is, first of all, a mental state, an attitude" (Castelfranchi and Falcone 2000, p. 801). Sociologists view trust as "a quality of relationship" (Sztompka 1999, p. 60). "From a sociological perspective, trust must be conceived as a property of collective units (...), not of isolated individuals. Being a collective attribute, trust is applicable to the relations among people rather than to their psychological states taken individually" (Lewis and Weigert 1985, p. 968). The research also differs with respect to whether trust is viewed as a prerequisite for an action or as the product of an action. Does an individual act because he or she trusts, or is trust only constituted in the moment in which the action is performed? As with many social processes, it is also still largely unclear in the case of trust which factors influence a relationship and in what ways.

What does trust refer to? A distinction that is commonly made in the literature is that between personal trust that applies to the relation between individuals and system trust that is related to supra-individual matters (Luhmann 1968). It is possible to further differentiate with respect to this rough distinction. Aside from personal relations (love, friendship), three possible points of reference can be distinguished from the perspective of a trustor:

- Trust in *people* as *role holders*. This refers, for example, to journalists in the media system, doctors in the health care system, teachers in the education system, politicians in politics, or managers in the economy.
- Trust in *institutions* or *organizations*. Newspapers or, for instance, the editorial department for politics at the New York Times—to use examples from the sphere of the media—or a hospital, a school, a political party, or a company would be examples of objects of trust at the level of organizations.
- Trust in *social systems*. Journalism or media, health care, education, politics, and the economy are trustees in this respect.

Trust relationships are not only relevant with regard to organizations and systems; they are also relevant within social groups and social subsystems. Journalists trust other journalists; media trust other media; doctors trust other doctors, and so forth.

This distinction between the micro, meso, and macro levels has consequences for the analysis of trust because trustors have different expectations and make different evaluations of trustworthiness depending on the point of reference. People have different forms of proving their trustworthiness (and of deceiving) to those of organizations. A person who trusts organizations and institutions directs his or her trust primarily at the performance of the relevant organization or institution—that is to say, it is directed at what the relevant organization or institution offers as content or as a product for use. In a study on trust in journalism, Kohring demonstrated that the point of reference for trust in this case is the reporting—and not the journalist, with whom recipients are not usually familiar. The trust that recipients have in journalism consists of four dimensions (Kohring 2004, p. 171ff.):

- Trust in *theme selectivity* refers to the selection of news that has relevance for recipients.
- Trust in *fact selectivity* concerns the notion that the relevant information pertaining to the selected themes, including background information, is provided.
- Trust in *the correctness of descriptions* relates to the notion that the facts are correct and the reporting is credible.
- Trust in *explicit evaluations* refers to the classification and weighing of information communicated by means of journalism.

The points of reference for trust are journalistic practices, namely the programs of research, selection, presentation, and coordination that pertain to journalism (Blöbaum 2014). In this sense, Kohring spoke of "trust in the system programming" (2004, p. 110, author's translation from the German). What has been described here with reference to the example of media can be applied to other organizations. Trust in a company relates to the notion that a service or a product will be made available at the expected level of quality. Just as trust in actors and institutions is concerned with the role holders and organizations functioning properly by delivering the performance required of them, system trust is constituted via the functioning of social subsystems. This reflects trustors' expectation that, for instance, politics will make decisions, science will yield true insights, and the media will provide up-to-date reports on relevant societal events and themes. System trust is a collective term that encompasses trust in the system programming, trust in the organizations, and trust in the role holders of a system.

Together, the three levels—system, organization, and role—form a stable structure. Whereas the existence of politics, science, health care, sport, the economy, and the media can be taken for granted as far as trustors are concerned, actors and organizations are subject to change. From the perspective of the trustors, the relation with subsystems comprises a state of familiarity. Luhmann interprets this as "an unavoidable fact of life" (2001, p. 144, author's translation from the German). Where this is the case, risks are not taken into account. It is possible to rest assured that politics, the economy, the media, and a health care system exist. Familiarity is based on experiences and extends these with respect to the future.

Familiarity indicates that everything is functioning without risk and in an unquestioned manner as it used to do.

In the case of actors and organizations, as well as in the case of programs that control the output of a system, the status of familiarity can be lost as a result of change. When this happens, trust has to be developed anew. Digitalization has created new actors, new organizations, and new ways of communicating, as well as new possibilities for gaining access to people and institutions. In so doing, it poses problems for trustors and trustees. This point can be illustrated by using media as an example. The Internet has provided a new form of communicating journalistic content. Traditional media and new providers have had to create new forms of presentation and new working and selection routines for the purpose of digital distribution. For recipients, this has meant that the objects of trust have changed. Many evaluations of the trustworthiness of media content can be taken from offline journalism and applied to online journalism. Blogs in which journalists give transparent accounts of their research activities and selection decisions, links to documents used as sources by journalists, and direct evaluations and comments on articles that are made by users are examples of digital innovations that are relevant to trust. Science blogs, open access, and digitally driven public relations work by universities in the sphere of science, e-government in the sphere of politics, virtual teamwork in the sphere of the economy, self-disclosure in social networks, and self-measurement in the spheres of health care and sport are effects of digitalization with respect to other objects of trust.

Four forms of trust relationship can be established from the perspective of a trustor: relationships with the output (performance, product), relationships with people, relationships with organizations, and relationships with the system.

Figure 1 illustrates these four points of reference pertaining to trust by using media as an example.

When carrying out studies on trust, it is necessary to establish in each case what it is that trust is being directed at in a specific situation. Whereas, in the health care system, the service is often provided within the scope of a direct interaction between the doctor and the patient, interactions between scientists and laypeople, politicians and citizens, and journalists and recipients are rather rare. In the case of the reception of a journalistic article, the object of trust is, first and foremost, the text, or its content. The following is an example. The English newspaper The Guardian reports on the decision of the British Prime Minister to permit 1000 refugees from Syria to enter the United Kingdom. A reader, after reading this

Performance of the system Journalistic article	**Representative** of the system Journalist	**Organization** of the system Medium/ Editorial department	**System** Media/ Journalism

Fig. 1 Objects of trust: Media system/Journalism

text, decides to criticize the political decision in a comment on Guardian Online. The basis of this decision is the article in the newspaper. The reader trusts that the information is accurate and bases his or her activity on this foundation. The trust in the correctness of the information may well have been influenced by the trust placed in The Guardian, the trust placed in the British press, and perhaps also the general trust placed in the media. However, the trigger for the action is the journalistic text.

This example provides a clear illustration of the fact that trust can have many points of reference (Fig. 2). Their order and the influence of individual levels are contingent. In the case of the media, the process of specifying objects of trust is made even more difficult by the fact that the media report on themes and events from other subareas of society. Therefore, in the example of a report about a political decision, it is not only the credibility of the reporting that is relevant to trust; so too are the political actors, the political institutions, and politics as a whole, which are addressed as themes of the article.

The differentiation of the objects of trust is elementary, but it indicates a problem faced by research. When surveys (such as the World Value Survey, the Eurobarometer, or the Edelman Trust Barometer) inquire about trust in politics, science, the economy, or media, it remains unclear what the values obtained by means of such surveys refer to. For instance, the relevant question in the Eurobarometer survey (2015) reads as follows: "I would like to ask you a question about how much trust you have in certain media and institutions. For each of the following media and institutions, please tell me if you tend to trust it or tend not to trust it." If a person indicates that he or she trusts media a lot or a little, it is possible that this statement refers to the media system in general (but then who reads all the newspapers and is capable of making an assessment in this respect?). The respondent could also be referring to the media that he or she uses because he or she has had experience with those media. The respondent might also be referring to journalists or to the content of the reporting. Studies of this kind, therefore, only

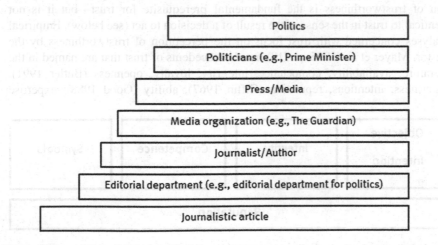

Fig. 2 Objects of trust: Political article

have limited analytical value. Studies that operate at the level of the journalistic article are faced with a similar problem. They have to identify which factors influence the evaluation of trustworthiness. These factors can pertain either to the object of trust—that is to say, the content, the form, and the editorial environment—or to the medium.

To date, there has not been sufficient clarification of how the individual planes of reference pertaining to trustworthiness relate to each other. For example, do knowledge and experiences that have been gained in instances of education and socialization cause people to trust media content? Or does the reception of media content generate trust in journalists, specific media, and the media system as a whole?

3 Trustees and Trustworthiness

Which factors pertaining to the trustee influence an act of trust? The factors differ depending on whether the object of trust is a performance, content, a person, an organization, or a sphere of society. In the literature, these features are discussed as antecedents of trust or as perceived trustworthiness (Mayer et al. 1995). At this point, a distinction is made between five elements that can be used to evaluate trustworthiness: trustee's objectives and intentions, trustee's integrity, trustee's competence, the symbols, and the reputation (Fig. 3).

How does a trustor recognize whether he or she can trust? Trustworthiness, which is also equated with trust in some studies, is rooted on both sides of the trust relationship. It is a set of characteristics pertaining to the trustee—in other words, it refers to "a characteristic of someone or something that is the object of trust" (Corritore et al. 2003, p. 741). At the same time, trustworthiness refers to an attribution of characteristics by the trustor on the basis of perception. The attribution of trustworthiness is the fundamental prerequisite for trust—but it is not identical to trust in the sense of the result of a decision to act (see below). Empirical analyses concerned with trust focus on the perception of trustworthiness by the trustor. Mayer et al. (1995, p. 718) listed antecedents of trust that are named in the literature: availability, competence, integrity, loyalty, openness (Butler 1991), expertness, intentions, reputation (Giffin 1967), ability (Good 1988), expertise

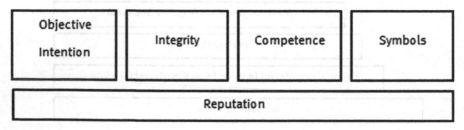

Fig. 3 Indicators for the evaluation of trustworthiness

(Hovland et al. 1953), competence (Lieberman 1981), and benevolence (Solomon 1960). They condensed these factors into three sets: ability, benevolence, and integrity. As the literature review by Fulmer and Gelfand (2012) and the overview by Schoorman et al. (2015) indicated, these antecedents are used in numerous studies. Castelfranchi and Falcone (2000, p. 802) described competence and benevolence as "the real cognitive kernel of trust."

The antecedents of trust are not ontological features of the trustee but the results of attributions and are therefore of a phenomenological nature. When making their evaluations, people have recourse to schemata and experiences that act as "cognitive shortcuts" (Müller 2013, p. 48) and thereby enable them to make a rapid assessment of trustworthiness.

Competence, with reference to actors, organizations, and subsystems, concerns the ability of the relevant parties to fulfill their tasks and always refers to the specific situation. "Ability is the group of skills, competencies, and characteristics that enable a party to have influence within some specific domain" (Mayer et al. 1995, p. 717). Quality is a key feature of competence with regard to content and performances.

Integrity, refers to "consistency of the party's past actions, credible communication about the trustee from other parties, belief that the trustee has a strong sense of justice. (...) the degree to which the party is judged to have integrity" (Mayer et al. 1995, p. 719; Ullmann-Margalit 2004).

Benevolence is understood by Mayer et al. to refer to "the extent to which a trustee is believed to want to do good to the trustor" (1995, p. 718). In this context, "to do good" directly refers to a good intention, and benevolence is positively connoted. Is online banking, as a service offered by a bank, guided by the motive of saving the customer the trip to the bank or by the motive of saving on personnel and increasing profits? Is the publication of a report in the daily newspaper always guided by the idea of informing people about an undesirable state of affairs? Or does the concern rest with the publisher's intention of making money in this way? Commercial enterprises aim to make profits; politics is about power—these motives are not characterized by good or bad intentions any more than the gaining of true insights is in science or the communication of up-to-date and relevant information is in journalism. Because it is difficult to distinguish good motives from bad motives, it seems useful to replace the positive construct of benevolence with the more neutral concepts of *"objectives"* and *"intentions"*.

As empirical studies show, the motives and interests that the trustee is perceived to have play a major role in the assessment of the trustee's trustworthiness:

- Those who pursue commercial interests are assessed as being less trustworthy than those who pursue intentions associated with civil society (Flanagin and Metzger 2000).
- Independent and professional organizations enjoy higher levels of trustworthiness than those that are perceived as being dependent and obliged to serve individual interests (Harris et al. 2011; Childs 2004).

– Informational messages appear more trustworthy than those that are delivered in a manner characteristic of efforts to persuade (Rabinovich et al. 2012).

Reputation Eisenegger and Imhof (2009) distinguished between functional, social, and expressive reputation. Functional reputation means that an organization or a system fulfills expectations. In short, it refers to whether it functions as the trustor expects it to function. This corresponds to the fundamental system trust or organization trust. Media have to deliver content reliably; politics has to make decisions, and science has to yield new insights. It follows from this that reputation refers to ability. Social reputation entails an evaluation of the integrity of an organization and can therefore be equated with integrity as a feature of trustworthiness. Among the questions asked is whether the interests of the trustor are taken into consideration. Expressive reputation concerns how external appearance is perceived; it concerns sympathy (Sztompka 1999, p. 71 ff.) Positive experiences improve reputation and thereby increase the level of trustworthiness. It is true that reputation takes into account competence and integrity, but it does not include expressive elements like the manner and the external appearance of role holders or organizations. "Reputation means simply the record of past deeds" (Sztompka 1999, p. 71). Reputation arises from first-hand experiences, such as direct observations, interactions, and memories. With regard to second-hand experiences, Sztompka (1999, p. 72) distinguished between "testimonials referring to reputation" (. . .) like "accounts by witnesses, CVs" and "more subtle, implicit signals of reputation" like the age of a company, membership in exclusive associations, and academic degrees (1999, p. 73). Reputation combines the indicators comprised of motives, integrity, competence, and symbols at the level of organizations and at the level of people. Products or performances, as objects of trust, only indirectly illustrate their trustworthiness via reputation. In their case, content-related features, such as quality (and hence competence), tend to matter instead.

With respect to the sphere of the media, Damm named genre (e.g., print, TV, quality media, tabloid media) and political perspectives, with which recipients associate moral judgments, as points of reference pertaining to reputation. Competence, appearance, and behavior are included in the evaluation of reputation in the case of journalists (Damm 2012).

Symbols For trustors, the antecedents of trustworthiness described so far—namely, integrity, ability, and motives—are difficult to identify. For this reason, they have recourse in trust situations to heuristics and circumstantial evidence that signal trustworthiness. Such "symbolic indicators" (Luhmann 1968, p. 28, author's translation from the German) enable evaluations to be made without expending major resources. Academic titles, the white coats worn by doctors, and the familiar lettering of newspaper titles, which is taken from the realm of offline journalism and applied to online presences, are examples of symbols. On the Internet, rankings, ratings, and recommendations have produced offerings that can be used as heuristics of trustworthiness by recipients without expending major resources. Buyer reviews on the Internet and, in the case of online journalism, recommendations of articles are provided in transparent ways for users. Symbols such as stars or scores are quality assessments that can be quickly comprehended and are made by other readers of the same article or by other users of the same service. Even though evaluations of this kind are susceptible to manipulation, they still create transparency with regard to how other users assess the required service. Symbols, therefore, are external validations provided by users with similar problems. They are able to minimize the perceived risk. On the basis of digitally available data, they condense the performances, abilities, and integrity of the trustee into straightforward indicators of trustworthiness. These elements are extremely relevant to assessments of trust for two reasons. One reason is that they are based on use and evaluation by other trustors; the other reason is that they are based on data and often appear in numerical form, a method of presentation that is considered to be particularly objective (Heintz 2010).

The features of trustworthiness that have been mentioned have different points of reference. Objectives and intentions can be situated at the level of a performance (e.g., the article has the objective of providing information), and they are firmly rooted—for example, as an organizational purpose—in the structure of an organization or of a system. Competence can also be situated in relation to the performance: In journalism, for example, this might refer to the quality of an article. A journalistic text, however, cannot have integrity. The expressive part of reputation can be situated in relation to the appearance of a text; social and functional elements of reputation, by contrast, are more aptly examined at the level of media editorial departments.

The evaluation of trustworthiness, therefore, both explicitly and implicitly includes various factors from a number of levels (cf. Fig. 2). Analytically distinguishing between these features and between their points of reference is a major challenge for research.

On the one hand, the following point is noted: "All clues of trustworthiness may be abused and subjected to manipulation" (Sztompka 1999, p. 74). On the other hand, digitalization is responsible for creating new and straightforward forms of transparency, for reducing the amount of resources that are expended on procuring information, and for enabling quick comparisons of the sort that are rarely possible outside the Internet.

4 Trustors

Whether a person or performance is assessed as being trustworthy depends on the above-outlined factors pertaining to the trustee. To put it more precisely, it depends on the perception and evaluation by the trustor. What influences the trustor with respect to his or her act of trust? In addition to the evaluation of integrity, competence, motives, reputation, and symbols, the following elements are relevant in this respect: experience and knowledge, personality features, the specific situation, and the communicative setting.

4.1 Knowledge and Experiences

Knowledge, in trust situations, has two points of reference. It refers to general knowledge about the organization or about the sphere of society to which the object of trust can be assigned. Those who know a lot about political matters or economic developments judge individual decisions in these spheres against a different backdrop than those who have little knowledge in this regard. Knowledge also refers to the specific content, to a political decision, or, in the case of the media, to the theme of an article. Those who are familiar with vaccination recommendations—perhaps because they have learned about the matter in educational institutions, for example, or because they deal with the matter in their professional capacity—will evaluate a newspaper article on this topic in a different way than those who do not have such knowledge. Studies on the influence of media knowledge on credibility have yielded no unequivocal findings (Vraga et al. 2012; Ashley et al. 2010).

Unlike general or specific knowledge, *experience,* as a factor in the evaluation of trustworthiness, is based on previous interactions. Experiences refer to "extrapolation from presently observed episodes of conduct to the future" (Sztompka 1999, p. 77). The recourse to experiences is "a kind of meta cue." "We are usually ready to trust more those whose trustworthiness has been tested before in relation to ourselves, for example, our proven friends, tested business partners, favorite authors of books, car makers who didn't fail us before" (Sztompka 1999, p. 96). In this respect, a distinction can be made between two forms: Experiences in which the trustor has directly experienced the trustee (first-hand experiences), and those that involve recourse to the experiences of others (second-hand experiences).

Little is known about the accumulation of experience in the building of trust. Mayer et al. (1995, p. 728f.) suspected that longer phases of positive experiences of a trustee strengthen trustworthiness. Good experiences are applied to future acts of trust. "The better and longer we are acquainted with somebody, and the more consistent the record of trustworthy conduct, the greater our readiness to trust" (Sztompka 1999, p. 72). Boon and Holmes (1991, p. 198) also viewed the generalization of earlier relations as a learning effect: "The particular history of a relationship may be considered a contextual variable of fundamental importance as it imparts a refined and perhaps unique quality of the expectations those involved possess about each other."

Digitalization facilitates access to knowledge and experience. On the Internet, many offerings enable users to have recourse both to other users' evaluations and to the experiences of those other users. Consequently, trustors have more possibilities to base acts of trust on solid foundations because risk evaluation seems easier to do digitally. However, knowledge and experiences must first of all be acquired for the new digital environments. In the sphere of the media, recipients of news prefer to have recourse to those brands with which they are familiar from the offline world (Reuters Institute 2013). Activities on the Internet are risky because of the possibilities for digital manipulation that need to be considered when assessing risk.

4.2 Features of the Person

Whereas the perception of trustworthiness, experience, and knowledge have a specific connection with the trustee or with the current trust situation, the personality features listed in the following part of the present chapter are exclusively linked to the trustor as a person. In this respect, a distinction can be made between sociodemographic factors, trust propensity, and risk propensity (Fig. 4).

Sociodemographics includes age, gender, and education, variables that are commonly used in empirical social research. It also includes factors such as cultural orientation, nationality, and social milieu. In studies that addressed the sphere of the media, age did not influence trust (Jackob 2010; Tsfati and Ariely 2014) when the matter concerned trust is placed in media in general. Comparisons between online and offline media have indicated that older people trust the traditional media formats a little more. Men and women do not differ with respect to general trust in the media (Jackob 2010; Matthes 2013). A higher level of formal education correlates with less trust in the media (Tsfati and Ariely 2014). Differences in education are less important with respect to digitally communicated media content (Xie and Zhao 2014).

General Trust Propensity Trust propensity, or disposition to trust, refers to a person's general ability to trust that goes beyond the scope of a specific situation. Mayer et al. (1995, p. 715) viewed it as "a stable within-party factor that will affect the likelihood the party will trust. People differ in their inherent propensity to trust. Propensity might be thought of as the general willingness to trust others." Early childhood experiences have been put forward as an explanation of the development of trust propensity (Sztompka 1999). According to Mayer et al., general trust propensity influences not only trust but also its antecedents. In the sphere of the media, evidence has indicated that there is a correlation between a generally high trust propensity and general trust in (political) institutions. Those who generally trust a lot also trust media (Gronke and Cook 2007).

A similar picture applies to *general risk propensity*: According to Das and Teng (2004), each individual has a specific risk propensity that influences both trust and the trust propensity of that individual. So far, little research has been carried out on this subject of risk propensity (Mayer et al. 1995, p. 710), which is also true of the relationship between trust propensity and risk propensity. However, it seems useful to treat these as two distinct constructs. It is conceivable that a generally high risk propensity would lead to an act of trust despite a perceived low level of trustworthiness. Those who generally avoid taking risks will refrain from performing the relevant action even if they assess the competence, reputation, and integrity of a

Fig. 4 Trustor: Personality features

Sociodemo-graphics	General trust propensity	General risk propensity

trustee as being very high. The operationalization and measurement of individual risk propensity is a task for future research.

4.3   Situational Features

General trust propensity and general risk propensity are unspecific. By contrast, a decision to trust, which leads to a concrete act of trust, is specific. In trust research, a major challenge is to determine the respective trust situations in a precise way. A distinction can be made between new situations arising for the first time in which initial trust is at stake and those which appear as a setting again and again. Reading a daily newspaper to which one has a subscription might be a constantly recurring situation; searching for information on a vaccination recommendation for traveling to a country in Asia, by contrast, might be an one-off occurrence that takes place before the journey.

As McKnight et al. demonstrated, the perception of the situation influences trust formation. "A person who enters a bank tends to expect a setting conducive to both customer service and fiduciary responsibility that is reflected in the workers' professional appearance, the prosperous and secure physical setting, and the friendly, yet safe, money-handling procedures. The individual's belief that the situation is normal helps that person feel comfortable enough to rapidly form a trusting intention toward the other party in the situation" (1998, p. 478). The example illustrates the fact that the evaluation of the situation is made against the backdrop of experience in the sense of conditioning and socialization. The notion that news media reliably provide information about current and relevant events is not one that recipients have to rediscover each time they make use of the media. They are able to draw on the experiences that they gained in various instances of socialization (family, school). To date, hardly any research has been carried out on the extent to which such attributions and experiences of socialization influence the perception of risk in trust situations. Face-to-face communication, online media, social media, and traditional media each constitute specific situations and each require different resources in order to realize an act of trust.

From the perspective of a trustor, a distinction is made at this point between four features that have effects on the execution of an act of trust: context, relevance, specific perception of risk, and communication situation (Fig. 5).

Context   It is both evident and elementary that trust propensity, risk evaluation, and the assessment of trustworthiness are different in private interactions than in public spaces and different in work contexts than in leisure contexts. In the sphere of work, the digital documentation of individual work steps can contribute to transparency and perhaps even replace trust. In private life, the documentation of statements and activities would tend to be perceived as surveillance and destroy trust.

Relevance describes how significant a trustor considers the situation in which he or she trusts to be. For a person affected by a threatening illness, the trustworthiness

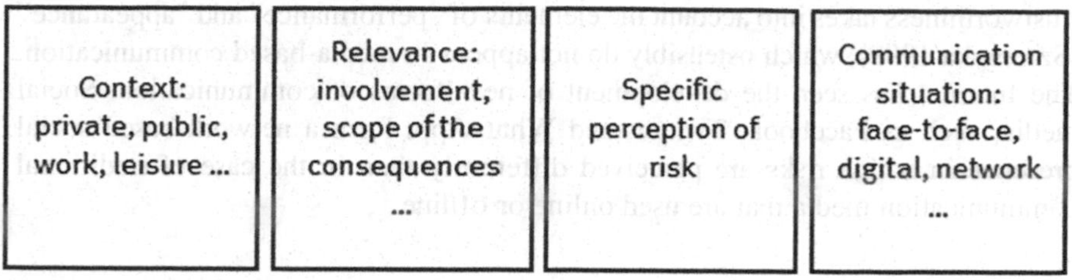

| Context: private, public, work, leisure ... | Relevance: involvement, scope of the consequences ... | Specific perception of risk | Communication situation: face-to-face, digital, network ... |

Fig. 5 Situational features

of sources is likely to have a different significance than in the case of a person who is looking to undergo treatment for a sprained ligament. In addition to an assessment of the consequences of an act of trust, relevance includes involvement. Involvement is reflected, for example, in fandom (Arpan and Raney 2003), personal importance (Gunther and Christen 2002), engagement, and group membership. A distinction is made between cognitive and affective forms of involvement (Matthes 2013).

Specific Perception of Risk   The risk always rests with the trustor. It can relate to all antecedents of trust (Das and Teng 2004). An actor runs the risk that the trustee is not competent, and the actor can be mistaken about the trustee's objectives and intentions or about the trustee's integrity. As mentioned above, the very construction of reputation by a trustee and the use of symbols, which lies in the trustee's hands, provide various possibilities for false conclusions to be drawn by the trustor. Reputation management and symbols can be strategically used to conceal risks. Risk in a trust relationship is not an objective feature but a subjective perception based on an evaluation of risk that is made by the trustor. Just as perceptions of trustworthiness vary, so too can perceptions of risk. The relationship between trust and risk is circular: A person who trusts risks something, and only a person who risks something can trust. The specific perception of risk relates to the concrete situation and is to be distinguished from the general risk propensity. The risk associated with trust that is placed in the content of online journalism differs from the risk that trustors take in disclosing personal information on Facebook. The perception of risk concerns the rational ("risk as analysis") or affective ("risk as feelings") form of weighing up the possible benefit of an act of trust against the negative consequences associated with it (Slovic and Peters 2006). This perception of risk tends to be intuitive and swift and tends less to involve thought-out assessments of advantages and disadvantages (Slovic 2010). The rating cues and indications of likes and shares that are emerging in the course of digitalization are features that can be quickly comprehended with a view to assessing risk. Few resources need to be expended in order to comprehend them.

Communication Situation   When analyzing processes of trust, various communicative settings need to be differentiated. Factors such as the willingness to take a risk and the assessment of trustworthiness depend on the communication situation. In face-to-face communication among those who are present, the evaluation of trustworthiness takes into account the elements of "performance" and "appearance" (Sztompka 1999), which ostensibly do not appear in media-based communication. The Internet has seen the development of new forms of communication. Social media, such as Facebook, Twitter, and WhatsApp, form a network-based social presence in which risks are perceived differently than in the case of traditional communication media that are used online or offline.

5 Trust: Acting on the Basis of Trustworthiness and Willingness to Take a Risk

Having described the factors influencing trust that pertain to the trustee and those that pertain to the trustor, the present chapter examines the act of trust in further detail. In the trust relationship, trust is only activated as a specific mode of social interaction when it takes the form of an action that is performed on the basis of trustworthiness and an evaluation of risk. From the perspective adopted here, trust, therefore, is not "the willingness of a party to be vulnerable" (Mayer et al. 1995, p. 712; Rousseau et al. 1998). The willingness to make oneself vulnerable on the basis of experiences and evaluations of previous interactions is a necessary but not sufficient condition for trust.

If trust only manifests itself by taking the form of an action, this has consequences for the status of risk in the process of trust. In the model by Mayer et al. (1995), the risk evaluation takes place after the decision to trust. Where trust is understood as an action, the risk evaluation takes place before the decision to trust; the risk itself, however, lies in the action.

Two forms of risk can be differentiated. There is the risk that is taken into account as a perception in the evaluation of the trust situation and of trustworthiness (risk evaluation). There is also the risk that is linked to the action because the action might have unintended consequences. "Risks, however, emerge only as a component of decision and action. (...) If you refrain from action you run no risk" (Luhmann 2000, p. 100). In the process of trust, the trustor reflects on external risks before he or she acts. "It is a purely internal calculation of external conditions which creates risk" (Luhmann 2000, p. 100).

A trustor only makes himself or herself vulnerable through his or her action and not through the assessment of trustworthiness. Only by completing the act of trust does the trustor become dependent on the trustee. The trustor only perceives the risk linked to the action if the objective that the act of trust was intended to accomplish is not achieved. If a person reads an academic text or a newspaper article, that person does not take a risk and make himself or herself dependent by reading it. Only if a person acts on the basis of his or her reading (e.g., the person cites the text or applies the content to his or her arguments) is a trust relationship constituted.

Because the risk lies in the act of trust, where the trustor subsequently reflects on this act, his or her reflection will always include a reflection on the risk. In this way, the outcome of the risky action is then taken into account as an experience with respect to the subsequent willingness to trust and evaluation of risk: "When a trustor takes a risk in a trustee that leads to a positive outcome, the trustor's perceptions of the trustee are enhanced. Likewise, perceptions of the trustee will decline when trust leads to unfavorable conclusions" (Mayer et al. 1995, p. 728). Longer and repeatedly positive experiences in a relationship would then be likely, it is presumed, to lead to a state of familiarity.

In the model by Mayer et al. (1995), the assessment of trustworthiness, together with the personal trust propensity, leads to trust. A person who evaluates a trustee positively in all dimensions and generally tends to trust, however, does not necessarily have to trust. If the risk in the situation is assessed as being too high, an act of trust will not take place. Therefore, trust is based on a combination of willingness to trust and evaluation of risk, and it manifests itself in a risky action.

The act of trust is preceded by the decision to trust (Dietz and Hartog 2006). The decision to trust does not yet entail risk: In making such a decision, a trustor does not yet make himself or herself dependent and vulnerable. "The decision is only an intention to act. For A to demonstrate unequivocally her/his trust in B, (s)he must follow through on this decision by engaging in any of the trust-informed risk-taking behaviors" (Dietz and Hartog 2006, p. 559).

Trust research is not only faced with the challenge of identifying the factors that influence the evaluation of risk and the willingness to trust; a no less difficult task consists in determining the risk that is associated with the acts of trust. The risk associated with journalistic texts, for instance, is that a recipient acts on the basis of false or incomplete information and evaluations. Negative consequences of these actions can therefore be attributed to the source of information. The concept of action or behavior is understood in a very broad sense in this respect: Information can increase knowledge and later have a bearing on decisions; it can lead to changes in attitude over the short or long term or to immediate actions. This can be illustrated by the following example with reference to a journalistic article. A person who reads about the intake of refugees in his or her city might immediately take this as a cue to go and help with this matter on a voluntary basis. However, that person might also store this information in his or her stock of knowledge, link it with other information, and become active later. The basis of the action is the trust that is placed in the media content. Contrary to the view put forward by Jackob (2012, p. 101), who proceeded from the assumption that "individuals enter a trust relationship (. . .) at the moment of reception", the reception in this case is regarded as a necessary but not sufficient condition for trust. The process of trust is only completed when an effect occurs that is based on the reception. This can also take the form of refraining from performing an action (the weather report forecasts rain and the person in question does not drive into the countryside). What is crucial is that there is a connection with the article that has been read—even if this connection is established at a considerably later point in time.

The act of trust is of a binary nature: One can act or not act. By contrast, willingness to trust and risk propensity are of a gradual nature: They can be high or low. Where surveys inquire about trust in politics or trust in the media, what they

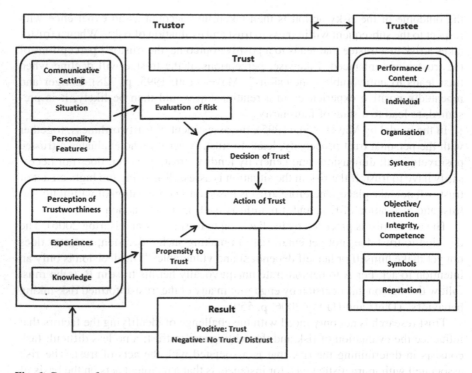

Fig. 6 Process of trust

identify in so doing, strictly speaking, is a general willingness to trust. A person who did not trust "the media" or "the newspapers" at all would not be able to perform any actions on the basis of media content—that is to say, that person would not be able to use any information from the media. Such a scenario is difficult to imagine.

The following figure presents a model of the influencing factors in the process of trust that are described in the present chapter (Fig. 6).

Irrespective of whether it is the willingness to trust as a state or trust as an action that is being examined, empirical analyses can only ever establish one part of the process of trust. Research is faced with the problem of operationalizing the individual components in appropriate ways. For example, in the case of journalistic texts, the following questions need to be asked:

– What is the risk associated with the reception of journalistic articles? (Construction of the risk)
– What action that is subsequent to the reception of a journalistic text can be plausibly constructed? (Construction of the act of trust) Instances in which reading a journalistic article directly entails an act of trust are probably very rare. The relevant experimental designs will therefore have to work with plausible actions that are imagined.

- How can existing knowledge be differentiated from knowledge that has just been acquired? The intake of information in the case of individuals can lead to knowledge, rules, and routines, and thereby lead to a state of familiarity that can hardly be distinguished from risk-fraught trust.
- How do rating cues, rankings, and other symbolic representations affect the willingness to trust?
- What experiences do recipients have with media in general and what experiences do they have with a specific medium?

6 Digitalization and Trust

The Internet—as noted several times above—influences the formation of trust. With reference to the example of media and journalism, a number of the effects of digitalization on trust shall be summarized at this point. It is to be noted that the following statements primarily have the status of research questions and hypotheses that need to be addressed in future. It is evident that digitalization is changing the relationship between public and journalism and hence the relationship between trustor and trustee (Sambrook 2012; Blöbaum 2014). Recipients are comprehensively equipped with digital communication technologies. The average Internet use time in Germany in 2015 was 108 min per day (ARD/ZDF Onlinestudie 2015). A great many people are "permanently online" and "permanently connected" (Vorderer and Kohring 2013). Even in the digital world, news continues to be important. Data from the Digital News Report (Reuters Institute 2013) indicated that, in most of the participating countries, more than 80 % of respondents consumed news on a daily basis.

Digitalization is changing media as objects of trust. Online offerings are emerging alongside traditional mass media. Within the digital environment, media are developing new forms of proving their trustworthiness. This represents a major challenge for journalism. Yet technological changes, such as the development of radio and television, have already presented the media with the task of adapting to new conditions on many occasions in the past. In the course of such developments, new forms of presentation have emerged in each case (Blöbaum 2014).

The media system as a whole and individual newspapers and broadcasting corporations have earned reputations over many years. Because the brand names carry reputations, traditional mass media are transferring their names into the realm of the Internet. This enables the online versions to benefit from tradition, from reputation from the offline world, and from the integrity and competence that have been established there. Those who avail themselves of news via a smartphone or tablet trust traditional media brands more than new providers (Reuters Institute 2013, p. 14). The reputation and expertise of the provider influence the assessment of trustworthiness (Flanagin and Metzger 2007). As is the case with traditional media, media use on the Internet is becoming a habitual behavior too.

Media have developed a number of features for the Internet that have the potential to document trustworthiness. In the case of online journalism, for instance, there is more information about the journalists in their capacity as authors of the articles. In online media, photos of journalists are often provided alongside their texts, and bylines are linked and enriched with additional information about the journalists, such as age, department, a short bio, or accolades. It is possible to follow authors on Facebook, and they can occasionally be addressed directly via email. On the Internet, the recipients get considerably more information about the people who are responsible for media coverage, and it is becoming easier to gain access to these people. This form of personalization paints a picture of the journalist and provides information about his or her skills and experience. Recipients can include these factors in the evaluation of trustworthiness.

Some journalists write blogs in which they report on their work, steps involved in research, and selection decisions. This activity is making journalistic work more transparent. Links to sources of reporting, such as documents or interviews, are frequently provided in the realm of online journalism. Media content, therefore, is becoming more accountable as a result of "disclosure transparency" (Karlsson 2010). Digitalization is creating transparency and providing recipients with possibilities regarding controls where such possibilities did not previously exist. Such controls influence the evaluation of risk: "When the risk in a situation is greater than the trust (and, thus, the willingness to take risk), a control system can bridge the difference by lowering the perceived risk to a level that can be managed by trust" (Schoorman et al. 2007, p. 346).

By means of like buttons and information about shared and recommended articles, digital media indicate which articles recipients particularly appreciate. Rating cues and other quantifications generate rankings for the digital content. These symbols have a high level of potential for documenting competence and integrity because they are, as it were, external validations provided by other recipients. They can be interpreted as signals of trustworthiness.

The examples from the sphere of the media illustrate the following points. With respect to the trustee, digitalization is changing the objects of trust, especially the performances and content that are being offered. Trustees are developing new forms of documenting their trustworthiness. Overall, trustors and trustees are moving closer together online. Internet users do not have to rely on a single source; instead, they can add further sources without any major effort (cf. Flanagin and Metzger 2008; Guenther and Möllering 2010). Accordingly, the need to trust can become superfluous because recipients have the opportunity to check information more effectively and because it is also possible to gain access to experts more quickly online. For the trustees, this increases the pressure to place stronger emphasis on their trustworthiness vis-à-vis recipients and to make this trustworthiness easily intelligible. The easy access to content on the Internet, however, also requires new forms of risk evaluation. Digital communication media bring users face to face with new situations for which new risk evaluation heuristics are necessary (Kelton et al. 2008). In the realm of online journalism, recipients have more possibilities to evaluate trustworthiness than in the case of traditional media.

In addition, the community itself is becoming a relevant variable in the process of trust. Media are creating new signals and symbols with an eye to recipients that make it possible to evaluate the performances of the relevant media outlets by means of a small number of features that can be quickly comprehended.

Digitalization is changing how trust is established and maintained in the relation between trustor and trustee. The act of trust, even in the digital world, remains one that is risky.

References

ARD/ZDF-Onlinestudie. (2015). http://www.ard-zdf-onlinestudie.de/

Arpan, L. M., & Raney, A. A. (2003). An experimental investigation of news source and the hostile media effect. *Journalism & Mass Communication Quarterly, 80*(2), 265–281.

Ashley, S., Poepsel, M., & Willis, E. (2010). Media literacy and news credibility: Does knowledge of media ownership increase skepticism in news consumers? *Journal of Media Literacy Education, 2*(1), 37–46.

Bachmann, R., & Zaheer, A. (Eds.). (2013). *Handbook of advances in trust research*. Cheltenham: Edward Elgar Publishing.

Blöbaum, B. (2014). *Trust and journalism in a digital environment* (Working paper). Accessed April 30, 2015, from https://reutersinstitute.politics.ox.ac.uk/sites/default/files/Trust%20and%20Journalism%20in%20a%20Digital%20Environment.pdf

Boon, S. D., & Holmes, J. G. (1991). The dynamics of interpersonal trust: Resolving uncertainty in the face of risk. In R. A. Hinde & J. Groebel (Eds.), *Cooperation and prosocial behaviour* (pp. 190–211). Cambridge: Cambridge University Press.

Butler, J. K. (1991). Toward understanding and measuring conditions of trust: Evolution of conditions of trust inventory. *Journal of Management, 17*, 643–663. doi:10.1177/014920639101700307.

Castelfranchi, C., & Falcone, R. (2000). Trust and control: A dialectic link. *Applied Artificial Intelligence, 14*, 799–823. doi:10.1080/08839510050127560.

Childs, S. (2004). Developing health website quality assessment guidelines for the voluntary sector: Outcomes from the judge project. *Health Information & Libraries Journal, 21*(s2), 14–26.

Corritore, C. L., Kracher, B., & Wiedenbeck, S. (2003). On-line trust: Concepts, evolving themes, a model. *International Journal of Human-Computer Studies, 58*(6), 737–758.

Damm, D. J. L. (2012). Medien-Reputation und Quellenzugang. In K.-D. Altmeppen & R. Greck (Eds.), *Facetten des Journalismus* (pp. 143–167). Wiesbaden: VS Verlag für Sozialwissenschaften.

Das, T. K., & Teng, B. S. (2004). The risk-based view of trust: A conceptual framework. *Journal of Business and Psychology, 19*(1), 85–116.

Dietz, G., & Hartog, D. N. D. (2006). Measuring trust inside organisations. *Personnel Review, 35* (5), 557–588.

Eisenegger, M., & Imhof, K. (2009). Funktionale, soziale und expressive Reputation–Grundzüge einer Reputationstheorie. In U. Roettger (Ed.), *Theorien der Public Relations* (pp. 243–264). Wiesbaden: VS Verlag für Sozialwissenschaften.

Eurobarometer. (2015). http://ec.europa.eu/public_opinion/index_en.htm

Flanagin, A. J., & Metzger, M. J. (2000). Perceptions of Internet information credibility. *Journalism & Mass Communication Quarterly, 77*, 515–540. doi:10.1177/107769900007700304.

Flanagin, A. J., & Metzger, M. J. (2007). The role of site features, user attributes, and information verification behaviors on the perceived credibility of web-based information. *New Media & Society, 9*, 319–342. doi:10.1177/1461444807075015.

Flanagin, A. J., & Metzger, M. J. (2008). Digital media and youth: Unparalleled opportunity and unprecedented responsibility. In *The John D. and Catherine T. MacArthur Foundation Series on Digital Media and Learning*. doi:10.1162/dmal.9780262562324.005.

Frevert, U. (2013). *Vertrauensfragen: Eine Obsession der Moderne*. Munich: CH Beck.

Fulmer, C. A., & Gelfand, M. J. (2012). At what level (and in whom) we trust: Trust across multiple organizational levels. *Journal of Management, 38*(4), 1167–1230.

Giddens, A. (1997). *Konsequenzen der Moderne*. Suhrkamp: Frankfurt am Main.

Giffin, K. (1967). The contribution of studies of source credibility to a theory of interpersonal trust in the communication process. *Psychological Bulletin, 68*(2), 104–120.

Good, D. (1988). Individuals, interpersonal relations, and trust. In D. Gambetta (Ed.), *Trust: Making and breaking cooperative relationships* (pp. 131–185). New York: Basil Blackwell.

Gronke, P., & Cook, T. E. (2007). Disdaining the media: The American public's changing attitudes toward the news. *Political Communication, 24*(3), 259–281.

Guenther, T., & Möllering, G. (2010). A framework for studying the problem of trust in online settings. In D. Latusek & A. Gerbasi (Eds.), *Trust and technology in a ubiquitous modern environment* (pp. 16–33). Hershey, PA: Information Science Reference.

Gunther, A. C., & Christen, C. T. (2002). Projection or persuasive press? Contrary effects of personal opinion and perceived news coverage on estimates of public opinion. *Journal of Communication, 52*(1), 177–195.

Harris, P. R., Sillence, E., & Briggs, P. (2011). Perceived threat and corroboration: Key factors that improve a predictive model of trust in internet-based health information and advice. *Journal of Medical Internet Research, 13*(3).

Heintz, B. (2010). Numerische Differenz. Überlegungen zu einer Soziologie des (quantitativen) Vergleichs/Numerical difference. Toward a sociology of (quantitative) comparisons. *Zeitschrift für Soziologie, 39*(3), 162–181.

Hovland, C. I., Janis, I. L., & Kelley, H. H. (1953). *Communication and persuasion. Psychological studies of opinion change*. New Haven, CT: Yale University Press.

Jackob, N. G. E. (2010). No alternatives? The relationship between perceived media dependency, use of alternative information sources, and general trust in mass media. *International Journal of Communication, 18*(4), 589–606.

Jackob, N. (2012). The tendency to trust as individual predisposition—Exploring the associations between interpersonal trust, trust in the media and trust in institutions. *Communications, 37*(1), 99–120.

Karlsson, M. (2010). Rituals of transparency: Evaluating online news outlets' uses of transparency rituals in the United States, United Kingdom and Sweden. *Journalism Studies, 11*(4), 535–545.

Kelton, K., Fleischmann, K. R., & Wallace, W. A. (2008). Trust in digital information. *Journal of the American Society for Information Science and Technology, 59*(3), 363–374.

Kohring, M. (2004). *Vertrauen in Journalismus*. Konstanz: UVK Verlagsgesellschaft.

Lewicki, R. J., Tomlinson, E. C., & Gillespie, N. (2006). Models of interpersonal trust development: Theoretical approaches, empirical evidence, and future directions. *Journal of Management, 32*(6), 991–1022.

Lewis, J. D., & Weigert, A. (1985). Trust as a social reality. *Oxford Journal, 63*, 967–985.

Lieberman, J. K. (1981). *The litigious society*. New York: Basic Books.

Luhmann, N. (1968). *Vertrauen. Ein Mechanismus der Reduktion sozialer Komplexität*. Stuttgart: Ferdinand Enke Verlag.

Luhmann, N. (2000). Familiarity, confidence, trust: Problems and alternatives. *Trust: Making and Breaking Cooperative Relations, 6*, 94–107.

Luhmann, N. (2001). Vertrautheit, Zuversicht, Vertrauen: Probleme und Alternativen. In M. Hartmann & C. Offe (Eds.), *Vertrauen. Die Grundlage des sozialen Zusammenhalts* (pp. 143–160). Frankfurt: Campus.

Matthes, J. (2013). The affective underpinnings of hostile media perceptions: Exploring the distinct effects of affective and cognitive involvement. *Communication Research, 40*(3), 360–387.

Mayer, R. C., Davis, J. H., & Schoorman, F. D. (1995). An integrative model of organizational trust. *Academy of Management Review, 20*(3), 709–734.

McKnight, D. H., Cummings, L. L., & Chervany, N. L. (1998). Initial trust formation in new organizational relationships. *Academy of Management Review, 23*(3), 473–490.

Müller, J. (2013). *Mechanisms of trust: News media in democratic and authoritarian regimes.* Frankfurt: Campus Verlag.

Nienaber, A.-M., Romeike, P., Searle, R., & Schewe, G. (2015). What makes the glue sticky? A qualitative meta-analysis of antecedents and consequences of trust in supervisor-subordinate relationships. *Journal of Managerial Psychology, 30*(5), 507–534.

Rabinovich, A., Morton, T. A., & Birney, M. E. (2012). Communicating climate science: The role of perceived communicator's motives. *Journal of Environmental Psychology, 32*(1), 11–18.

Reuters Institute for the Study of Journalism. (2013). *Reuters Institute Digital News Report 2013.*

Rousseau, D. M., Sitkin, S. B., Burt, R. S., & Camerer, C. (1998). Introduction to special topic forum: Not so different after all: A cross-discipline view of trust. *Academy of Management Review, 23*(3), 393–404.

Sambrook, R. (2012). *Delivering trust: Impartiality and trust in the digital age.* Accessed April 30, 2015, from https://reutersinstitute.politics.ox.ac.uk/sites/default/files/Delivering%20Trust%20Impartiality%20and%20Objectivity%20in%20a%20Digital%20Age.pdf

Schoorman, F. D., Mayer, R. C., & Davis, J. H. (2007). An integrative model of organizational trust: Past, present, and future. *Academy of Management Review, 32*(2), 344–354.

Schoorman, F. D., Wood, M. M., & Breuer, C. (2015). Would trust by any other name smell as sweet? Reflections on the meanings and uses of trust across disciplines and context. In B. Bornstein & A. Tomkins (Eds.), *Motivating cooperation and compliance with authority* (pp. 13–35). New York: Springer International Publishing.

Simmel, G. (1908/2009). *Sociology: Inquiries into the construction of social forms* (2 vols., A. J. Blasi, A. K. Jacobs, & M. J. Kanjirathinkal, Trans.). Leiden: Brill.

Slovic, P. (2010). *The feeling of risk. New perspectives on risk perception.* London: Earthscan.

Slovic, P., & Peters, E. (2006). Risk perception and affect. *Current Directions in Psychological Science, 15*(6), 322–325.

Solomon, L. (1960). The influence of some types of power relationships and game strategies upon the development of interpersonal trust. *The Journal of Abnormal and Social Psychology, 61*(2), 223–230.

Sztompka, P. (1999). *Trust: A sociological theory.* Cambridge: Cambridge University Press.

Tsfati, Y., & Ariely, G. (2014). Individual and contextual correlates of trust in media across 44 countries. *Communication Research, 41*, 760–782. doi:10.1177/0093650213485972.

Ullmann-Margalit, E. (2004). Trust, distrust, and in between. In R. Hardin (Ed.), *Distrust* (pp. 60–82). New York: Russel Sage Publications.

Vorderer, P., & Kohring, M. (2013). Comm research—Views from Europe|Permanently online: A challenge for media and communication research. *International Journal of Communication, 7*, 188–196.

Vraga, E., Tully, M., Akin, H., & Rojas, H. (2012). Modifying perceptions of hostility and credibility of news coverage of an environmental controversy through media literacy. *Journalism, 13*, 942–959. doi:10.1177/1464884912455906.

Xie, W., & Zhao, Y. (2014). Is seeing believing? Comparing media credibility of traditional and online media in China. *China Media Research, 10*(3), 64.

Relational Trust and Distrust: Ingredients of Face-to-Face and Media-based Communication

Anil Kunnel and Thorsten Quandt

Abstract The analysis of relational trust and distrust between human actors is a promising but underdeveloped part of trust research. Instead of a scenario in which a trustor observes a trustee and therefore strategically gives him or her a credit of trust, the concept of relational trust focuses on the interaction and trust relationship between the actors. Here, we argue that relational trust and distrust are both part of an intersubjective "shared identity" between the interactants. We further explore their role in reciprocal face-to-face and media-based relationships. In this context, relational trust is defined as an essential communicational ingredient that enables interaction and the growth of human relationships through mutual confidence. Relational distrust, in contrast, helps interactants avoid risky relationships because it leads to skepticism within the relationship. We consider both relational trust and distrust to be ongoing communicational parts of any interaction. Based on our definition, we introduce an analytical model for further examination.

Keywords Relational trust • Relational distrust • Intersubjectivity • Copresence • Social presence

1 Introduction

In the discipline of Communication Studies, trust is a term with different interpretations. Most of the attention is focused on questions regarding the credibility of sources (Reich 2011a; Lankes 2008) or the systemic trust in and reliability of institutionalized journalism (Kohring 2004; Blöbaum 2014; Dernbach 2005; Quandt 2012). Fewer studies have been published about the role of mass communication in building media-based trust relationships. For instance, traditional mass media play an essential role in how we trust public actors such as politicians, corporations and entire systems, e.g., the health system (compare Sandvoss 2012). The introduction of social media brought new types of media-based trust relationships with people who appear publicly through their online profiles: Renting sites such as *AirBnB* offer cheap lodging in private apartments, dating apps such as

A. Kunnel (✉) • T. Quandt
University of Münster, Münster, Germany
e-mail: anil.kunnel@uni-muenster.de; thorsten.quandt@uni-muenster.de

© Springer International Publishing Switzerland 2016   27
B. Blöbaum (ed.), *Trust and Communication in a Digitized World*, Progress in IS,
DOI 10.1007/978-3-319-28059-2_2

Tinder offer romance based on social relatedness, and transportation apps such as *Lyft* offer a cheap ride based on geographical proximity (Tanz 2014). Although the concepts behind these services are nothing new, people use these applications with a whole new type of involvement. Many areas of their private lives, such as their living space and their cars, are commoditized in a way that they can be used and shared by others.

These examples show that more future research should focus on how trust is mediated through the use of mass communication and what the differences are, depending on the various types of communication. In this theoretical chapter, we would like to address this research gap and explore the role of trust in "connecting" people through media-based interaction. Although most of the current trust research is based on a rational concept of trust that has originated in game theory and introduces a scenario in which individuals make themselves strategically vulnerable to others (Loomis 1959; compare Mayer et al. 1995), we would like to explore a different perspective on trust that defines it as a social "connective tissue" between people (compare Endreß 2008). It is our belief that this type of *relational* trust should be considered an integral part of reciprocal relationships. In this context, we will define relational trust as a form of an assumed "shared identity" between two or more actors that is established through face-to-face or media-based interaction.

In the first part of this chapter, we will develop a concept of relational trust and distrust as a "shared identity" in face-to-face situations. In the second part, we will use social presence theory (Short et al. 1976) to apply this basic definition to mediated relationships, focusing on three scenarios: (1) the mediated relationship between interactants who are connected by *traditional information and communication technologies (ICT)*, (2) the mediated relationship between recipients and public actors who are covered by *institutionalized mass media* and (3) the mediated relationship between users in online social networks generated by *social media*. Finally, we will propose a general model of relational trust and distrust that should be further discussed and explored.

2 Interpersonal Relational Trust and Distrust

2.1 Relational Trust and Distrust as Components of Reciprocal Relationships

Trust research is a complex, cross-disciplinary field that includes different definitions and theories. It can be better described as a "meso" concept, "integrating micro-level psychological processes and group dynamics with institutional arrangements" (Rousseau et al. 1998, p. 393). Although economists view trust as "either calculative [. . .] or institutional", psychologists "focus on a host of internal cognitions that personal attributes yield". Sociologists, on the other side, "find trust in socially embedded properties and relationships among people [. . .] and institutions" (Rousseau et al. 1998, p. 393).

Although we understand trust as a social construct, we see these definitions as complementary rather than contradictory. In our understanding, relational trust is a multi-dimensional meta-cognitive but social process that constitutes human relationships by giving both sides the individual assumption of a "shared identity". This is a deviation from a traditional understanding: Trust is usually marked by a unidimensional approach that defines it as a cognitive and emotional psychological state. A trustor, under risky circumstances, develops a willingness to become vulnerable towards a trustee based on the perceived ability, benevolence, and integrity (Mayer et al. 1995; compare McKnight and Chervany 2001; Wang and Emurian 2005).

Recently, more scholars have used a "two-dimensional" approach that deviates from the idea that trust and distrust are on two symmetrical sides of the same scale (Lewicki et al. 1998, p. 446). Instead, they are understood as two different and sometimes competing constructs. Following this other consideration, trust can be defined in terms of "confident positive expectations regarding another's conduct, and distrust in terms of confident negative expectations regarding another's conduct" (Lewicki et al. 1998, p. 439).

In other words, relational trust and distrust exist simultaneously, and they both shape interdependent multiplex relationships. To emphasize their point, Lewicki et al. combine *high trust, low trust, high distrust* and *low distrust* to explain four scenarios (2006, p. 1003):

1. Relationships that feature *low distrust* and *low trust* are characterized by "casual acquaintances" and "limited interdependence" and allow for "professional courtesy".
2. Relationships that feature *low distrust* but *high trust* are characterized by "high value congruence" and allow for "new initiatives", which, in many situations, is basically an ideal scenario.
3. Relationships that feature *high distrust* and *high trust* are "highly segmented and bounded relationships" in which "opportunities are pursued and downside risks [and] vulnerabilities [are] continually monitored".
4. Relationships that feature *high distrust* and *low trust* are characterized by the assumption of "harmful motives" and "paranoia".

These four combinations demonstrate that relational trust and distrust are reciprocal and multiplex, which allows for various types of interaction in different situations. If two friends are working together, it is possible that there is *high trust* and *low distrust* on a private level but on that a professional level, there is *high distrust* and *less trust*. This suggests that in "all but the most primitive and simplistic relationships, we relate to each other in multiple ways" (Lewicki et al. 1998, p. 442). A human relationship can be defined through various contexts simultaneously, e.g., through friendship, professions, social milieu or experiences. Each different context comes with a different set of positive or negative assumptions about another's conduct and therefore with a different set of relational trust and distrust.

2.2   The Non-Rationality of Relational Trust and Distrust

The concept of trust as a multifaceted construct that leads to different types of relationships focuses on the complexity of *intersubjectivity* between two sides rather than on only one trustor "observing" a trustee. For all the reasons mentioned above, the concept of "relational trust" can be separated from more reflective concepts such as "deterrence-based trust", "calculus-based trust" or "institution-based trust" (Rousseau et al. 1998, pp. 398–401) because it is not dependent on only one "spectator". This concept emphasizes that "trust must be conceived as a property of collective units (ingoing dyads, groups and collectivities), not of isolated individuals. Being a collective attribute, trust is applicable to the relations among people rather than to their psychological states taken individually" (Lewis and Weigert 1985, p. 968). We will argue that relational trust and distrust are assumptions that are based on both a psychological process and the interaction between actors in a relationship.

In some parts of the literature, distrust, in contrast to trust, is defined as rationally based expectations and a form of social control (Barber 1983, pp. 21–23). Based on the definition of Lewicki et al., and contrary to a rational explanation, we understand relational distrust as a social construct that is equally intuitive and interdependent as relational trust. To be precise, *relational trust* is better understood as a social bonding mechanism that reduces vigilance and the awareness of potential risks in this relationship through an induced optimism (compare Sperber et al. 2010). *Relational distrust* is a mechanism that divides people by inducing skepticism and vigilance towards each other. This might lead to a higher reflection of the other side but not necessarily to rational behavior. According to Luhmann, distrust has a function similar to trust because it also creates order and reduces complexity but with a higher effort of control (1968, pp. 69–76). For instance, a professional business relationship might be successful when both parties involved perceive a level of distrust and therefore introduce careful negotiations about mutual expectations.

The general idea behind this non-rational approach on relational trust and distrust is the difficulty of a worldview that defines social relationships as entirely subjective and rational transactions. In trust or distrust scenarios defined by rationality, two parties perceive each other as potentially dangerous and give each other some type of "credit of trust", which can be a "willingness to be vulnerable" (Mayer et al. 1995). In the "trust game", a popular behavioral measure of trust and trustworthiness and a variation of the "dictator game", the trust credit is given by an isolated individual as an often conscious and rational decision (Johnson and Mislin 2011). In these scenarios, it is assumed that people are constantly "taking a risk" in social relationships, if only on a cognitive and emotional level. It is our assumption that most informal relationships that include a high degree of relational trust do not feature this type of high risk awareness. In our understanding, relational trust and distrust are basically features of *any* informal reciprocal relationship and might vary in their degree, alignment and "openness" for transactions.

For an observation of relational trust and distrust from *within* social relationships, we need to emphasize that relationships, in this context, are defined as continuous, growing interdependencies. Relationships build dynamic, ongoing ties that have a timeframe and a varying degree of reciprocity. These ties *change*; they can grow or shrink. From a network theory perspective, humans are connected through either weak or strong (undirected or directed) ties, whose strength is defined by reciprocal services, time, (emotional) intensity and mutual confiding or intimacy (Granovetter 1983). We assume that these factors of tie strength are influenced by the relational trust and distrust found in a tie. In the literature, additional features such as social distance, emotional support and the social structure have been investigated (Goldbeck 2013, pp. 66–68). These are primarily features of *undirected* ties. Although there are several open questions regarding the strength of *directed* ties (Ruef 2002, pp. 430–432), we assume that the strength of directed ties can be measured through directed features such as participation, support and emotional involvement.

It should be noted that Granovetter chooses not to define trust explicitly in his original theory, "regarding trust as a property either of individuals or of the emotional content, common understandings, or reciprocities of their interpersonal relationships" (Shapiro 1987, p. 625). Above all, relational trust and distrust are considered basic ingredients of social ties and human relationships, and they are only possible if at least two sides, which individually perceive each other, are involved. Although trust is "functionally necessary for the continuance of harmonious relationships, its actual continuance in any particular social bond is always problematic" (Lewis and Weigert 1985, p. 969).

Without the reflective, calculus-driven interpretation of trust, new questions arise. Instead of asking how humans manage dangerous situations or interactions with potentially malevolent others in a world full of risks, we should ask why they interact with each other or, alternatively, what stops them from connecting. We assume that relational trust and distrust are present once two or more actors develop a reciprocal relationship. This means that relational trust and distrust are linked directly to interdependence. This intuitive and non-calculative type of trust (or distrust) is less prominent in the literature but is arguably a major incentive (or disincentive) for interpersonal or interorganizational interaction (Endreß 2012)[1]. Consequently, its role in face-to-face and media-based communication should be further explored.

2.3 Relational Trust and Distrust as "Shared Identity"

In the literature, relational trust is often referred to as "identity-based trust". In most definitions, this type of trust is linked only to longer-term relationships that have

---

[1] See Endreß' concept of pre-reflective, "operating trust" ("fungierendes Vertrauen") for a similar approach.

developed a deep sense of familiarity (Rousseau et al. 1998, p. 399). For instance, when two colleagues have worked together for over 20 years, they have developed an affective, identity-based form of trust.

In this chapter, we would like to use a broader concept of identity-based trust that can also be applied to new relationships and is more dynamic in nature. This type of trust is not a static entity but a constant ongoing social identification process that "involves not only personal identities but also collective identities" (Möllering 2013, pp. 7–9). If we believe that human beings are in a continuous state of social identification with other actors (including people, groups or institutions), we can argue that on a meta-cognitive level, they constantly process other actors with each observation or interaction through the perception of "shared identities".

In this context, the term "shared identity" is not necessarily limited to similarities or commonalities, as suggested by the psychological research on "shared reality" (compare Echterhoff 2014). It also goes beyond an "encapsulated interest", in which one side includes the other side into their cognition (Hardin 2004, pp. 7–11). Moreover, "shared identity" refers to an assumed mutual horizon, an *intersubjective identity* that is based on actual copresence (compare Lewicki 2003). According to Goffman, "copresence renders persons uniquely accessible, available, and subject to another" (Goffman 1963, p. 22). In this sense, copresence refers to the "psychological connection to and with another [interaction partner]", requiring that "interactants feel they [are] able to perceive their interaction partner and that their interaction partner actively perceive[s] them" (Nowak and Biocca 2003, p. 482).

According to Schütz, we constantly construct current meaning in any interaction by internally processing our past and future as retentive and protective narrations (1974, pp. 62–95). This enables us to act regarding the future based on the knowledge of the past. We argue that in many situations that feature other actors, this narration is defined by a "togetherness" of at least two parties. In the context of the theory of "collective identity", our concept of trust as a shared identity can be described as "an interactive and shared definition" regarding future conduct (Melucci 1995, p. 44).

Based on the consideration of shared identity as an interactional process, our definition of *relational trust* refers to the assumption that the other side has convergent expectations about future conduct and will talk, behave and act as one (ideally) would. In contrast, *relational distrust* refers to the assumption that the other side has divergent expectations about future conduct and will not act as one (ideally) would. Therefore, negotiation and monitoring are more necessary in a high-distrust scenario.

We assume that based on this concept of a perceived convergent or divergent "shared identity", humans are more capable of coping with the general insecurity of social relationships. As an extension of the definition featured in Lewicki et al. 1998, we propose the following definitions of relational trust and distrust:

1. We define relational trust as the *assumption of convergent mutual expectations about future conduct* between one actor and other actors in social relationships.

2. We define relational distrust as the *assumption of divergent mutual expectations about future conduct* between one actor and other actors in social relationships.

In a sense, relational trust and distrust are ways of using one's own individual horizon of experience and self-reflected conduct as an intuitive assumption tool for another's conduct. By synchronizing our past actions, experiences and observations with the idea of our own (idealized) future behavior, we are able to assume converging or diverging expectations about the future conduct of others. We believe that this happens continuously with each interaction. Relational trust and distrust as assumptions make it easy to form new relationships without effort and avoid relationships that might be stressful or do us harm.

Consequently, a relationship that is characterized by *high mutual relational trust* usually has a great degree of retentive familiarity (regarding past experiences) and mutual protective confiding (regarding future conduct; compare definitions in Luhmann 2001; Schütz 1974). In an ongoing tie, trust "self-regulates" social relationships and allows us to have a continuous, confident "default status" without effort. This "connective" role marks its significance. When there is *high mutual trust*, we are not overly vigilant, and we perceive low risks of future conduct. Even when there is no continuous reciprocity, we assume that the relationship is working to our advantage. A relationship that is characterized by *high mutual distrust* can be considered equally self-regulated because both sides fail to become involved with each other, negotiate behavioral rules and sanctions or even refuse to interact (compare Lewicki et al. 2006, p. 1003). A diverging mutual expectation about future conduct can help us avoid risky relationships or help us to negotiate, monitor or control. The degree of distrust, much like the degree of trust, might vary from relationship to relationship or even culturally (Whaley 2001).

We have described trust and distrust as part of shared identities that are perceived on both sides individually but not necessarily in sync. It must be emphasized that this type of assumption is true only for social relationships that are not completely formalized. In a hypothetical setting of a completely formalized relationship (e.g., between a school teacher and a student), there is no need for relational trust or distrust because this relationship is defined and structured by behavioral rules and sanctions. A person can interact without the need of assuming the other side's expectations. Relational trust and distrust are necessary only when there are risks. By reflecting our own behavior onto others and creating an intersubjective space as we interact with them, we are able to draw assumptions about others' conduct similar (or different) to ours without the need to negotiate it. According to the definition of Renn and Klinke[2], risks in relationships are defined as the uncertainty, complexity or ambiguity of future conduct (compare Renn and Klinke 2003)—which is particularly true for (partly) informal and multiplex relationships. We assume that the salience of risks and securities could be influenced by

---

[2] Risks must not be confused with an actual threat or a specific danger. In this context, a risk can be defined as an insecurity about the contingencies of an interaction, including potential threats and opportunities. Contrary to risks such as uncertainty, ambiguity and complexity, relationships can also feature securities such as certainty, disambiguity or simplicity

external stimuli such as new information, individual disposition, e.g., one's trust propensity, or the degree of familiarity with that interactional partner.

2.4 Dimensions of Relational Trust and Distrust

So far, we have established a dynamic concept of relational trust and distrust that defines them as features of ongoing relationships, focusing on the uncertainty, ambiguity or complexity (risks) of future conduct. According to Lewicki et al., relational trust and distrust lead to confident or skeptical behavior within a relationship (2006, p. 1003). This marks their importance for the strength of relational ties; for instance, a tie that features *high trust* and *low distrust* likely features *high confidence* and *low skepticism*. In this case, intimate types of interaction such as reciprocal services or mutual confiding are more likely. To examine the role of relational trust and distrust for traditional and media-based relationships, we need to address the communicational aspect of our definition. According to Lewis and Weigert, the underlying process behind trust can be divided into three distinctive analytical dimensions of communicated content: *behavioral*, *cognitive* and *affective*[3] dimensions. These are, in reality "interpenetrating and mutually supporting aspects of the one, unitary experience and social imperative we simply call 'trust'" (1985, p. 972).

According to Lewis and Weigert, all three types of content are communicated simultaneously and also interfere with each other. Although their multi-dimensional definition stems from a tradition that defines trust as subjective and unidirectional, we would like to use their framework for our relational definition, which is defined by the perception of reciprocity and a shared identity. As we have noted, we understand the concept of intersubjectively shared identity as the assumption of a "shared" horizon. To better understand this concept of a shared identity in the context of a multi-dimensional definition, we would like to refer again to the theory of "collective identities". According to Melucci, collective identities are, similarly to Lewis and Weigert's concept of trust, developed on a behavioral, cognitive and affective dimension[4]. They are all part of a process that is "constructed and negotiated through a repeated activation of the relationships that link individuals (or groups)" (Melucci 1995, pp. 44–46). It is our objective to define relational trust as a shared identity that, in reciprocal relationships, is communicated on these three dimensions and encourages repeated activation of the relationship (see Table 1 and Fig. 1)

---

[3] Lewis and Weigert use *affective* and *emotional* synonymously.
[4] See Melucci's definitions of "cognitive definitions", "active relationships" and "emotional investment".

Table 1 Communication of relational trust and distrust through copresence

Dimension	Intersubjectivity through	Content	Communicated by
Behavioral	Exchange	Experience of interaction	Direct interaction such as *attendance, eye contact, exchange, conversation, competition, cooperation, collaboration, accommodation, transaction,...*
Cognitive	Reflection	Perceived trustworthiness	Personal information such as *reputation, image, credibility, reliability,...*
Affective	Association	Sense of belonging	Emotional intensity through *social relatedness, attitude, wish fulfillment, ideology, beliefs, symbolic tokens,...*

Behavioral Dimension

For traditional face-to-face-relationships, *direct interaction* is most likely a key factor for the development of relational trust and distrust (compare Hiltz et al. 1986). In this most basic dimension, the assumption of a shared identity is based on the *experience of interaction*. If a person directly interacts with another person or group, e.g., in a collaboration or in a conversation, this will influence their assumption about convergent or divergent expectations and produce a high or low level of confidence and skepticism[5]. This experience can be marked by different types of conduct, such as *eye contact, conversations* and *simple exchanges*, or through more complex types of interaction, such as *cooperation, collaboration* and *accommodation*. The point that we would like to make here is that *any* interaction, even without further reflection, inhabits some type of relational trust or distrust. Endreß argues that we are constantly in a relational mode when we interact with other people (compare 2008, p. 8). This means that trust is a constant part of the experience of others; it enables the mutual, ongoing perception of each other that is necessary for any interaction. This is not only true for dyads but can also be applied to larger groups. All members of a soccer team, for instance, need to trust each other without the constant necessity of monitoring each other or surveying their perception of each other. In this sense, relational trust and distrust are directly interwoven with the interaction itself and not a result or a prerequisite of interaction. According to Endreß, the interaction itself is the core[6] of relational trust (2008, pp. 14–15). This means that there is no trust or distrust without interaction or perceived reciprocity.

---

[5] This is particularly true for children, who even more strongly rely on the testimony of others and process past experiences such as "the informant's past inaccuracy, ignorance, uncertainty, or apparent idiosyncrasy" to feed their perceived profile of the other side (Harris 2007, p. 138).

[6] Translation from the German term "Kernphänomen".

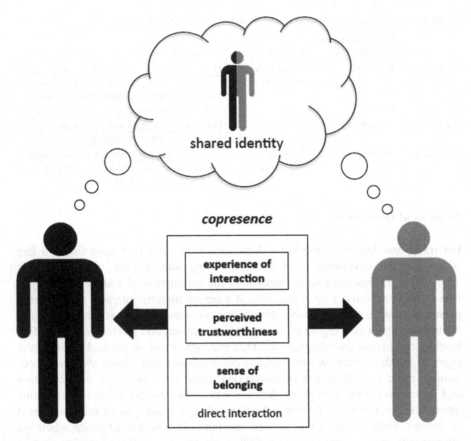

Fig. 1 Relational trust and distrust as shared identity through copresence

Cognitive Dimension

Every interaction with another actor includes a frequent cognitive process of mutual *reflection*. In the interaction itself, but also through the judgment of others, we receive personal information about the other side. "Information processing that is relevant for trust does not happen solely within individual minds of course, but also in all kinds of social processes of communicating and sense-making [...] and is shaped by organizational and institutional contexts as well as social networks" (Möllering 2013, p. 6). Whereas Lewis and Weigert define the cognitive dimension of trust more as a ground for rationality (1985, p. 973), we would like to define this type of information processing as reflective but non-rational (Endreß 2008, p. 8). In our definition, relational trust and distrust are based on the mostly subconscious reflection of the other side. The information on which this reflection is based is the other side's *trustworthiness*. In our understanding, trustworthiness is a type of information through which trust is communicated or perceived and should "not to be equated with trust" (Möllering 2013, p. 6). It is not an attribute of a person (compare Bierhoff and Rohmann 2010, p. 78). It can be indicated and communicated through personal information such as a person's *reputation* (others' perception), his or her *image* (self-portrayal) or specific factors such as the *reliability* of his or actions or the *credibility* of what he or she says (compare definitions by Eisenegger 2005, pp. 19–24; Fombrun 1996, pp. 70–72). It is our assumption that by receiving and reflecting personal information, relational trust and distrust can develop in an interaction or, based on the judgment of others, even without any previous mutual exchange. For instance, if we perceive a person as good-looking or if they manage to present themselves in a favorable light, this information will most likely positively influence our relational trust. If we hear other people speak ill of this person, this information will most likely positively influence our relational distrust.

Affective Dimension

On an emotional level, assumptions about shared expectations about future conduct can be caused by the feeling of *association*, resulting in the perception of a shared *sense of belonging*. This might refer not only to a "shared identity" but also to a "collective identity" that can understood as "the experience of personal involvement in a system or environment so that persons feel themselves to be an integral part of that system or environment" (Hagerty et al. 1992, p. 173; as cited in Zhao et al. 2012, p. 576). According to Putnam, this identification and sense of belonging between members of community is directly linked to the social capital of that community (Putnam 2000, pp. 133–147). A strong indicator of the sense of belonging might be the *social relatedness* to a person, group or institution (compare Knox et al. 2006, pp. 133–136). For instance, if the other side is or includes a friend of a friend, it will be easier for us to assume convergent expectations about future conduct based on the emotional intensity of the tie. If the other side is a stranger, we might be much more careful with our assumptions. Other potential indicators are, e.g., *shared beliefs* and *ideologies* or, on a more abstract level, *symbolic tokens* such as logos or brands (compare Reich 2011b, p. 99; Giddens 1991, p. 90). Even more than the cognitive dimension, the affective dimension of relational trust and distrust becomes salient not only when we connect with each other but also when we *exclude* other people, groups or institutions from future interactions. In this case, reflection and association can be even more effectively mobilized to build or affirm assumptions about *diverging* expectations of future conduct. In the most extreme scenarios, this associative relational distrust can be based on emotional reflections regarding ethnicity or political views (compare Whaley 2001; Krastev 2012).

3 Media-based Relational Trust and Distrust

3.1 Social Presence as a Foundation for Media-based Relational Trust and Distrust

So far, we have aimed to explain how relational trust and distrust are features of interpersonal relationships whose interdependence is defined primarily by direct interaction and direct copresence. With the expansion and growing complexity of modern societies and the growing importance of mediated communication, trust has become a frequently used and fragmented resource (Frevert 2013). In the transformation from a "face-to-face society to one of widespread anonymity in a demographically large and structurally complicated system, a person often interacts with others who are not known well or even at all" (Lewis and Weigert 1985, p. 973). According to Giddens, these trust relations "are basic to the extended time-space distanciation associated with modernity", allowing us to use the opportunities of an interconnected, globalized world (1991, p. 87).

To explain how relational trust and distrust can develop in "disembedded", media-based relationships (compare Giddens 1991, p. 79), we would like to take a look at how in mediated communication, the perception of *copresence* (e.g., in face-to-face situations) is replaced by the *social presence* of the interaction partner. Although social presence and copresence are sometimes used synonymously in parts of the literature (Bailenson et al. 2005), they can be understood as two different concepts. In this context, we use a definition in which social presence is a type of copresence that is perceived not directly but through mediated communication. According to Short et al., "social presence" is defined as "the degree of salience of the other person in a mediated communication and the consequent salience of their interpersonal interactions" (1976, p. 65). In this context, social presence is linked to the perceived "immediacy" and "intimacy" of mediated communication.

Although the original concept of social presence has often been interpreted as the *attribute* of the medium itself, we would like to use a definition that focuses on the *perception* of participants in mediated interactions (Gunawardena 1995, p. 163). This perception is characterized by the "awareness" of another actor and the feeling of "connectedness" with another actor (Rettie 2003). As we have noted, the perception of interaction and the awareness of another actor are, in our understanding, a requirement for relational trust and distrust to develop (compare de Vries 2006). We argue that with this "relational view" on social presence in media-based relationships (Kehrwald 2008, p. 91), relational trust and distrust as assumptions of expectations about future conduct are part of coordinating the future of that relationship.

In the context of our argumentation, the term "media-based relationships" refers to (1) the mediated relationship between interactants who are connected by *traditional information and communication technologies (ICT)*, (2) the mediated relationship between recipients and public actors who are covered by *institutionalized mass media* or (3) the mediated relationship between users in online social networks generated by *social media*. We believe that in all three types of mediated relationships, the basic mechanics behind relational trust and distrust are the same but are based on different alterations of social presence: To distinguish these three scenarios, we use the terms *interactional presence*, *public presence* and *network presence* as subcategories.

Interactional Presence

We use the term "interactional presence" to refer to the social presence between interactional partners in direct interactions that are based on the use of telecommunications or ICT and are not face-to-face (similar to Short et al.'s original definition (Short et al. 1976)). In this context, Hwang and Park suggest that "when we try to distinguish the experiences of individuals in physical environments from those in mediated environments, our understanding of what it means to feel present and what creates that feeling of social presence becomes a more important issue" (Hwang and Park 2007, p. 846). This means that the feeling of mutual awareness and connectedness, similar to the copresence in face-to-face-situations, is important for the effective use of communication technologies in interpersonal communication such as computer-mediated collaboration (Hwang and Park 2007, pp. 847–848; Weinel et al. 2011). Based on the limitations of the technology's "interactivity", which is their potential for interactional use (Neuberger 2007, pp. 43–47), trust content is communicated in direct exchange, either synchronously or disembedded in terms of time and space (see Fig. 2).

Public Presence

Although the concept of social presence has more recently been used for digital and interactional media, we assume that in relationships between recipients and public actors that are covered by institutionalized mass media (such as broadcast media or the printing press), recipients relationally trust or distrust those actors based on their "public presence". This alteration of social presence is understood as an attribute not of the media but of the "public sphere" created by institutionalized mass media. From a theoretical point of view, this public sphere can be described as "a network of communicational flows"[7] that generates interactional space for individuals and organizations (Imhof 2008, p. 73). Only through this "public arena" is a broader observation of and participation in what we call society possible (Imhof 2008, p. 74). Through public content, recipients are aware of and feel connected to public actors such as politicians, movie stars and athletes but also groups or institutions.

---

[7] We use this as a translation of the German description "Netzwerk von Kommunikationsflüssen".

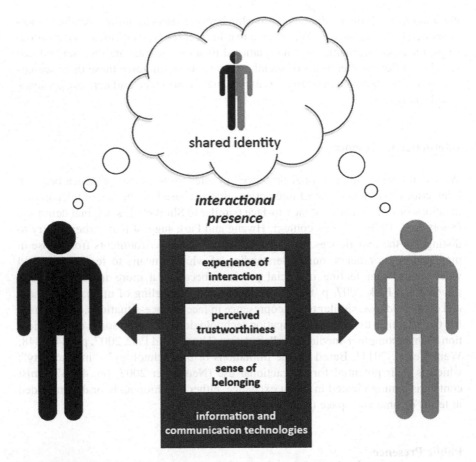

Fig. 2 Relational trust and distrust as shared identity through interactional presence

Professional journalism, public relations and marketing are some of the essential administrators of content that produce this type of media-based immediacy.

In public elections, for instance, an individually shared identity with politicians might be a major reason why citizens are capable of voting (Greene 2004). Public elections usually feature a degree of insecurity and a degree of perceived reciprocity as voters influence the fate of politicians or parties. This is why assumptions about converging or diverging expectations about future conduct are of importance. Particularly if someone lacks political knowledge or expertise, this feeling of connectedness and interactivity with a politician or a party may be a motivation behind his or her voting decision. In this case, relational trust and distrust in a politician reduce complexity (compare Luhmann 1968, p. 8) and might be a voter's "access point" to the complex dynamics of politics (compare Giddens 1991, p. 115). If there is high relational trust, the tie between voters and politicians might be strengthened by participation, emotional involvement or support on the voter's side. In contrast, the assumption of diverging expectations about future

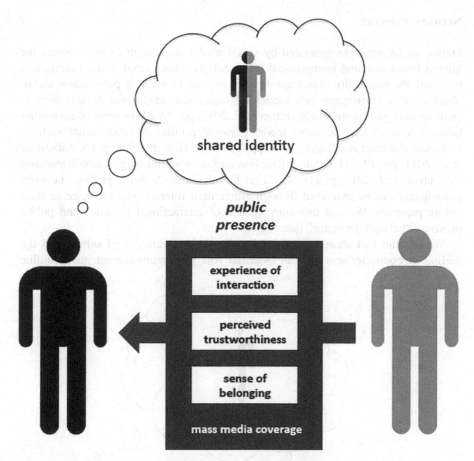

Fig. 3 Relational trust and distrust as shared identity through public presence

conduct may be helpful to decide whom not to vote for and weaken that tie (Zeineddine and Pratto 2014).

Because the relationship between recipients and public actors is primarily unidirectional and usually does not involve much direct interaction, our focus lies on the role of *mass media coverage* for relational trust and distrust in public actors. According to Koopman, in many situations, a feeling of interaction with public actors is salient through the visibility, resonance and perceived legitimacy of mass media content (2004, pp. 373–376). Because this content produces and shapes the individually perceived public presence of an actor and, with it, a level of immediacy, recipients are capable of relationally trusting and distrusting it. It is our assumption that in relationships between recipients and public actors, relational trust and distrust are equally communicated through the experience of interaction, perceived trustworthiness and an affective sense of belonging (see Fig. 3).

Network Presence

Online social networks generated by social media are complex environments for human interaction and interpersonal relationships. Most social media portals feature both the possibility to interact directly with other network participants and to observe them. Participants can interact through communicational devices such as chats or wall posts (compare Sherchan et al. 2013, pp. 20–21) or observe each other through features such as news feeds, personal profiles or reputational systems (compare Botsman and Rogers 2011, pp. 140–143; Howard 2008, p. 16; Astheimer et al. 2011, pp. 19–21). Often, interaction and observation happen simultaneously (Sherchan et al. 2013, p. 21). Based on this dynamic "hybrid" process, network participants can be perceived through either their interactional presence or their public presence. We call this convergence of interactional presence and public presence "network presence" (see Fig. 4).

We assume that shared identities based on the awareness of others and the feeling of connectedness play an essential role in communication inside online

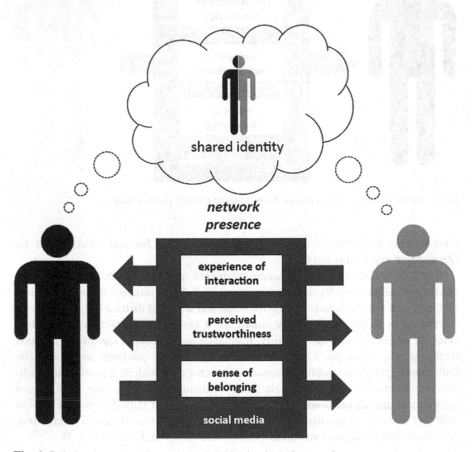

Fig. 4 Relational trust and distrust as shared identity through network presence

social networks. Particularly with new relationships, shared identities are needed to clarify contingencies (compare Thiedeke 2007, pp. 193–197). For instance, if a user wants to book a room on the renting site *AirBnB*, he or she will use the site's search engine to find suitable options. If there are several rooms that are similar (e.g., featuring the same price, location or tidiness), there might be still risks (uncertainties, ambiguities or complexities (compare Renn and Klinke 2003)) regarding the different hosts. Based on reception of the host's personal profiles, their ratings or shared friends, the user will perceive a varying degree of converging or diverging expectations about future conduct for each host. He or she is further incentivized to personally contact and directly interact with them, whereby their mutual relational trust or distrust is further developed.

This example shows that relational trust and distrust based on network presence are communicated through information that appears to be private (e.g., on personal profiles) but is distributed publicly inside networks (Münker 2009, pp. 115–119). Through this *network diffusion*, e.g., through recommendation systems (compare Andersen et al. 2008), relational trust and distrust can stabilize or destabilize the organizational and systemic structures of the network (compare Zucker 1985). For instance, a high level of relational distrust within a network might nurture social panic or inefficiency, whereas a high level of relational trust might raise the number of reactivations in collaborations or the degree of innovation (compare Karlan et al. 2009; Diekmann et al. 2014; Sundararajan et al. 2013). This "network effect" might also influence network participant's future ability to develop relational trust or distrust.

3.2 A Model of Relational Trust and Distrust

As we have seen, the concept of social presence offers a framework in which relational trust and distrust can be applied to media-based relationships. We need to emphasize that in each of our examples, the perception of a social presence is a fundamental requisite for relational trust and distrust to develop, much as the perception of a copresence is a requisite for relational trust and distrust in face-to-face situations. If recipients or users perceive a sense of reciprocity or "interactional space", relational trust and distrust are not only possible but also beneficial. This sense of connectedness is also based on the feeling of reliability of the medium itself or the institutions behind it. On a broader level, citizens are dependent on the functionality of the institutions behind traditional mass media and social media. In a sense, they need to trust or rely on these institutions to be able to trust other actors through the use of media. This is true not only for institutionalized journalism (Blöbaum 2014, pp. 37–40) but also for institutions in the new digital economy, such as *Facebook* or *Google,* that have recently been negatively linked to the NSA surveillance scandal (compare Zuboff 2013). If people perceive institutionalized journalism as a "liar press" (Connolly 2015) or social media sites as data surveillance systems, it will be hard for them to profit from the connective power of mass

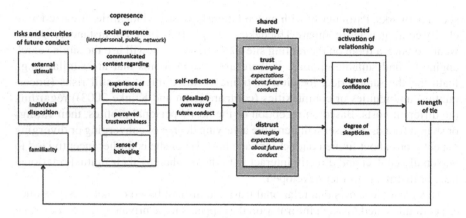

Fig. 5 Relational trust and distrust as shared identity in social relationships

communication. This is why both institutionalized media and new dynamic online social networks are competing for people's trust and attention (Quandt 2012, pp. 13–14; Castells 2012; Leiterer 2014).

Based on these restrictions, we propose the following model to emphasize how relational trust and distrust are part of a multi-dimensional meta-cognitive social process that affects the repeated activation of relationships and, ultimately, the strength of social ties (see Fig. 5): Informal relationships usually feature a degree of risks (uncertainty, ambiguity or complexity) and a degree of securities (certainty, disambiguity and simplicity) of future conduct. These perceived risks and securities might be influenced by *external stimuli* (e.g., new information), *individual dispositions* (e.g., the propensity to trust) and the *familiarity* between two or more actors. Through relational trust and distrust, people are capable of self-regulating relationships beyond the presence of risks or the lack of securities. By processing the *experience of interaction*, the *perceived trustworthiness* and the *sense of belonging* through *copresence* or an alteration of *social presence* and by balancing them with their own *self-reflection*, people are capable of assuming *converging* or *diverging* *expectations of future conduct*. We call these assumptions *relational trust* and *distrust*. Together, they form a perceived *shared identity* between two or more actors and influence the *repeated activation of relationships* by raising *confidence* or *skepticism*. We assume that this affects the *strength of ties*, which is directly linked to the *familiarity* and "shared history" between all actors involved.

4 Conclusion

Throughout this chapter, we have integrated several theoretical concepts into our model of relational trust and distrust. Such an approach usually comes with certain limitations and downsides, particularly in the space of a book chapter. On a basic level, further work needs to be put into the theoretical fusion of the ideas behind these theories, particularly considering the implications regarding the concepts of perceived intersubjectivity and shared identity. Nonetheless, this approach demonstrates the general cross-disciplinarity of trust research and offers an understanding of trust that is not based entirely on a rational perspective in which individuals strategically make themselves vulnerable. Only by exploring the complex dynamics behind human face-to-face and media-based interaction is it possible to understand the role of relational trust as a consistent part of human communication. Through our model, we were able to consider the following further research questions:

First, we were able to argue not only that trust is relevant when there are specific dangers or threats but that the insecurity about future conduct is a basic characteristic of informal relationships that are not strictly regulated. In the context of media-based communication, it will be interesting to find out how, for instance, external stimuli such as a public scandal regarding a public person change our perception of the person and what effect they have on the perceived familiarity. Further research should also answer the question how familiarity, e.g., through interaction or media coverage, progresses in the constant reactivation of a relationship.

Based on the research of Lewicki and colleagues, we have also argued that we see trust and distrust not as the strategic actions implied in most of the literature but as assumptions that constantly regulate the induced confidence and skepticism in relationships. This is a much more dynamic understanding of trust and distrust; they "accompany" every communicative act in a relationship. Further research should address the effect of confidence and skepticism on the reactivation of relationships and on the strength of ties between interactants, measuring indicators of directed and undirected strength (e.g., support, or intimacy).

Another implication of our model is that trust and distrust are linked to constant self-reflection. This is an argument that can rarely be found in the specific literature, which usually focuses on trust based on rational observations. The idea that relational trust and distrust as a shared identity intersubjectively emerge out of a reflection of the interactant and a reflection of one's own leads to further research opportunities, in which both types of reflection should be analyzed, measured and put into relation. This is particularly true for the field of media reception.

We have also argued that in media-based relationships, copresence is "substituted" by different forms of social presence. In this context, it will be necessary to analyze how communicated trust content differs depending on the type of media, e.g., how reputation as an indicator of trustworthiness is communicated through institutionalized mass media or social media. Further research should also focus on relational trust and distrust that are based simultaneously on different forms of (mediated) interaction. For instance, how does a meet-and-greet with a politician influence the perception of his or her institutionalized media appearance or her *Twitter* account?

Based on our model, we hope we have demonstrated the limitations and opportunities of a relational view on trust and distrust in face-to-face and media-based relationships and have offered a framework for future research in the field of Communication Studies.

References

Andersen, R., et al. (2008). Trust-based recommendation systems: An axiomatic approach. In *WWW'08 Proceedings of the 17th international Conference on World Wide Web*, Beijing, 170–199.

Astheimer, J., Neumann-Braun, K., & Schmidt, A. (2011). My face. Portrait photography on the social web. In U. P. Autenrieth & K. Neumann-Braun (Eds.), *The visual worlds of social networks sites. Images and image-based communication on Facebook and Co* (pp. 15–60). Baden-Baden: Nomos.

Bailenson, J. N., et al. (2005). The independent and interactive effects of embodied agent appearance and behavior on self-report, cognitive, and behavioral markers of copresence in immersive virtual environments. *Presence: Teleoperators and Virtual Environments, 14*(4), 1–34.

Barber, B. (1983). *The logic and limits of trust*. New Brunswick, NJ: Rutgers University Press.

Bierhoff, H.-W., & Rohmann, E. (2010). Psychologie des Vertrauens. In M. Maring (Ed.), *Vertrauen—zwischen sozialem Kitt und der Senkung von Transaktionskosten* (pp. 71–89). Karlsruhe: KIT Scientific Publishing.

Blöbaum, B. (2014). *Trust and journalism in a digital environment* (Working Paper). Oxford: Reuters Institute for the Study of Journalism.

Botsman, R., & Rogers, R. (2011). *What's mine is yours: How collaborative consumption is changing the way we live*. London: Collins.

Castells, M. (2012). *Networks of outrage and hope. Social movements in the internet age*. Cambridge: Polity Press.

Connolly, K. (2015). Pegida: What does the German far-right movement actually stand for? *The Guardian Online*. http://www.theguardian.com/world/shortcuts/2015/jan/06/pegida-what-does-german-far-right-movement-actually-stand-for. Accessed 3 Apr 2015.

De Vries, P. (2006). Social presence as a conduit to the social dimensions of online trust. In W. Ijsselsteijn, Y. de Kort, & C. Midden (Eds.), *Persuasive technology. First International Conference on Persuasive Technology for Human Well-Being* (pp. 55–59). Berlin: Springer.

Dernbach, B. (2005). Was schwarz auf weiß gedruckt ist... Vertrauen in Journalismus, Medien und Journalisten. In B. Dernbach & M. Meyer (Eds.), *Vertrauen und Glaubwürdigkeit. Interdisziplinäre Perspektiven* (pp. 135–154). Wiesbaden: VS Verlag für Sozialwissenschaften.

Diekmann, A., et al. (2014). Reputation formation and the evolution of cooperation in anonymous online markets. *American Sociological Review, 79*(1), 65–85.

Echterhoff, G. (2014). Achieving commonality in interpersonal communication: Shared reality and memory processes. *Asian Journal of Social Psychology, 17*(2), 104–107.

Eisenegger, M. (2005). *Reputation in der Mediengesellschaft. Konstitution—Issues Monitoring—Issues Management*. Wiesbaden: Springer Fachmedien.

Endreß, M. (2008). Fungierendes Vertrauen—Eine prä-reflexive wie meta-reflexive Ressource. *Vortrag Berlin Juli 2008*, 1–17. http://www.bildungsvertrauen.de/material/endress_nw1.pdf. Accessed 3 Apr 2015.

Endreß, M. (2012). Vertrauen und Misstrauen—Soziologische Überlegungen. In C. Schilcher, M. Will-Zocholl, & M. Ziegler (Eds.), *Vertrauen und Kooperation in der Arbeitswelt* (pp. 81–102). Wiesbaden: Springer.

Fombrun, C. J. (1996). *Reputation: Realizing value from the corporate image*. Harvard: Harvard Business School Press.

Frevert, U. (2013). *Vertrauensfragen. Eine Obsession der Moderne*. München: C.H. Beck.

Giddens, A. (1991). *The consequences of modernity*. Cambridge: Polity Press.

Goffman, E. (1963). *Behavior in public places: Notes on the social organization of gatherings*. New York: The Free Press.

Goldbeck, J. (2013). *Analyzing the social web*. Waltham: Morgan Kaufman.

Granovetter, M. (1983). The strenght of weak ties: A network theory revisited. *Sociological Theory, 1*, 201–233.

Greene, S. (2004). Social identity theory and party identification. *Social Science Quarterly, 85*(1), 136–153.

Gunawardena, C. N. (1995). Social presence theory and implications for interaction and collaborative learning in computer conferences. *International Journal of Educational Telecommunications, 1*(2/3), 147–166.

Hagerty, B. M. K., et al. (1992). Sense of belonging: A vital mental health concept. *Archives of Psychiatric Nursing, 6*(3), 172–177.

Hardin, R. (2004). *Trust and trustworthiness*. New York: Russell Sage.

Harris, P. L. (2007). *Trust. Developmental science, 10*(1), 135–138.

Hiltz, S. R., Johnson, K., & Turoff, M. (1986). Experiments in group decision making. Communication process and outcome in face-to-face versus computerized conferences. *Human Communication Research, 13*(2), 225–252.

Howard, B. (2008). Analyzing online social networks. *Communications of the ACM, 51*(11), 14–16.

Hwang, H. S., & Park, S. (2007). Being together: User's subjective experience of social presence in CMC Environments. In *Human-computer interaction, Part 1* (pp. 844–853). Berlin: Springer.

Imhof, K. (2008). Theorie der Öffentlichkeit als Theorie der Moderne. In C. Winter, A. Hepp, & F. Krotz (Eds.), *Theorien der Kommunikations- und Medienwissenschaft. Gundlegende Diskussionen, Forschungsfelder und Theorienentwicklung* (pp. 65–89). Wiesbaden: VS Verlag für Sozialwissenschaften.

Johnson, N. D., & Mislin, A. A. (2011). Trust games: A meta-analysis. *Journal of Economic Psychology, 32*, 865–889.

Karlan, D., et al. (2009). Trust and social collateral. *The Quarterly Journal of Economics, 124*, 1307–1361.

Kehrwald, B. (2008). Understanding social presence in text-based online learning environments. *Distance Education, 29*(1), 89–106.

Knox, H., Savage, M., & Harvey, P. (2006). Social networks and the study of relations: Networks as method, metaphor and form. *Economy and Society, 35*(1), 113–140.

Kohring, M. (2004). *Vertrauen in Journalismus. Theorie und Empirie*. Konstanz: UVK Verlagsgesellschaft.

Koopmans, R. (2004). Movements and media: Selection processes and evolutionary dynamics in the public sphere. *Theory and Society, 33*, 367–391.

Krastev, I. (2012). Can democracy exist without trust? *TedGlobal*. Available at: http://www.ted.com/talks/ivan_krastev_can_democracy_exist_without_trust. Accessed 5 June 2014.

Lankes, D. R. (2008). Credibility on the internet: Shifting from authority to reliability. *Journal of Documentation, 64*(5), 667–686.

Leiterer, A. (2014). ZAPP Studie: Vertrauen in Medien ist gesunken. *Zapp—Das Medienmagazin*. http://www.ndr.de/fernsehen/sendungen/zapp/ZAPP-Studie-Vertrauen-in-Medien-gesunken, medienkritik100.html. Accessed 15 Mar 2015.

Lewicki, R. (2003). Trust and shared identity. *Beyond intractability*. http://www.beyondintractability.org/audiodisplay/lewicki-r-12-shared-identity1. Accessed 30 Mar 2015.

Lewicki, R. J., McAllister, D. J., & Bies, R. J. (1998). Trust and distrust: New relationships and realities. *Academy of Management Review, 23*(3), 438–458.

Lewicki, R. J., Tomlinson, E. C., & Gillespie, N. (2006). Models of interpersonal trust development: Theoretical approaches, empirical evidence, and future directions. *Journal of Management, 32*(6), 991–1022.

Lewis, J. D., & Weigert, A. (1985). Trust as a social reality. *Social Forces, 63*(4), 967–985.

Loomis, J. L. (1959). Communication, the development of trust, and cooperative behavior. *Human Relations, 12*(4), 305–315.

Luhmann, N. (1968). *Vetrauen. Ein Mechanismus der Reduktion sozialer Komplexität*. Stuttgart: Ferdinand Enke Verlag.

Luhmann, N. (2001). Vertrautheit, Zuversicht, Vertrauen: Probleme und Alternativen. In M. Hartmann & C. Offe (Eds.), *Vertrauen. Die Grundlage des sozialen Zusammenhalts* (pp. 143–160). Frankfurt: Campus Verlag.

Mayer, R. C., Davis, J. H., & Schoorman, F. D. (1995). An integrative model of organizational trust. *Academy of Management Review, 20*(3), 709–734.

McKnight, D. H., & Chervany, N. L. (2001). Trust and distrust definitions: One bite at a time. In R. Falcone, M. Singh, & Y.-H. Tan (Eds.), *Trust in cyber-societies. Integrating the human and artificial perspectives. Lecture Notes in Artificial Intelligence* (pp. 27–54). Heidelberg: Springer.

Melucci, A. (1995). The process of collective identity. In H. Johnston & B. Klandermans (Eds.), *Social movements and culture* (pp. 41–63). Minneapolis, MN: University of Minnesota Press.

Möllering, G. (2013). Process views of trusting and crises. In R. Bachmann & A. Zaheer (Eds.), *Handbook of advances in trust research* (pp. 285–306). Cheltenham: Edward Elgar.

Münker, S. (2009). *Emergenz digitaler Öffentlichkeit*. Suhrkamp: Frankfurt am Main.

Neuberger, C. (2007). Interaktivität, Interaktion, Internet. Eine Begriffsanalyse. *Publizistik, 52*(1), 33–50.

Nowak, K. L., & Biocca, F. (2003). The effect of the agency and anthropomorphism on users' sense of telepresence, copresence, and social presence in virtual environments. *Presence: Teleoperators and Virtual Environments, 12*(5), 481–494.

Putnam, R. D. (2000). *Bowling alone. The collapse and revival of American community*. New York: Simon & Schuster Paperbacks.

Quandt, T. (2012). What's left of trust in a network society? An evolutionary model and critical discussion of trust and societal communication. *European Journal of Communication, 27*(1), 7–21.

Reich, Z. (2011a). Source credibility and journalism. *Journalism Practice, 5*(1), 51–67.

Reich, Z. (2011b). User comments. The transformation of participatory space. In J. B. Singer et al. (Eds.), *Participatory journalism. Guarding open gates at online newspapers* (pp. 96–117). Malden: Wiley-Blackwell.

Renn, O., & Klinke, A. (2003). Risikoabschätzung und -bewertung. Ein neues Konzept zum Umgang mit Komplexität, Unsicherheit und Ambiguität. In J. Beaufort, E. Gumpert, & M. Vogt (Eds.), *Fortschritt und Risiko. Zur Dialektik der Verantwortung in (post-) modernen Gesellschaften* (pp. 21–52). J.H. Roll: Dettelbach.

Rettie, R. (2003). Connectedness, awareness and social presence. In *6th Annual International Workshop on Presence*. Aalborg. http://eprints.kingston.ac.uk/2106/.

Rousseau, D., et al. (1998). Not so different after all: A cross discipline view of trust. *Academy of Management Review, 23*(3), 393–404.

Ruef, M. (2002). Strong ties, weak ties and islands: Structural and cultural predictors of organizational innovation. *Industrial and Corporate Change, 11*(3), 427–449.

Sandvoss, C. (2012). Enthusiasm, trust and its erosion in mediated politics: On fans of Obama and the Liberal Democrats. *European Journal of Communication, 27*(1), 68–81.

Schütz, A. (1974). *Der sinnhafte Aufbau der sozialen Welt. Eine Einleitung in die verstehende Soziologie*. Frankfurt am Main: Suhrkamp.

Shapiro, S. P. (1987). The social control of impersonal trust. *American Journal of Sociology, 93* (3), 623–658.

Sherchan, W., Nepal, S., & Paris, C. (2013). A survey of trust in social networks. *ACM Computing Surveys, 45*(4), 1–33.

Short, J., Williams, E., & Bruce, C. (1976). *The social psychology of telecommunications*. London: Wiley.

Sperber, D., et al. (2010). Epistemic vigilance. *Mind & Language, 25*(4), 359–393.

Sundararajan, A., et al. (2013). Research commentary—Information in digital, econonic, and social networks. *Information Systems Research, 24*(4), 883–905.

Tanz, J. (2014). How Airbnb and Lyft finally got Americans to trust each other. *WIRED*. http://www.wired.com/2014/04/trust-in-the-share-economy/. Accessed 13 Nov 2014.

Thiedeke, U. (2007). *Trust, but test! Das Vertrauen in virtuellen Gemeinschaften*. Konstanz: UVK Verlagsgesellschaft.

Wang, Y. D., & Emurian, H. H. (2005). An overview of online trust: Concepts, elements, and implications. *Computers in Human Behavior, 21*, 105–125.

Weinel, M., et al. (2011). A closer look on social presence as a causing factor in computer-mediated collaboration. *Computers in Human Behavior, 27*(1), 513–521.

Whaley, A. L. (2001). Cultural mistrust: An important psychological construct for diagnosis and treatment of African Americans. *Professional Psychology: Research and Practice, 32*(6), 555–562.

Zeineddine, F. B., & Pratto, F. (2014). Political distrust: The seed and fruit of popular empowerment. In J.-W. van Prooijen & P. A. M. van Lange (Eds.), *Power, politics, and paranoia. Why people are suspicious of their leaders* (pp. 106–129). Cambridge: Cambridge University Press.

Zhao, L., et al. (2012). Cultivating the sense of belonging and motivating user participation in virtual communities: A social capital perspective. *International Journal of Information Management, 32*(6), 574–588.

Zuboff, S. (2013). Be the friction—Our response to the New Lords of the Ring. *Frankfurter Allgemeine*. http://www.faz.net/-gqz-7adzg. Accessed 1 June 2014.

Zucker, L. G. (1985). Production of trust: Institutional sources of economic structure, 1840 to 1920. In L. L. Cummings & B. Staw (Eds.), *Research in organizational behavior* (pp. 53–111). Greenwich: JAI Press.

Part II
Concepts and Models of Trust Research in Media, Sport, Science, Economy, and Social Relations

Trust in Online Journalism

Katherine M. Grosser, Valerie Hase, and Bernd Blöbaum

Abstract With professional journalism being subject to major changes due to the process of digitalization, the development of the recipients' trust in journalism must be reconsidered. In this paper, we propose a conceptual model for trust in online journalism which takes into consideration both influential characteristics of the recipients and changes within journalism itself. This conceptualization is based on a sociological and psychological understanding of trust as well as a systems-theoretical definition of journalism. We thereby argue that socio-demographic, personal and situational aspects regarding the recipients (as the trustors) affect trust in journalism (as the trustee). While socio-demographics and political ideologies lose influence on the development of trust compared to offline journalism, specific media behavior gains in importance. Furthermore, changes within the criteria for the correct functioning of the existing journalistic programs, which are considered antecedents of trustworthiness, as well as the emergence of new antecedents within these programs and external factors influence whether journalism is perceived as trustworthy in the online context. In sum, we posit that the development of trust in online journalism becomes more difficult, especially due to changes within journalism itself. Our model enables further research by laying the groundwork for empirical measurement regarding the difference between trust in offline and online journalism.

Keywords Trust • Journalism research • Online journalism • Offline journalism • Digitalization • Recipients

K.M. Grosser (✉) • V. Hase • B. Blöbaum
University of Münster, Münster, Germany
e-mail: k.grosser@uni-muenster.de; valerie.hase@uni-muenster.de; bernd.bloebaum@uni-muenster.de

© Springer International Publishing Switzerland 2016
B. Blöbaum (ed.), *Trust and Communication in a Digitized World*, Progress in IS,
DOI 10.1007/978-3-319-28059-2_3

1 Introduction

With the complexity of society continuously growing, the functioning of everyday
life is becoming indisputably more difficult.[1] In a world where no one has the
resources to know everything about one another, trust and distrust are of central
importance for the functioning of society (Barber 1983, p. 165; Kohring 2004,
p. 11) as they both reduce complexity (Luhmann 1979, pp. 71–72). Trust and
distrust are often not created through direct interaction, but rather through interme-
diaries such as journalism (Blöbaum 2014, p. 22). However, in order for journalism
to create trust and distrust, its recipients first need to trust journalism itself (Kohring
2004, p. 104). In recent years, journalism has undergone many changes, first and
foremost due to digitalization. The process of digitalization affects society as a
whole and has especially brought forth new developments in online journalism. Not
only journalism itself has changed though—its relationship to the recipients, who
have a much more active role in the news production online, has developed further
as well. The audience as a whole has become more relevant to journalism—online
and offline. Trust in online journalism is therefore an issue that has to be analyzed
both theoretically and empirically to define its status quo, to discern differences and
similarities in comparison to trust in traditional offline journalism and to discover
possible consequences for both journalism research and journalistic practices.

The aim of this paper therefore is to conceptualize the development of trust in
online journalism under consideration of changes regarding both the recipients and
journalism itself due to digitalization. To this end, we will develop a model of trust
in online journalism based on a sociological understanding of trust in systems and a
systems-theoretical definition of journalism. While this conceptualization is the
main accomplishment of the paper, the model is followed by a comparison of trust
for online and offline journalism as well as an enumeration of starting points for
journalism to deal with trust problems.

It is important to note two things regarding the scope of this paper. First, the
focus of the analysis is on professional news journalism; it does not deal with
citizen or participatory journalism and activities like blogs. While citizen journalism as a phenomenon is growing, this limitation seems justified by the fact that
professional journalism has much higher user numbers and is therefore more
relevant (Wolf and Schnauber 2014, p. 11). From this follows that, whenever we
use the term *news media*, we mean professional journalism. Furthermore, this paper
deals explicitly with trust in journalism and not with journalism's credibility. This
is important because trust and credibility have often been treated as the same in
Communication Studies, especially regarding its operationalization in empirical
research (Kohring and Matthes 2007, p. 232).

---

[1] Some aspects of this chapter were previously expounded upon in an article published in
DIGITAL JOURNALISM, published online on 26 January, 2016, copyright by Taylor & Francis,
available online: http://www.tandfonline.com/10.1080/21670811.2015.1127174

The relevance of this paper is illustrated by the following two reasons: First, more and more people are going online to get their daily information (Pew Research Center for the People and the Press 2012, p. 1; Reuters Institute 2014), meaning that trust in online journalism as a prerequisite for the emergence of trust and distrust in society is becoming increasingly more important. And second, analyzing changes in journalism is one of the most important tasks of Communication Studies (Blöbaum 2005, p. 57).

2 Basics: Trust and Journalism

Before specifically considering trust in professional journalism, it is important to clarify this paper's understanding of trust in social systems as well as journalism as a social system.

2.1 Trust in Systems

Trust is defined as a state, specifically the "willingness of a party [namely the trustor] to be vulnerable to the actions of another party [namely the trustee]" (Mayer et al. 1995, p. 712). This state is therefore relevant in a relationship between two entities: an individual, an organization or a system as the trustor and an individual, an organization or a system as the trustee. Since the trustor must first perceive a risk in order for this willingness to become relevant (Luhmann 1979, p. 24; Giddens 1991, p. 30; Rousseau et al. 1998, p. 395; Kohring 2004, p. 89), this willingness to be vulnerable, i.e., to trust, can also be described as the willingness to take a risk. This risk is perceived subjectively by each trustor according to the specific situation (Jungermann and Slovic 1993, p. 171). It results from the internal considerations of external circumstances (Luhmann 1988, p. 100). Risk can be related to several possible trust outcomes, e.g., the aimed goal being failed due to unfulfilled expectations regarding the trustee or to the trustor having invested unnecessary resources (Castelfranchi and Falcone 2000, p. 804; Das and Teng 2004, pp. 101–103). Since this paper focuses on recipients' trust in journalism, in the following we deal solely with the relationship between an individual as the trustor and a system as the trustee.

The trustor's willingness to trust is mainly influenced by two things: his characteristics and the perceived trustworthiness of the trustee (Mayer et al. 1995, pp. 715–724). On the one hand, the trustor's socio-demographic background and personal characteristics such as his general propensity to trust and his general propensity to take risks as a personal trait (Sitkin and Pablo 1992, pp. 12–13; Das and Teng 2004, p. 97; Blöbaum 2014, p. 49) may have an influence. Furthermore, situational aspects such as his prior experience with the trustee may affect his willingness to trust. The willingness to trust therefore depends greatly on the trustor and his characteristics (Blöbaum 2014, p. 17).

On the other hand, the perceived trustworthiness as an attributive characteristic of the trustee is based on specific expectations the trustor has regarding the trustee's actions. The relevant action for a system as the trustee is its correct functioning (Luhmann 1979, p. 50; Giddens 1991, pp. 33–34). Therefore, the trustworthiness of a system is based on the extent to which the trustor perceives his expectations regarding the correct functioning to be fulfilled (Kohring 2004, p. 110). Seeing as the correct functioning of a system is determined by the correct functioning of the system's programs (ibid.)—the guidelines and operation processes which manage a system (Luhmann 1990, p. 91)—the antecedents of a system's trustworthiness can consequently be derived from the criteria for or expectations regarding the correct functioning of the system's programs (Kohring 2004, p. 124).

We term the trustor finally making himself vulnerable to the system's actions as the *trusting action*. This trusting action is only taken when the trustor's willingness to trust surpasses his level of perceived risk (Mayer et al. 1995, p. 726). In this paper, the weighing of the willingness to trust against the perceived risk—the outcome of which can be a trusting action—is termed as the *trust mechanism*.

While Mayer et al.'s (1995) trust mechanism therefore serves as the basis of our model, their conceptualization, which was developed for interpersonal and organizational trust, must be adapted for trust in systems, as done here. It also must be transferred to journalism research, which is undertaken below. Along similar lines, Kohring's (2004) understanding of trustworthiness being based on the correct functioning of the system's programs serves as a starting point for our conceptualization. However, our model is advantageous insofar as it goes beyond Kohring and thus makes progress in points in which his model comes up short, thereby expanding the concept of trust in journalism. Specifically, our model deals with the role the recipients play within the trust mechanism and with trust in the era of digitalization, thus allowing us to draw a comparison between the development of trust in offline and online journalism. Before describing trust in both offline and online journalism, we first outline our understanding of journalism as a system.

2.2 Journalism as a System

In this paper, we understand journalism as a social system with the function of selecting and communicating current information (Blöbaum 1994, p. 261). This enables follow-up action and follow-up communication to its recipients. The journalistic system consists of the following three structural elements: organizations, roles and programs (Blöbaum 2016, p. 151). The journalistic programs are: research, selection, editing—which comprises presentation, proofing and revision—and coordination (ibid., pp. 156–158). Altogether, they refer to "journalistic practices, work routines and professional norms" (Blöbaum 2014, p. 10). The recipients—often also referred to as the audience—are thereby seen as a part of the journalistic system. Whether they are an internal or an external part with regard to journalism differs within theoretical perspectives (Marcinkowski 1993, pp. 79–98; Blöbaum 1994, pp. 167–170; Scholl and Weischenberg 1998, pp. 120–124). According to Luhmann (1995, pp. 140–143), communication is only complete if the information that is communicated is also received (and there, either understood or misunderstood). As the recipients therefore complete journalistic communication, their importance for the comprehension of journalistic information is undisputed (Meusel 2014, p. 61).

Since journalism is not defined by the way media content is distributed, but rather by its function (Blöbaum 2016, p. 153), the journalistic system comprises both offline and online journalism. For professional journalism fulfills the same function (Neuberger et al. 2009, p. 174) and is determined by the same processes and guidelines in both contexts (Neuberger and Quandt 2010, p. 64). Thus, the programs themselves are the same in both offline and online journalism. The developments digitalization has triggered in the journalistic system consequently do not change the programs themselves—they rather lead to changes *within* the programs, namely with regard to the antecedents of trustworthiness. This will be shown in the third chapter.

2.3 Trust in Offline Journalism

Based on our understanding of trust in systems and journalism as a system, trust in journalism can be defined as the willingness of the trustor—in our case the recipients—to be vulnerable to the journalistic system's selection and communication of current information by making the information the basis of their follow-up communication and follow-up action. Trust therefore is based on the expectation that the selection and communication of current information is done correctly, i.e., in such a way as to enable adequate follow-up on the recipient's part.

First, the willingness to trust is determined by the characteristics of the recipient. As mentioned in our introduction, many studies in this field do not differentiate between trust and credibility when measuring the recipients' relationship with journalism. Therefore, both types of studies are similar enough in their operationalization to enable us to transfer empirical results regarding the recipients' characteristics from credibility studies to trust. In the offline context, the recipient's characteristics, though an influential and integral part of the relationship of trust, have long been neglected apart from a few theoretical notes that the trustor's traits are influential (Blöbaum 2014, p. 49). Even less interest has been shown in compiling a comprehensive empirical overview. If anything, *socio-demographic characteristics* and *personal aspects* such as media behavior have been considered (Carter and Greenberg 1965; Westley and Severin 1964; Greenberg 1966; Abel and Wirth 1977; Burgoon et al. 1986; Rimmer and Weaver 1987; Bentele 2008; Jackob 2010). As research proceeded, more elaborate designs started to measure the influence of personal characteristics other than media behavior, such as political attitudes, the general propensity to trust other people or (political) institutions, as well as interpersonal discussions or media literacy. More knowledge about the media for example seems to lead to a more critical view regarding news reports. Also, *situational characteristics*, such as involvement in the topics journalism reports on or the anticipation of risk, have been shown to affect the views on the media (e.g., Gunther and Lasorsa 1986; Gunther 1988; Kiousis 2001; Eveland and Shah 2003; Jones 2004; Kohring 2004; Schmitt et al. 2004; Lee 2005, 2010; Choi et al. 2009; Ashley et al. 2010; Jackob 2010, 2012; Ladd 2012; Tsfati and Ariely 2014). Regarding offline journalism, one can state that female, younger and less-educated recipients trust television more than or even instead of newspapers, although education (often related with media literacy) seems to be a factor undermining general trust in the media. Also, politically liberal as well as generally trusting recipients perceive the media as more credible, especially the ones they use frequently. Depending on the context, it might also be important whether someone tends to have a stronger attitude regarding a news topic.

All these characteristics may—apart from the actual willingness to trust—also have an influence on how much trustworthiness the recipients grant the trustee. But how do they evaluate journalistic trustworthiness, which is the second determining factor with regard to the recipients' willingness to trust in journalism as a system?

Giddens posits that trust in systems is often not focused on the abstract system as a whole. Instead, there are so-called access points, at which the trustor encounters representatives of the system (Giddens 1991, p. 83). While Giddens understands such representatives to be mainly individuals or groups (ibid.), this paper focuses on journalistic pieces as representatives of the journalistic system. For, unlike journalistic organizations or journalists themselves, recipients encounter journalistic pieces on a regular basis, though this certainly does not exclude organizations and journalists from being possible representatives as well. Following Giddens' conceptualization of access points, the trustworthiness of the journalistic piece therefore functions as an antecedent of the represented system's overall trustworthiness, which is crucial for the recipient's willingness to trust. Whether a journalistic piece is regarded as trustworthy or not is therefore determined by the perceived fulfillment of the recipient's expectations regarding the journalistic programs for the journalistic piece in question. Each of these programs in turn comprises several antecedents of trustworthiness.

For the *offline* context, these criteria and expectations are as follows (Blöbaum 2016, pp. 156–158): The guidelines on how to collect information are provided in the *research* program. The main aim being to communicate previously unknown or hidden information, the most important criteria for good information are the currentness, newness, relevance, completeness and timeliness of the information. Furthermore, the information should be presented from various perspectives. The guidelines regarding the manner in which journalists select certain topics for further treatment and finally for communication can be found in the *selection* program. Similarly, the selection of topics is determined by their currentness, newness, timeliness and relevance. The *presentation* program determines the way in which researched and selected information is presented. Two criteria are important here:

Table 1 Antecedents of trustworthiness—offline context

Factor of trustworthiness	Antecedents of trustworthiness
Trustworthiness of research	• Currentness of information • Newness of information • Relevance of information • Completeness of information • Diversity of information • Timeliness of information
Trustworthiness of selection	• Currentness of topic • Newness of topic • Timeliness of topic • Relevance of topic
Trustworthiness of presentation	• Putting the information in its context • Explicit assessment of information
Trustworthiness of proofing	• Correctness of information • Reliability of source • Verifiability of information
Trustworthiness of revision	• Understandability of the journalistic piece • Comprehensibility of the journalistic piece
Trustworthiness of coordination	• Weighting of the topic • Putting the topic in its context • Independence of the editorial department

first, putting the information in its context through various presentation formats, and second, assessing the information, which is most often done in journalistic commentary. The guidelines on how to proof the information before communication are provided in the *proofing* program. The aspects of the correctness of information, the reliability of the source and the verifiability of information are important here. The *revision* program concerns the editing process, which comprises the stylistic and linguistic correction of the journalistic piece in order to make it understandable and comprehensible. And lastly, the *coordination* program determines the guidelines for the operational processes in the editorial department. Here, the publishing of a piece within a certain section determines the weighting of the topic and its assignment to a certain desk decides over its contextual placement. Moreover, this program encompasses the guidelines on how the editorial department deals with other parts of the media organization in such a way as to maintain its independence. An overview can be found in Table 1.

It is important to note that while the outlined criteria are derived from a scholarly and professional perspective, several studies have shown that recipients' expectations regarding the correct functioning of the journalistic system by and large reflect this perspective—both for offline and online expectations, which we will delve into in the following chapter (Neuberger 2012, p. 52; Urban and Schweiger 2013, p. 4; Scholl et al. 2014, pp. 25–27). Moreover, it should be pointed out that the journalistic practices and routines themselves are not the basis for the recipient's perception of trustworthiness, but rather their results are. The recipient can see these results within the journalistic piece. Trustworthiness is therefore based not on the perception of the actual "behind the scenes" practices and routines—on *how* the function has been fulfilled—but rather on the perception of *whether* the function has been fulfilled at all.

In line with our understanding of the trust mechanism according to Mayer et al. (1995), the following assumption can be made: the more the antecedents of trustworthiness for each program are perceived as being fulfilled by the recipient, the higher in turn the perceived trustworthiness of the journalistic piece and, in consequence, the willingness to trust the overall journalistic system should be. This willingness to trust is then weighed against the perceived risk. The perceived risk with regard to the journalistic system is the risk of making the journalistic information the basis of one's follow-up action or communication (Kohring 2002, p. 103). A trusting action in the journalistic system means taking this risk, which specifically lies in the consequences of an action based on incorrectly selected and communicated information. Depending on whether the willingness is higher or lower than the perceived risk, the trusting action will or will not take place. While there are different views (e.g., Kohring 2002, p. 96; Blöbaum 2014, p. 43) within journalism research on what exactly a trusting action entices, we have a broad definition in this paper. A trusting action, as understood here, can manifest itself as an action, an omitted action, a change of attitude in both a positive or negative direction, or a maintaining of attitude.

In the following chapter we now present our conceptual model of trust in the online context based on the changes both the recipients and journalism itself have undergone due to digitalization.

3 Conceptual Model: Trust in Online Journalism

The way the trust mechanism works remains the same in the online context as it does in the offline context: The willingness to trust is weighed against the perceived risk, which may or may not lead to a trusting action. The journalistic programs themselves, as previously stated, also remain the same. However, two important changes can be identified: First, especially socio-demographic characteristics seem to have less influence on the recipient's trust while other characteristics such as specific media behavior gain in importance. Second, the developments due to digitalization impact the antecedents of trustworthiness within the programs and bring forth new antecedents as well as external factors, thereby changing the way in which trustworthiness is perceived.

3.1 The Trustor in the Online Context

Analyzing influential characteristics on the part of the trustor seems even more important considering that trust in journalism is generally explained more by individual rather than national or cultural differences (Tsfati and Ariely 2014,

p. 769). With the influential characteristics of the recipients regarding offline journalism in mind, socio-demographic, personal and situational aspects seem to determine the willingness to trust in the offline word. But how does the influence of these characteristics change when it comes to online journalism? Which characteristics play a decisive role when predicting trust and which do not?

Regarding online journalism, age seems to have an especially strong influence and gender a moderate one, with male and younger users tending to have more trust, although there might be differences between online media types (Johnson and Kaye 2000, pp. 869–871; Bucy 2003, pp. 253–255; Johnson and Kaye 2010, pp. 11–13; Wenjing and Yunze 2014, pp. 68–69). Nevertheless, some studies did not find any or only few socio-demographic differences (Johnson and Kaye 2002, p. 630; Greer 2003, p. 21; Kim and Johnson 2009, p. 295). Particularly, indicators such as education or income are rarely reported as influential. While there might have been slight differences in prior studies, newer reports do not show any predicting role of education or income in contrast to offline journalism (Kim and Johnson 2009, p. 295; Johnson and Kaye 2010, pp. 11–13). In sum, socio-demographic differences are less important as a predictor of trust in online journalism compared to offline journalism, where especially differences in dimensions of social class such as education (e.g., Tsfati and Ariely 2014, p. 770) are regarded as more influential. Johnson and Kaye (2004, p. 25) see this as a result of the Internet becoming more and more of a mainstream medium that is equally used and evaluated by all social groups.

If these differences have less influence, what about the personal characteristics of the trustor? While studies have shown that, for example, having a liberal political attitude is associated with trust in offline journalism (Lee 2010, pp. 12–17), the results for online journalism are conflicting, to say the least. Some studies show that political interest or party ideology may have an influence while others say they do not. This is the case especially when it comes to general trust in online journalism that is not exclusively related to political information but rather to general information (Johnson and Kaye 2000, pp. 869–871, 2002, p. 630, 2010, pp. 11–13; Mackay and Lowrey 2011, p. 52; Netzley and Hammer 2012, pp. 55–56; Wenjing and Yunze 2014, pp. 68–69). While the personal attitude to politics loses influence, another indicator gains in importance. Several studies have shown experience with and reliance on the Internet, such as daily time spent online or years of experience, is at least partly associated with trust in online journalism (Flanagin and Metzger 2000, p. 528; Kiousis 2001, p. 394; Johnson and Kaye 2002, p. 630; Greer 2003, p. 21; Stavrositu and Sundar 2008, p. 67). This effect, however, is weakened by newer studies. The difference between heavy and light users wears off as a result of the Internet moving into the mainstream (Flanagin and Metzger 2007, p. 332; Mackay and Lowrey 2011, p. 52; Wenjing and Yunze 2014, pp. 68–69). Nevertheless, the *specific* media behavior regarding traditional, but partly also online, journalism is still a strong factor positively influencing trust in online journalism (Johnson and Kaye 2000, pp. 869–871; Johnson and Kaye 2002, p. 630; Kim and Johnson 2009, p. 295; Johnson and Kaye 2010, pp. 11–13). Relying on the media for information boosts trust in the online environment, therefore making media behavior regarding traditional and online media relevant for developing trust.

Finally, a short look on situational aspects predicting trust in online journalism seems important, although this aspect has not yet been fully explored by scientific research. While context-related aspects of the trustee, here journalism, such as technical modalities, have been analyzed (Kiousis 2006; Sundar et al. 2007), situational evaluations regarding the trustor have been neglected. As trust is always specific (Barber 1983; Kohring 2004), researchers should align their studies with specific situations. This said, analyses should not concentrate on general evaluations of the media but rather explore the influence of both the news topic and the trustor's attitude regarding the news topic as predictors of trust. Kohring and Matthes showed that the further away a topic is from the trustor, the more differentiated his trust in offline journalism is (Kohring and Matthes 2007, pp. 247–248). Nevertheless, only a few studies considered the influence of news topics for trust in online journalism. Flanagin and Metzger (2000, p. 525) proved that the attributed credibility of news media differs within news themes. Hard news is perceived as more credible than soft news. On the part of the trustor, interest in a topic can support trust in online journalism's reporting (Netzley and Hammer 2012, pp. 55–56). A strong attitude regarding a specific topic can either boost or weaken the perceived trustworthiness of the Internet as a news medium, depending on whether the recipients expect to find information supporting or not supporting their own views (Choi et al. 2006, p. 221). In sum, situational aspects have not been studied enough, especially by communication research. Methodologically, interest in or attitudes regarding specific news topics should be used at least as a control variable to consider possible bias perceptions specific to the trustor (see for example Meyer et al. 2010, pp. 107–110).

Summing up the influence of trustor-related aspects influencing trust, three assumptions can be made. Namely, that while socio-demographic differences and political characteristics of the trustor are regarded as less influential compared to their importance in the offline world, other aspects such as specific media behavior gain in importance. Furthermore, situational aspects need to be considered for further research as trust is always specific and specific topics stimulate different attitudes within the mass of recipients. Altogether, the majority of communication studies have not yet controlled or considered most of these aspects in the online context. Not only the trustor, but also the trustee undergoes many changes due to digitalization, which we explore in the following chapter.

3.2 The Trustee in the Online Context

The following seven developments in online journalism have an impact on the recipient's perception of trustworthiness. First, *transparency* is more pronounced in the online than in the offline context, specifically in two ways. On the one hand, product transparency comprises naming sources and their interests in the journalistic piece as well as clarifying which questions remain unanswered. On the other hand, process transparency concerns editorial decisions but also entails explaining and justifying the selection, placement, and assessment of both topics and information as well as dealing with reporting errors (Meier and Reimer 2011, pp. 138–139; Porlezza and Russ-Mohl 2013, pp. 56–57). Second, *reputation transfer* is an important factor in online journalism, since the reputation of strong brand names from the offline world is transferred to their online brand and their journalistic pieces there (Blöbaum 2014, p. 37). Third, *user-generated content* (UGC) is much more common in online journalism than in offline journalism due to the technical possibilities of the Internet (Bivens 2008, p. 117). This content contributed by recipients—e.g., eye-witness accounts and pictures—is used by journalists to supplement their own professional content (Hermida and Thurman 2008, pp. 343–344). Fourth, *rating cues* have become increasingly important since the beginning of the new century and most often connect journalistic pieces with social networks (Knobloch-Westerwick et al. 2005, p. 297). They function as a proxy for other recipients' consummation and appreciation of a news piece (ibid., p. 299). Fifth, online journalistic pieces are not limited to text, sound or pictures but can combine all these and other media formats (Deuze 2004, p. 140). This concept is called *multimedia* and is one of the most important developments in online journalism (Franklin 2008, p. 365; Russial 2009, p. 52). Sixth, the Internet and the online-first mantra have brought forth a *new understanding of what it means to be current*. Lacking the periodicity of offline media, online journalism has the potential for constant currentness (Karlsson and Strömbäck 2010, p. 4). Seventh and finally, *interactivity* is more easily achieved online and is gaining increasing importance (ibid., p. 3; Boczkowski and Mitchelstein 2012, p. 2). While there is no standard definition of interactivity (ibid., p. 3), in this paper it is understood as user comments on journalistic pieces and journalistic replies.

These developments impact the perception of trustworthiness in three ways: They lead to changes in the expectations regarding already existing antecedents of trustworthiness, to the emergence of new antecedents unique to online journalism and, finally, to the emergence of external factors that influence not only the perceived trustworthiness but also the perceived risk.

Regarding the already existing antecedents, only diversity of information (research program) is positively influenced, namely by UGC. This development allows journalists to include new perspectives in their reporting (Hermida and Thurman 2008, p. 352; McNair 2013, p. 81), which in turn can positively influence the recipient's perception of the diversity. Four antecedents can be both positively and negatively influenced: the three antecedents within the proofing program and the currentness of information (research program). In the proofing program, product transparency can actually enhance the perception of the fulfillment of the three antecedents (De Maeyer 2012, p. 693). UGC, on the other hand, can have a negative impact, as it leads to problems of credibility (Jacobson 2010, p. 74; Singer 2010, p. 133; Oswald 2013, p. 68), which itself refers to the expectations in this program (Kohring 2004, p. 174). Moreover, today's online-first mantra can also have a negative impact on the perceived fulfillment of the proofing program's antecedents, since this policy can cause insufficiently proofed pieces to be published (Porlezza and Russ-Mohl 2013, p. 55). Due to the online-first policy and the new understanding of what it means to be current, recipients also expect constant currentness instead of periodicity in online journalism (Wolf and Schnauber 2014, p. 8). This new expectation can actually impede recipients from perceiving information as current (research program). At the same time, UGC can also enhance this perception, since it allows journalists to report information while an event is happening without having to be there themselves (Bivens 2008, p. 117; Hermida 2011, p. 28). Finally, two antecedents are negatively influenced by the developments. Perceptions of the completeness of information (research program) and currentness of topic (selection program) are both impeded by the new understanding of what it means to be current. Currentness in the online world often takes precedence over completeness of information (Karlsson and Strömbäck 2010, p. 4; Porlezza and Russ-Mohl 2013, p. 55), leaving recipients' expectations regarding completeness unfulfilled. In line with the currentness of information, it is also hard for the topics of journalistic pieces to be as current as recipients expect them to be in the online world.

Besides these impacts, four new antecedents of trustworthiness have emerged. When using UGC in the journalistic pieces, journalists retain their gate-keeping role insofar as they select UGC based on its correctness, newness and relevance (Hermida and Thurman 2008, p. 353; Jacobson 2010, p. 74; McNair 2013, p. 81). This leads to a new antecedent in the selection program, as recipients expect only adequate UGC to be selected. Furthermore, three new antecedents emerge within the coordination program. The comments cause changes within journalism's routines and operational processes insofar as journalists take an active part in the communication between recipients by either deleting comments perceived as problematic both by recipients and journalists themselves or by participating with their own comments (Domingo 2008, pp. 694–695; Heise et al. 2014, p. 415; Dohle and Loosen 2014, p. 7). Thus emerges the new antecedent of managing the comments. The possibility of process transparency has led more and more journalists to blog about their editorial decisions (Bivens 2008, p. 124; Heise et al. 2014, p. 414) and therefore the recipients expect journalists to transparently correct and also own up to made mistakes (ibid., p. 14; Porlezza and Russ-Mohl 2013, pp. 45–46, pp. 55–56). Here we now find the new antecedent of process transparency. Finally, the various multimedia elements not only need to be coordinated so that they are consistent and optimally complement each other, the issue of which media format and which combination of elements is appropriate must also be decided (Oswald 2013, pp. 69–70; Radü 2013, pp. 178–179). The recipients expect an adequate management of the multimedia elements.

As previously indicated, not only changes in the antecedents of trustworthiness have occurred due to developments in online journalism, but three external factors have also emerged. Interactivity in form of comments, as described above, leads to a new antecedent. However, comments can also have a general negative impact both on the overall perceived trustworthiness and on the perceived risk. Recipients often comment in order to educate others, ask or answer questions, add information, share experience and knowledge, clarify issues, point out missing or incorrect information, and balance a discussion (Diakopoulos and Naaman 2011, pp. 5–6; Graham 2013, pp. 121–122). Arguments supporting news coverage are found only seldom (ibid., p. 119). It therefore stands to reason that comments can make recipients aware of various problems regarding the antecedents of trustworthiness perceived by the commentator. At the same time, comments can also point out risks the recipients might previously have been unaware of based solely on the journalistic piece. Comments as an external factor therefore seem to impede the emergence of a trusting action both via the perceived trustworthiness and risk. Rating cues as a second external factor can serve as a proxy for trustworthiness (Blöbaum 2014, p. 59). Research on this phenomenon is scarce so far. Nevertheless, studies show that—depending on the amount of likes or shares and positivity or negativity of the ratings—rating cues can both facilitate and impede the overall perceived trustworthiness (Seely 2014, pp. 27–28). Reputation transfer is the third external factor. Reputation is an indicator of trustworthiness (Eisenegger 2009, p. 12). Therefore, reputation transfer can enhance the trustworthiness of an established offline brand's online offshoot (Banning and Sweetser 2007, p. 452; Melican and Dixon 2008, p. 161) and thus appears to have a facilitating effect on trust in online journalism.

3.3   The Model: Trust in the Online Context

The considerations regarding the trustor and trustee in the online context lead to the following model of trust (Fig. 1). As it features, on the part of the trustee, four new antecedents of trustworthiness and three external factors, the development of online trust can be regarded as more complex than offline trust. Regarding the trustor, online trust is shaped less by socio-demographics and political aspects, while

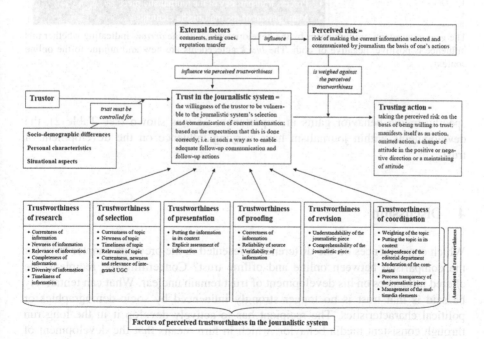

Fig. 1 Model of trust in online journalism

Table 2 Antecedents of trustworthiness—online context

Factor of trustworthiness	Antecedents of trustworthiness
Trustworthiness of research	• → Currentness of information • Newness of information • Relevance of information • ↘ Completeness of information • ↗ Diversity of information • Timeliness of information
Trustworthiness of selection	• ↘ Currentness of topic • Newness of topic • Timeliness of topic • Relevance of topic • Currentness, newness and relevance of integrated UGC
Trustworthiness of presentation	• Putting the information in its context • Explicit assessment of information
Trustworthiness of proofing	• → Correctness of information • → Reliability of source • → Verifiability of information
Trustworthiness of revision	• Understandability of the journalistic piece • Comprehensibility of the journalistic piece
Trustworthiness of coordination	• Weighting of the topic • Putting the topic in its context • Independence of the editorial department • Moderation of the comments • Process transparency of the journalistic piece • Management of the multimedia elements

The *grey* antecedents are influences by the developments, with the *arrows* indicating whether this influence is positive, negative or both. The *black* antecedents are new and unique to the online context

specific media behavior gains in importance. As was shown (see Table 2), the developments within journalism have varying influence on the development of trust.

4 Discussion

Which consequences do the differences presented in the previous chapter have for the comparison between online and offline trust? Concerning the recipient, the altered influences on his development of trust remain unclear. What can tentatively be said is that trust is no longer strongly influenced by socio-demographics or political characteristics. The recipient has to actively develop it in the long run through consistent media behavior, which in turn means that the development of trust could become harder in the online world. However, we feel it is important to point out that as the Internet has moved into the mainstream, the development of trust in online journalism is surely easier now than it was in the early days of online journalism due to media socialization.

Concerning journalism, it is important to note that a minimum of trustworthiness must be perceived with regard to each and every antecedent in order for trust to emerge (Mayer et al. 1995, p. 271; Kohring 2004, p. 171). The complexity of the online model, especially with regard to the additional antecedents, therefore impedes the emergence of trust in the online context. While the influence of the external factors seems to be both positive and negative, the overall negative influence of the developments on the already existing antecedents of trustworthiness strengthens the supposition of a more difficult development of trust in online journalism. Overall, therefore, we posit that while the difference between the trust in online and offline journalism is not a very striking one, it does seem more difficult for recipients to develop trust in online journalism than in offline journalism. This difference is more due to the developments in journalism than due to the characteristics of the recipient.

The model not only serves as a heuristic to study the development of trust, it also helps explain the emergence of trust problems in journalism which are currently being so heavily discussed and even points out starting points for journalism to enhance or even rebuild trustworthiness. The development of UGC, which has a negative impact on several antecedents, is especially problematic, as are the developments of transparency, interactivity and multimedia, which lead to the emergence of new expectations and therefore of three new antecedents. However, while UGC can be problematic, it also offers great potential for journalism's trustworthiness. More actively reviewing the currentness, newness and relevance of UGC could counteract the negative impact of UGC. If product transparency was created additionally by naming sources and their interests, the positive impact of UGC could be enhanced at the same time. The three new antecedents in the coordination program also display the potential to increase trustworthiness, if tackled correctly. A good comment culture, the implementation of clear guidelines regarding process transparency, as well as innovative multimedia formats could contribute to the fulfillment of recipients' expectations towards online journalism. While these measures entail a lot of work, especially in the coordination program, they are important—and not only for journalism itself with regard to its trustworthiness. Trust in journalism— which can be enhanced by these measures—also remains a prerequisite for the emergence of trust and distrust in individuals, groups, organizations and systems (Kohring 2004, p. 104) and therefore for the functioning of society as a whole (Luhmann 1979, p. 13; Barber 1983, p. 165; Kohring 2004, p. 11).

5 Conclusion: Limitations and the Road Ahead

The aim of this paper was to develop a theoretical model of trust in online journalism and conceptualize how it emerges with regard to both recipients and journalism itself. Although our approach can serve as a heuristic, it needs to be empirically tested. This is especially true for the trustor, with regard to whom future research is of great importance because of the current insufficiencies. Additionally, the expectations of the recipients regarding online journalism, which might actually differ from topic to topic, should be empirically examined to determine the accuracy of this model. Due to continuously emerging new developments, online journalism is a moving target and the recipients' expectations as well as their own characteristics are constantly changing. The model should therefore be regularly updated. Regarding theoretical limitations, our model only captures one moment of trust and does not take into consideration long-term or short-term developments in the trust relationship between recipients and online journalism. Also, the role of risk regarding trust has not been fully cleared—neither is there a theoretical consensus on the exact role perceived risk plays in the formation of trust in journalism (Blöbaum 2014, p. 15) nor is there an agreement on its empirical measurement.

In sum, both the influence of the external factors and certain characteristics of the trustor need more research. Moreover, future studies should consider that some of the online developments also influence the trustworthiness of offline journalism. While developments such as multimedia and rating cues are not relevant for offline journalism, television and radio, for example, also make use of UGC, which was shown to have both positive and negative consequences for perceived trustworthiness. And reputation transfer can of course also take the direction from online to offline and lead to positive or negative impacts. While we contend that offline journalism is perceived as more trustworthy than online journalism even allowing for the developments' offline impact, it is important to study the repercussions of digitalization on offline journalism as well. Hypotheses and research questions for this continuative research should be derived from the proposed model and empirically examined. A focus could lie on media effects research, in particular on testing the impact of recipients' trust in online journalism on their actions and attitudes, and there especially on the emergence of trust and distrust through journalism.

References

Abel, J. D., & Wirth, M. O. (1977). Newspaper vs. TV credibility for local news. *Journalism Quarterly, 54*(2), 371–375.
Ashley, S., Poepsel, M., & Willis, E. (2010). Media literacy and news credibility: Does knowledge of media ownership increase skepticism in news consumers? *Journal of Media Literacy Education, 2*(1), 37–46.
Banning, S., & Sweetser, K. (2007). How much do they think it affects them and whom do they believe?: Comparing the third-person effect and credibility of blogs and traditional media. *Communication Quarterly, 55*, 451–466. doi:10.1080/01463370701665114.
Barber, B. (1983). *The logic and limits of trust.* New Brunswick, NJ: Rutgers University Press.
Bentele, G. (2008). *Objektivität und Medienglaubwürdigkeit: Medienrealität konstruiert* [Objectivity and media credibility: media reality constructed]. Wiesbaden: VS Verlag für Sozialwissenschaften.

Bivens, R. K. (2008). The internet, mobile phones and blogging. *Journalism Practice, 2*, 113–129. doi:10.1080/17512780701768568.

Blöbaum, B. (1994). *Journalismus als soziales System. Geschichte, Ausdifferenzierung und Verselbstständigung* [Journalism as a social system. Formation, differentiation and independence]. Opladen: Westdeutscher Verlag.

Blöbaum, B. (2005). Wandel und Journalismus—Vorschlag für einen analytischen Rahmen [Journalism and change—proposal for an analytic concept]. In M. Behmer, B. Blöbaum, A. Scholl & R. Stöber (Eds.), *Journalismus und Wandel. Analysedimensionen, Konzepte, Fallstudien* [Journalism and change. Dimensions of analysis, concepts and case studies] (pp. 41–60). Wiesbaden: VS Verlag für Sozialwissenschaften.

Blöbaum, B. (2014). *Trust and journalism in a digital environment.* Working Paper. https://reutersinstitute.politics.ox.ac.uk/sites/default/files/Trust%20and%20Journalism%20in%20a%20Digital%20Environment.pdf. Accessed 11 Feb 2015.

Blöbaum, B. (2016). Journalismus als Funktionssystem der Gesellschaft [Journalism as a functional system of society]. In M. Löffelholz & L. T. Rothenberger (Eds.), *Handbuch Journalismustheorien [Handbook journalism theories]* (pp. 151–162). Wiesbaden: VS Verlag für Sozialwissenschaften.

Boczkowski, P., & Mitchelstein, E. (2012). How users take advantage of different forms of interactivity on online news sites: Clicking, e-mailing, and commenting. *Human Communication Research, 38*, 1–22. doi:10.1111/j.1468-2958.2011.01418.x.

Bucy, E. P. (2003). Media credibility reconsidered: Synergy effects between on-air and online news. *Journalism & Mass Communication Quarterly, 80*, 247–264. doi:10.1177/107769900308000202.

Burgoon, J., Burgoon, M., & Buller, D. B. (1986). Newspaper image: Dimensions and relation to demographics, satisfaction. *Journalism Quarterly, 63*(4), 771–781.

Carter, R. F., & Greenberg, B. S. (1965). Newspaper and television: Which do you believe? *Journalism Quarterly, 42*(1), 29–34.

Castelfranchi, C., & Falcone, R. (2000). Trust and control: A dialectic link. *Applied Artificial Intelligence, 14*, 799–823. doi:10.1080/08839510050127560.

Choi, J. H., Watt, J. H., & Lynch, M. (2006). Perceptions of news credibility about the war in Iraq: Why war opponents perceived the internet as the most credible medium. *Journal of Computer-Mediated Communication, 12*, 209–229. doi:10.1111/j.1083-6101.2006.00322.x.

Choi, Y., Yang, M., & Chang, J. J. C. (2009). Elaboration of the hostile media phenomenon. The roles of involvement, media skepticism, congruency of perceived media influence, and perceived opinion climate. *Communication Research, 36*, 54–75. doi:10.1177/0093650208326462.

Das, T. K., & Teng, B. S. (2004). The risk-based view of trust: A conceptual framework. *Journal of Business and Psychology, 19*(1), 85–116.

De Maeyer, J. (2012). The journalistic hyperlink. Prescriptive discourses about linking in online news. *Journalism Practice, 6*, 692–701. doi:10.1080/17512786.2012.667273.

Deuze, M. (2004). What is multimedia journalism? *Journalism Studies, 5*, 139–152. doi:10.1080/1461670042000211131.

Diakopoulos, N., & Naaman, M. (2011). Towards quality discourse in online news comments. *Proceedings of the ACM 2011 conference on computer supported cooperative work*, March 19–23, 2011, Hangzhou, China.

Dohle, M., & Loosen, W. (2014). Journalismusforschung und Rezeptions- und Wirkungsforschung: Intradisziplinäre Trennung oder selbstverständliche Verbindung [Journalism research and audience and reception research: interdisciplinary separation or self-evident connection]? In W. Loosen &. M. Dohle (Eds.), *Journalismus und (sein) Publikum. Schnittstellen zwischen Journalismusforschung und Rezeptions- und Wirkungsforschung* [Journalism and (its) audience. Points of contact between journalism research and audience and reception research] (pp. 1–13). Wiesbaden: VS Verlag für Sozialwissenschaften.

Domingo, D. (2008). Interactivity in the daily routines of online newsrooms: Dealing with an uncomfortable myth. *Journal of Computer-Mediated Communication, 13*, 680–704. doi:10.1111/j.1083-6101.2008.00415.x.

Eisenegger, M. (2009). Trust and reputation in the age of globalization. In J. Klewes & R. Wreschniok (Eds.), *Reputation capital: Building and maintaining trust in the 21st century* (pp. 11–22). Berlin: Springer.

Eveland, W. P., & Shah, D. V. (2003). The impact of individual and interpersonal factors on perceived news media bias. *Political Psychology, 24*, 101–117. doi:10.1111/0162-895X.00318.

Flanagin, A. J., & Metzger, M. J. (2000). Perceptions of internet information credibility. *Journalism & Mass Communication Quarterly, 77*, 515–540. doi:10.1177/107769900007700304.

Flanagin, A. J., & Metzger, M. J. (2007). The role of site features, user attributes, and information verification behaviors on the perceived credibility of web-based information. *New Media & Society, 9*, 319–42. doi:10.1177/1461444807075015.

Franklin, B. (2008). The future of newspapers. *Journalism Studies, 9*, 630–641. doi:10.1080/17512780802280984.

Giddens, A. (1991). *The consequences of modernity*. Cambridge: Polity Press.

Graham, T. (2013). Talking back, but is anyone listening? Journalism and comment fields. In C. Peters & M. J. Broersma (Eds.), *Rethinking journalism. Trust and participation in a transformed news landscape* (pp. 114–127). London: Routledge.

Greenberg, B. S. (1966). Media use and believability: Some multiple correlates. *Journalism Quarterly, 43*, 665–670. doi:10.1177/107769906604300405.

Greer, J. D. (2003). Evaluating the credibility of online information: A test of source and advertising influence. *Mass Communication & Society, 6*, 11–28. doi:10.1207/S15327825MCS0601_3.

Gunther, A. (1988). Attitude extremity and trust in the media. *Journalism Quarterly, 65*(2), 279–287.

Gunther, A., & Lasorsa, D. L. (1986). Issues importance and trust in mass media. *Journalism Quarterly, 63*(4), 844–848.

Heise, N., Loosen, W., Reimer, J., & Schmidt, J.-H. (2014). Including the audience. *Journalism Studies, 15*, 411–430. doi:10.1080/1461670X.2013.831232.

Hermida, A. (2011). Mechanisms of participation: How audience options shape the conversation. In J. B. Singer, A. Hermida, D. Domingo, A. Heinonen, S. Paulussen, T. Quandt, Z. Reich, & M. Vujnovic (Eds.), *Participatory journalism: Guarding open gates at online newspapers* (pp. 13–33). Oxford: Wiley-Blackwell.

Hermida, A., & Thurman, N. (2008). A clash of cultures: The integration of user-generated content within professional journalistic frameworks at British newspaper websites. *Journalism Practice, 2*, 343–356. doi:10.1080/17512780802054538.

Jackob, N. G. E. (2010). No alternatives? The relationship between perceived media dependency, use of alternative information sources, and general trust in mass media. *International Journal of Communication, 18*(4), 589–606.

Jackob, N. G. E. (2012). The tendency to trust as individual predisposition-exploring the associations between interpersonal trust, trust in the media and trust in institutions. *Communications, 37*, 99–120. doi:10.1515/commun-2012-0005.

Jacobson, S. (2010). Emerging models of multimedia journalism: A content analysis of multimedia packages published on nytimes.com. *Atlantic Journal of Communications, 83*, 63–78. doi:10.1080/15456870903554882.

Johnson, T. J., & Kaye, B. K. (2000). Using is believing: The influence of reliance on the credibility of online political information among politically interested internet users. *Journalism & Mass Communication Quarterly, 77*, 865–879. doi:10.1177/107769900007700409.

Johnson, T. J., & Kaye, B. K. (2002). Webelievability: A path model examining how convenience and reliance predict online credibility. *Journalism & Mass Communication Quarterly, 79*, 619–642. doi:10.1177/107769900207900306.

Johnson, T. J., & Kaye, B. K. (2004). For whom the web toils: How internet experience predicts web reliance and credibility. *Atlantic Journal of Communication, 12*, 19–45. doi:10.1207/s15456889ajc1201_3.

Johnson, T. J., & Kaye, B. K. (2010). Choosing is believing? How web gratifications and reliance affect internet credibility among politically interested users. *Atlantic Journal of Communication, 18*, 1–21. doi:10.1080/15456870903340431.

Jones, D. A. (2004). Why Americans don't trust the media: A preliminary analysis. *The International Journal of Press/Politics, 9*, 60–75. doi:10.1177/1081180X04263461.

Jungermann, H., & Slovic, P. (1993). Die Psychologie der Kognition und Evaluation von Risiko [The psychology of cognition and evaluation of risk]. In G. Bechmann (Ed.), *Risiko und Gesellschaft. Grundlagen und Ergebnisse interdisziplinärer Risikoforschung* [Risk and society. Foundations and results of interdisciplinary risk research] (pp. 167–207). Opladen: Westdeutscher Verlag.

Karlsson, M., & Strömbäck, J. (2010). Freezing the flow of online news. Exploring approaches to the study of the liquidity of online news. *Journalism Studies, 11*, 2–19. doi:10.1080/14616700903119784.

Kim, D., & Johnson, T. J. (2009). A shift in media credibility. Comparing internet sources and traditional news sources in South Korea. *The International Communication Gazette, 71*, 283–302. doi:10.1177/1748048509102182.

Kiousis, S. (2001). Public trust or mistrust? Perceptions of media credibility in the information age. *Mass Communication and Society, 4*, 381–403. doi:10.1207/S15327825MCS0404_4.

Kiousis, S. (2006). Exploring the impact of modality on perceptions of credibility for online news stories. *Journalism Studies, 7*, 348–359. doi:10.1080/14616700500533668.

Knobloch-Westerwick, S., Sharma, N., Hansen, D. L., & Alter, S. (2005). Impact of popularity indications on readers' selective exposure to online news. *Journal of Broadcasting and Electronic Media, 49*, 296–313. doi:10.1207/s15506878jobem4903_3.

Kohring, M. (2002). Vertrauen in Journalismus [Trust in journalism]. In A. Scholl (Ed.), *Systemtheorie und Konstruktivismus in der Kommunikationswissenschaft* [Systems theory and constructivism in communication research] (pp. 91–110). Konstanz: UVK.

Kohring, M. (2004). *Vertrauen in Journalismus* [Trust in journalism]. Konstanz: UVK.

Kohring, M., & Matthes, J. (2007). Trust in news media: Development and validation of a multidimensional scale. *Communication Research, 34*, 231–252. doi:10.1177/0093650206298071.

Ladd, J. M. (2012). *Why Americans hate the media and how it matters*. Princeton, NJ: Princeton University Press.

Lee, T.-T. (2005). The liberal media myth revisited: An examination of factors influencing perceptions of media bias. *Journal of Broadcasting & Electronic Media, 49*, 43–64. doi:10.1207/s15506878jobem4901_4.

Lee, T.-T. (2010). Why they don't trust the media: An examination of factors predicting trust. *American Behavioral Scientist, 54*, 8–21. doi:10.1177/0002764210376308.

Luhmann, N. (1979). *Trust and power: Two works by Niklas Luhmann*. Chichester: Wiley.

Luhmann, N. (1988). Familiarity, confidence, trust: Problems and alternatives. In D. Gambetta (Ed.), *Trust. Making and breaking cooperative relations* (pp. 94–107). New York: Basil Blackwell Ink.

Luhmann, N. (1990). *Ökologische Kommunikation. Kann die moderne Gesellschaft sich auf ökologische Gefährdungen einstellen* [Ecological communication. Can modern society adapt to environmental dangers]? Opladen: Westdeutscher Verlag.

Luhmann, N. (1995). *Social systems*. Stanford: Stanford University Press.

Mackay, J. B., & Lowrey, W. (2011). The credibility divide: Reader trust of online newspapers and blogs. *Journal of Media Sociology, 3*(1–4), 39–57.

Marcinkowski, F. (1993). *Publizistik als autopoietisches System. Politik und Massenmedien. Eine systemtheoretische Analyse* [Journalism as an autopoietic system. Politics and mass media. A systems-theoretical analysis]. Opladen: Westdeutscher Verlag.

Mayer, R. C., Davis, J. H., & Schoorman, F. D. (1995). An integrative model of organizational trust. *Academy of Management Review, 20*(3), 709–734.

McNair, B. (2013). Trust, truth and objectivity: sustaining quality journalism in the era of the content-generated user. In C. Peters & M. J. Broersma (Eds.), *Rethinking journalism. Trust and participation in a transformed news landscape* (pp. 75–88). London: Routledge.

Meier, K., & Reimer, J. (2011). Transparenz im Journalismus. Instrumente, Konfliktpotentiale, Wirkung [Transparency in Journalism. Instruments, conflicts, effects]. *Publizistik, 56*(2), 133–155.

Melican, D. B., & Dixon, T. L. (2008). News on the net. Credibility, selective exposure, and racial prejudice. *Communication Research, 35*(2), 151–168.

Meusel, J. (2014). Die Beziehung zwischen Journalisten und ihrem Publikum. Kritische Betrachtung und alternative theoretische Fundierung [The relationship between journalists and their audience. A critical analysis and alternatives for theory building]. In W. Loosen & M. Dohle (Eds.), *Journalismus und (sein) Publikum. Schnittstellen zwischen Journalismusforschung und Rezeptions- und Wirkungsforschung* [Journalism and (its) audience. Points of contact between journalism research and audience and reception research] (pp. 53–69). Wiesbaden: VS Verlag für Sozialwissenschaften.

Meyer, H. K., Marchionni, D., & Thorson, E. (2010). The journalist behind the news: Credibility of straight, collaborative, opinionated and blogged "news.". *American Behavioral Scientist, 54*, 100–119. doi:10.1177/0002764210376313.

Netzley, S. B., & Hammer, M. (2012). Citizen journalism just as credible as stories by pros, students say. *Newspaper Research Journal, 33*(3), 49–61.

Neuberger, C. (2012). Journalismus im Internet aus Nutzersicht [Online journalism as seen by the audience]. *Media Perspektiven, 25*(1), 40–55.

Neuberger, C., Nuernbergk, C., & Rischke, M. (2009). Journalismus im Internet: Zwischen Profession, Partizipation und Technik. [Online journalism. *Between profession, participation and technology] Media Perspektiven, 22*(4), 174–188.

Neuberger, C., & Quandt, T. (2010). Internet-Journalismus: Vom traditionellen Gatekeeping zum partizipativen Journalismus [Online journalism: Developing from traditional gate keeping to participating journalism]? In W. Schweiger & K. Beck (Eds.), *Handbuch Online-Kommunikation* [Handbook online communication] (pp. 59–79). Wiesbaden: VS Verlag für Sozialwissenschaften.

Oswald, B. (2013). Vom Produkt zum Prozess [From product to process]. In L. Kramp, L. Novy, D. Ballwieser & K. Wenzlaff (Eds.), *Journalismus in der digitalen Moderne. Einsichten—Ansichten—Aussichten* [Journalism in digital modernity. Insights—views—perspectives] (pp. 63–79). Wiesbaden: VS Verlag für Sozialwissenschaften.

Pew Research Center for the People and the Press. (2012). *Trends in news consumption: 1991-2012. In changing news landscapes, even television is vulnerable.* http://www.people-press.org/files/legacy-pdf/2012%20News%20Consumption%20Report.pdf. Accessed 16 Mar 2015.

Porlezza, C., & Russ-Mohl, S. (2013). Getting the facts straight in a digital era. Journalistic accuracy and trustworthiness. In C. Peters & M. J. Broersma (Eds.), *Rethinking journalism. Trust and participation in a transformed news landscape* (pp. 45–59). London: Routledge.

Radü, J. (2013). Technologie als Chance. Auf welche Weise Smartphones, Tablets und die Medientechnologie der Zukunft journalistische Qualität sichern helfen [Technology as a chance. How smartphones, tablets and media technology might support journalism's quality in the future]. In L. Kramp, L. Novy, D. Ballwieser & K. Wenzlaff (Eds.), *Journalismus in der digitalen Moderne. Einsichten – Ansichten—Aussichten* [Journalism in digital modernity. Insights—views—perspectives] (pp. 173–183). Wiesbaden: VS Verlag für Sozialwissenschaften.

Reuters Institute for the Study of Journalism. (2014). *Reuters institute digital news report 2014.* https://reutersinstitute.politics.ox.ac.uk/sites/default/files/Reuters%20Institute%20Digital%20News%20Report%202014.pdf. Accessed 3 Mar 2015.

Rimmer, T., & Weaver, D. (1987). Different questions, different answers? Media use and media credibility. *Journalism Quarterly, 64*(1), 28–44.

Rousseau, D. M., Sitkin, S. B., Burt, R. S., & Camerer, C. (1998). Introduction to special topic forum: Not so different after all: A cross-discipline view of trust. *Academy of Management Review, 23*(3), 393–404.

Russial, J. (2009). Growth of multimedia not extensive at newspapers. *Newspaper Research Journal, 30*(3), 58–74.

Schmitt, K. M., Gunther, A. C., & Liebhart, J. L. (2004). Why partisans see mass media as biased. *Communication Research, 31*, 623–641. doi:10.1177/0093650204269390.

Scholl, A., Malik, M., & Gehrau, V. (2014). Journalistisches Publikumsbild und Publikumser-wartungen. Eine Analyse des Zusammenhangs von journalistischen Vorstellungen über das Publikum und Erwartungen des Publikums an den Journalismus [Journalists and their audience. An analysis of the relationship between journalists' perception of their audience and what the audience expects from them]. In W. Loosen & M. Dohle (Eds.), *Journalismus und (sein) Publikum. Schnittstellen zwischen Journalismusforschung und Rezeptions- und Wirkungs-forschung* [Journalism and (its) audience. Points of contact between journalism research and audience and reception research] (pp. 17–33). Wiesbaden: VS Verlag für Sozialwissenschaften.

Scholl, A., & Weischenberg, S. (1998). *Journalismus in der Gesellschaft. Theorie, Methodologie und Empirie* [Journalism within society. Theory, methodology and empiricism]. Opladen: Westdeutscher Verlag.

Seely, N. (2014). *Social indicators in online news environments: The influence of bandwagon cues on news perceptions.* Unpublished Master Thesis, The Ohio State University, Ohio, USA.

Singer, J. B. (2010). Quality control. *Journalism Practice, 4*, 127–142. doi:10.1080/17512780903391979.

Sitkin, S. B., & Pablo, A. L. (1992). Reconceptualizing the determinants of risk behavior. *Academy of Management Review, 17*(1), 9–38.

Stavrositu, C., & Sundar, S. S. (2008). If internet credibility is so iffy, why the heavy use? The relationship between medium use and credibility. *CyberPsychology & Behavior, 11*, 65–68. doi:10.1089/cpb.2007.9933.

Sundar, S., Knobloch-Westerwick, S., & Hastall, M. R. (2007). News cues: Information scents and cognitive heuristics. *Journal of the American Society for Information Science and Technology, 58*, 366–378. doi:10.1002/asi.20511.

Tsfati, Y., & Ariely, G. (2014). Individual and contextual correlates of trust in media across 44 countries. *Communication Research, 41*, 760–782. doi:10.1177/0093650213485972.

Urban, J., & Schweiger, W. (2013). News quality from the recipients' perspective. *Journalism Studies, 15*, 821–840. doi:10.1080/1461670X.2013.856670.

Wenjing, X., & Yunze, Z. (2014). Is seeing believing? Comparing media credibility of traditional and online media in China. *China Media Research, 10*(3), 64–73.

Westley, B. H., & Severin, W. J. (1964). Some correlates of media credibility. *Journalism Quarterly, 41*, 325–335.

Wolf, C., & Schnauber, A. (2014). News consumption in the mobile era. *Journalism Practice, 3*, 759–776. doi:10.1080/21670811.2014.942497.

Examining Journalist's Trust in Sources: An Analytical Model Capturing a Key Problem in Journalism

Florian Wintterlin and Bernd Blöbaum

Abstract In order to maintain its credibility, news journalism largely depends on the accuracy of facts. One key factor necessary for building trust in journalism is the trustworthiness and reliability of its sources. News journalism needs to trust its sources to deliver accurate information in order to fulfill journalistic standards. Journalists always have to balance the risk of reporting selected parts of the constant flow of information. The process of fact checking to verify news material is of great importance in minimizing the risk. However, digitalization and the dramatic increase in possible news sources, demand new and better ways to cope with the issue of source trustworthiness. With a few exceptions, journalism research has not dealt with trust issues in the relationship between journalists and sources. In order to bridge this gap, we propose a reflexive understanding of journalistic trust in sources which is based on the perception of risk and trustworthiness.

Based on an analytical model of journalism and an examination of the role of recipient's trust in journalism, trust in journalistic sources is conceptualized building on source credibility research, as well as on sociological and psychological trust theory, respectively. An analytical model for trust in journalistic sources is developed for further research in this field and trust building in journalistic practices is described.

Keywords Trust • Journalism • Sources • Digitalization • Verification

1 Introduction

Since journalism has become an important institution of modern society in the nineteenth century, it has undergone continuous change. Political, economic and— most importantly—technological changes have influenced the development of news media as organizations, the differentiation on the level of roles in journalism vary and the way journalists and media organizations gather, select and present information and coordinate their action, communication and decisions. Without doubt, digitalization constitutes the predominant challenge for contemporary

F. Wintterlin (✉) • B. Blöbaum
University of Münster, Münster, Germany
e-mail: florian.wintterlin@uni-muenster.de; bernd.bloebaum@uni-muenster.de

© Springer International Publishing Switzerland 2016   75
B. Blöbaum (ed.), *Trust and Communication in a Digitized World*, Progress in IS,
DOI 10.1007/978-3-319-28059-2_4

journalism. News media have to develop new and better business models in order to survive. Journalists have to enhance their competences as well as create new forms of cooperation and coordination. Data journalism and new forms of narration (storytelling), highlight alterations in terms of content and presentation formats. Data which is available in a digital form offers new opportunities for whistle-blowers—with Wikileaks and Edward Snowden as prominent examples—and it enhances journalism's ability to access information, pictures and footage from events that would have been less accessible in the past.

Journalism, be it offline and online, is based on trust. The public is unable to control and verify the facts and figures, journalism delivers in a constant flow. Readers, users, listeners and viewers have to trust journalism as an institution and they have to trust, in particular, news organizations as well as journalists, that those issues and events presented in the news media are true and reliable. Digitalization influences the relationship between recipients and journalism, which is built on trust.

This paper conceptualizes and discusses one aspect of this process: trust in sources. Due to digitalization, news media have access to more sources than ever before, but they also have to develop new and better ways of verifying information from social media and users, that reaches newsrooms via digital channels. The importance of trust and trust building in the relationship between sources and journalism is an issue that bothers on the theoretical and empirical relevance of journalism research.

Based on an analytical model of journalism, we emphasized the role of the recipient's trust in journalism. In order to develop and maintain the trust in journalism, it is essential for news media to deliver reliable information. The quality of news depends on various factors such as relevance, comprehensiveness and accuracy. But first and foremost, the news has to be correct. And to present factual information largely depends on the quality of sources. This is the starting point in conceptualizing the process of trust building between journalism and sources, leading to a model for further research in this field. The scope of this paper is limited to news journalism, which focuses on the dissemination of relevant information to the general public.

2 Trust and Its Antecedents

Regarding journalism, there are three areas where trust seems to be an important explanatory factor: trust through journalism, trust in journalism and trust building within journalism (Blöbaum 2014). Trust through journalism means the contribution of journalism to trust in societal systems (for example, Politics), organizations (For example, Parties) and individuals (For example, Politicians). From the perspective of the audience, we can analyze the different dimensions of trust in Journalism (Kohring and Matthes 2007). In order to derive the concept of trust building within journalism as in the case of its relation to sources, we turn to sociological and psychological trust theory.

Although, a common understanding of trust has not emerged in science, so far, there are some basic elements, scholars widely agree upon (Levi and Stoker 2000). First, trust enables the trustor to act in the face of uncertainty. Situations lacking the required knowledge and the possibility or capacity to control the counterpart trust is crucial for social actions (Coleman 1990). According to Luhmann, trust reduces social complexity by suspending certain future developments (Luhmann 1979). Consequently, Simmel (1908) describes trust as an intermediate between knowledge and ignorance, which means that trust cannot evolve with either complete knowledge or ignorance. Second, trust refers to a relationship. The willingness to maintain the relationship is crucial for trust relations (Hardin 2002). Contrary to other disciplines, sociology deals with trust as a social category. But it is based on the cognitive process of forming expectations about another's future behavior (Müller 2013; Barber 1983). Third, trust is therefore, aimed at the future. Trust as a reflexive process is based on knowledge about past actions, refers to a present action and is orientated towards the future. The trusting actor acts as if only one certain future is possible based on inferences about the past (Luhmann 1979). According to Sztompka (1999, p. 70), the "most important and common ground for trust is the estimate of the trustworthiness of the target". Factors contributing to trustworthiness are ability, benevolence and integrity as perceived by the trustor (Mayer et al. 1995). Fourth, trust entails risk. The trustor's expectations can be disappointed by the trustee. The willingness to take a risk in a certain situation depends largely on the perception of the amount of risk required for this particular action. According to Mayer et al. (1995, p. 725), trust as an action is the result of a specific calculation "weighing the likelihoods of both positive and negative outcomes". Only if the level of trust is higher than the level of perceived risk, will the trustor take action. Fifth, trust needs preconditions. It not only depends on the trustworthiness of the trustee and the perceived risk of the trustor, but also, on characteristics of the trustor like the general willingness to trust or to take a risk. The "propensity to trust is proposed to be a stable within-party factor that will affect the likelihood the party will trust" (Mayer et al. 1995, p. 715). The named factors and their antecedents can be called reasons to trust. Sixth, trust is limited to a subject and specific matter. A trusts B to do X; but A may not trust B to do Y (Hardin 2002).

Taking into account all these elements, trust can be described as a superordinate concept, entailing trust as trusting beliefs, intentions and trust-related behavior (McKnight and Chervany 2001; Kohring 2001). Trusting beliefs means the relative security that the trustee has characteristics beneficial to one's self, such as ability, benevolence or integrity. Basically, it can be described as the judgment of his trustworthiness. Trusting intentions incorporate the willingness to declare the trust to B with regard to X and therefore, depend on B. Mayer et al. (1995, p. 712) defined trust as "the willingness of a party to be vulnerable to the actions of another party, based on the expectation that the other will perform a particular action important to the trustor, irrespective of the ability to monitor or control the other party". Trust-related behavior means that a trustor voluntarily depends on a trustee, even though he is aware of the possible negative consequences. "Social Actor A selectively connects his or her own action with a certain action of Social Actor B, under the condition of a perceived risk" (Kohring and Matthes 2007).

According to Endreß (2010), most of the literature on trust, can be categorized as reflexive trust in differentiation with operating trust, which describes trust as a given tacit frame reference for every social interaction. We define reflexive trust as a willingness to selectively connect one's action to a certain action of the trustee, based on the latter's perceived trustworthiness and the possible risk of negative consequences. Trust becomes manifest in the trust action and is based on reasons to trust. According to Zucker (1986), trust can be institution-based, characteristics-based and process-based. Process-based trust is tied to interactions in the past between trustor and trustee or mediated experiences by a third party. As an exemplary indicator, reputation can serve as a process-based reason to trust. Characteristics-based trust rests on the judgement of the actor or on the content as trustworthy or credible. Institution-based trust becomes important, especially in modernized societies where the exchange partners may remain anonymous and the institutional context in the form of memberships or professional certificates, for example, becomes the main reason to trust.

3 Journalism and Trust

The terms "media" and "journalism" are often used synonymously. In social sciences, "media" includes the organizational structure (certain newspapers, TV stations, and so on.), different types and forms of media (print, TV, radio, online) and refers to a social system of modern society, arranged on the same level as the economy, religion, politics, sports. . ... Media is also used as an expression for media content. It is more or less common sense (at least in Western societies) that the media play an important societal role. The performance of the media is essential within the field of norm-building in various parts of society. "In a democratic society, the media are expected to be accountable, relatively free of undue intrusion from the state, and provide an opportunity for various members and groups to be reflected fairly" (Reese 2008, p. 2990).

Scholars analyzing media content usually focus their attention primarily to articles and news pieces selected and put together by journalists (Wahl-Jorgensen and Hanitzsch 2009). Even the normative function of media in the process of political communication, and the role of media as a social actor are associated with the performance of journalism.

Journalism can be seen as a process connected to an organizational context, usually, the organizational environment of a news department. Journalists perform their tasks as professional actors in a certain division of labour (editors, reporters, managing editors . . .), by observing a specific part of the societal environment: politics, economy, sports, science, and so on. Journalists use certain forms, formats and professional routines to select events (news values) and to put them into a specific form, using journalistic patterns of presenting (news, reports, interviews . . .). An article marks the end of a long process of editing and coordination in a news organization. McQuail noted that journalism "is typically undertaken within a larger news organization, by skilled or trained persons, following established and transparent rules and procedures" (2013, p. 15).

Dissemination of relevant information to the public marks the main function of journalism in modern society. Journalism reduces complexity by publishing events and circumstances of public significance. To fulfil this function, the journalistic system basically takes three steps: (1) Researching and acquiring information, (2) Selecting information and (3) Presenting information. The working process in journalism is very much organized or revolve around these steps.

Programs (or practices) are one structural element of journalism. Other elements of the journalistic structure are journalistic organization (mainly editorial offices) and journalistic roles (journalists and recipients) (Blöbaum 2014). Journalism research distinguishes between four types of programs:

– Research: The information-collecting program is essential for journalism. Researching information represents a fundamental activity. It is essential that media content is "based on the information acquired from reliable sources" (McQuail 2013, p. 15).
– Selection: As there are more topics and events than journalism is able to convey, selection is crucial.
– Coordination: This program assigns an event or a topic to a certain part of a newspaper, broadcast program, and so on. Coordination by means of different forms of conferences and meetings, enables journalism to handle the huge amount of content.
– Presentation: Journalists have to decide how to convey information of public interest that has been researched, selected and has undergone various decision-making steps in the process of coordination (Blöbaum 2014).

Journalism—like other institutions of modern society—depends on trust. But at the same time, journalism plays an important role in *creating* trust for other parts of society. Covering current affairs in politics, economy, sport, science, and so on conveys a certain image of the organizations and actors of the respective societal field. Although, it is not the predominant mission of journalism to create or destroy trust, the coverage of events and affairs has at least the potential to influence public trust in politics, economy and other systems. By reporting malfunctions and violations of general societal norms or those rules and moral foundations which apply in social systems, journalism is capable of developing, enhancing or reducing trust. Journalism's autonomy to gather and present information, journalistic norms of objectivity and transparency, intellectual autonomy and independence are principles supporting the social function and responsibility of journalism. Journalism's capability to distrust itself is based on public trust in the journalistic system.

There are three reference points for recipient's trust in journalism: Trust in the system of journalism, in journalistic organizations and roles and finally, in journalistic practices. By looking at journalism's role in creating trust and distrust in different areas of society, journalism could be viewed as a trustor (with organizations and actors in politics, economy, sport and so on as trustees). Focusing on journalism from the viewpoint of the general public, however, reverses the roles: the public becomes the trustor with journalism being the trustee. Acting as trustor and trustee simultaneously, entails certain implications: Journalism as a trustor for example, has to develop and maintain trust with its sources; as a trustee it has to prove its trustworthiness continuously.

Trust in journalism reflects a historical achievement that has been gained from severe fights for press freedom and a constant struggle to remain independent of political and economic impact. But recipient's trust in journalism is also a product of socialization. In modern (Western) societies, it is more or less common sense and part of collective and individual knowledge, that people can rely on news content. Information about current affairs is usually not based on personal experience, but on media coverage presented by journalists. Generally speaking, there is no reason to question the credibility of media content. In this respect, trust in journalism is renewed permanently, by an ongoing process (Blöbaum 2014).

Public trust in journalism is first and foremost based on the system's ability to act professionally. As with all other systems, laypersons are unable to control what is offered by news media. By relying on journalism, a recipient makes himself vulnerable. Trust in media content does not only mean to believe the facts and figures presented in the news. Trust in journalism is rooted in the programs and practices performed by journalism (Kohring 2002). "The news media can be trusted by the audience if it selects relevant facts and positions from public discourses and presents them without bias and distortion" (Müller 2013, p. 81). Readers, users, listeners and viewers trust those guidelines, journalists follow in their newsrooms— without necessarily being aware of them. These manuals include norms (For example, objectivity), rules (be first, but first be right) and routines of gathering, selecting and presenting valid information. Violation of professional norms is always the objects of concern within journalism. "Journalistic practices that violate norms of journalistic independence and appropriateness are scandalized by news media" (Müller 2013, p. 55).

Recipients expect relevant and appropriate information. In order to obtain information, journalists have privileged access to sources and the right to protect sources, for example, not to disclose the names of whistleblowers. This capacity to publish information not intended for the public realm is an important prerequisite for gaining public trust.

Journalism itself and the trust relationship between journalism and recipients is challenged mainly by two developments: economization and digitalization. In the following, we shall focus on digitalization, without neglecting the fact that this process is closely linked to economic pressure in news media. The Internet has several impacts on journalism. Via digital paths, institutions, and actors gain access to the public, without having to rely on journalism any longer. The internet and social media offer direct links between political institutions and politicians, clubs and athletes, companies and consumers and scientific institutions and lay people.

Although, this process of bypassing journalism has sometimes been labelled as the end of the predominant gatekeeping function of journalism, it has to be considered that the news media still play an important role in the process of agenda setting. "The internet has not killed the newspaper" (Nielsen 2012, p. 27). Journalism as a system is still alive—but it has to change, in order to remain a relevant and reliable institution. Nevertheless, in the digital era, journalism remains first and foremost journalism.

The Internet has not only become a new distribution channel for legacy media. It also stimulates journalism to develop new formats, forms of storytelling, new forms of coordination in newsrooms and new forms of research. From a journalistic point of view, digitalization enhances the possibilities of research. In the digital world, more sources are available and accessible than ever before. In terms of trust, digitalization influences journalism's role, both as trustor and as trustee. Internet journalism requires the same level of trust as journalism of the pre-Internet era. Impartiality and objectivity are norms that are not suspended in digital journalism. Similarly, journalistic principles such as the protection of sources or scrutinizing and double checking important facts are not dismissed in online journalism.

Yet, as a trustee, journalism has to prove its trustworthiness in the digital environment. To provide the public with relevant, correct and current facts as well as contextualisation is by far the strongest means to maintain trust in journalism. The Internet offers the opportunity to facilitate communication between journalistic media and recipients. To comment becomes easy for the audience, and online journalism provides an instant feedback. Answering comments and correction columns, stress journalism's concern regarding accountability and appropriate relationship with its audience. The digital world bridges the gap between journalism and the public. Social media has become a channel for media organizations to inform recipients about relevant topics. Facebook and Twitter have also become a medium for gathering information, becoming alert of events and actions. Many sources find an easier way into newsrooms via digital channels. This does not only amplify the problem of selection, but also demands new methods to evaluate the credibility of the digital material. This is also true for user-generated content. Media users, both experts and laypersons, deliver footage, pictures and other forms of content that has to be checked.

With regard to journalism and sources, we observe the following changes due to digitalization:

- The number of (possible) sources has increased dramatically
- Institutions and persons can bypass news media more easily
- Recipients can reach newsrooms without major obstacles
- More data and information than ever before are available for journalists
- News organizations have to organize techniques and to develop criteria, in order to make a useful selection of information
- News media have to develop techniques to check and verify digital information

4 Trust in Sources

4.1 Trust in Journalistic Sources

For some time now, journalism research has dealt with questions on trust under the label of media credibility (Kohring and Matthes 2007). Studies have been undertaken concerning source credibility (Hovland et al. 1953), the credibility of media like newspapers, television and radio in comparison (Roper 1985), and the different dimensions of credibility, using factor analytical studies (Gaziano and McGrath 1986). According to this research, trustworthiness and competence are subfactors of credibility. Trustworthiness refers to the intentions of the communicator and is operationalized, on the one hand by impartiality and, on the other hand, the motivation to lie about the topic. Later, researchers interpreted this variable as benevolence, because a high benevolence is inversely related to the motivation to lie (Mayer et al. 1995). Although, research on credibility gained much attention in science, many researchers criticized its lack of theoretical foundation (Metzger et al. 2003; Earle and Cvetkovich 1995; Self 2009). Instead, they turned to the concept of trust for describing the relationship between listeners, speakers and their messages and conceptualized trustworthiness as the superordinate concept, with credibility, being only one dimension (Giffin 1967; Kohring and Matthes 2007). This differentiation notwithstanding, many dimensions identified in credibility research can be integrated into trust research, as reasons to trust sources.

This contribution focuses on trust building within journalism and takes a closer look at the relationship between journalists and their sources. Integrating studies of source credibility into sociological and psychological trust literature seem a promising way to gain new insights into the relationship between journalists and their sources.

The importance of credibility as a norm for journalists has been widely documented. Getting the facts right is a core principle of journalism, and codes of ethics feature credibility as a central principle (Tsfati 2008; Zelizer 2004). Standards of source credibility determine access to the news as well as the capacity of journalism to produce fair, accurate and unbiased news (Reich 2011a). According to Reich (2011a, p. 51) and Yoon (2005), "source credibility may be defined as the person's believability as a source of information or as the degree to which information from a source is perceived by a journalist as accurate, fair, unbiased and trustworthy". According to Gans (1979, p. 130), "when reliability cannot be checked quickly enough, story selectors look for trustworthy sources: those who do not limit themselves to self-serving information, try to be accurate, and, above all, are honest." Journalists have to balance continuously between losing time when being over-suspicious and losing their face or job when being under-suspicious (Reich 2011b). "Viewing all sources as questionable, news reporters must spend time verifying their statements" (Tuchman 1978, p. 84). Journalists prefer more credible sources because they are less likely to require further verification (Fishman 1980). Therefore, judging the credibility of a source is decisive for their everyday work. According to a study by Powers et al. (1994), journalists considered credibility to be the most important factor in source selection. "The extent to which information sources, that stand behind virtually all the news, are perceived by journalists as credible is a key determinant of the likelihood of their obtaining news access and public voice" (Reich 2011a, p. 51).

The issue of credibility is gaining importance in the context of online sourcing, where journalists constantly have to balance between maintaining professional standards of accuracy and tapping the full potential of social media, in order to gain access to free and fast sources (Jurisic and Sipic 2013). In a study of U.S. journalists, Cassidy (2007) found that Internet news information was viewed as moderately credible overall, and identifies the Internet as being a medium where anyone can publish information as the main reason for this perception. Reich identified four strategies, journalists employ in avoiding erroneous publications: Typecasting, which means building up a ring of credible sources they can rely on; practical skepticism by using cross-verification and additional sources only in inverse proportion to source credibility; prominent presentation for credible sources; and distancing from less credible sources by explicit attributes in published items (Reich 2011b). According to the literature, there exists a hierarchy of credibility, with official sources, scoring highest and PR practitioners and ordinary citizens lowest (Becker 1970; Sigal 1973; Manning 2001). In a study of Israeli journalists, Reich (2011b) found that less credible sources face more cross-checking, more sources were used and less space was granted. Attributing credibility to a source often means, easing journalistic practices like cross-checking and the use of additional sources (Fishman 1980; Gans 1979). According to Reich (2011a), the major source characteristic, the journalists' judgment of credibility is based upon, is previous contact. This refers to the process character of trust in the sources, which so far, has not gained much attention in credibility research. Trustworthiness and credibility as seen by journalists in general, is widely neglected in journalism research and is not at all theoretically examined (Yoon 2005). In order to focus on the relevant factors, an analytical model of trust is presented and applied to journalistic trust in sources (Fig. 1).

At the center of the model, stands the perceived likelihood of positive or negative outcomes the trustor gains, from weighing factors in the relationship with the trustee (that is, the perceived trustworthiness) and factors outside the relationship that makes it uncertain (that is, the perceived risk) (Mayer et al. 1995). According to Mayer et al., "the level of trust is compared with the level of perceived risk in a situation. If the level of trust surpasses the threshold of perceived risk, then, the trustor will engage in the RTR (Risk Taking in Relationship)" (Mayer et al. 1995, p. 726). This cognitive process, which leads to the willingness to take risks in the relationship, may be described as reflexive trust or trust intention. "Trusting Intentions mean one is willing to depend or intends to depend, on the other party with a feeling of relative security, in spite of lack of control over that party, and even though negative consequences are possible" (McKnight and Chervany 2001, p. 34). One connects his or her action with a certain action of the other party under the condition of perceived risk (Kohring and Matthes

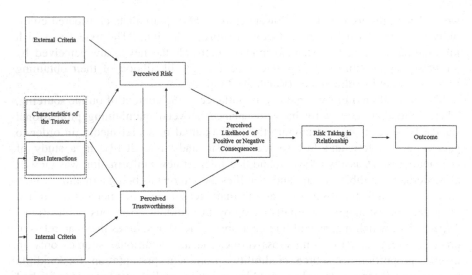

Fig. 1 Model of reflexive trust

2007). Trust, in this reflexive sense, is a calculative resource in social interactions and a cognitive mode (Endreß 2010). It is based on specific expectations about specific future actions of the trustee (Luhmann 2001; Gambetta 1988). RTR is the behavioural manifestation of trust or how McKnight and Chervany (2001), call it: trust-related behaviour. "Trust is the willingness to assume risk; behavioral trust is the assuming of risk" (Mayer et al. 1995, p. 724).

On the other hand, risk and trustworthiness are perceived by considering other factors. In the case of risk, these are external criteria "outside of considerations that involve the relationship with the particular trustee" (Mayer et al. 1995, p. 726), like the effectiveness of control mechanisms and context variables, such as relevance and familiarity of the situation (Sitkin and Pablo 1992). In addition, the risk propensity of the trustor (Das and Teng 2004) and past interactions with the trustee play a decisive role in the judgment about the level of risk involved in a given situation. Past interactions can be primarily and secondarily mediated.

The trustworthiness as perceived by the trustor is judged based on internal criteria, his trust propensity and past interactions. Internal characteristics entail three factors: the characteristics of the trustee and the content he offers as well as his institutional embedment.

1. Characteristics of the trustee or trusting beliefs include ability, benevolence, integrity and predictability (Mayer et al. 1995; McKnight and Chervany 2001). Based on studies of source credibility, other dimensions are dynamism, similarity and affiliation to the community (Self 2009; Metzger et al. 2003). In the case of journalism, the perceptions, whether the source is able and willing to deliver accurate information are the main factors of trustworthiness.
2. According to the literature on message credibility, there are three superordinate factors contributing to the judgement of the characteristics of the content:

structure, content and delivery (Metzger et al. 2003). Content indicators for message credibility in the relationship between sources and journalists are for example, references to other sources and background information. Structure refers to the clarity and organization of the message (Metzger et al. 2003). Message delivery captures the way in which the message is presented by a source. Regarding journalism and the use of social media, technical features like metadata of pictures and videos are taken into account by journalistic inquiry.

3. The institutional embedment of a source entails its reputation, its belonging to a group, network characteristics and the type of source. Most importantly, the type of source, whether it is official, professional or non-professional, is decisive for the judgement of its trustworthiness. According to Flanagin and Metzger (2008), credibility can be endorsed in a digital environment by group and social engagement. Ziegler and Lausen (2005), hint at possible network effects on the judgements of trustworthiness by considering the ratings of trustworthiness of other users in the network.

Besides these internal criteria, characteristics of the trustor, such as trust propensity (Mayer et al. 1995) and past interactions (Endreß 2010) are important reasons for the perceived trustworthiness, as with the case of perceived risk.

To highlight the process character of trust, our model connects the outcome of risk taking in relationship with reasons of perceived trustworthiness and risk. The consideration of internal criteria as well as past interactions is largely determined by the history of past interactions with the trustee.

4.2 Trust Building in Journalistic Practices

To apply the category of trust in the special case of journalism, means describing journalistic practices as trust processes. The silver bullet to bestow journalism's credibility and believability are adequate verification processes (Silverman 2014). Kovach and Rosenstiel (2001, p. 71), described journalism as a "discipline of verification". To control as much of the internal factors as possible, journalism has developed a means of verification to judge the trustworthiness of sources. There are some recent studies which focus on verification processes in general (Shapiro et al. 2013), whereas, research on the verification of social media content is rare (Brandtzaeg et al. 2015).

Comparing the norm of verification with daily practice, Rosner (2008) questioned whether verification is a workable norm for routine news, because journalism would be paralyzed if all information were checked before reporting. Despite acknowledging the norm of verification, Shapiro et al. (2013), found pragmatic compromises when selecting sources. "Statements were frequently relayed, with or without attribution, based on a single subject's word" (Shapiro et al. 2013, p. 657). Some of the verification process seems to rest on the reporter's earlier work. "Trust for a source was derived from previous interviewing" (Shapiro et al. 2013, p. 668). Journalists have to balance between verifying everything possible and trusting the source because of a common background of interactions. Whether or not reporters check sources, largely depends on three factors: sensitivity of information, availability of alternate sources and the reliability of the original source (Shapiro et al. 2013).

Especially in the context of new media, journalism has to develop new strategies to deal with the speed and the amount of material popping up in social media. The old top-down routine of traditional journalism in determining the accuracy and validity of events is called into question, by the rise of social media. Sources outside the established structures of journalism deliver short information fragments, the journalist has to deal with (Hermida 2012). The accelerated speed is the main challenge, which causes concern about an "erosion of the discipline of verification" (Hermida 2012, p. 661). Journalists constantly have to strike a balance between being first and being right. To fulfil journalistic norms of accuracy and impartiality, effective ways of verifying social media sources and contents are demanded (Brandtzaeg et al. 2015). One way to cope with these new developments is to develop a "discipline of collaborative verification" (Hermida 2012, p. 663) or "crowd-verification" (Shapiro et al. 2013, p. 659), with users being active contributors in the process of ensuring the accuracy of the sources. In theory, journalists use networks like Twitter, to determine the truth in an iterative process (Hermida 2012). Social Media used as interfaces between journalism and the public, offer the potential that every single user contributes to the verification of journalistic content and therefore, accelerates the speed of detecting errors. According to Kovach (2006, p. 41), "journalists must find tools that will enlist a methodology of verification in a more citizen-oriented way". However, journalistic organizations—with only a few exceptions—have not yet realized this potential of social media (Hermida 2012). Employing rather classic journalistic strategies to cope with the new material, there are several online tools like the Google Image Search, Streetview, Exif and TinEye, journalists may use to verify social media content. According to Wardle (2014), there are three elements in verifying social media content: provenance, source, date and location. Practical examples suggest a three-step verification process, including content (frequency, style, personality), context (provenance, followers, in correlation with other sources) and code (URL, caches, source code) analysis (Bruno 2011). However, often lacking resources such as time or technical skills, result in certain media, outsourcing the verification process to external organizations like Storyful, to mention just a popular one (Brandtzaeg et al. 2015). Others create new professional positions called "social media editors" or establish desks like the BBC Hub (Turner 2012). Bruno suggests that with social media becoming an integral part of the news gathering process, the new positions of social media curators will be created (Bruno 2011). Social media not only offer new possibilities on the content level, but also, offer the potential to gain access to expert discourses and knowledge in digital discussion panels. However, the role of social media as a channel to connect with experts, eye witnesses or other sources is widely neglected in journalism research. Alternative ways of coping with social media content include, new storytelling methods like, live-blogs to integrate the continuous stream of information by combining unverified social media content with professional reports (Hermida 2012). Especially in crisis, events user-generated-content helps to fill the news vacuum. "The Twitter effect, allows you to provide live coverage without any reporters on the ground, by simply newsgathering user-generated content available online" (Bruno 2011, p. 8). It allows reporters to gain first-hand material or information from the ground, even if no correspondents are present in the area (Bruno 2011). Looking at media organizations in Britain and in the U.S., Bruno states that The Guardian and CNN chose the "tweet first, verify later" approach in contrast to the BBC, who verified all information before publishing (Bruno 2011). However, journalism is far away from standard rules on how to verify sources and materials online. Apart from a few studies examining verification strategies, which refer to a time-consuming evaluation of the trustworthiness of the source, trust between sources and journalists based on other factors like previous interactions, has not yet been studied and requires further consideration.

5 Conclusion

Based on an analytical model of journalism, we focused on the challenges of digitalization and the dwindling trust in journalism. In Germany, examples like the coverage of the Ukraine crisis, called the trustworthiness of journalism into question. Journalists as trustees have to prove their trustworthiness constantly, therefore, it is essential to deliver accurate information. One key factor for ensuring the reliability of news is the trustworthiness of journalistic sources and journalists as trustors, need adequate ways to prove it. Challenged by technological developments, journalism has to change depending on the level of programs, organizations and roles. New journalistic programs which are aimed to gather, select and present information, especially in the context of social media have been discussed and described in trust building in journalism. Journalism develops verification strategies to prove the trustworthiness of sources online. Previous studies have examined different steps in the verification process as well as new strategies like crowd-verification, however, much more qualitative research is needed to understand changes caused by the network characteristics of social media. On the level of journalistic organizations, some media outlets decided to outsource the process of verification and social media monitoring to external partners, like Storyful and that it would be a fruitful way to examine in details this new development of outsourcing the verification process, as one of the key elements of journalism. Another avenue for journalism to deal with the challenges of online sources, is by creating new jobs labelled "social media editor". Specialized in verification, these experts demand new competences exceeding traditional journalism. Concerning the organizational level, more research is needed to encompass changes in journalism caused by social media. On the level of journalistic roles, new expectations are to be met by those performing the roles. Dealing with online sources demands technological competencies as well as a different role perception by journalists. Approaches conceptualizing journalistic organizations as nodes in a network of sharing and exchanging information, question the gatekeeper function of journalists (Heinrich 2011). The formation of news should be seen as a collaboration between professional journalists and lay communicators (Beckett and Mansell 2008), and journalists have to ask themselves, whether they are reporters, editors, critics or just talking among friends (Farhi 2009, p. 21). The gatewatching concept also deals with these questions of journalistic roles (Bruns 2005).

In order to examine one important part of the trust process, we proposed an analytical model of reflexive trust, which was derived from sociological and psychological trust literature and long established credibility research. Applied to journalism, the model describes factors contributing to the reflexive trust of journalists in the sources. It is based on the distinction of trust, reasons such as trustworthiness, trusting intentions and trust-related behaviour highlights the process character of trust by connecting the outcome of trust-related behaviour to trust reasons. The perception of risk and trustworthiness are crucial for the intention to trust, by weighting the possibilities of positive or negative outcomes. Reasons for risk and trustworthiness perceptions are clustered both in internal and external criteria, characteristics of the trustor and past interactions. This distinction offers the possibility to differentiate between trust, mainly based on high trustworthiness or low risk perceptions. Trust in this sense is a cognitive mode of the trustor, grounded in a reciprocal relationship with the trustee. Much more research using in-depth interviews with journalists has to be done concerning the process character of trust, particularly, with regard to previous interactions as the main reason to trust. According to Endreß (2010), this might be called operating trust and future research has to examine its importance in the relationship between journalists and sources.

References

Barber, B. (1983). *The logic and limits of trust*. New Brunswick, NJ: Rutgers University Press.
Becker, H. S. (1970). Whose side are we on? In J. D. Douglas (Ed.), *The relevance of sociology* (pp. 99–111). New York: Meredith Corporation.
Beckett, C., & Mansell, R. (2008). Crossing boundaries: New media and networked journalism. *Communication, Culture and Critique, 1*(1), 92–104. doi:10.1111/j.1753-9137.2007.00010.x.
Blöbaum, B. (2014). *Trust and journalism in a digital environment*. Working Paper. Oxford: Reuters Institute for the Study of Journalism.
Brandtzaeg, P. B., Lüders, M., Spangenberg, J., Rath-Wiggins, L., & Følstad, A. (2015). Emerging journalistic verification practices concerning social media. *Journalism Practice*. doi:10.1080/17512786.2015.1020331.
Bruno, N. (2011). *Tweet first, verify Later? How real-time information is changing the coverage of worldwide crisis events*. Working Paper. Oxford: Reuters Institute for the Study of Journalism.
Bruns, A. (2005). *Gatewatching: Collaborative online news production*. New York: Peter Lang.
Cassidy, W. P. (2007). Online news credibility: An examination of the perceptions of newspaper journalists. *Journal of Computer-Mediated Communication, 12*(2), 478–498.

Coleman, J. S. (1990). *The foundations of social theory*. Cambridge, MA: Harvard University Press.

Das, T. K., & Teng, B. (2004). The risk-based view of trust: A conceptual framework. *Journal of Business and Psychology, 19*(1), 85–116.

Earle, T. C., & Cvetkovich, G. T. (1995). *Social trust. Toward a cosmopolitan society*. Westport, CT: Praeger Publishers.

Endreß, M. (2010). Vertrauen—soziologische Perspektiven. In M. Maring (Ed.), *Vertrauen— zwischen sozialem Kitt und der Senkung von Transaktionskosten*. Karlsruhe: KIT Scientific Publishing.

Farhi, P. (2009). The Twitter explosion. *American Journalism Review, 31*, 1–6. Retrieved from http://www.ajr.org/Article.asp?id=4756.

Fishman, M. (1980). *Manufacturing the news*. Austin, TX: University of Texas Press.

Flanagin, A. J., & Metzger, M. J. (2008). Digital media and youth: Unparalleled opportunity and unprecedented responsibility. In *The John D. and Catherine T. MacArthur Foundation Series on Digital Media and Learning* (pp. 5–28). Cambridge, MA: MIT Press. doi:10.1162/dmal. 9780262562324.005.

Gambetta, D. (1988). Can we trust trust? In D. Gambetta (Ed.), *Trust: Making and breaking cooperative relations* (pp. 213–237). New York: Basil Blackwell.

Gans, H. (1979). *Deciding what's news: A study of CBS Evening News, NBC Nightly News, Newsweek, and Time*. Evanston, IL: Northwestern University Press.

Gaziano, C., & McGrath, K. (1986). Measuring the concept of credibility. *Journalism Quarterly, 63*, 451–462.

Giffin, K. I. M. (1967). The contribution of studies of source credibility to a theory of interpersonal trust. *Psychological Bulletin, 68*(2), 104–120.

Hardin, R. (2002). *Trust and trustworthiness*. New York: Russell Sage.

Heinrich, A. (2011). *Network journalism: Journalistic practice in interactive spheres*. New York: Routledge.

Hermida, A. (2012). Tweets and truth. *Journalism Practice, 6*(5–6), 659–668.

Hovland, C. I., Janis, I. L., & Kelley, H. H. (1953). *Communication and persuasion: Psychological studies of opinion change*. New Haven, CT: Yale University Press.

Jurisic, J., & Sipic, I. (2013). Social networking sites: (Un)trustworthy news sources? *Communication Management Quarterly, 26*, 51–72.

Kohring, M. (2001). *Vertrauen in Medien—Vertrauen in Technologie*. Working Paper. Stuttgart: Akademie für Technikfolgenabschätzung in Baden-Württemberg.

Kohring, M. (2002). Vertrauen in Journalismus. In A. Scholl (Ed.), *Systemtheorie und Konstruktivismus in der Kommunikationswissenschaft* (pp. 91–110). Konstanz: UVK.

Kohring, M., & Matthes, J. (2007). Trust in news media: Development and validation of a multidimensional scale. *Communication Research, 34*(2), 231–252.

Kovach, B. (2006). Toward a new journalism with verification. *Nieman Reports, 60*(4), 39–41.

Kovach, B., & Rosenstiel, T. (2001). *The elements of journalism*. New York: Crown Publishers.

Levi, M., & Stoker, L. (2000). Political trust and trustworthiness. *Annual Review of Political Science, 3*(1), 475–507.

Luhmann, N. (1979). *Trust and power. Two works by Niklas Luhmann*. Chichester: Wiley.

Luhmann, N. (2001). Vertrautheit, Zuversicht, Vertrauen: Probleme und Alternativen. In M. Hartmann & C. Offe (Eds.), *Vertrauen. Die Grundlage des sozialen Zusammenhalts* (pp. 143–160). Frankfurt: Campus-Verlag.

Manning, P. (2001). *News and news sources: A critical introduction*. London: Sage.

Mayer, R. C., Davis, J. H., & Schoorman, F. D. (1995). An integrative model of organizational trust. *Academy of Management Review, 20*(3), 709–734.

McKnight, D. H., & Chervany, N. L. (2001). Trust and distrust definitions: One bite at a time. In R. Falcone, M. Singh, & Y.-H. Tan (Eds.), *Trust in cyber-societies. Integrating the human and artificial perspectives* (pp. 27–54). Berlin: Springer.

McQuail, D. (2013). *Journalism and society*. London: Sage.

Metzger, M. J., Flanagin, A. J., Eyal, K., Lemus, D. R., & McCann, R. M. (2003). Credibility for the 21st century: Integrating perspectives on source, message, and media credibility in the contemporary media environment. *Communication Yearbook, 27*, 293–336.

Müller, J. (2013). *Mechanisms of trust: News media in democratic and authoritarian regimes.* Frankfurt: Campus Verlag.

Nielsen, R. K. (2012). *Ten years that shook the media world. Big questions and big trends in international media developments.* Oxford: Reuters Institute for the Study of Journalism.

Powers, A., Fico, F., & Jackson, J. (1994). Influences on use of sources at large U.S. newspapers. *Newspaper Research Journal, 15*(4), 87–98.

Reese, S. (2008). Media production and content. In W. Donsbach (Ed.), *The international encyclopedia of communication* (pp. 2982–2994). Malden, MA: Blackwell.

Reich, Z. (2011a). Source credibility and journalism. *Journalism Practice, 5*(1), 51–67.

Reich, Z. (2011b). Source credibility as a journalistic work tool. In B. Franklin & M. Carlson (Eds.), *Journalists, sources, and credibility: New perspectives* (pp. 19–36). New York: Routledge.

Roper, B. W. (1985). *Public attitudes toward television and other media in a time of change.* New York: Television Information Office.

Rosner, C. (2008). *Behind the headlines: A history of investigative journalism in Canada.* Don Mills, ON: Oxford University Press.

Self, C. C. (2009). Credibility. In D. W. Stacks & M. B. Salwen (Eds.), *An integrated approach to communication theory and research* (2nd ed., p. 592). New York: Routledge.

Shapiro, I., Brin, C., Bédard-Brûlé, I., & Mychajlowycz, K. (2013). Verification as a strategic ritual. *Journalism Practice, 7*(6), 657–673.

Sigal, L. V. (1973). *Reporters and officials: Organization and politics of newsmaking.* Lexington, MA: Heath.

Silverman, C. (2014). *Verification handbook: An ultimate guide on digital age sourcing for emergency coverage.* Maastricht: European Journalism Centre.

Simmel, G. (1908). *Soziologie, Untersuchungen über die Formen der Vergesellschaftung.* English edition, K. H. Wolff (1950). *The Sociology of Georg Simmel* (K. H. Wolff, Trans). New York: Free Press.

Sitkin, S. B., & Pablo, A. L. (1992). Reconceptualizing the determinants of risk behavior. *The Academy of Management Review, 17*(1), 9–38.

Sztompka, P. (1999). *Trust: A sociological theory.* Cambridge: Cambridge University Press.

Tsfati, Y. (2008). Journalists, credibility of. In W. Donsbach (Ed.), *The international encyclopedia of communication* (pp. 2597–2600). Malden, MA: Wiley.

Tuchman, G. (1978). *Making news: A study in the construction of reality.* New York: Free Press.

Turner, D. (2012). Inside the BBC's verification hub: Technology and human intervention are key. *Nieman Reports, 66*(2), 10–13.

Wahl-Jorgensen, K., & Hanitzsch, T. (Eds.). (2009). *The handbook of journalism studies.* New York: Routledge.

Wardle, C. (2014). Verifying user-generated content. In C. Silverman (Ed.), *Verification handbook: An ultimate guide on digital age sourcing for emergency coverage* (pp. 24–30). Maastricht: The European Journalism Centre.

Yoon, Y. (2005). Examining journalists' perceptions and news coverage of stem cell and cloning organizations. *Journalism & Mass Communication Quarterly, 82*(2), 281–300.

Zelizer, B. (2004). When facts, truth, and reality are God-terms: On journalism's uneasy place in cultural studies. *Communication and Critical/Cultural Studies, 1*(1), 100–119.

Ziegler, C.-N., & Lausen, G. (2005). Propagation models for trust and distrust in social networks. *Information Systems Frontiers, 7*(4–5), 337–358.

Zucker, L. G. (1986). Production of trust: Institutional sources of economic structure, 1840–1920. *Research in Organizational Behavior, 8*(1), 53–111.

Trust in Organizations: The Significance and Measurement of Trust in Corporate Actors

Christian Wiencierz and Ulrike Röttger

Abstract For organizations, the trust of their stakeholders is of enormous significance because it is the basis on which organizations are able to achieve their objectives in the long run in a modern, differentiated society. The public perception of organizations and their products also depends heavily on the assessment of their trustworthiness. It is therefore all the more surprising that questions concerning what stakeholder trust in organizations actually is and how it can be measured have so far only been sparsely addressed in communication science. In the present contribution, trust in organizations is conceptualized with reference to sociological theories of trust, among other ideas. According to these theories, trust is a mechanism that makes the risk perceived by stakeholders in their relationships with organizations tolerable. Following the model by Mayer, Davis, and Schoorman, which originates from organizational psychology, trust in organizations is significantly based on their perceived trustworthiness. The empirical analysis of the factors of the perceived trustworthiness of organizations is performed with reference to the example of political parties and non-governmental organizations. The results illustrate the significance of organizational trustworthiness for the relevant organizations and provide valuable implications for organizational practice. The contribution also sheds light on the methodological challenges associated with measuring the trustworthiness of organizations and looks at the resultant challenges for interdisciplinary trust research.

Keywords Trust in organizations • Trust in political parties • Trust in non-governmental organizations (NGOs) • Campaign communication

The following observations are primarily based on the studies by Wiencierz (2016) and by Wiencierz et al. (2015).

C. Wiencierz (✉) • U. Röttger
University of Münster, Münster, Germany
e-mail: christian.wiencierz@uni-muenster.de; ulrike.roettger@uni-muenster.de

B. Blöbaum (ed.), *Trust and Communication in a Digitized World*, Progress in IS,
DOI 10.1007/978-3-319-28059-2_5

1 Introduction

Trust, in general, is a multi-layered phenomenon as well as a topical subject. The significance of trust for modern societies and for social coexistence is emphasized in sociological approaches in particular (e.g., Luhmann 1979, p. 4; Kohring 2004, p. 80; Barbalet 2009). According to these approaches, a society without trust cannot exist (Barber 1983, p. 19; Deutsch 1962). For organizations, the trust of their stakeholders represents a valuable, intangible resource. This trust is significant for organizations because it promotes acceptance of their actions, leads to support for their activities, and, ultimately, expands their scope of action (Morgan and Hunt 1994). In addition, trust is seen as a key factor for an enduring, loyal relationship with their stakeholders (Ki and Hon 2007; Aurier and N'Goala 2010; Grayson et al. 2008). Despite the significance of stakeholder trust in organizations, this field of research has received hardly any systematic examination to date. The present contribution addresses this research gap.

In this contribution, we consider the questions of what stakeholder trust in organizations specifically looks like and how it can be measured accordingly. The focus of this examination is on the trust of external stakeholders. Yet, engaging with trust is a challenge in general because nothing resembling a common understanding of what the term means has so far been established, which is why the field of research is diffuse and heterogeneous (Barbalet 2009). The diverse individual results of the numerous theoretical approaches and empirical studies on trust each relate to a specific problem, which makes it all the more difficult to combine them to form a coherent image of the current state of research (Möllering 2006, pp. 128–129).

We will describe the function and significance of stakeholder trust for organizations primarily on the basis of the sociological assumptions by Luhmann (1979), Kohring (2004; Kohring and Matthes 2007), and Giddens (1991), which we shall apply to trust in organizations. We will also consider the approach to trust originating from organizational psychology that is taken by Mayer et al. (1995; see also Mayer and Davis 1999; Schoorman et al. 2007) because this approach describes trust as a process. This makes the elusive entity of trust into something concrete that can be operationalized. Although the approach of Mayer et al. was developed to research interpersonal trust within organizations, it can also be applied to trust that is placed in organizations (Schoorman et al. 2007). We will describe our experiences of applying the approach with reference to two studies in which we examined trust in non-profit organizations (NPOs). For the examination, we focused on the perceived trustworthiness of organizations because this factor is central to the process of trust. We will present the problems that we encountered in measuring the trustworthiness of organizations and critically discuss the approach. Despite the problems with measurement and the resultant limitations, our application of the approach so far has enabled us to reveal valuable implications both for further trust research and for the strategic communication of organizations. We will present these as part of our conclusion.

2 Trust in Organizations: Theoretical Derivation

When discussing trust in an organizational context, a distinction must be made between two different types of trust relationships: the trust of internal stakeholders and the trust of external stakeholders. In the first type of trust relationship, the focus is on the trust that members of an organization place in the organization or on intraorganizational trust, which describes the trust between members of an organization (Schweer and Thies 2003, p. 57). In our contribution, we will concentrate on the trust that external stakeholders place in NPOs. Before we depict this type of trust with reference to the example of political parties and non-governmental organizations (NGOs), we shall first define the term "trust". Such a definition of the term is necessary because trust is a "[...] contested term [...]" (Levi and Stoker 2000, p. 476) and there are different views concerning what is meant by the term (McKnight and Chervany 2001). We will theoretically demonstrate why trust in organizations is a necessity in modern, differentiated societies and what the function of trust consists of before finally describing trust as a process following Mayer et al. (1995).

2.1 The Necessity of Trust in Organizations

Organizations are often described as corporate actors with a specified structure that is formalized or schematized to an above-average degree. Organizations exhibit a specific purpose orientation and pursue defined objectives (Endruweit 1981, pp. 17–18). The actions of organizations consist of the actions of the relevant organization members, which are decisively influenced by the organizational mechanisms. These mechanisms cause the motives of the organization members to become generalized and lead to a specification of behavior. Consequently, it is possible for the diverse actions of the organization members to be substantively and temporally generalized (Luhmann 2005, p. 14)[1]. Organizations are of vital significance to members of a modern society because expert knowledge is integrated in them. This knowledge is used to provide certain goods and services for certain target groups. Stakeholders are dependent on organizations because they are not able to produce these goods and services themselves in a society shaped by the division of labor and specialization. They lack the knowledge, skills, and resources

---

[1] Luhmann (2005, pp. 13–14, translated from the German) provides the following definition of organizations: "We can describe as being organized those social systems which link membership to specific conditions, that is, which make entrance and exit dependent on conditions. It is assumed that the behavioral requirements of the system and the behavioral motives of the members can vary independently of each other but can, under certain circumstances, be linked together to form relatively long-lasting constellations. With the help of such membership rules [...] it becomes possible, in spite of voluntarily chosen and shifting membership, to reproduce highly artificial modes of behavior over a relatively long stretch of time."

required to do so. Moreover, they often do not have the opportunity or do not wish to acquire the requisite knowledge, skills, and resources (Giddens 1991, pp. 83–84).

However, there are fundamental problems in the relationship between stakeholders and organizations that can make it risky for stakeholders to link an action of their own with the actions of organizations. Firstly, organizations, just like their stakeholders, have a plethora of possible courses of action available to them. Organizations can choose the courses of action expected by the stakeholders, but they can also make a different choice. The actions of corporate actors are therefore contingent; in other words, it is also always possible for everything to be done differently. The contingency of the actions makes it more difficult for stakeholders to anticipate the actions of organizations. It is therefore possible and likely that the expectations placed on organizations will be disappointed by the organizations. Consequently, stakeholders are able to perceive uncertainties and risks when they enter into relationships with the organizations. Secondly, the organizations usually have an edge in terms of knowledge that can be used to the advantage or to the disadvantage of the stakeholders. If stakeholders have insufficient information about the abilities and characteristics of the organizations and about their intended actions and objectives, it is difficult for them to anticipate or recognize what might be opportunistic actions that are being taken by the organizations (Schichtmann 2007; Sztompka 1999, p. 23; Möllering 2008). Finally, the intensity and pace of processes of social change are making it increasingly difficult for organizations to fulfill the expectations of the stakeholders. Processes of change such as globalization and internationalization create complexity, uncertainties, and incalculabilities—that is, life's risks. These risks also have an effect on the actions of organizations and make it more difficult for them to perform their tasks (Sztompka 2006; Cook and Cook 2011; Giddens 1991, pp. 109–110).

If, owing to the aforementioned problems, stakeholders perceive a risk in the relationship with an organization, problems ensue. As laypeople, stakeholders are dependent on organizations and on their goods and services in a society shaped by the division of labor (Giddens 1991, pp. 83–92). At the same time, the purchasing of goods and services is vitally significant to organizations. So that relationships between stakeholders and organizations can exist under the condition of perceived risks, a suitable mechanism is required in order to be able to deal with these risks in the relationships. Trust is such a mechanism.

2.2 The Function of Trust in Organizations

Sociological approaches often primarily describe trust in systems, where these take the form of subareas or functional systems of society, such as politics or the economy. According to these approaches, personal trust is increasingly turning into system trust in modern, differentiated societies (Giddens 1991, pp. 100–111; Luhmann 1979, pp. 48–58). Individuals have to make themselves dependent on the functioning of highly complex, inscrutable systems together with their actors.

Although trust in organizations or institutions—which are understood as being corporate actors—is indicated in these approaches, they do not clearly and compellingly represent and define it as such. Nevertheless, many of the assumptions can be applied to organizations.

Kohring (2004, pp. 110–111) explains that system trust is dependent on the social function of the relevant functional or expert system. This refers to the proper functioning of the system as seen from the subjective perspective of the layperson. According to this understanding, trust in systems develops on the basis of generalized specific expectations about the future performance of the system (Kohring 2004, p. 131). As well as being based on expectations, system trust, according to Giddens (1991, p. 83), is based on the assessment of the trustworthiness of established expert knowledge pertaining to these systems[2]. This perceived trustworthiness serves the assessment of benefits and risks in trust-related situations[3].

According to Luhmann (1979, pp. 93–94), the function of trust in general is to reduce social complexity. Missing information is replaced with an internally guaranteed certainty. Yet, the use of trust to establish complete certainty must be seen in a critical light because the fundamental problems that make trust necessary, but also risky, continue to exist objectively. Because of the contingency of the actions, the information asymmetry that favors organizations, and the processes of social change, the risk to stakeholders that their expectations will be disappointed remains objectively present. Rather, trust has the function of making it possible to tolerate the risk perceived by a stakeholder in his or her relationship with the organization. Trust "[...] is the selective linking of the actions of another with one's own actions under the condition of the toleration of the perceived risk in a way that cannot be legitimated by means of factual arguments" (Kohring 2004, p. 131, translated from the German). A pretense is made that the desirable outcomes of the act of trust are likely to occur:

> [T]rust is an ongoing process of building on reason, routine, and reflexivity, suspending irreducible social vulnerability and uncertainty *as if* they were favorably resolved, and maintaining thereby a state of favorable expectation toward the actions and intentions of more or less specific others. (Möllering 2006, p. 111)

From the perspective of the organizations, toleration of the perceived risk leads to an increase in their legitimacy and effectiveness. Organizations that are trusted can

---

[2] Kohring (2004, pp. 122–123) stresses that the focus of an empirical examination of trust must be placed on the expectations of the trustors and not on the preconditions. According to this view, trust describes a relation between social actors and not an assessment of certain (learnable) characteristics of the object of trust by the trustor. In this contribution, the characteristics of the object of trust will nevertheless be taken into consideration because the expectations have to be formed by the stakeholders beforehand and the possible actions of the object of trust have to be anticipated accordingly. Anticipation of the possible actions of the object of trust is, however, only possible if its characteristics are assessed at a previous stage.

[3] Giddens (1991, p. 83) uses the concept of the "calculation" of benefits and risks in this context. This concept was replaced by that of assessment in order to avoid the impression of describing a theory of trust that is based on rational choice theory.

maintain or expand their scope of action owing to the fact that stakeholder trust increases the acceptance of their activities. However, if organizations lack stakeholder trust, their legitimacy, stability, and scope of action are threatened (Hoffjann 2011, pp. 65–66).

2.3 Trust in Organizations as a Process

Following our description of the function of trust for organizations, our next step will be to theoretically derive an understanding of what trust specifically is. For this purpose, the elaborated approach to trust taken by Mayer et al. (1995; see also Schoorman et al. 2007; Mayer and Davis 1999), which originates from organizational psychology, will be taken into consideration. This approach describes trust as a process and thereby makes the elusive entity of trust into something concrete that can be operationalized. The sociological explanations considered previously lack this kind of specific process description. Although the approach was developed to research interpersonal trust within organizations, it can also be applied to trust that is placed in organizations (Schoorman et al. 2007).

Applied to organizations, trust, following Mayer et al. (1995), is the willingness to make oneself vulnerable to an organization in a certain situation in a relationship with that organization. Trust is

[...] the willingness of a party to be vulnerable to the actions of another party based on the expectation that the other will perform a particular action important to the trustor, irrespective of the ability to monitor or control that other party. (1995, p. 712)

In addition, Mayer et al. describe trust as a state of willingness to take a risk in a relationship. Whether or not stakeholders enter such a state depends, firstly, on their propensity to trust—that is, their "[...] general willingness to trust others" (Mayer et al. 1995, p. 715). Secondly, trust is significantly determined by the trustworthiness of the organizations as perceived by the stakeholders. The assessment of an organization's trustworthiness is made on the basis of factors that comprise the organization's ability, benevolence, and integrity (Mayer et al. 1995). These antecedents of perceived trustworthiness are also explicitly or implicitly present in many other approaches and studies that describe, among other things, trust in organizations (e.g., Grayson et al. 2008; McKnight and Chervany 2001; Schichtmann 2007; Hon and Grunig 1999, p. 3; Renn and Levine 1991, pp. 179–180). With respect to organizations, the ability factor describes skills, competencies, and characteristics that enable a specific task to be carried out in a specific situation. Consequently, ability is always domain-specific. Benevolence relates to the stakeholders' perception of whether organizations have a benevolent disposition toward them and act in their interests or whether they will instead pursue egocentric motives. Finally, the assessment of integrity takes into account the principles, values, and beliefs of the organization. The consistency of the actions and reliability are also assigned to this factor. The three antecedents of perceived trustworthiness vary independently of each other and are able to influence each other (Mayer et al. 1995).

Yet, trust, understood as a state, does not automatically lead to the behavioral manifestation of trust. Nevertheless, trust does increase the likelihood that stakeholders will take the risk in the relationship with the organization and make themselves vulnerable to it. Within the model, context factors can have a moderating effect on the connection between trust and the taking of a risk in a relationship. The risk is only taken if trust manifests itself in an action (Mayer et al. 1995).

The construct of perceived trustworthiness, with the factors "ability", "benevolence", and "integrity", is central to trust in organizations, which is why our following analyses will concentrate on this construct. Moreover, we do not restrict the understanding of trust to that of a state. When defining trust, we also include the associated action and refer to it as the act of trust. The process is only complete when the act of trust is performed. We also take the view that the risk does not just have an effect after there has been a willingness to make oneself vulnerable. Rather, the perceived risk in the relationship with the organization is the precondition for the process of trust because it is only in that case that a mechanism for dealing with this risk is required. However, we do agree with the assumption that context factors are able to influence the process of trust (Luhmann 1979, p. 33). Accordingly, whether and how trust is able to arise and exist also depends on the situation and on the context.

It is also necessary to establish that, although the stakeholder expectations primarily relate to the outcome of the organization's actions, other aspects of the organization also have to be considered in regard to the formation of expectations. Lepsius (1997, pp. 286–288) provides a theoretical description of three dimensions that shape the expectations placed on institutions. In our opinion, these insights can also be applied to organizations. According to this idea, a distinction must be made between an organization's central idea, its internal order, and its material results. Each of these dimensions can shape stakeholder expectations, and trust can relate to each of these dimensions. If, for example, the results of an organization are not satisfactory, the central idea as well as the internal order or structure of the organization can be called into question. If the central idea is no longer recognized, it becomes difficult to gain trust with the material results of the organization.

Finally, the representatives of the organizations must be considered in the process of trust (Lepsius 1997, p. 289). Giddens (1991, pp. 83–92) describes representatives of abstract systems as access points because it is through them that a connection is established between stakeholders as laypeople and the expert system to which these stakeholders do not belong. If this idea is applied to organizations, it follows that stakeholders have experiences in encounters with representatives of organizations that can form, maintain, or strengthen trust in organizations. However, trust can also be undermined through incorrect conduct by the representatives.[4] For this reason, this is a place where the organization is vulnerable (Grayson et al. 2008).

---

[4] However, direct contact with access points is not always necessary or possible in order to be able to assess the trustworthiness of an abstract system or in order to be able to form trust in that system.

3 Measuring Trust in Organizations

Having provided a general outline of stakeholder trust in organizations, we will describe our experiences of measuring trust in organizations in this next part of the contribution. To reduce complexity and because of practical research consider-ations, we placed two delimitations on the research. Firstly, we are analyzing NPOs, specifically political parties and non-governmental organizations. Secondly, we are concentrating on perceived trustworthiness because this construct is the basis for the process of trust. On the basis of perceived trustworthiness, stakeholders assess whether or not organizations are able to fulfill their expectations. This assessment plays a decisive role in determining whether stakeholders will link their actions with those of the organizations. As soon as they link their actions, the results of the stakeholders' own acts of trust are dependent on the results of the actions taken by the organizations. Therefore, the assessment of trustworthiness is crucial in deter-mining whether or not the stakeholders will make themselves vulnerable to orga-nizations. In addition to our analysis concerning the question of whether the construct of perceived trustworthiness posited by Mayer et al. (1995) can be applied to organizations, we will also summarize the central findings of the studies.

3.1 Trust in Political Parties

The object of the first study was citizens' trust in political parties (Wiencierz 2016). For the parties, as political corporate actors, this trust is significant because it leads to the acceptance of the party activities and increases the parties' legitimacy, ability to act, and effectiveness (Hetherington 1998; Braithwaite and Levi 1998; Benz 2002). Moreover, trust in parties is essential to the functioning of a party democracy such as that of Germany: Without a minimum degree of trust in parties—that is to say, trust placed in intermediary actors or links between citizen and state—a party democracy cannot function smoothly (Benz 2002; Höhne 2006, p. 42; Strøm 2009). There is, therefore, a risk that a lack of trust in parties will diminish not only the ability to act and the effectiveness of the parties, but also, ultimately, the ability to act and the effectiveness of the entire political system.

Because of the significance of interpersonal influence for political opinion formation, we examined whether eligible German voters talked about election advertising by the political parties and about the content of such advertising; we also examined what effect these conversations had on trust in parties. Such an analysis had so far been largely neglected in communication science. For the examination, a three-stage panel survey was used in which $N = 496$ (18–84 years, $M = 47.21, SD = 15.98$) for the first survey wave, $N = 322$ (18–84 years, $M = 47.93$,

---

For these purposes, information from the mass media and from personal contacts can also be taken into account (Coleman 1990, pp. 180–185; Giddens 1991, pp. 90–91).

$SD = 15.83$) for the second survey wave, and $N = 264$ (18–84 years, $M = 48.85$, $SD = 15.49$) for the third survey wave. The samples obtained were comparable across all three survey times.

We phrased the items for measuring the trustworthiness of political parties following those of Mayer and Davis (1999). We took these items, which were designed for measuring interpersonal trust in organizations, into consideration as a basis for creating four items in each case for the factors of perceived trustworthiness, namely ability, benevolence, and integrity. The items had to be evaluated by using a five-point Likert scale (1 = "Strongly disagree" through 5 = "Strongly agree"). Because voting by citizens is understood as being a cumulative action, which takes into consideration different facts and circumstances, such as financial and economic policy, family policy, environmental policy, etc., we phrased the items in a general way (see Table 1). In some cases, German translations of the original items of Mayer and Davis (1999) were used; in other cases, items had to be adapted. For example, the original item "X is very capable of performing its job.", which measures ability, was—as per the example of the CDU, the German liberal-conservative Christian democratic party—rephrased as follows: "The CDU demonstrates competence in solving problems relevant to society." We removed other items, such as "Top management is well qualified.", because they did not seem plausible for the party context. Instead, we added items, such as "I consider the CDU to be credible." We assigned the credibility of political parties to the dimension of integrity.

To test whether the derived items actually did relate to citizens' existing expectations, we first conducted an exploratory survey to determine the expectations by using five items that were phrased on the basis of the factors of perceived trustworthiness ($\alpha = .93$). It was apparent that citizens had clear expectations in relation to ability, according to which the parties were supposed to have suitable solutions for the most important problems, for example. In a similar way, it was possible to assign the expectation that the focus should be on citizens' needs, for example, to the dimension of the benevolence of the political parties; likewise, it was possible to assign the expectation that the party will keep its word to the dimension of integrity.

To test the construct of perceived trustworthiness adopted from Mayer et al., with its three antecedents, we first checked the intercorrelations of the 12 trustworthiness items with the data from the first survey wave with reference to the example of the CDU. The analysis of the correlation ($n = 387$) according to Pearson, with a listwise deletion, revealed high intercorrelations from $r = .60$ to $r = .82$ (see Table 1). Contrary to expectations, intercorrelations did not only occur between the relevant four items of the assumed subdimension, namely ability, benevolence, and integrity, in each case. The results also showed intercorrelations between all 12 items. For a more detailed examination, we carried out a principal component analysis with the 12 items for measuring the perceived trustworthiness of the CDU with an oblique rotation (oblimin) and with a listwise deletion owing to some missing values. The Kaiser-Meyer-Olkin measure indicated very good suitability for a principal component analysis, with a KMO value of .97. The individual values

Table 1 Items (translated from the German) and intercorrelations concerning the measurement of the CDU's trustworthiness (all correlations: $p < .001$)

	1	2	3	4	5	6	7	8	9	10	11	12
Ability												
1. The CDU demonstrates competence in solving problems relevant to society.	1											
2. The CDU is known to be successful at the things it tries to do.	.782	1										
3. The CDU knows exactly which important tasks must be dealt with.	.723	.716	1									
4. The CDU has specialist knowledge that is necessary for solving the problems relevant to society.	.743	.718	.725	1								
Benevolence												
5. The CDU is concerned about the welfare of the citizens.	.770	.753	.665	.669	1							
6. The CDU would do everything possible to protect the citizens from harm.	.706	.709	.600	.655	.709	1						
7. The CDU considers the needs of the citizens in its decisions.	.794	.788	.717	.716	.824	.768	1					
8. The CDU knows about the needs of the citizens.	.712	.684	.746	.676	.717	.626	.732	1				
Integrity												
9. The CDU has a sense of justice.	.779	.773	.641	.683	.768	.755	.800	.699	1			
10. I am sure that the CDU will keep its word.	.729	.733	.609	.638	.756	.704	.740	.625	.739	1		
11. I like the values that the CDU stands for.	.757	.733	.681	.662	.708	.669	.707	.652	.740	.685	1	
12. I consider the CDU to be credible.	.806	.794	.685	.694	.791	.741	.815	.706	.822	.784	.788	1

of the KMO statistic for the individual variables, which were taken from the anti-image matrix, were $> .95$. This exceeded the acceptable value of .5. Bartlett's test of sphericity $\chi^2(66) = 4886.47$, $p < .001$, indicated that the variables in the survey population were correlated. Taking into account Kaiser's criterion (eigenvalue > 1) and the analysis of the scree plot, the analysis indicated a one-factor solution. This factor explained 74.7 % of the variance. Therefore, the results clearly contradicted the assumption of the distinct subdimensions of perceived trustworthiness, namely ability, benevolence, and integrity. The factor loadings ranged from .91 to .82. The Cronbach's alpha value of .97 indicated very high reliability of the trustworthiness scale with all 12 items taken into account.

We carried out the test of the construct of the three factors of perceived trustworthiness with the data of the CDU and the SPD, the social democrats, from all three survey waves. The results of the six principal component analyses carried out in total also supported a general factor of trustworthiness in each case. The results therefore refuted the assumption of the three distinct factors of perceived trustworthiness, which is why the application of the trustworthiness construct posited by Mayer et al. was unsuccessful in this study.

Nevertheless, it was possible to derive important insights about the significance of trustworthiness for parties from the results that were calculated with the general factor[5]: The results showed a clear connection between the perceived trustworthiness of the parties and the willingness to vote for them, which we interpreted in this study as being the willingness to trust. There was also a clear connection between perceived trustworthiness and the actual vote, cast as a postal vote, which we interpreted as being an act of trust.

In addition, the study made it clear that the subjects talked about the election advertising by the CDU and by the SPD—especially election posters and TV advertisements—and that these conversations had an influence on perceived trustworthiness. The more positive the conversations about election advertising that took place and were investigated as part of the survey, the more positive the evaluation of the trustworthiness of the parties. The more negative the evaluation of these conversations, the more negative the evaluation of trustworthiness. The way in which the parties were talked about depended considerably on party affiliation

3.2 Trust in Non-Governmental Organizations (NGOs)

In the second study, which is presented below, we examined the trust placed by potential donors in NGOs. For NGOs, trust is significant because it generally

---

[5] With the exception of the derivation of perceived trustworthiness, the findings of the studies in this contribution are not demonstrated with figures. Detailed accounts of the specific analyses are provided in the publications by Wiencierz (2016) and by Wiencierz et al. (2015).

promotes a willingness to donate and leads to support for an NGO's activities (e.g., Bekkers 2003; Sargeant and Lee 2004; Beldad et al. 2014). Therefore, trust is a critical variable in the success of NGOs in general and those soliciting donations in particular, and it has a decisive influence on whether reference groups support the relevant organization (Bryce 2007; Lambright et al. 2010). At the same time, NGOs put further donations at risk if stakeholders lose trust in the relevant organization and feel deceived by it (Sisco 2012).

Because interpersonal influence can also be extensive in relation to the effect of donation campaigns, we examined the effect of user comments about campaign motifs published on the social networking site Facebook and of like counts on the perceived trustworthiness of NGOs in our experimental study. The object of investigation was a campaign motif of the World Wide Fund for Nature (WWF). The study was conducted as an online experiment with a 3 (connotation: positive vs. negative vs. positive and negative comments) x 2 (likes: high amount of likes vs. no likes) between-subject design and a control group without comments and likes. The experiment was implemented as an online survey of the German population with interlocked quotas according to age and sex. The sample contained 369 people, who were randomly assigned to the experimental conditions (18–69 years, $M = 44.36$; $SD = 14.06$).

We operationalized the expectations placed on the WWF in the donation context examined in the study by postulating that the expectations were that the NGO would use the donations efficiently in accordance with the declared objectives. In contrast to the first study described in this contribution, we incorporated the expectations directly into the trustworthiness items for the experiment. In other words, expectations were formulated simultaneously with the trustworthiness items because the assessment of trustworthiness referred to the expectations (for example, "I expect the WWF to have the competence to save the jaguar." was an item used to measure the perceived ability of the WWF) (see Table 2).

The items for measuring the perceived trustworthiness of the WWF were also phrased following Mayer and Davis (1999). We analyzed the trustworthiness scale analogously to the study about the political parties. The item intercorrelations showed a range from $r = .29$ to $r = .86$ (see Table 2). A PCA (oblique rotation: oblimin) on the 12 items of the trustworthiness scale (KMO $= .95$; Bartlett's test of sphericity: $\chi^2(66) = 4463.91$, $p < .001$) permitted either a one-factor solution (explaining 68 % of total variance) considering the scree plot, or a two-factor solution according to Kaiser's criterion with just two items loading clearly on the second factor (explaining 79 % of total variance). Therefore, the application of the trustworthiness construct posited by Mayer et al., with ability, benevolence, and integrity as distinct factors, also did not work in this study. Because of the results, we also decided in this study to consider the general factor solution with factor loadings ranging from .57 to .92. The reliability test revealed a Cronbach's α of .95.

Despite this limitation, this study also made it clear how important it is for organizations to be seen as trustworthy. Our analyses showed that the willingness to trust exists if the NGO is perceived as trustworthy: The more trustworthy the WWF was perceived to be, the more the participants were willing to donate to the relevant

Table 2 Items (translated from the German) and intercorrelations concerning the measurement of the WWF's trustworthiness (all correlations: $p < .001$)

I expect the WWF...	1	2	3	4	5	6	7	8	9	10	11	12
Ability												
1. ...to have the competence to save the jaguar.	1											
2. ...to be successful in saving the jaguar.	.663	1										
3. ...to know what needs to be done to save the jaguar.	.792	.656	1									
4. ...to have specialist knowledge to save the jaguar.	.832	.639	.815	1								
Benevolence												
5. ...to also look out for my well-being as a donor when it comes to saving the jaguar.	.356	.430	.348	.294	1							
6. ...to make me feel good by donating to save the jaguar.	.561	.565	.538	.509	.533	1						
7. ...to consider my wishes as a donor when it comes to saving he jaguar.	.455	.539	.453	.416	.785	.578	1					
8. ...to act in the interest of its donors when it comes to saving the jaguar.	.708	.710	.668	.663	.479	.647	.568	1				
Integrity												
9. ...to keep its word with regard to saving the jaguar.	.717	.777	.708	.689	.424	.626	.498	.767	1			
10. ...to be credible with regard to saving the jaguar.	.769	.749	.760	.730	.411	.610	.500	.777	.821	1		
11. ...to base its actions on reasonable principles with regard to saving the jaguar.	.734	.714	.697	.710	.419	.599	.527	.774	.804	.794	1	
12. ...to act responsibly when it comes to saving the jaguar.	.783	.725	.755	.775	.421	.628	.522	.813	.825	.855	.846	1

campaign and the more they could envisage inviting others to support this campaign. Nearly half of the participants indicated that they would comment on the WWF donation campaign; the higher they rated the trustworthiness of the WWF, the more positive this comment would be. We did not collect data on the actual act of trust, such as the actual donation, in this study.

Finally, in regard to the study's research question, the results showed that user comments on social media influence the perceived trustworthiness of NGOs. Negative comments result in a lower level of perceived trustworthiness. No additional effect of the positive comments could be demonstrated when compared with the control group, which showed the pure campaign effect without manipulations. According to these findings, negative comments have a negative bearing on the campaign effects, whereas positive comments have no additional effect. Similarly, with regard to the like counts, no significant effect was identified.

3.3   Critical Discussion

In the studies presented, we tested our approach to trust empirically with reference to the example of NPOs, specifically political parties and an NGO. We gave particular attention to the construct of the perceived trustworthiness of organizations because stakeholders base their trust on this assessment. We tested whether the construct of perceived trustworthiness posited by Mayer et al. (1995), with subdimensions consisting of ability, benevolence, and integrity, could also be applied to organizations. However, the results clearly do not support the assumption of distinct subdimensions comprised of ability, benevolence, and integrity. Moreover, they allow the inference that the items of Mayer and Davis (1999), which were developed to examine interpersonal trust in an organizational context, are not suitable for measuring the trustworthiness of organizations. Admittedly, it must be made clear in this context that the items of Mayer and Davis were not adopted on a one-to-one basis. For instance, some items were rephrased so that they could be applied in a political context to political parties or in a donation context to conservation organizations. Nevertheless, the items used were primarily based on those of Mayer and Davis, which is why doubts remain regarding the suitability of these items for analyzing the perceived trustworthiness of organizations. There is also the question of whether the construct of perceived trustworthiness posited by Mayer et al. can be applied to organizations at all.

As studies already show, organizations can be perceived as being able, benevolent and/or of integrity, or, alternatively, organizations are associated with attributes that can be assigned to these factors. Accordingly, it must also be fundamentally possible to examine trust in organizations following Mayer et al.'s approach. A lack of information on the part of the subjects might be a reason for the failure to identify the three factors of the perceived trustworthiness of organizations on the basis of the items of Mayer and Davis in both studies presented. It is possible that the subjects were not able to make a clear assessment of the ability, benevolence, and integrity of the organization because, in most cases, they did not have sufficiently good knowledge about the organization. Whereas relationships with work colleagues are much clearer, more specific, and more concrete, the experience of dealing with an organization often merely consists of the purchase of products or the use of services. Direct contact with organizations is frequently limited to the use of their services and offerings; in some cases, it also includes interpersonal exchanges with individual representatives of the organizations. Ultimately, information about organizations is mostly perceived indirectly via the mass media. Consequently, it might have been the case that the subjects had difficulty in judging the relevant organizations, as abstract entities, and in anticipating their actions, which meant that they had corresponding difficulty in assessing the presented trustworthiness items.

If it is true, then, that the three subdimensions of perceived trustworthiness often cannot be judged by stakeholders owing to a lack of information, the following questions arise: In the case of incomplete information about an organization, is a generalized, undifferentiated form of perceived trustworthiness the basis of the process of trust? If so, how can this type of trustworthiness be measured? These are key questions, which remain unanswered at this point and will need to be examined in future research on organizational trust. With the general factor that we formed, we did describe a type of undifferentiated trustworthiness pertaining to the relevant organization. However, it is questionable whether this general factor actually includes all of the factors that lead to an undifferentiated assessment of the trustworthiness of an organization. This is because in the case of trust in organizations, in contrast to that of interpersonal trust, factors such as the central idea of an organization, its internal order, and its material results can also play a role and shape the impression of an organization. Therefore, it is necessary to achieve a still much more precise, differentiated observation of the functional relationship between the stakeholder and the organization than the one made in the studies presented in this contribution. It can be useful to inquire about knowledge of the central idea, internal order, and material results of an organization in conjunction with ability, benevolence, and integrity. For instance, an organization can be assessed as being able if stakeholders evaluate the internal order as being efficient and the material results correspond to the expectations held by the stakeholders themselves. The central ideas of an organization and its internal order can play a crucial role in determining benevolence and integrity. If, as already suggested, there is a lack of the necessary knowledge about the organization, it is necessary to examine, by way of a next step, which of these factors are crucial and what a generalized, undifferentiated form of trustworthiness looks like.

Apart from the problems associated with measuring the factors of perceived trustworthiness, there is also the question that arises from a communication science perspective with regard to whether the antecedents of perceived trustworthiness described by Mayer et al. actually do measure trustworthiness or whether they instead measure phenomena such as reputation or image. In the literature, the relationship between these phenomena is consistently described as being very close but with considerable variation between them in terms of detail (e.g., Meijer

2009; Reputation Institute 2015; Einwiller et al. 2005; Koch et al. 2000). From a communication science perspective, Eisenegger's (2005) approach to reputation is the most theoretically substantial and comprehensive one that can be applied to various organization types. Following Jürgen Habermas's three-world concept, Eisenegger distinguishes between three types of reputation: functional, social, and expressive reputation (Eisenegger and Imhof 2008). Functional reputation relates to dominant performance goals and success criteria in the relevant social sphere of activity. The central question is whether an organization is perceived as successful within its scope of action. Social reputation describes the organization's ability to act in accordance with moral and normative requirements and social values. Finally, expressive reputation describes an organization's emotional power to fascinate and its perceived authenticity. The focus is on the emotional sensation experienced by the stakeholders, which is based in particular on the attractiveness, sympathy, and fascination associated with a person or organization (Eisenegger and Imhof 2008). A comparison of Eisenegger's concept of reputation (2005; Eisenegger and Imhof 2008) and the model of trust by Mayer et al. (1995) makes it clear that Eisenegger, particularly with his reputation types of functional and social reputation, is essentially describing the factors of perceived trustworthiness put forward by Mayer et al.

In conducting our WWF study, we made an initial attempt to address this research gap and examine the relationship between trustworthiness and reputation. We hypothesized that an NPO's reputation influences its trustworthiness decisively (Ingenhoff and Sommer 2010). We understand reputation to mean

> [. . .] the generalized, collective assessment of an object (e.g., a company) by its stake-holders [. . .], which they cumulatively obtain through direct and indirect experiences of it and also perceive via media and multipliers (Liehr et al. 2009, p. 4, translated from the German).

A comparison of Eisenegger's concept of reputation (2005; Eisenegger and Imhof 2008) and the model of trust by Mayer et al. (1995) indicates the similarity of functional reputation to the antecedent ability, whereas social reputation includes the components of the antecedents benevolence and integrity. The decisive difference between these reputation and trust dimensions is seen in the time factor. Functional reputation is the subjective assessment of the generalized, collective perception of ability; social reputation is the assessment of the generalized, collective perception of benevolence and integrity. These assessments relate to public information from the past. In the case of trustworthiness, the assessment of ability, benevolence, and integrity relates to the task of solving a certain problem in the future. Trust is the future-oriented assessment of the extent to which the organization will act in the interests of the stakeholder. In addition, the assessment of emotional influences, such as the evaluation of attractiveness, sympathy, and fascination, is summarized under the category of expressive reputation. The outputs of acts of trust are ultimately experiences that, in turn, are able to influence reputation.

Our analyses showed that reputation can be seen as a predictor of trustworthiness. We conducted a simple regression to specify how much the perceived trustworthiness of the WWF was affected by its reputation. The perceived trustworthiness of the WWF was predicted by the evaluation of reputation. Thus, a prediction of the level of trustworthiness is significantly improved by taking into consideration perceived reputation; however, the proportion of the explained variance was lower than expected (27 %). With regard to the link between the constructs of reputation and trustworthiness, the results indicated that reputation and trustworthiness are two distinct, correlating constructs.

4 Outlook

Further research is still required to clarify how exactly trust in organizations, or, specifically, the trustworthiness of organizations, can be measured. In the studies presented in this contribution, we gave particular consideration to the approach to trust taken by Mayer et al. (1995). In so doing, we encountered problems in measuring the factors of perceived trustworthiness. However, the critical discussion of the operationalization of trustworthiness undertaken in this case should not create the impression that we are arguing for the approach to trust taken by Mayer et al. to be fundamentally rejected for the examination of trust in organizations. This approach represents one of the most well-elaborated approaches to trust to date (Fulmer and Gelfand 2012; Nienaber et al. 2015). Moreover, other approaches to trust also describe factors that can be interpreted as antecedents of the perceived trustworthiness of organizations. These factors include the ability or competence of organizations and their benevolence or fairness as well as their integrity or principles and their values or other equivalents. Despite the diffuse field of research, therefore, there are at least indications that suggest that the factors described in relation to the assessment of perceived trustworthiness play a role.

Instead, it is necessary to reconsider the operationalization of trustworthiness. In this context, moreover, we argue for the relationship between reputation, image, and trustworthiness to be clarified. These constructs are very similar to each other. An engagement with these concepts seems useful in order to achieve a better understanding of the construct of the trustworthiness of organizations and in order to refine the concept of trustworthiness.

Despite the problems encountered in measuring stakeholder trust in organizations, the studies that we have described are able to make a contribution to the discussion about the significance and measurement of trust in organizations and thereby provide implications for practice. Firstly, we have been able to make trust in organizations, such as that placed in political parties and NGOs, at least theoretically concrete. Secondly, we have been able to clearly demonstrate the connection between the trustworthiness of organizations and the willingness to use their goods and services.

Because of the significance of trust, organizations ought to take trust into consideration when planning, implementing, and evaluating their communication efforts, especially in light of the fact that trust primarily arises as a result of the way in which the object of trust presents itself (Luhmann 1979, pp. 39–46; Giddens 1991, pp. 85–86). The strategic communication of organizations, such as that which takes the form of campaigns, therefore plays a central role in building the trust of their stakeholders (Hon and Grunig 1999, pp. 10, 19; Ledingham and Bruning 1998; Ball et al. 2004; Morgan and Hunt 1994). Accordingly, strategic organizational communication can be an important link in building trust relationships between organizations and their stakeholders (Schweer and Thies 2003, p. 128). If the antecedents of perceived trustworthiness presented in this contribution are taken into account, organizations, as potential objects of trust, ought to emphasize their ability, benevolence, and integrity accordingly (Beckert 2002). Although we were unable to analyze these subdimensions in a way that clearly distinguishes them from each other, they are nevertheless included in the general factor of trustworthiness that was created. Moreover, numerous other studies have also identified factors of trust to which the subdimensions ability, benevolence, and integrity can be assigned. Perhaps organizations merely have to convey greater quantities of better targeted information in which they present themselves as being able, benevolent, and of integrity. If that were the case, the possibility of making the relevant assessment would also be greater and trustworthiness could increase.

When carrying out communication activities aimed at appearing trustworthy, organizations should, however, pay attention to interpersonal influence on the effect of their communication activities. In the two studies, we were able to provide a clear illustration of this influence. Likewise, organizations always ought to be aware that trust cannot be demanded. In addition to public image, the most effective method of appearing trustworthy is, ultimately, to act consistently in the interests of the trustor (Kuhlen 2008). If the expectations that have been formed are repeatedly confirmed by the object of trust, trust and the object of trust's perceived trustworthiness increase: "He who stands by what he has allowed to be known about himself, whether consciously or unconsciously, is worthy of trust." (Luhmann 1979, p. 39)

References

Aurier, P., & N'Goala, G. (2010). The differing and mediating roles of trust and relationship commitment in service relationship maintenance and development. *Journal of the Academy of Marketing Science, 38*(3), 303–325.

Ball, D., Coelho, P. S., & Machás, A. (2004). The role of communication and trust in explaining customer loyalty. *European Journal of Marketing, 38*(9/10), 1272–1293.

Barbalet, J. (2009). A characterization of trust, and its consequences. *Theory and Society, 38*(4), 367–382.

Barber, B. (1983). *The logic and limits of trust.* New Brunswick, NJ: Rutgers University Press.

Beckert, J. (2002). Vertrauen und die performative Konstruktion von Märkten [Trust and the performative construction of markets]. *Zeitschrift für Soziologie, 1,* 27–43.

Bekkers, R. (2003). Trust, accreditation, and philanthropy in the Netherlands. *Nonprofit and Voluntary Sector Quarterly, 32*(4), 596–615.

Beldad, A., Snip, B., & van Hoof, J. (2014). Generosity the second time around: Determinants of individuals' repeat donation intention. *Nonprofit and Voluntary Sector Quarterly, 43*(1), 144–163.

Benz, A. (2002). Vertrauensbildung in Mehrebenensystemen [Trust-building in multi-level systems]. In R. Schmalz-Bruns & R. Zintl (Eds.), *Politisches Vertrauen. Soziale Grundlagen reflexiver Kooperation* [Political Trust] (pp. 275–291). Nomos: Baden-Baden.

Braithwaite, V., & Levi, M. (1998). Introduction. In V. Braithwaite & M. Levi (Eds.), *Trust and governance* (pp. 1–5). New York, NY: Russell Sage.

Bryce, H. J. (2007). The public's trust in nonprofit organizations: The role of relationship marketing and management. *California Management Review, 49*(4), 112–131.

Coleman, J. S. (1990). *Foundations of social theory.* Cambridge, MA: Havard University Press.

Cook, K. S., & Cook, B. (2011). Social and political trust. In G. Delanty & S. P. Turner (Eds.), *Routledge international handbook of contemporary social and political theory* (pp. 236–247). New York, NY: Routledge.

Deutsch, M. (1962). Coproation and trust: Some theoretical notes. In M. R. Jones (Ed.), *Nebraska symposium on motivation 1962* (pp. 275–318). Lincoln: University of Nebraska Press.

Einwiller, S., Herrmann, A., & Ingenhoff, D. (2005). Vertrauen durch Reputation—Grundmodell und empirische Befunde im E-Business [Trust through reputation—Basic model and empirical findings in e-business]. *Marketing Zeitschrift für Forschung und Praxis (Marketing ZFP), 1,* 25–40.

Eisenegger, M. (2005). *Reputation in der Mediengesellschaft. Konstitution—Issues Monitoring—Issues Management* [Reputation in media society. Constitution—Issues Monitoring—Issues Management]. Wiesbaden: VS Verlag für Sozialwissenschaften.

Eisenegger, M., & Imhof, K. (2008). The true, the good and the beautiful: Reputation management in the media society. In A. Zerfass, B. van Ruler, & S. Krishnamurthy (Eds.), *Public relations research. European and international perspectives and innovations* (pp. 125–146). Wiesbaden: VS Verlag für Sozialwissenschaften.

Endruweit, G. (1981). *Organisationssoziologie* [Organizational sociology]. Berlin: de Gruyter.

Fulmer, C. A., & Gelfand, M. J. (2012). At what level (and in whom) we trust: Trust across multiple organizational levels. *Journal of Management, 38*(4), 1167–1230.

Giddens, A. (1991). *The consequences of modernity.* Stanford, CA: Stanford University Press.

Grayson, K., Johnson, D., & Chen, D.-F. R. (2008). Is firm trust essential in a trusted environment? How trust in the business context influences customers. *Journal of Marketing Research (JMR), 45*(2), 241–256.

Hetherington, M. J. (1998). The political relevance of political trust. *The American Political Science Review, 92*(4), 791–808.

Hoffjann, O. (2011). Public relations in society. A new approach to the difficult relationships between PR and its environment. *Central European Journal of Communication, 4*(1), 63–76.

Höhne, B. (2006). *Vertrauen oder Misstrauen? Wie stehen die Ostdeutschen 15 Jahre nach der Wiedervereinigung zu ihrem politischen System?* [Trust or mistrust]. Marburg: Tectum.

Hon, L. C., & Grunig, J. E. (1999). Guidelines for measuring relationships in public relations. *The Institute for PR.* http://www.instituteforpr.org/research_single/guidelines_measuring_relation ships. Accessed 12 Mar 2015.

Ingenhoff, D., & Sommer, K. (2010). Spezifikation von formativen und reflektiven Konstrukten und Pfadmodellierung mittels Partial Least Squares zur Messung von Reputation [Specification of formative and reflective constructs and path modeling with Partial Least Squares for the measurement of reputation]. In J. Woelke, M. Maurer, & O. Jandura (Eds.), *Forschungsmethoden für die Markt- und Organisationskommunikation* [Research methods for market and organizational communication] (pp. 246–248). Cologne: Herbert von Halem.

Ki, E.-J., & Hon, L. C. (2007). Reliability and validity of organization-public relationship measurement and linkages among relationship indicators in a membership organization. *Journalism & Mass Communication Quarterly, 84*(3), 419–438.

Koch, M., Möslein, K., & Wagner, M. (2000). Vertrauen und Reputation in Online-Anwendungen und virtuellen Gemeinschaften [Trust and reputation in online applications and virtual communities]. In M. Engelien & D. Naumann (Eds.), *Virtuelle Organisation und Neue Medien. Dokumentation des Workshops GeNeMe2000—Gemeinschaften in Neuen Medien—TU Dresden, 5. und 6. Oktober 2000* [Virtual organizations and new media] (pp. 69–84). Lohmar: Josef Eul-Verlag.

Kohring, M. (2004). *Vertrauen in Journalismus. Theorie und Empirie* [Trust in journalism. Theoretical and empirical investigations]. Konstanz: UVK Verlagsgesellschaft.

Kohring, M., & Matthes, J. (2007). Trust in news media—Development and validation of a multidimensional scale. *Communication Research, 34*(2), 231–252.

Kuhlen, R. (2008). Vertrauen in elektronischen Räumen [Trust in electronic spaces]. In D. Klumpp et al. (Eds.), *Informationelles Vertrauen für die Informationsgesellschaft* [Informational trust for the information society] (pp. 37–52) Wiesbaden: Westdeutscher Verlag.

Lambright, K. T., Mischen, P. A., & Laramee, C. B. (2010). Building trust in public and nonprofit networks: Personal, dyadic, and third-party influences. *The American Review of Public Administration, 40*(1), 64–82.

Ledingham, J. A., & Bruning, S. D. (1998). Relationship management in public relations: Dimensions of an organization-public relationship. *Public Relations Review, 24*(1), 55–65.

Lepsius, R. M. (1997). Vertrauen zu Institutionen [Trust in institutions]. In S. Hradil (Ed.), *Differenz und Integration. Die Zukunft moderner Gesellschaften. Verhandlungen des 28. Kongresses der Deutschen Gesellschaft für Soziologie in Dresden 1996* [The future of modern societies] (pp. 283–293). Frankfurt a. M.: Campus.

Levi, M., & Stoker, L. (2000). Political trust and trustworthiness. *Annual Review of Political Science, 3,* 475–507.

Liehr, K., Peters, P., & Zerfaß, A. (2009). *Reputationsmessung: Grundlagen und Verfahren (communicationcontrolling.de Dossier Nr. 1)* [Reputation measurement: Background and procedure]. Berlin, Leipzig. http://www.communicationcontrolling.de/fileadmin/communicationcontrolling/pdf-dossiers/communicationcontrollingde_Dossier1_Reputationsmessung_April2009_o.pdf. Accessed 21 Jan 2015.

Luhmann, N. (1979). *Trust and power: Two works by Niklas Luhmann.* Chichester: Wiley.

Luhmann, N. (2005). *Soziologische Aufklärung 2. Aufsätze zur Theorie der Gesellschaft. 5. Auflage* [Sociological enlightenment 2]. Wiesbaden: VS Verlag für Sozialwissenschaften.

Mayer, R. C., & Davis, J. H. (1999). The effect of the performance appraisal system on trust for management: A field quasi-experiment. *Journal of Applied Psychology, 84*(1), 123–136.

Mayer, R. C., Davis, J. H., & Schoorman, F. D. (1995). An integrative model of organizational trust. *Academy of Management Review, 20*(3), 709–734.

McKnight, D. H., & Chervany, N. L. (2001). Trust and distrust definitions: One bite at a time. In R. Falcone, M. Singh, & Y.-H. Tan (Eds.), *Trust in cyber-societies SE—3* (pp. 27–54). Berlin Heidelberg: Springer.

Meijer, M. M. (2009). The effects of charity reputation on charitable giving. *Corporate Reputation Review, 12*(1), 33–42.

Möllering, G. (2006). *Trust: Reason, routine, reflexivity.* Amsterdam: Elsevier.

Möllering, G. (2008). *Inviting or avoiding deception through trust? Conceptual exploration of an ambivalent relationship.* MPIfG Working Paper 08/1, Cologne.

Morgan, R. M., & Hunt, S. D. (1994). The commitment-trust theory of relationship marketing. *Journal of Marketing, 58*(3), 20–38.

Nienaber, A. M., Hofeditz, M., & Romeike, P. D. (2015). Vulnerability and trust in leader-follower relationships. *Personnel Review, 44*(4), 567–591.

Renn, O., & Levine, D. (1991). Credibility and trust in risk communication. In R. E. Kasperson & P. J. M. Stallen (Eds.), *Communicating risks to the public. Technology, risk, and society* (pp. 175–218). Dordrecht: Kluwer Academic Publishers.

Reputation Institute. (2015). The RepTrak® System. http://www.reputationinstitute.com/ thoughtleadership/. Accessed 21 Jan 2015.

Sargeant, A., & Lee, S. (2004). Donor trust and relationship commitment in the U.K. charity sector: The impact on behavior. *Nonprofit and Voluntary Sector Quarterly, 33*(2), 185–202.

Schichtmann, C. (2007). An analysis of antecedents and consequences of trust in a corporate brand. *European Journal of Marketing, 41*(9/10), 999–1015.

Schoorman, F. D., Mayer, R. C., & Davis, J. H. (2007). An integrative model of organizational trust: Past, present, and future. *Academy of Management Review, 32*(2), 344–354.

Schweer, M. K. W., & Thies, B. (2003). *Vertrauen als Organisationsprinzip* [Trust as an organizational principle]. Bern: Verlag Hans Huber.

Sisco, H. F. (2012). The ACORN story: An analysis of crisis response strategies in a nonprofit organization. *Public Relations Review, 38*(1), 89–96.

Strøm, K. (2009). Parties at the core of government. In R. J. Dalton & M. P. Wattenberg (Eds.), *Parties without partisans. Political change in advanced industrial democracies* (pp. 181–207). Oxford: Oxford University Press.

Sztompka, P. (1999). *Trust: A sociological theory.* Cambridge: Cambridge University Press.

Sztompka, P. (2006). New perspectives on trust. *American Journal of Sociology, 112*(3), 905–919.

Wiencierz, C. (2016). *Vertrauen in Parteien durch Gespräche über Wahlwerbung. Der Einfluss interpersonaler Kommunikation über Wahlwerbung auf das Vertrauen in politische Parteien* [Trust in political parties by talking about electoral advertising] (forthcoming).

Wiencierz, C., Pöppel, K. G., & Röttger. (2015). Where does my money go? How online comments on a donation campaign influence the perceived trustworthiness of a nonprofit organization. *International Journal of Strategic Communication, 9*(2), 102–117.

Trust as an Action: About the Overrated Significance of Trust in Information Sources in a Digitized World

Sarah Westphal and Bernd Blöbaum

Abstract This paper demonstrates that trust, which actually informs the actions of people, can only be identified under specific preconditions and is relevant less often than it appears to be by the frequent and manifold use of the term. Using online information as an example, it is pointed out, that, when defining trust with a focus on the trusting action, trust can only apply to one specific, pre-selected information source. Therefore, it is then argued, that trust is an especially rare and special phenomenon with information sources on the Internet.

Keywords Trust • Information sources • Action • Trust process • Preconditions • Internet

1 Trust as an Omnipresent and Fundamentally Relevant Phenomenon in Social Interactions

"Today nearly everyone seems to be talking about 'trust'. Presidential candidates, political columnists, pollsters, social critics, moral philosophers, and the man in the street all use the word freely and earnestly" (Barber 1983, p. 1). What Barber wrote as introducing words in his book in 1983 seems still to be the case today. Be it trust in the context of intelligence agencies and Edward Snowden, trust in banks in the face of financial crises, or trust in sports in light of doping—in media coverage as well as in everyday language trust is an omnipresent phenomenon.

Two aspects of scientific research on trust also contribute to the fact that trust seems to be a concept of relevance in every context. First, in sociological research on trust,[1] which looks at trust from a macro-perspective, trust is regarded as a social mechanism of fundamental importance in modern society. From this perspective, trust becomes relevant in relationships of dependency in contexts of risk (Luhmann

---

[1] This is also true for some works in philosophy and political science, which shares some views of sociological research.

S. Westphal (✉) • B. Blöbaum
University of Münster, Münster, Germany
e-mail: sarah.westphal@uni-muenster.de; bernd.bloebaum@uni-muenster.de

© Springer International Publishing Switzerland 2016   113
B. Blöbaum (ed.), *Trust and Communication in a Digitized World*, Progress in IS,
DOI 10.1007/978-3-319-28059-2_6

1968; Barber 1983; Giddens 1995; Endreß 2002). From this perspective, however, essentially every social interaction bears a risk because one cannot know how the other actor will act (Müller 2013, pp. 42–43; Giddens 1995, p. 114; Hartmann 2010, p. 20). Especially in modern societies, which are so complex that individuals have to enter into numerous relationships of dependency with unfamiliar actors and institutions they cannot control (Giddens 1995, p. 103; Luhmann 1968, p. 43), risk becomes pervasive. In these contexts, trust becomes relevant as a social mechanism to reduce the complexity of social interactions (Luhmann 1968, p. 13; Kohring 2004, p. 94, 102; Lewis and Weigert 1985, p. 696; Seligman 2000, pp. 18–19) so that individuals are still able to act in these contexts. Other researchers do not even confine the relevance of trust to situations of risk, but state that trust shadows all social interactions in a non-reflexive way (Endreß 2010, p. 95, 98; Lagerspetz 1998, p. 30).

Second, from the perspective advocated in this contribution, some works on trust confound the concept of trust with other comparable concepts and mix up situations of trust with similar situations in which those other concepts come into effect, e.g., calculation (Coleman 1990; Lewicki and Bunker 1996), confidence (Lewicki et al. 1998; Guenther and Möllering 2010; Barber 1983), or familiarity (Endreß 2012; Lagerspetz 1998).

This confounding of concepts and the fundamental relevance in many or all social interactions make it difficult to narrow down the meaning of trust as a concept, which is generally hard to grasp (Ripperger 2003, p. 34; Gambetta 1988, pp. IX–X).

2 Definition of Trust as an Action in Specific Social Interactions

Since there a several alternatives to trust, such as calculation, confidence, and familiarity (Kohring 2004, pp. 135–136), that come into effect in similar situations and are also capable of reducing complexity, it is argued here that trust does not come into effect in all social interactions and that the circumstances of the situation should be carefully considered before defining a situation or a social interaction as one of trust. To implement this, trust is conceptualized from a micro-perspective as a social mechanism enabling actions in a concrete social interaction that only comes into effect under specific preconditions and fulfills a specific function for the trustor that exceeds the overall function to reduce complexity.

In a situation of trust, an actor (the trustor) voluntarily enters into a relationship of dependency with another actor (the trustee; Gambetta 2001, p. 213; Hartmann 2010, p. 20; Preisendörfer 1995, p. 266; Ripperger 2003, p. 37), because he[2] has a

---

[2] The male form is used in the following for reasons of simplicity, but this is a reference to both sexes.

specific problem he cannot or does not want to solve on his own since he lacks the resources or does not want to invest them (Kohring 2004, p. 94; Preisendörfer 1995, p. 267). Depending on the problem and the trustee, the trustor has specific expectations of the trustee (Hardin 2001). However, the trustor is uncertain about whether the trustee will fulfill these expectations because of the contingency of the trustee's actions and because the trustor lacks sufficient information about the trustee (Simmel 1999, p. 393). In a situation of trust, the trustor remains in this state of uncertainty until the end of the interaction and can only say retrospectively whether the trustee lived up to expectations (Kohring 2004, p. 130; Preisendörfer 1995, p. 265; Seligman 2000, p. 21). The trustor perceives this contingency and uncertainty as a risk (Kohring 2004, p. 91), meaning that, next to the advantages of using the resources of the trustee, the trustor is also aware of the negative side of this dependency that the trustee could fall short of his expectations and that negative consequences could be the result for the trustor (Kohring 2006, p. 124; Ripperger 2003, pp. 41–42). In a trust situation, however, the trustor tolerates the risk (Kohring 2004, p. 95; Lewis and Weigert 1985, S. 969) and focuses on the advantages of the dependency (Kieserling 2012, p. 141).

If these preconditions (relationship of dependency, lack of sufficient information about the trustee, uncertainty about the fulfillment of expectations, risk perception and tolerance of risk) are not met, the situation is not one of trust, but rather one of the functional equivalents of trust (e.g., confidence, familiarity or calculation) that reduces complexity in this situation. For example, if the actor is not uncertain about whether the other actor will fulfill his expectations but is able to predict the actions of the other actor because the latter is entirely bound by his role and rules, the situation is one of confidence rather than trust (Kohring 2004, p. 112; Seligman 2000, p. 19). If the actor does not tolerate the risk that the other actor could not live up to his expectations but tries to reduce this risk by seeking further information about this actor, the situation is one of calculation rather than trust (Kohring 2004, p. 119). If the actor has a lot of information about the other actor from past interactions and experience so that he does not perceive any contingency in the others actions and thus no risk of unfulfilled expectations but assumes that the other will act as always, the situation is one of familiarity but not of trust (Luhmann 1968, p. 71).

These prerequisites of a trust situation also shape the definition of trust. The focus of the definition used here is the action of the trustor. Based on the work of Kohring (2004) trust is defined as

> a social mechanism that enables the trustor to engage in a particular form of action, which is connected to a contingent action of a preselected and responsible trustee, to whom the trustor holds a relationship of dependency he perceives as risky. This particular form of action and the associated tolerance of the risk, which can only be legitimated by few nonfactual arguments, yield the advantage of economizing resources for the trustor.

Thus, trust describes a specific relationship of dependency in which a trustor transfers responsibility for actions to the trustee (Kohring 2004, p. 112) and connects his own actions to the actions of the trustee. More than reducing

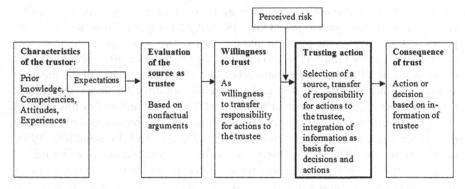

Fig. 1 Trust in information sources as a process (image of the authors based on Mayer et al. 1995; Kohring 2004)

complexity, trust as an action fulfills a specific function for the trustor: it economizes the resources of the trustor. By engaging in a trusting action, the trustor is able to save his own resources because of several reasons. First, in a situation of trust, the trustor only uses nonfactual arguments like for example the white coat of the doctor (see Fig. 1). Such arguments provide insufficient information about the trustee, because they do not indicate whether the trustee will fulfill the expectations of the trustor (Kohring 2004, p. 113), but are much easier to access and process than factual arguments like medical knowledge. Second, the trustor renounces seeking so much information to be able to control (Mayer et al. 1995, p. 712) or calculate the actions of the trustee (Kohring 2004, pp. 112–119). Third, the trustor tolerates the risk and renounces further efforts to reduce it (Kohring 2004, p. 95). Fourth, the trustor lets the trustee perform actions instead of performing them personally (Kohring 2004, p. 112).

The definition of trust as a mechanism enabling a specific action can be illustrated by an example of a trust situation. Consider the case of a sick person who consults a new doctor to cure a disease. The sick person connects his own actions (choosing and contacting the doctor as well as entrusting himself to the charge of the doctor for an operation) to the actions of the doctor he wants to profit from (the operation) and which he cannot perform on his own. Therefore, the patient transfers the responsibility for the operation to the doctor although he is not certain whether the doctor, with whom he does not have any prior experience, will meet his expectations. He is aware that the doctor has liberties in choosing a diagnosis and selecting between different ways of operating and that it is possible that the doctor might not live up to the patient's expectations of an operation without complications. But the patient tolerates the risk that the doctor could possibly fall short of his expectations and produce negative consequences for him (e.g., health damage). The patient can only legitimate his positive expectations that the doctor will perform the operation successfully by using nonfactual knowledge about the doctor (e.g., his title, the white coat), but no factual or professional knowledge (Kohring 2007,

p. 30). Since the patient relies on this symbolic knowledge instead of controlling the doctor, and because he can use the resources of the doctor, he can save up his own resources.

From our perspective, trust can only be defined with a focus on the trusting action. It cannot be defined as an expectation (Lewicki et al. 1998, p. 439; Luhmann 1968, p. 37), because expectations are not a sufficient criterion to define trust, since they also play a role in similar concepts such as hope and confidence (Kohring 2006, p. 125; Seligman 2000, p. 19), as well as quality (Wolling 2004). Trust can also not be defined with a focus on the evaluation of trustworthiness (McKnight et al. 1998; Butler and Cantrell 1984), since similar evaluations are also connected to the concept of credibility (Hovland et al. 1953) and "knowing that A considers B trustworthy is of little use if A does not intend to act on that basis [...]" (Dietz and Den Hartog 2006, p. 565). Trust as a psychological state with the intention or willingness to trust as a willingness to be vulnerable is the focus of many (psychological) definitions of trust (Mayer et al. 1995; Baier 1986; Corritore et al. 2003; Kramer 1999; Möllering 2001; Warren 1999). In contrast, in the sociological perspective on trust followed here, trust can only be seen as part of a social relationship, whereas applying it only to a psychological state of one individual is seen as a reduction or restriction (Lewis and Weigert 1985, p. 968; Endreß 2002, p. 71). In line with this, the mere willingness to be vulnerable is insufficient to define trust because the formerly described prerequisites of trust and the specific function of trust only come into effect in the trusting action. As Dietz and Den Hartog (2006) stated: "[...] The decision is only an intention to act. For A to demonstrate unequivocally her/his trust in B, (s)he must follow through on this decision by engaging in any of the trust-informed risk-taking behaviors [...]" (p. 559). First, the prerequisite of a relationship of dependency in a trust situation is only fully accomplished if the trustor engages in a trusting action. Because only with the trusting action does the trustor transfer responsibilities for actions to the trustee, connect his own actions to those of the trustee, and thus make the success of his actions dependent on the actions of the trustee (Kohring 2004, p. 132). In contrast, the willingness to be vulnerable is an attitude of the trustor towards the trustee and thus a one-way relation.

Second, the risk of the trust situation is only taken if the trustor engages in a trusting action. "Risks [...] emerge only as a component of decision and action. [...] If you refrain from action you run no risk" (Luhmann 2000, p. 100). Therefore, in being willing to make himself vulnerable the trustor runs no risk (Mayer et al. 1995, p. 724). Moreover, the willingness to be vulnerable does not necessarily mean that the trustor also engages in a trusting action, actually makes himself vulnerable, and takes a risk (Dietz and Den Hartog 2006, p. 560). This can be the case if the trustor is willing to trust the trustee and to make himself vulnerable, because he thinks him trustworthy, but he does not engage in an action because he perceives the risk that the trustee might not meet his expectations as too high, based on the understanding that a high amount of damage is possible if his expectations are not met. External risks that are not related to the trustee can also prevent the trustor from engaging in a trusting action even if he is willing to make himself vulnerable to the trustee (Mayer et al. 1995, p. 726).

Third, the advantage of trust to economize resources for the trustor (Kohring 2004, p. 99) only comes into effect if the trustor engages in a trusting action. The willingness to be vulnerable does not economize resources for the trustor. Instead, he must invest some of his own resources to form this willingness when evaluating whether the trustee is trustworthy. Not until he engages in a trusting action is the trustor able to economize his resources because then he lets the trustee perform actions for him and connects his own actions to them.

Therefore, the focus of the definition in this contribution lies on the trusting action, whereas expectations, the evaluation of the trustee's trustworthiness, and the willingness to trust are conceptualized as prerequisites for the trusting action, as shown in Fig. 1.

3   Significance of Trust in Information Sources on the Internet

The definition of trust with a focus on the trusting action can also be transferred to (online) information sources. *Trust as a social mechanism enables the trustor to make a specific selection that is based on the contingent selection of a preselected and responsible (online) information source to which the trustor holds a relationship of dependency he perceives as risky. This particular form of selection and the associated tolerance of the risk, which can only be legitimated by a few nonfactual arguments, yield the advantage of economizing resources for the trustor.* The action which the trustor transfers to the online information source as a trustee is the selection of relevant information, and the risk is that the online information source provides false, biased or incomplete information to the trustor (Corritore et al. 2003, p. 742).

When dealing with trust in online information sources, it is important to consider that trust comes into effect to achieve a specific goal for the trustor and is not an end in itself (Hartmann 2010, p. 19). By trusting online information sources, the trustor's goal is to solve a problem, such as to make a decision or take an action on the basis of the information from the trustee. Therefore, the selection as a trusting action is not a mere selection, but a selection of an online information source that has an effect on subsequent decisions and actions of the trustor (Kohring 2004, p. 182). Because of this, trust is a key variable for media effects (Kohring 2004, p. 183). These consequences of trust are also important aspects of the trust situation, because only through these consequences of trust (actions and decisions) does the risk of the trust situation—that the trustee might not live up to the expectations of the trustor—become a real risk. False, biased, and incomplete information is not a risk in itself, but only becomes a risk if the recipient acts upon this information like making a false decision or engaging in a wrong action, which are associated with negative consequences for the trustor (Lagerspetz 1998, p. 41; Luhmann 2000, p. 100).[3]

These remarks demonstrate that trust as an action comes into effect in risky relationships of dependency to reduce complexity. The Internet, with its flood of information and variety of information sources that are difficult to evaluate, is a context of high complexity. It is also a context of risk because gatekeepers and quality controls are lacking on the Internet (Neuberger 2009, pp. 38–39; Kelton et al. 2008, p. 363; Guenther and Möllering 2010, p. 31) and thus there is a high risk of false, biased, and incomplete information. Because of this, trust seems to be a relevant issue with online information sources.

In the following the opposite is argued, that *trust is a rare and special situation in the context of online information sources* if it is defined with a focus on the trusting action in a special relationship of dependency in which responsibility for actions is transferred to the trustee and the trustor bases his own actions or decisions on those of the trustee. There are several arguments for the hypothesis that trust occurs only rarely in the context of online information sources. First, for trust to become relevant, a recipient has to want to use information to solve a problem and make a decision or engage in an action. But a lot of (online) information is not immediately relevant for actions and decisions of recipients, e.g., information about crises in other countries that have no direct consequences for recipients.

Second, situations in which the trustor lacks information are different from situations in which the trustor lacks other resources (e.g., abilities to carry out an operation or to repair a car). When lacking other resources, the trustor cannot acquire those resources without considerable effort, like studying medicine or automotive repair, and therefore cannot solve his problem on his own. When lacking information, the trustor is still in a position to solve his problem on his own. He can select information autonomously by considering several information sources and generating his own understanding of the issue. Therefore, he does not have to trust an information source and does not have to transfer responsibility for information selection to this source. This is likely a frequent occurrence on the Internet because various sources can be reached very easily and quickly with just a few clicks.

Third, from a perspective of trust as a special form of dependency and action as advocated here, it is no longer a situation of trust if a recipient considers several information sources because the recipient does not transfer responsibility for actions to an information source but simply solves his own lack of information problem independently. An example with the TV show "Who Wants to Be a Millionaire" can illustrate this argument. In this TV show, the candidate trusts several people in the audience, whose multiple choice answer he uses as a basis for his own answer in the game, so he therefore depends on those people (Kohring

---

[3] This is why only decisions and actions can be conceptualized as consequences of trust but not attitudes or opinions, because only actions and decisions are associated with risks (see above, Luhmann 2000, p. 100).

2004, p. 95). But in effect, every person that the candidate trusts in the audience says exactly the same thing, for example, answer "B". In this specific scenario, trust in several sources of information (here, people from the audience) is possible. If the scenario in the show was comparable to the reception of online information sources, the people in the audience would provide not only the answer but also arguments for choosing this answer over the others. At this point, the candidate is able to weigh those arguments and connect them to his own knowledge and experience. This way, he can build up an argumentation and come to a conclusion on his own without depending on people in the audience, who only assist him in finding his answer. But the responsibility lies with the candidate to deduce the right answer from the different arguments. There is no relationship of dependency when a recipient consults several information sources because he does not transfer but retains responsibility for the selection of information.

Moreover, there are further reasons that, from the perspective of trust chosen here, trust is not possible with several (online) information sources. First, the relationship between the recipient and the information source is broken if the recipient consults several information sources because the sources fade into the background and their information remains in the foreground: "[. . .] Consumers collect bits and pieces of information from different Web sites without necessarily paying a lot of attention to who authored each information bit" (Eysenbach 2008, p. 140).

Second, trust is not possible with several sources because, in a trusting action, the action of the trustor (here: the selection of a source and its information as a basis for a decision or an action) is causally linked to the action of the trustee (here: the selection of information by the source; Kohring 2004, p. 170). Such a causal link is not possible if the recipient consults several information sources and uses only bits and pieces of information to get an idea of the topic.

Third, the tolerance of risk has been described as a central aspect of a trust situation and a trusting action. However, if the recipient consults several information sources, he does not have to tolerate the risk of false, biased, or incomplete information because he reduces this risk by cross-checking information among the various sources. He can compare the information of several sources to check their adequacy, complete his understanding of the information, and gain different perspectives on the topic. Some researchers have stated that, even after reducing the risk, there is still some risk left that can then be surmounted by trust (Mayer et al. 1995). However, in cases where some risk still remains, the recipient has the opportunity to seek as much information as needed until the risk of false information is subjectively overcome and he is able to make his decision. Moreover, in a trust situation as it is viewed here, the risk only exists because of the relationship of dependency to the trustee (Ripperger 2003, p. 38). Since there is no relationship of dependency to a specific trustee when the recipient consults several information sources, the only risk is that the recipient selects false information, fails to understand the topic, and draws erroneous conclusions. This is a risk that has nothing to do with depending on an information source, but rather is based on the recipient depending on his own abilities. For this reason, consulting several information sources is not a case of trust but rather of self-confidence (Kohring 2004, p. 112).

Fourth, the saving of resources for the trustor was a further aspect of the definition of trust. If the recipient as a trustor hands over responsibility for the selection of information to one specific source and takes only the information of this source as a basis for his decision or action, he does not have to invest his own resources to solve his problem of a lack of information. If the recipient consults several online information sources, however, he must invest his own cognitive and temporal resources to seek information and evaluate both the information and the sources, which is especially difficult on the Internet due to its lack of quality control (Flanagin and Metzger 2008, p. 5; Kelton et al. 2008, p. 363). Moreover, he has to select which information of which source he wants to explore further and then has to piece the information together to make sense of it and to get an idea of the topic. This can be troublesome because conflicting perspectives on a topic produce new complexity (Babrow and Kline 2000, p. 1811) that the recipient has to reduce again. Therefore, the recipient has to invest a lot more resources when consulting several resources compared to when he trusts one specific source, then depends on this source and adopts its perspective on the topic. Therefore, with its advantage of saving resources for the trustor, trust is a very effective way of reducing complexity (Kohring 2004, p. 134).

But this advantage of saving resources loses some of its effect on the Internet, because new Internet sources can be consulted more quickly than in the offline world because they are only a few clicks away, and search engines, which are frequently employed (van Eimeren and Frees 2014), make this task very easy. This quick and easy access to a lot of different information supports the recipient's opportunity to solve his problem of a lack of information on his own. For this reason, it can be assumed that it is a rather rare case that a recipient depends only on one specific source on the Internet and that trust, as it is defined here, rarely becomes relevant on the Internet. Therefore, on the one hand, digitization enhances problems of trust because of a high complexity, quality problems, and possibly conflicting sources that are difficult to assess. On the other hand, digitization reduces problems of trust because of the possibility of cross-checking information quickly and easily, and because there is no need to depend on one specific information source.

Nevertheless, it is not entirely impossible for trust to become relevant in the online context. Trust is especially likely to come into effect with recipients who lack resources, for example cognitive resources, as the experience and ability to search for and evaluate online information sources can be difficult for those recipients due to the flood of information and problems of quality (Eysenbach and Jadad 2001, p. 24). Trust also becomes relevant if people do not want to invest their own resources, e.g., if they do not want to invest a lot of time to solve their problem. Even if it is much easier and quicker to get additional information from several other sources on the Internet than with sources in the offline context, the recipient still has to invest more resources when looking for online information from additional sources than if he just depends on one specific source and adopts the perspective this source has on the topic.

When trust becomes relevant, it enables the source as a trustee to have a high impact on the recipient as a trustor. When trusting a source, the recipient depends only on this source and its perspective on a topic without using other online information sources, and consequently, the source has a far-reaching impact on his decisions and actions. Therefore, the situation of trust is a special situation and very desirable from the perspective of information sources.

4 Conclusion

In this contribution it was argued that trust becomes relevant more seldom than previous research and the general use of the term in everyday language and the media may make us believe. This was demonstrated in the context of online information sources in which trust is assumed to be an especially rare and special occasion.

Specific preconditions for trust to come into effect showed that trust is not relevant in every social interaction but that other similar concepts come into effect in situations that share some aspects of a trust situation. For this reason, it is necessary, on the Internet as well as in other contexts, to precisely look at the situation and the relationship between actors to decide whether trust is relevant in this context or not.

Since these preconditions and the specific function of trust only really come into effect if the trustor engages in an action, trust was defined with a focus on the trusting action instead of an expectation, evaluation, or willingness. If applied to information sources, this definition conceptualizes trust as an action of selection that impacts the consequent decisions and actions of the trustor, which makes trust an important factor in media effects. Nevertheless, if defined this way, trust is not relevant in all information contexts but only if that information is directly relevant for people's decisions and actions.

On the Internet, the complexity of which seems to be a fitting context for trust to be relevant, trust is less omnipresent and relevant in fewer contexts than previously assumed. Since trust is defined here as a specific relationship of dependency between a recipient and a source in which the recipient transfers responsibility for the selection of information to the source, trust can only be conceptualized with reference to one specific source but not several information sources. Because several sources are very easily and quickly accessible on the Internet, which supports the opportunity for the recipient to solve his problem of a lack of information on his own, trust might become a rather rare case in this context.

Even if trust might be only rarely relevant in the context of online information sources, it is still important to analyze trust in this context for two reasons. First, research on trust in online information sources is needed to explore empirically the real significance that trust has in this context. Second, even if it might be rare, the high impact that a trusted information source can have on a recipient is another reason that research on trust in online information sources is relevant.

References

Babrow, A. S., & Kline, K. N. (2000). From "reducing" to "coping with" uncertainty: Reconceptualizing the central challenge in breast self-exams. *Social Science & Medicine, 51*(12), 1805–1816.

Baier, A. (1986). Trust and antitrust. *Ethics, 96*(2), 231–260.

Barber, B. (1983). *The logic and limits of trust.* New Brunswick, NJ: Rutgers University Press.

Butler, J. K., & Cantrell, R. S. (1984). A behavioral decision theory approach to modeling dyadic trust in superiors and subordinates. *Psychological Reports, 55,* 19–28.

Coleman, J. S. (1990). *Foundations of social theory.* Cambridge, MA: The Belknap Press of Havard University Press.

Corritore, C. L., Kracher, B., & Wiedenbeck, S. (2003). On-line trust: Concepts, evolving themes, a model. *International Journal of Human-Computer Studies, 58,* 737–758.

Dietz, G., & Den Hartog, D. (2006). Measuring trust inside organisations. *Personnel Review, 35* (5), 557–588.

Endreß, M. (2002). *Vertrauen.* Bielefeld: transcript Verl.

Endreß, M. (2010). Vertrauen: Soziologische Perspektiven. In M. Maring (Ed.), *Vertrauen: Zwischen sozialem Kitt und der Senkung von Transaktionskosten* (Vol. 3, pp. 91–114). Karlsruhe: KIT Scientific Publishing.

Endreß, M. (2012). Vertrauen und Misstrauen—Soziologische Überlegungen. In C. Schilcher, M. Will-Zocholl, & M. Ziegler (Eds.), *Vertrauen und Kooperation in der Arbeitswelt.* Wiesbaden: Springer Verlag für Sozialwissenschaften.

Eysenbach, G. (2008). Credibility of health information and digital media: New perspectives and implications for youth. In A. J. Flanagin & M. J. Metzger (Eds.), *Digital media, youth, and credibility* (pp. 123–154). Cambridge: The MIT Press.

Eysenbach, G., & Jadad, A. R. (2001). Evidence-based patient choice and consumer health informatics in the Internet age. *Journal of Medical Internet Research, 3*(2), e19.

Flanagin, A. J., & Metzger, M. J. (2008). Digital media and youth: Unparalleled opportunity and unprecedented responsibility. In A. J. Flanagin & M. J. Metzger (Eds.), *Digital media, youth, and credibility* (pp. 5–28). Cambridge: The MIT Press.

Gambetta, D. (1988). Foreword. In D. Gambetta (Ed.), *Trust: Making and breaking cooperative relations* (pp. IX–X). New York: Basil Blackwell.

Gambetta, D. (2001). Können wir dem Vertrauen vertrauen? In M. Hartmann & C. Offe (Eds.), *Vertrauen: Die Grundlage des sozialen Zusammenhalts* (pp. 204–237). Frankfurt am Main: Campus-Verl.

Giddens, A. (1995). *Konsequenzen der Moderne.* Suhrkamp: Frankfurt am Main.

Guenther, T., & Möllering, G. (2010). A framework for studying the problem of trust in online settings. In D. Latusek & A. Gerbasi (Eds.), *Trust and technology in a ubiquitous modern environment: Theoretical and methodological perspectives* (pp. 16–34). Hershey: IGI Global.

Hardin, R. (2001). Conceptions and explanations of trust. In K. S. Cook (Ed.), *Trust in society* (pp. 3–39). New York: Russell Sage.

Hartmann, M. (2010). Die Komplexität des Vertrauens. In M. Maring (Ed.), *Vertrauen: Zwischen sozialem Kitt und der Senkung von Transaktionskosten* (Vol. 3, pp. 15–26). Karlsruhe: KIT Scientific Publishing.

Hovland, C. I., Janis, I. L., Irving, L., & Kelley, H. (1953). *Communication and persuasion: Psychological studies of opinion change.* New Haven: Yale University Press.

Kelton, K., Fleischmann, K. R., & Wallce, W. A. (2008). Trust in digital information. *Journal of the American Society for Information Science and Technology, 59*(3), 363–374.

Kieserling, A. (2012). Vertrauen: Ein Mechanismus der Reduktion sozialer Komplexität (1968). In O. Jahraus, A. Nassehi, M. Grizelj, I. Saake, C. Kirchmeier, & J. Müller (Eds.), *Luhmann-Handbuch: Leben—Werk—Wirkung* (pp. 140–144). Stuttgart: Metzler.

Kohring, M. (2004). *Vertrauen in Journalismus: Theorie und Empirie.* Konstanz: UVK Verlags-Gesell.

Kohring, M. (2006). Zum Verhältnis von Wissen und Vertrauen: Eine Typologie am Beispiel öffentlicher Kommunikation. In K. Pühringer & S. Zielmann (Eds.), *Vom Wissen und Nicht-Wissen einer Wissenschaft* (Vol. 7, pp. 121–134). Berlin: Lit Verlag.

Kohring, M. (2007). Vertrauen statt Wissen—Qualität im Wissenschaftsjournalismus. In G. Kienzlen, J. Lublinski, & V. Stollorz (Eds.), *Fakt, Fiktion, Fälschung: Trends im Wissenschaftsjournalismus* (pp. 25–38). Konstanz: UVK Verlags-Gesell.

Kramer, R. M. (1999). Trust and distrust in organizations: Emerging perspectives, enduring questions. *Annual Review of Psychology, 50*, 569–598.

Lagerspetz, O. (1998). *Trust: The tacit demand*. Dordrecht: Kluwer.

Lewicki, R. J., & Bunker, B. B. (1996). Developing and maintaining trust in work relationships. In R. M. Kramer & T. R. Tyler (Eds.), *Trust in organizations: Frontiers of theory and research* (pp. 114–139). Newbury Park, CA: Sage.

Lewicki, R. T., McAllister, D. J., & Bier, R. J. (1998). Trust and distrust: New relationships and realities. *The Academy of Management Review, 23*(3), 438–458.

Lewis, J. D., & Weigert, A. (1985). Trust as a social reality. *Social Forces, 63*(4), 967–985.

Luhmann, N. (1968). *Vertrauen: Ein Mechanismus der Reduktion sozialer Komplexität*. Stuttgart: Ferdinand Enke Verlag.

Luhmann, N. (2000). Familiarity, confidence, trust: Problems and alternatives. In D. Gambetta (Ed.), *Trust: Making and breaking cooperative relations* (pp. 94–107). Cambridge, MA: Basil Blackwell.

Mayer, R. C., Davis, J. H., & Schoormann, F. D. (1995). An integrative model of organizational trust. *The Academy of Mangament Review, 20*(3), 709–734.

McKnight, D. H., Cummings, L. L., & Norman, L. C. (1998). Initial trust formation in new organizational relationships. *The Academy of Management Review, 23*(3), 473–490.

Möllering, G. (2001). The nature of trust: From Georg Simmel to a theory of expectation, interpretation and suspension. *Sociology, 35*, 403–420.

Müller, J. (2013). *Mechanisms of trust: News media in democratic and authoritarian regimes*. Frankfurt: Campus-Verl.

Neuberger, C. (2009). Internet, Journalismus und Öffentlichkeit: Analyse des Medienumbruchs. In C. Neuberger (Ed.), *Journalismus im Internet. Profession—Partizipation—Technisierung*. Wiesbaden: VS Verlag für Sozialwiss.

Preisendörfer, P. (1995). Vertrauen als soziologische Kategorie: Möglichkeiten und Grenzen einer entscheidungstheoretischen Fundierung des Vertrauenskonzepts. *Zeitschrift für Soziologie, 24* (4), 263–272.

Ripperger, T. (2003). *Ökonomik des Vertrauens: Analyse eines Organisationsprinzips* (2nd ed.). Tübingen: Mohr Siebeck.

Seligman, A. B. (2000). *The problem of trust* (2nd ed.). Princeton, NJ: Princeton University Press.

Simmel, G. (1999). *Soziologie: Untersuchungen über die Formen der Vergesellschaftung*. Frankfurt am Main.

van Eimeren, B., & Frees, B. (2014). Ergebnisse der ARD/ZDF-Onlinestudie 2014: 79 Prozent der Deutschen online—Zuwachs bei mobiler Internetnutzung und Bewegtbild. *Media Perspektiven, 7–8*, 378–396.

Warren, M. E. (1999). *Democracy and trust*. Cambridge: Cambridge University Press.

Wolling, J. (2004). Qualitätserwartungen, Qualitätswahrnehmungen und die Nutzung von Fernsehserien: Ein Beitrag zur Theorie und Empirie der subjektiven Qualitätsauswahl von Medienangeboten. *Publizistik, 49*, 171–193.

Trust Processes in Sport in the Context of Doping

Dennis Dreiskämper, Katharina Pöppel, Daniel Westmattelmann,
Gerhard Schewe, and Bernd Strauss

Abstract Trust is a relatively rare explored research field in sport. This is surprising, because different trust constellations can be expected in sport. Besides, constructs intrinsic to sport, like self-efficacy, social resources or group cohesion, might at least be correlated with trust.

Doping seems to place the trustworthiness of sport itself at serious risk. The doping problem is a constant part of elite-sports, which displays a new dynamic due to increased digital media use. The Olympic sports federations and anti-doping agencies are responsible for the fight against doping. The aims of doping prevention are to encourage a clean environment and to control athlete's behaviour. Sport in general is attacked by the public on two grounds: that that sport is neither able nor willing to fight doping successfully.

Using the model of trust proposed by Mayer et al. (The Academy of Management Review, 20:709–734, 1995), we aim to adapt the construct of trustworthiness in terms of the different trust relationships in elite-sports by referring to current circumstances in sports, including the use of digital media. The possibilities of transferring this trust model are discussed. Therefore, as well the antecedents of trust as the risk factors for athletes, sports federations and spectators are to be reflected. Furthermore, the importance of the trustworthiness of the different protagonists in sport for the success of the fight against doping will be discussed. A special focus is on the changes of communication between athletes, spectators, federations and anti-doping agencies because of the effects of the digitization and forthcoming mediatisation of communication methods.

Keywords Sport • Doping • Trustworthiness • Anti-doping agency • Substance abuse treatment

D. Dreiskämper (✉) • K. Pöppel • D. Westmattelmann • G. Schewe • B. Strauss
University of Münster, Münster, Germany
e-mail: dreiskaemper@uni-muenster.de; katharina.poeppel@uni-oldenburg.de; daniel.
westmattelmann@uni-muenster.de; 19gesc@wiwi.uni-muenster.de; bstrauss@uni-muenster.
de

© Springer International Publishing Switzerland 2016   125
B. Blöbaum (ed.), *Trust and Communication in a Digitized World*, Progress in IS,
DOI 10.1007/978-3-319-28059-2_7

1   Doping and Trust

Doping is a risk for every athlete: The risk of being detected is combined with a risk of conviction, a long suspension or a serious loss of image. Also, an athlete can lose the opportunity to reach his or her highest aim in life in terms of success as an athlete, because the athlete's career might be ended or at least suffer a devastating setback.

Health consequences, or social effects like exclusion from a sports team or the loss of friends and social support in the setting of sport, might be further risks for athletes who engage in doping.

But what would it mean if not only doping itself but also not to dope were a risk for the athlete? This would be the case if the athlete could be sure that his or her opponents were taking performance-enhancing drugs without being detected. In this case the athlete would be at a disadvantage in competition against his or her opponents if he or she did not also take performance-enhancing drugs.

At first glance, this scenario, in which a whole sport is affected by doping, seems unrealistic. But if we consider cycling, which has suffered huge damage to its image due to doping over the last 20 years, it seems that such a situation has existed in sport: In the late 90s cycling was at its peak: athletes like Marco Pantani, Bjarne Rijs, Jan Ullrich or a bit later Lance Armstrong were competing against each other in extreme rivalry. The average speed of the Tour de France increased annually, even as the demands of the routes became greater. Years later it was shown that almost all the top competitors used doping during these years. What had happened? An explanation could be that different trust relationships were seriously damaged by the occurrence of doping possibilities. An athlete has to evaluate his or her probability of winning. The athlete must take into consideration whether he or she is disadvantaged in comparison with others by not taking performance-enhancing drugs. This is in particular the case if doped athletes are not detected by the responsible agencies for the control of doping, like sports federations and the World Anti-Doping Agency (WADA). If other elements in the sport system like physicians, support staff or team chiefs not only tolerate doping but also support the use of dope by athletes, the athlete who does not use such drugs would probably estimate his or her chances of winning as being quite low. In that case the risk that accompanies a decision not to dope and to accept a disadvantage in relation to a large proportion of one's opponents might be perceived as greater than the risk of one's use of dope being detected. Accordingly, the athlete has to consider whether there is a higher risk in doping or in not doping, when he decides for or against doping. To renounce doping, the athlete must trust the system in his or her sport averts a situation in which opponents can take performance-enhancing drugs without being detected. Here, the athlete has not only to assess the trustworthiness of his or her opponents but also the trustworthiness of sports federations, which have the task of ensuring doping-free conditions and of prohibiting doping, and of the anti-doping agencies, which detect and sanction doping. Only if the athlete has trust that the other parties stand for a doping-free system, in which he or she can be

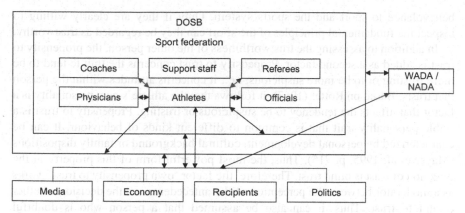

Fig. 1 Trust relations in sport

competitive and will suffer no disadvantages without resorting to any doping substances, might he or she take the risk of rejecting doping and trying to be a "clean" athlete (Fig. 1).

In the following sections the trustworthiness of the three main protagonists (athletes, sports federations and WADA/NADA) in respect of doping is analysed from different perspectives. We examine not only the relationships within the sport but also the influence and demands of external factors that invest in sport, like politics, economics, spectators and media.

2   Definitions of Trust

To evaluate the trustworthiness of the different protagonists in sport, the model from economical science that is introduced at the beginning of this book is adapted to the setting of sport. Mayer et al. (1995, p. 712) define trust as follows: "the willingness of a party to be vulnerable to the actions of another party based on the expectation that the other will perform a particular action important to the trustor, irrespective of the ability to monitor or control that other party."

This willingness to trust is based on the evaluation of the person or organisation that is to be trusted. Mayer et al. (1995) summarize these assessments under the three antecedents of trust: ability, benevolence and integrity. In the case of doping, athletes have to evaluate whether the other athletes are able to reach their desired level of performance without the use of any illegal substances. In addition, they evaluate whether another athlete will try to get an advantage in comparison with themselves and other athletes and wants to harm the chances of the other athletes (failure of benevolence); and whether an athlete actually believes in the basic principles of sport, like fair play or equality of chances, and behaves in accordance with those principles (integrity). This applies with respect to both the integrity of the athletes, and so to their values, principles and attitudes to sport, and also to their benevolence to sport and the sports system. Only if they are clearly willing to respect the fundamental principles of the sport can they be regarded as trustworthy.

In addition to assessing the trustworthiness of the other person, the propensity to trust is added as a second factor. Propensity to trust concerns the trait to tend to be more trusting or to be more suspicious, i.e., it concerns attitudes within the person that trusts. Based on Rotter (1967), it follows that the athlete's own personality is a factor that affects the tendency to be suspicious or trusting. Propensity to trust is a stable personality trait that is common to different kinds of behaviour. It can be characterized by personal development, cultural background or family dispositions (Mayer et al. 1995, p. 715). Thus, the most powerful form of this property in the direction of trust is blind trust. Therefore, the factor 'own propensity to trust' works as a moderator between the perception of the antecedents and the decision whether or not to trust. Thus, it can also be assumed that a person who is doubtful unconvinced that a sports system prosecutes and prevents doping tends to use doping more than a person who believes in the integrity, ability and benevolence of other athletes, the sports federation or the WADA.

The existence of trust does not necessarily mean that trusting behaviour results. Besides the perception of trustworthiness there is another important factor that effects the decision: the perception of risk. There is a consensus that risk is necessary for the existence of a trust situation. The perception of the extent of a risk might lead to a decision not to trust even though both perceived trustworthiness and own propensity are high. In the model of trust proposed by Mayer et al. (1995) the evaluation of the circumstances is a factor that moderates the relationship between trust and risk-taking behaviour. However, this moderation can be maximal: In sport, an athlete could have maximum trust in his or her opponents and the anti-doping system, but nevertheless use doping substances to be sure of reaching the highest level of competition.

Finally, after a decision to trust or not to trust, the trustor will evaluate the outcome of the situation. For an athlete who renounces doping because he or she believes that one can be successful without doping in his or her sport, a case of doping would be a reason to change his or her behaviour in the future.

Where the result of the trust decision is to reject the risk, the outcome will be evaluated by analysing which decision would have been better for the trustor. An athlete would assess whether it was necessary to take performance enhancements or whether he or she would have been as successful without them. This evaluation of the results will be incorporated in further trust decisions and has a direct influence on the perception of the antecedents of the trustees.

Another factor Mayer et al. (1995) emphasize is the relationship between trust and control. Conceptualising the model of trust, Mayer et al. (1995) neglect this factor, but in their own review (Schoorman et al. 2007, p. 346) they add that these two factors are not necessarily mutually dependent, but that control might moderate the interrelation between trust and risk. For the situation of athletes it can be assumed that they have comparatively little control on doping behaviour in their sport. They can control their own behaviour only and will compare it with the perceived attitudes of the other protagonists.

3   Trustworthiness of Athletes

When an athlete is announced as a member of a national youth team or reaches a certain performance level in team sports, he or she is already obliged to comply with the rules of the anti-doping code. That athletes reach an arrangement to adhere to the rules established by the WADA means here is an internal contract to reduce the complexity of the possibilities in sport. Athletes trust their opponents meet the laws and will not try to evade them. This might mean there is a risk for athletes, because they cannot control whether other athletes meet the demands of the anti-doping code. Control is entrusted to sports federations and the WADA. Sports federations are responsible for preventing, prohibiting, and punishing doping. The WADA has a legislative and oversight function, making the rules and checking that they are met by all protagonists. The trustworthiness of these three players in sport (i.e., athletes, sports federations and WADA) is to be examined in this and later sections of this chapter.

To evaluate whether athletes are trustworthy in terms of their doping behaviour it seems first to be necessary to analyse the possible reasons for doping use. A first model to predict doping behaviour of athletes is by Donovan et al. (2002). It was developed based on a request of the American anti-doping agency and can be reduced to an analysis of given literature in sport science and health science. The authors developed a model that is based on cost/benefit considerations (Fig. 2). Besides threats, costs and benefits the authors add social, individual, and objectively given parameters to the model.

The model itself is hermeneutic, which means that there is a lack of empirical evidence for the parameters named in the model (Mazanov and Huybers 2010). The actual influence of the analysis of costs and benefits and the accuracy of the somewhat vague explanations of parameters like personality and reference groups cannot be proved. But parallels to the ideas of trust research can be found. For example, the influence of personality traits and the assessment of legality or morality of the behaviour (comparable to the antecedent integrity) are similar to the trust model of Mayer et al. (1995).

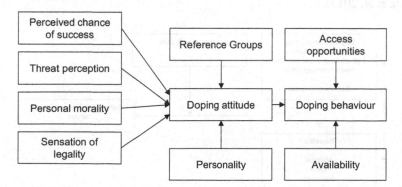

Fig. 2 Adaption of the model by Donovan et al. (2002) explaining possible factors of doping behavior

Strelan and Boeckmann (2003) focus, in another explanatory approach, on possible deterrence mechanisms that influence doping behaviour, such as controls and education work, moral concerns, social effects and health consequences. They argue that doping behaviour is due to rational reasons in that thoughts about deterrence arguments and positive effects of doping are weighed against each other. The weight assigned to factors leads to a decision about doping; and the pathway to that decision can be moderated by situational factors like the perception of the prevalence of doping in a sport, experiences with penalties, the perception of actual competitiveness, the professionalism of the sport, the perception of the sports federation as the responsible agent, and the kind of substance involved in doping. Strelan and Boeckmann (2003) consider three possible kinds of sanction: first, legal consequences that would create high personal costs; second, social sanctions like exclusion from social groups (e.g., training groups); and self-centred consequences like a sense of guilt or a lack of self-worth. In addition, health consequences can appear as a deterrent (Strelan and Boeckmann 2003).

Benefits can be assumed to include material benefits like prize money and sponsorship; and the chance of greater success for the athlete's own career. Also, social factors like appreciation or personal factors like satisfaction with the results might be consequences (Strelan and Boeckmann 2003; Fig. 3).

A further model by Petróczi (2007) considers attitudes towards doping and doping behaviour. Based on the theory of planned behaviour (TPB, Ajzen 1985), it integrates perceived competitiveness as a part of behaviour control. This component can be seen as the perception of the given conditions in a sport, which also means evaluating the risk that goes along with a non-doping behaviour.

The model shows two further predictors of doping: Petróczi and Aidman (2008) argue that the motivation of the athletes has a significant influence on their doping attitude and behaviour: The higher the orientation of a person towards winning, the greater is the probability that the person will be open to doping. For this hypothesis she finds only partial evidence in an empirical study: Direct influence can be found only for the kind of motivation in terms of athlete's attitudes, not in terms of athlete's actual behaviour. However, other authors also point out the fact that an athlete's general motivation might be an important influence on doping attitudes (Dietz et al. 2013).

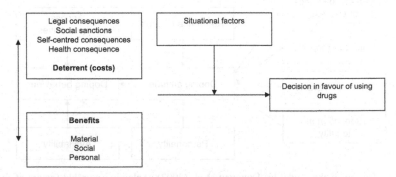

Fig. 3 Model of doping behaviour, adopted by Strelan and Boeckmann (2003)

A second factor Petróczi includes in her model refers to athletes' beliefs about doping. Beliefs about doping are defined as the attitudes of athletes towards the question whether performance-enhancing drugs, such as those currently banned by the WADA, should be legalized. This parameter can be compared with the antecedents benevolence and integrity in the trust model by Mayer et al. (1995).

Petróczi's (2007) model was used and expanded in further research (Mazanov et al. 2008; Petróczi et al. 2011). Petróczi and Aidman (2008) highlight that besides doping attitudes and beliefs about doping other factors that are not intrinsic to athletes influence the doping decisions of athletes. This represents a kind of paradigm shift in psychological research on doping: Whereas in former studies the athlete using dope was at the centre as the only responsible party, now other elements of the sport system have become the focus of research for the first time. Social and situational factors are also said to be potential reasons for doping behaviour. In the model that has not been empirically proved, next to personality factors systemic parameters influence athletes' decision making regarding doping. These systemic factors are described as the perception of beliefs about doping within the sports federation, and the general and the subjective perception of the prevalence of doping in the sport and within the opponents. These factors, and actual events like new doping substances, new detection formats or actual cases of doping are considered to influence behaviour. The model (Fig. 4) also shows reciprocal effects between factors within and around the athletes. For example, personality traits might influence the perception of the particular sport system and the sports federation.

Athletes have different reasons to use performance-enhancing drugs. These reasons are influenced by systemic and situational arguments and the evaluation of those arguments by athletes. Further, not only costs and benefits but also motives and beliefs about existing doping behaviours influence the decision-making process. There are parallels found between the paradigms concerning athletes' attitudes to doping and the trust model of Mayer et al. (1995): e.g., the suggestion in the doping paradigm that other parties in the system are evaluated regarding their

Fig. 4 Reciprocal influence on the situation in which an athlete uses or does not use doping substances (adapted by Petróczi and Aidman 2008)

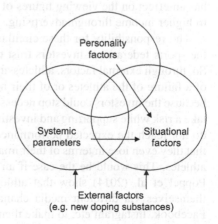

behavior is paralleled in the trust model by the antecedents to trust; the own personality seems to be a significant factor in both models (cf. propensity to trust) and the situation in a sport and the given parameters that are to be estimated might be compared with the risk perception in the trust model.

Athletes are in direct competition with each other and therefore evaluate the trustworthiness of their opponents and draw conclusions related to their doping behaviour. At the same time they will also estimate situational factors, risks and the intentions of others. While these are reciprocal effects of trust, athletes are also in one-sided trust relationships: customers and investors in sport, politics, media, economics and spectators also judge the athletes regarding their trustworthiness and behave in ways that are based on these judgements. One of the new digital options for athletes to present themselves as trustworthy or to evaluate opponents as trustworthy are social media like Facebook or Twitter, where athletes have the opportunity to provide a personal channel for self-presentation. In contrast to times of traditional media like television or newspapers, athletes now have the chance to contact their recipients more directly and thus try to have an impact on the recipients' perception of themselves.

For economics and for media representatives, athletes are promotional items. They invest in sports by sponsorship or buying broadcasting rights or by funding elite sports. These investors hope for benefits and advantages to themselves from their commitment. For sponsors, these benefits are economic income through promotional activity or an increase in their perceived image by association with the extraordinary performance of an athlete. They might hope that recipients associate the success of an athlete with the success of the company or brand mark. Policy supports sport for at least two reasons: On the one hand, sport is an important part of civil society. On the other hand, countries compete with each other and, as a question of prestige, it is important that national athletes are successful compared with athletes from other countries. Elite sport also creates role models for society. Media invests in sport because they believe in the entertainment effect of sports. This leads to a greater perception and use of the offers of a media programme. For example, a higher perception of sports that media present has an effect on the viewing figures of television programmes, which in turn leads to higher income through advertising.

The responsibility for these circular processes is the obligation of athletes and the sports federations. Investors trust that players in sport will meet expectations. So, through external factors, athletes are put under pressure: Possible consequences of a failure of the athletes or of their not meeting demands can be extremely high, because the investors could stop necessary financial support. The customers of sport take a risk while supporting and investing in sport. These risks could be that athletes do not reach the expected performance, so that the investment is not efficient; or that they even lose in terms of their image and reputation because of a failure by the athletes. This would be the case if an athlete took performance-enhancing drugs. Pöppel et al. (2014) show that athletes have different possibilities to promote themselves via different media channels. They can use platforms like Twitter, Facebook, Instagram etc. to make themselves more popular. Also, these platforms give the opportunities to publish own statement about competitions, results and also suspicions like in doping issues to save their own image and reputation.

However, these two risks—to fail performance or to get addicted to doping—conflict with each other: Bette and Schimank (2006) emphasize that all investors expect maximum performance of the athletes, but for some athletes the consumption of performance-enhancing drugs can be necessary to meet the demands. For the athletes this creates a dilemma, in which they have to weigh the risks and reach the desired performance. That doping cases mean an immediate decrease of trust can be shown by different examples: the withdrawal of German public television from broadcasting the Tour de France can be explained by an extreme decrease of trust in cycling and in the protagonists of this sport. This decision had far-reaching consequences for all parties involved. Other examples are the termination of sponsor's contracts after the revelation of the Lance Armstrong doping case or the petition of the German political party Bündnis 90/Die Grünen to cancel all financial support for cycling sport after the doping cases in 2005. But not only politics, media, and economics can withdraw their trust, also spectators can lose their trust in athletes. Scandals like doping cases, game manipulation or cheating can lead to a lack of trust by the public (Breuer and Hallmann 2013).

4 Trustworthiness of Sports Federations

If the model of trust by Mayer et al. (1995) is transferred to the relationship between athletes (trustor) and sports federations (trustee) it is first to be clarified whether a risk relationship between the federation and the athlete exists. In the previous section the cost/benefit model of Strelan and Boeckmann (2003) was introduced, in which doping has a high risk of being detected. This opinion, that doping creates a higher risk than non-doping, must be questioned if the trustworthiness of sports federations is our focus. In Petróczi and Aidman's (2008) paper a possible interpretation of the decision to dope or not to dope is that athletes use performance-enhancing drugs because it is the better, or even the only, decision for success in their sport. If the conditions in sport or in some sports disciplines actually are characterized this way, it is not doping behaviour but non-doping that is a behaviour that carries risk. The athlete would be vulnerable to having a disadvantage in comparison with other (doping) athletes. The subjective norm (TPB, Ajzen 1985) of the sport would be constructed by doping as the normal behaviour of participants.

The sports federations, as the organizers of sport, are responsible for setting the norms in a sport. They are responsible for the prosecution and sanction of doping. So, the sports federations regulate the penalties for doping, because it is their task to guarantee fair conditions to the athletes (WADA 2014). If the sports federation fails to suppress doping, a non-doping athlete will be at a disadvantage compared with his opponents, who exploit the failure of the federation by taking performance-enhancing drugs. Petróczi and Aidman (2008) underline that athletes care about being surrounded by doped athletes, which signifies a perceived vulnerability for the athletes.

Therefore, an athlete will evaluate his or her sports federation by judging whether the federation handles its tasks successfully and will weigh the risks of doping and non-doping. In other words, the athlete weighs whether the anti-doping work of the federation is trustworthy or not. This means that the ability of a sports federation to provide fair conditions for athletes can be interpreted as the assessment of its professional and technical competencies in anti-doping work, e.g., sufficient and efficient doping controls. The benevolence of a sports federation can be assessed by the effort it makes to help athletes. In that regard, athletes will evaluate whether the federation takes the side of those athletes who take performance-enhancing drugs by protecting them or of those who reject doping. The perception of the integrity of a sports federation can be explained by its endeavour to provide fair conditions for all athletes. Also, an athlete could ask whether the federation fights doping transparently or tries to obscure it. Figure 5 shows the model of trustworthiness adapted to the setting of athletes who trust their sports federation regarding its anti-doping work.

Bette and Schimank (2006) mention in this context the double accusation against sports federations regarding their anti-doping work. On the one hand, it is questioned whether federations have the ability to prohibit doping. This is supported by the fact that the search for new doping substances would always be one step ahead of research into doping detection. So, sports federations are only able to react to the behaviour of athletes. Further, it is argued that comprehensive control of athletes in training and competition is not possible. Also, a lack of financial resources for the fight against doping is assumed. A further aspect deals with the international comparability of anti-doping work. While in industrial

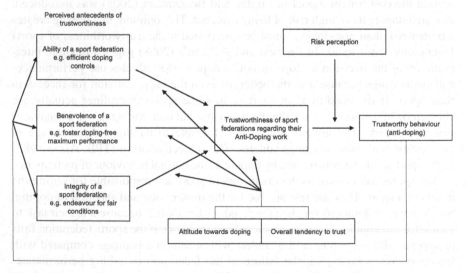

Fig. 5 Trustworthiness of sports federations regarding their anti-doping work

nations the national anti-doping agencies are sufficiently supported by the state, comprehensive monitoring of doping is not possible in many other countries. So the competencies of national and international sports federation to fight doping successfully are often questioned.

Even more serious is the accusation of some media representatives that not all sports federations are willing to fight doping (Bette et al. 2012). This suggestion refers to the antecedent of benevolence and to the antecedent of integrity. It is argued that federations do not want to detect doping because they depend financially on the success of their elite athletes. This would lead to a neglect of, or even support for, doping (which would mean a benevolent attitude to doped athletes). Furthermore, the federations are accused of not wanting to detect doping, because not only would negative consequences damage the athlete, but also they would damage the federations' image.

What must sports federations do to protect themselves against these critical opinions and to appear trustworthy regarding their anti-doping work? Sports federations should present the doping issue in a way in which they seem to be a credible enemy of doping. Being idealistic and emphasizing complete solutions to the doping problem is not to be considered as trustworthy (Bette and Schimank 2006). Therefore, anti-doping work is not to be perceived as a symbolic appeasement of a problem. Thus, anti-doping seems to be successful if the sports federation presents itself as a trustworthy player in the system. Augustin (2007a, b) points to the necessity of a positive image of the fight against doping. This can be achieved by:

- Giving anti-doping a positive image in public.
- Promoting the increase of health consciousness.
- Sending transparent messages.
- Inviting public and media to dispute doping critically.
- Promoting the fun of sport as well as individual performance.
- Showing a transparent and broad support of the fight against doping

However, it seems to be important not only that federations focus on winning the fight against doping, but also that their position is credible and reliable. Nevertheless, for any sports federation a doping case or even a suspicion of doping means a high level of organizational stress the federations have to avoid or even to minimize (Bette and Schimank 2006).

New possibilities to meet these expectations are given by new media and new ways of communication: Using digital campaigns or a well-structured homepage with information about their own Anti-Doping work, sport federations are able to change the perception of their trustworthiness (Dreiskämper 2014).

By focussing on own trustworthiness regarding their anti-doping work, sports federation might take a big step to reach the aims of anti-doping. Thus, successful anti-doping work does not totally prevent doping, but is possible for sports federations to be perceived as trustworthy and reliable. Therefore they have to state their position quickly and transparently if necessary (Dreiskämper 2014). This behaviour might counteract the double accusation levelled at sports federations. Also, it can be an important contribution to the reduction of the contradiction between reaching the maximum performance and the fair spirit of sport. In particular, anti-doping work would be a central part of prevention f all protagonists in sport, investors and competitors, could believe in the trustworthy attitude and role of sports federations, as they are the organizing umbrella for all parties.

5   Trust and National and World Anti-Doping Agencies

Similar to the fact that sports federations present themselves as reliable parts of the anti-doping work, national as well as international anti-doping agencies behave analogously. In 2004, under the World Anti-Doping Code (WADC), a catalogue was released which was supposed to manage all kinds of matters and corresponding consequences with regard to doping (WADA 2015). The catalogue is based on two fundamental principles which can be seen as the aim of WADA: 'the protection of the athlete's basic right to participate in doping-free sport' (WADA 2009, p. 6), which aims to encourage athletes in terms of health, fairness and equal treatment; and the 'securing of harmonized, coordinated and effective anti-doping programs in an international as well as national context' (WADA 2009, p. 6), which enables the detection of violations against anti-doping regulations to hinder or prevent doping (WADA 2009). WADA itself assumes the role of a legislator and controller since it is responsible for current anti-doping regulations as well as for doping tests and the prosecution of doping athletes through its national layers (Haug 2006, p. 71).

Consequently, WADA does not risk being accused of not fighting doping because it possesses a neutral, superior role within the anti-doping fight. Nevertheless, it also faces reproaches that it is one step behind dopers (Kayser et al. 2007, p. 3; Haug 2006, p. 91). However, WADA's establishment has been a decisive point in the trust relationship between doping inspectors and athletes, caused by different regulations anchored in the WADC. Under these regulations a control mantle is installed which serves as a substitute for the trust in athletes and other protagonists in sport. Thus, professional athletes are encouraged to inform WADA about their current residence at any time. In fact, WADA's 'whereabouts-rule' is extremely controversial and has been criticized from a contextual perspective (Bojsen-Møller and Christiansen 2010) as well as from an ethical perspective (Pawlenka 2012). Although the rule leads to the fact that athletes at a certain level of performance are constrained to reduce their privacy, the risk of undetected usage of doping substances is said to be reduced by it. Information about 'whereabouts' is secured digitally by the ADAMS-system (WADA 2009, p. 88). Thus, through this system athletes' confidential data are available all over the world (Kayser et al. 2007, p. 2). This example is not the only one showing that effects of digitization have changed the sports, and especially the doping, environment. Because on the other hand it is easier for athletes to get information about the current anti-doping regulations respectively list of banned substances and methods via homepage or Apps (WADA 2015).

6   Effects of Digital Communication on Trust

Trust is not only necessary for sports federations in respect of their anti-doping work or for athletes in respect of combating doping. According to Luhmann (1979) it is an essential part of cooperation, because it reduces the complexity of life. Sports, especially at the most competitive levels, are complex systems, characterized by complicated relations between coaches, athletes, federations, support staff, and also media, economics, and politics. In addition, social intercourse has become even more complex due to digitization. Whereas sports events were formerly characterized by a time lag as information was transmitted solely by journalistic sources, such as television, radio or newspapers, the emergence of social media has changed this system completely (Sanderson and Hambrick 2012). Not only journalists report on sport events: athletes, federations, or recipients also disseminate information instantaneously (Hutchins 2011). These changes enable athletes and federations to appear more active and to present their services. Homepages are central information channels for athletes, federations and sports clubs. Media channels like Twitter, Facebook, or Instagram are used for commercials or reporting (Wallace et al. 2011). For recipients, like spectators or representatives from economics or sports, sport and opinion making become more complicated due to these changes of digitization. Whereas, in the times traditional media were paramount a small amount of already filtered and evaluated information was available, recipients now have to choose the information themselves from a high number of sources (Agichtein et al. 2008). Thus, the recipient has to decide which source is trustworthy and credible. For the doping discourse, this means that and sports federations are able to decide themselves whether they want to clarify their position in cases of doping. As the history of doping in German sport from the 1990s on reveals (Krüger et al. 2014), the increase of information sources also enhanced the complexity of the issue. When numerous German media reported on doping practices in the old West and East German states, the doping problem became more complex. Recipients, but also sport and media, are introduced to the doping problems more intensely. Due to the possibilities of the Internet, sports recipients not only expect a sophisticated clarification of the doping problem, but also statements from the parties involved. Therefore, digital communication is both a chance to enhance trustworthiness and a danger to perceptions of the trustworthiness of sports people and organizations: On the one hand, attitudes, actions, and intentions in the fight against doping can be presented transparently. On the other hand, federations and athletes are measured by how they position themselves in relation to doping. If such positioning is not successful or if another source is more credible in presenting a federation as non-trustworthy in their actions against doping, this can have negative consequences for the specific federation. These consequences encompass not only the image of a certain type of sport, but can also include far reaching financial losses, such as a cancellation of subsidies by the Governments or the cancellation of sponsorship agreements. Therefore, digitization forces athletes and federations to refer to topics like anti-doping measures in a transparent and a trustworthy manner.

7 Discussion

Doping is one of the greatest risks to trust in sports and in sport's protagonists (Meinberg 2010). Certain types of sports or sports federations have already suffered significant reputational and other losses as a result of doping scandals in the last decades (see Krüger et al. 2014). Not only because of that, trust should be a point of focus if the phenomenon of doping is observed. As shown in the previous sections, relations within the sports system are complex. Thus, the use of illegal performance-enhancing drugs is not determined solely by the athlete, his or her moral transgressions or personality traits. The athlete is part of a system, which he or she analyses and evaluates. It can be assumed that the decision for or against doping is based on an evaluation of the single components, chances and risks in top-class sports. Trust in the single components is a basic requirement for decision making: If the athlete is not convinced that he or she can compete successfully and win on fair terms because of a lack of trust in the anti-doping measures in place and the behaviour of other competitors, the decision will be seriously influenced.

The integrative model of organizational trust (Mayer et al. 1995) has been successfully transferred to various scientific domains (see also the chapters within this book referring to communication, psychology, or information systems), but it remains in question whether a transfer to the complicated trust relationships in sport is feasible. By adapting the trust model to sports, several parallels to the current doping research can be identified: It is assumed that the protagonists in sports evaluate each other and thus refer to parameters like integrity, benevolence, and ability. In addition, personality traits (see Strelan and Boeckmann 2003) or the assessment of own risk (Petróczi and Aidman 2008) have an influence on decision making in sports. The existence of risk is an integral part of the trust model, combined with a surrendering of control. Exactly this phenomenon occurs in the case of athletes: If they trust their sport as free from doping they give up control to the sports federation and anti-doping agencies. Further, those parties with a control function in sports have to trust athletes to stick to the rules and principles. However, trust is reduced due to the amount of controls and regulations that exist. This fact can be transferred to an analysis of trust: Because of the high number of doping cases in the different types of sport like cycling or track and field, anti-doping interventions have been extended, which leads to a new evaluation of the antecedents of trustworthiness of the specific actors, as in the trust model of Mayer et al. (1995). Thus, adaptation of the existing model to sports appears to be reasonable.

Nevertheless, limitations to the adaptation of the trust model to sports can be named: Further research is necessary to answer the question whether the relationship between sports' protagonists is a trust relationship, which can also be understood as an interpersonal trust relation. The relationships between the customers of sport, like media, economics, politics, and spectators, and athletes and federations can be regarded as forms of initial trust (see Rousseau et al. 1998) without extended prior knowledge to assess the antecedents of trustworthiness. A direct relationship is, mostly, not involved. Further research is necessary to clarify why sponsors invest in sports, teams or athletes and thus engage in a trusting action.

A further question refers to the perception of risk and alternatives to athletes' behaviour. Whereas risks are apparent for athletes, the complexity of the system becomes obvious when we consider the debate concerning the double accusation made against top-class sport: for federations, trust is accompanied by the risk that their athletes might engage in doping. If they reduce this risk by more frequent use of doping controls, they increase the danger of own losses. The concept of risk is even more challenging when we consider the incorporation of recipients of sport. They face the risk of being disappointed by their idols in whom they have invested time, money, or passion, but it is unclear whether this is an interpersonal relationship accompanied by an obvious risk. The current trust model does not encompass these complex and branched relations: further research is necessary.

Current research regarding the doping problem and the prevalence of doping (Pitsch and Emrich 2012; Pitsch et al. 2007) indicates that sport might face a trust crisis in the near future. Also, stimulated for example by the clarifications regarding the history of the institute for sports medicine in Freiburg, including several proofs of doping in diverse types of sport the current doping discourse shows that doping is a major threat for the ideas and principles of sport. The opportunities to conduct the fight against doping successfully are supported by the dissemination of new media and their ability to contact athletes, federations, recipients and media directly. In this chapter, several parties that are involved in the doping issue are introduced. They all are to be trustworthy parts of the system and they all have different possibilities, including new media, to avoid further doping crises for sport in future.

References

Agichtein, E., Castillo, C., Donato, D., Gionis, A., & Mishne, G. (2008). *Finding high-quality content in social media*. Paper presented at the Proceedings of the 2008 International Conference on Web Search and Data Mining.

Ajzen, I. (1985). From intentions to actions: A theory of planned behavior. In J. Kuhl & J. Beckman (Eds.), *Action-control: From cognition to behavior* (pp. 11–39). Heidelberg: Springer.

Augustin, R. (2007a). Die Rolle der Nationalen Anti-Doping-Agentur (NADA) in der nationalen und internationalen Dopingbekämpfung—Grundlagen und Perspektiven. In R. Nickel & T. Rous (Eds.), *Das Anti-Doping-Handbuch, Band 1* (pp. 80–92). Aachen: Meyer & Meyer.

Augustin, R. (2007b). Gesamtkonzeption der Dopingprävention. In R. Nickel & T. Rous (Eds.), *Das Anti-Doping-Handbuch, Band 1* (pp. 206–244). Aachen: Meyer & Meyer.

Bette, K.-H., Kühnle, F., & Thiel, A. (2012). *Dopingprävention: Eine soziologische Expertise*. Bielefeld: Transcript.

Bette, K.-H., & Schimank, U. (2006). *Die Dopingfalle: Soziologische Betrachtungen*. Bielefeld: Transcript Verlag.

Bojsen-Møller, J., & Christiansen, A. V. (2010). Use of performance- and image-enhancing substances among recreational athletes: A quantitative analysis of inquiries submitted to the Danish anti-doping authorities. *Scandinavian Journal of Medicine and Science in Sports, 20* (6), 861–867. doi:10.1111/j.1600-0838.2009.01023.x.

Breuer, C., & Hallmann, K. (2013). *Dysfunktionen des Spitzensports: Doping, Match-Fixing und Gesundheitsgefährdungen aus Sicht von Bevölkerung und Athleten*. Bonn: Bundesinstitut für Sportwissenschaft.

Dietz, P., Ulrich, R., Dalaker, R., Striegel, H., Franke, A. G., Lieb, K., et al. (2013). Associations between physical and cognitive doping—A cross-sectional study in 2.997 triathletes, *PLoS ONE, 8*(11): e78702. doi:10.1371/journal.pone.0078702.

Donovan, R., Egger, G., Kapernick, V., & Mendoza, J. (2002). A conceptual framework for achieving performance enhancing drug compliance in sport. *Sports Medicine, 32*(4), 269–284.

Dreiskämper, D. (2014). *Die Vertrauenswürdigkeit der Anti-Doping Arbeit von Sportverbänden*. Dissertation. Münster: WWU Münster.

Haug, T. (2006). *Dilemma des Leistungssports*. Hamburg: merus Verlag.

Hutchins, B. (2011). The acceleration of media sport culture: Twitter, telepresence and online messaging. *Information Communication and Society, 14*(2), 237–257.

Kayser, B., Mauron, A., & Miah, A. (2007). Current anti-doping policy: A critical appraisal. *BMC Medical Ethics, 8*(1), 2.

Krüger, M., Becker, C., Nielsen, S., & Reinold, M. (2014). *Doping und Anti-Doping in der Bundesrepublik Deutschland 1950 bis 2007. Genese—Strukturen—Politik*. Hildesheim: Arete.

Luhmann, N. (1979). *Trust and power*. Chichster: Wiley.

Mayer, R. C., Davis, J. H., & Schoorman, F. D. (1995). An integrative model of organizational trust. *The Academy of Management Review, 20*(3), 709–734. doi:10.5465/AMR.1995.9508080335.

Mazanov, J., & Huybers, T. (2010). An empirical model of athlete decisions to use performance-enhancing drugs: Qualitative evidence. *Qualitative Research in Sport and Exercise, 2*(3), 385–402. doi:10.1080/19398441.2010.517046.

Mazanov, J., Petróczi, A., Bingham, J., & Holloway, A. (2008). Towards an empirical model of performance enhancing supplement use: A pilot study among high performance UK athletes. *Journal of Science and Medicine in Sport, 11*, 185–190. doi:10.1016/j.jsams.2007.01.003.

Meinberg, E. (2010). Vertrauen im Sport. In M. Schweer (Ed.), *Vertrauensforschung 2010: A state of the art* (pp. 191–206). Frankfurt am Main: Peter Lang.

Pawlenka, C. (2012). Ethik, Natur und Doping im Sport. *Sportwissenschaft, 42*(1), 6–16. doi:10.1007/s12662-011-0223-7.

Petróczi, A. (2007). Attitudes and doping: A structural equation analysis of the relationship between athletes' attitudes, sport orientation and doping behaviour. *Substance Abuse Treatment, Prevention, and Policy, 2*, 2–34. doi:10.1186/1747-597x-2-34.

Petróczi, A., & Aidman, E. (2008). Psychological drivers in doping: The life-cycle model of performance enhancement. *Substance Abuse Treatment, Prevention, and Policy, 3*, 3–7. doi:10.1186/1747-597x-3-7.

Petróczi, A., Mazanov, J., & Naughton, D. P. (2011). Inside athletes' minds: preliminary results from a pilot study on mental representation of doping and potential implications for anti-doping. *Substance Abuse Treatment, Prevention, and Policy, 6*(10), 1–8. doi:10.1186/1747-597X-6-10.

Pitsch, W., & Emrich, E. (2012). The frequency of doping in elite sport: Results of a replication study. *International Review for the Sociology of Sport, 47*(5), 559–580.

Pitsch, W., Emrich, E., & Klein, M. (2007). Doping in elite sports in Germany: Results of a www survey. *European Journal of Sport & Society, 4*(2), 89–102.

Pöppel, K., Dreiskämper, D., Dreiskämper, D., & Hoof, M. (2014). "Ich bin sauber"!?!—Die Wirkung von Anti-Doping Statements in Abhängigkeit vom Medienkanal über den sie verbreitet werden. In R. Frank, I. Nixdorf, F. Ehrlenspiel, et al. (Eds.), *Performing under pressure* (p. 194). Hamburg: Feldhaus Edition Czwalina.

Rotter, J. B. (1967). A new scale for the measurement of interpersonal trust. *Journal of personality, 35*(4), 651–665. doi:10.1111/j.1467-6494.1967.tb01454.x.

Rousseau, D. M., Sitkin, S. B., Burt, R. S., & Camerer, C. (1998). Not so different at all: A cross-discipline view of trust. *Academy of Management Review, 23*(3), 393–404.

Sanderson, J., & Hambrick, M. E. (2012). Covering the scandal in 140 characters: A case study of Twitter's role in coverage of the Penn State saga. *International Journal of Sport Communication, 5*(3), 384–402.

Schoorman, F. D., Mayer, R. C., & Davis, J. H. (2007). An integrative model of organizational trust: Past, present, and future. *Academy of Management Review, 32*(2), 344–354. doi:10.5465/amr.2007.24348410.

Strelan, P., & Boeckmann, R. J. (2003). Research notes: A new model for understanding performance-enhancing drug use by elite athletes. *Journal of Applied Sport Psychology, 15* (2), 176–183. doi:10.1080/10413200390213795.

Wallace, L., Wilson, J., & Miloch, K. (2011). Sporting Facebook: A content analysis of NCAA organizational sport pages and Big 12 Conference Athletic Department pages. *International Journal of Sport Communication, 4*(4), 422–444.

World Anti-Doping Agency. (2009). *World anti-doping code.* http://www.wada-ama.org/World-Anti-Doping-Program/Sports-and-Anti-Doping-Organizations/The-Code/. Accessed 28 July 2014.

World Anti-Doping Agency. (2014). *2013 anti-doping testing figures—Laboratory report.* http://www.wada-ama.org/en/Resources/Testing-Figures/. Accessed 28 July 2014.

World Anti-Doping Agency. (2015). *World anti-doping code.* https://wada-main-prod.s3.amazonaws.com/resources/files/wada-2015-world-anti-doping-code.pdf. Accessed 28 July 2014.

Trust in Science and the Science of Trust

Friederike Hendriks, Dorothe Kienhues, and Rainer Bromme

Abstract When risky technologies are debated in the media or when cases of scientific misconduct are made public, inevitable discussions arise about public loss of trust in science. However, trust in science reaches far beyond such incidents: trust is of much more fundamental importance for science. Clearly, trust is pivotal in *doing* science, since researchers in their everyday practice rely on the knowledge produced by other experts with different specialization and expertise. In the same way, trust is fundamental for the public *understanding* of science. Laypeople depend on the knowledge of scientific experts when developing a personal stance on science-based issues and arriving at decisions about them. Laypeople only possess a bounded understanding of science, but nowadays they are able to rapidly access all kinds of scientific knowledge online. To deal with scientific information, laypeople have to trust in scientists and their findings. We will at first describe the role of trust in doing and understanding science. Then a summary of international survey results on the general public's trust in science are presented. Starting from these results and questions that arise from them, we extend and revise past conceptualizations of trust, arriving at a conceptualization of *epistemic trust*. Epistemic trust rests not only on the assumption that one is *dependent* on the knowledge of others who are more knowledgeable; it also entails a *vigilance* toward the risk to be misinformed. Drawing on empirical findings, we argue that the critical characteristics that determine the epistemic trustworthiness of a source of science-based information (for example, a scientist or a scientific institution) are the source's expertise, integrity and benevolence. These characteristics have already been described in the model of trust provided by Mayer et al. (1995), but when it comes to trust in context of science, they must be redefined. Furthermore, trust judgments are not based solely on these characteristics, but depend on further constrains, which will be discussed in this chapter.

Keywords Epistemic trust • Trust in science • Trust • Public understanding of science • Science communication • Division of cognitive labor

F. Hendriks (✉) • D. Kienhues • R. Bromme
University of Münster, Münster, Germany
e-mail: f.hendriks@uni-muenster.de; kienhues@uni-muenster.de; bromme@uni-muenster.de

© Springer International Publishing Switzerland 2016   143
B. Blöbaum (ed.), *Trust and Communication in a Digitized World*, Progress in IS,
DOI 10.1007/978-3-319-28059-2_8

1   Introduction

Public loss of trust in science is a topic of much discussion, especially when scientific misconduct becomes evident. For example in 2011, Diederik Stapel was suspended from Tilburg University after it became known that he had manipulated data and faked the results of various experiments. Investigations brought to light that more than 30 publications were based on fraudulent data, a misdemeanor he has since admitted (Stapel 2012). His legal case received considerable attention, leading to a discussion about the effects that fraud in science might have on public trust in science. Confronted with news about plagiarism or manipulation of data, it becomes obvious for the public that the everyday practice of scientific work and science communication is based on trust (Vetenskap and Allmanhet 2015).

But trust is not only an issue when researchers abandon the rules of scientific conduct (for example, by deliberately faking scientific results). Such cases are actually exceptional. In reality, trust is inevitable and essential for scientists for doing science (trust *within* science) as well as for the general public dealing with science-related topics in their everyday life. In other words, trust is critical for 'insiders' as well as 'outsiders' (Feinstein 2011).

In the following chapter, we will at first elaborate why trust is essential in the context of science and why it is therefore an important topic for empirical research about science and its public understanding. Second, we will provide an overview about the state of public trust in science as it has been depicted in surveys on public attitudes toward science. Referring to these findings, we will then discuss the specificities of 'trust' in the context of public understanding of science. In doing so, we will start from the same general understanding of trust as it applies to trust research in other domains and, henceforth, as most of the other chapters in this volume. We will then specify and extend this research toward epistemic trust as conceptual framework and point to the special importance of epistemic trust in a digitized knowledge society.

2   Why Trust is Essential in the Context of Science

'Trust' is most typically ascribed as a kind of assumption about others. Whenever people are dependent on agents (persons, organizations) and whenever they are willing to accept the risks that come along with this dependency, they put trust into these agents (the trustees) (see Blöbaum 2016). This general notion of trust implies that there are degrees of freedom for the trustor (for example he/she does not have to purchase products offered by the trustee) and that there is some risk that he/she cannot control (for example, the trustor cannot be sure if the product works as promised, and if the product fails, this would be detrimental according to the goals of the trustor). This has been described as the willingness to be *vulnerable* to another person (e.g., Mayer et al. 1995). However, this core idea of 'trust' has to be refined and specified when it comes to knowledge. In this case, the goods that the trustee provides to the trustor is 'knowledge', and the risk to the trustor is his/her vulnerability to a *lack of truth* or *validity* of that knowledge.

The Paradox of Trust in Science Trust in Science[1] does address a paradox, as Science has evolved as a means to question and readdress established 'facts'. As such, the very idea of modern Science is to know the truth instead of just trusting what you are told. This is based on the enlightenment idea that everybody should be able to overcome the vulnerability of not being told 'the truth' by empowering their own capabilities to think and to know. The emergence of modern Science in the sixteenth century was based on the idea that the truth of knowledge could be established by epistemic acts (by seeing, hearing, or providing correct impressions about nature) and by rational conclusions based on such impressions. Thus, Science is no longer based on the faith in assertions that have been put forward by authorities. As mentioned by Sperber et al., "Historically, this individualistic stance could be seen as a reaction against the pervasive role in Scholasticism of arguments from authority" (2010, p. 361). Understanding and doing Science is a way of *controlling* the risk of not getting 'the truth'.

Referring back to the core notion of trust described above, this might at first glance imply that trust conflicts with Science. The legacy of modern Science, as a way of knowing and learning about the world that does not rely on trust, might be the reason why many seminal accounts on the philosophy of Science even do not mention the concept of trust at all. Only a small group of philosophers and historians of Science have emphasized the role of trust in Science, mostly on how it relates to doing Science and on communication among scientists (to a lesser degree on Science communication with the public). For example, in his seminal paper, Hardwig (1991) points to some proofs in modern mathematics that cannot be checked personally by most mathematicians. Thus, they must trust the claims of those who have processed the proofs. Obviously, interdisciplinary work is deeply reliant on cooperation and trust between experts of different knowledge areas (Origgi 2010; Whyte and Crease 2010; Wilholt 2013). Even within the same research team, trust in the knowledge of others is essential for everyday scientific practice. "Whenever the relevant evidence becomes too extensive or too complex for any one person to gather it all" (Hardwig 1991, p. 698), it is more advantageous to rely on the testimony of others than on one's own empirical evidence (Chinn et al. 2011).

The Division of Cognitive Labor The perpetual construction of new knowledge and the discovery of new scientific phenomena leads not only to individuals gaining

---

[1] 'Science' is a notion for a cognitive as well as a concrete social endeavor. The notion of Science is used to refer to distinguished bodies of knowledge (Science in a cognitive sense) as well as to abstractly refer to the institutions and people who are producing and maintaining these bodies of knowledge (Science in a social sense, see also Longino 2002). In order to emphasize that both meanings are covered, when not specified otherwise, we use a capital S.

ever more specialized expertise, but it also transforms scientific disciplines as new sub-disciplines evolve. The need for trust within as well as in Science is an immediate result of the specialization of knowledge (areas) (Barber 1987; Rolin 2002). Insofar, the constitutive role of *trust* for doing, using and understanding Science follows immediately from the division of cognitive labor (Bromme et al. 2010; Bromme and Thomm 2015; Keil 2010; Keil et al. 2008). Theoretical approaches on trust in Science point out that trust is a constituent for our contemporary society in which specialization and complexity are ubiquitous (Barber 1987; Rolin 2002). However, the body of scientific knowledge is not the only thing that is continuously growing: so is the public's need for information about scientific topics. For example, in the realm of citizenship the public is continuously challenged to form opinions about Science related issues (e.g., "do I oppose nuclear energy?") or even act upon those opinions (e.g., "should I then invest in solar power for my personal home").

The Complexity of Scientific Knowledge As mentioned above, trust is not only essential for scientists (trust *within* Science), but also and even more so for the general public, the 'outsiders' (trust *in* Science). The emergence of Science in modern history has also been a history of separating a scientific understanding from an everyday understanding of the world (Wolpert 1992). Scientific knowledge has become more and more abstract, tied to cognitive artifacts (like mathematical models) and technological tools (like microscopes, MRT devices) for the production of data (Daston and Galison 2007). The division of cognitive labor between scientists and the general public raises boundaries for the *Public Understanding of Science* (Bromme and Goldman 2014). Most scientific phenomena defy firsthand experience, as observation is impossible (e.g., oxygen, electrons, genes) without means that are only accessible to scientists. Furthermore, fully comprehending information about such phenomena does require specialized knowledge possessed by only a few experts (e.g., understanding why oxygen is existential in some concentrations but toxic in others). Also many topics of everyday interest to the public ('socio-scientific' topics) cannot be fully understood without deep scientific knowledge. Consider discussions about nuclear energy, climate change or stem cells, to name just a few. Most people possess only a bounded understanding of the underlying Science of such topics (while political or social consequences may be more easily accessible to them). Thus, we can conclude from the division of cognitive labor, going hand in hand with the complexity of our knowledge society, that a full Public *Understanding* of Science is unfeasible. Instead, a public trust in Science is essential.

Easy Access to Science-Related Information in Digitized Societies The need for trust in Science has increased because of digitalization (especially the Internet). Nowadays, people in many countries (except those in which economical, educational or political conditions prevent it) have easy access to scientific information via the Internet. Young people especially search online to find out about scientific issues and research information (Anderson et al. 2010). In the U.S. in 2012 (Besley 2014), around 42 % of survey respondents mentioned that the Internet is their primary source of information about Science and technology, replacing the TV, which was only named by 32 % of respondents. Of all the respondents that named the Internet as their number one source of science-based information, 63 % said that they actually read online newspapers, while less than 10 % mentioned blogs. When searching for information about specific scientific issues, 63 % of Americans make use of online sources (Besley 2014). The *Wellcome Trust Monitor* found that in the United Kingdom, 63 % of adults and 67 % of young people choose to search the Internet when they were actively looking for scientific information (Wellcome Trust 2013). In all of Europe, similar results are found (European Commission 2013). This concurs with a disintermediation through digital technologies (Eysenbach 2008)—as opposed to in traditional news media, there are far fewer gatekeepers, like journalists or editors, online. This is due to very low costs of publishing and lack of quality control when compared to traditional publications, which employ peer review (Eysenbach 2008). Hence, recipients must take it upon themselves to gather and evaluate information about a (scientific) topic. One can imagine that finding reliable information is difficult when considering thousands of potentially relevant websites that are published by an equally great number of sources of varying trustworthiness. Consequently, for laypeople in a digitized world who are confronted with an overwhelming amount of information, it is essential that they are able to judge whom to believe. That is, judgments about who is a trustworthy source of information and who may provide relevant information about an issue are crucial (Bromme et al. 2010; Bromme et al. 2015; Hendriks et al. 2015a).

3   How much does the Public Trust Science?

As argued above, a full *understanding* of even of those segments of scientific knowledge that are relevant for our lives is unfeasible. In consequence, it is crucial that the public *trusts* Science. In fact, various representative research attempts that claim to study the general Public's *Understanding* of Science focus instead on attitudes, behaviors and activities of the general public—these issues are more closely related to people's trust in rather than their understanding of Science.

Therefore, in the following section we will overview such recent representative survey studies, as they give various hints about how much the public trusts Science. We took the liberty to subsume all items (printed in italics) that point to public trust in Science, and subdivided these topic into items that focus on the public's *general appreciation of Science*, *general trust in Science*, and *trust in Science in the context of specific topics*. We chose surveys from the U.S. and from several European countries (see appendix for detailed survey information). Data on the U.S. public's views on Science are presented in the National Science Board's report on attitudes about Science and technology in its *Science and Engineering Indicators* (Besley 2014) and in the Pew Research Center's survey on *Public and Scientist's Views on Science and Society* (Pew Research Center 2015). Data from representative samples of all 27 European Union member states are provided by a *Special Eurobarometer*: *Responsible Research and Innovation (RRI), Science and Technology* (European Commission 2013). Furthermore, we include three European national surveys, the Ipsos Mori *Public Attitudes to Science* survey from the United Kingdom (Castell et al. 2014), the German *Wissenschaftsbarometer* (Wissenschaft im Dialog [WiD] 2014) and the Swedish *VA Barometer* (Vetenskap and Allmanhet 2015).

The General Appreciation of Science In all surveys, when asked about the outcomes of Science, the public holds a rather positive and optimistic view about Science in general. Respondents of all surveys mostly agree with the statement *science makes life easier*: namely, 79 % of American (Pew Research Center 2015), 81 % of British (Castell et al. 2014), 66 % of European (asked does science make life easier, more comfortable and healthier) (European Commission 2013) and 74 % of Swedish (asked if *scientific developments in the last 10–20 years have made life easier for ordinary people*) respondents agree (Vetenskap and Allmanhet 2015). Moreover, most Americans (90 %) have a great deal or some *confidence in the leaders of the scientific community*; only the military is trusted more (Besley 2014). In addition, 70 % of Americans (Besley 2014) and 55 % of British (Castell et al. 2014) respondents agree that the benefits of science outweigh the harmful effects. The German *Wissenschaftsbarometer* (Wissenschaft im Dialog [WiD] 2014) asked if *science is more harmful than beneficial*, and 68 % of respondents reject the statement. Furthermore, 77 % of Europeans agree that *science has a positive influence on society*, and among them 17 % regard the influence as very positive. In contrast, only 10 % of respondents to this question think that science has a negative impact on society (European Commission 2013). In the United Kingdom, 90 % of respondents agree (among them, 46 % strongly agree) that *scientists make a valuable contribution to society* (Castell et al. 2014).

Also, regarding scientists and their actions within the realm of Science, it seems that that the public mainly perceives scientists to have good intentions. In the U.S., 86 % of respondents think that *scientists work for the good of humanity* and the same amount of respondents thinks that *scientists work on things that will make life better for the average person* (Besley 2014). In Europe, 82 % of respondents think that *scientists working at a university behave responsibly toward society by paying attention to the impact of their science or technology related activities*. Only 66 % of respondents agreed with this statement when it concerned scientists working in private company laboratories (European Commission 2013). In the United Kingdom, scientists' intentions are judged with a bit more reservation. Of respondents, 83 % agree (among them, 27 % strongly agree) that *scientists want to make life better for the average person*. However, 27 % of respondents agree with the statement that *science benefits the rich more than the poor*. Still, 48 % of respondents disagree with this statement (Castell et al. 2014).

General Trust in Science In current surveys, only a few items focus directly on the trust people put in scientific knowledge claims. For example, 52 % of British respondents agree that the *information they hear about science is generally true*, elaborating that they had no reason to doubt it (40 %) or that they believed other scientists had checked it (15 %). Regarding scientists' assumed competence, in the *Eurobarometer* survey, 66 % of respondents agree that *university scientists are qualified to give explanations about the impact of scientific and technological developments on society*, outdoing all other groups. In contrast, scientists working in private company laboratories are regarded to be qualified in this regard by only 35 % of respondents (European Commission 2013). Also, there are some data suggesting that respondents not only regard scientists to be able to inform and advise society, but also that they have the integrity to make truthful claims. Regarding the attitudes of the public about the honesty, ethicality and integrity of scientists, only data from Europe are available. In the *Eurobarometer*, 54 % of respondents are concerned that the *application of science and technology can threaten human rights* and 61 % think that *researchers should not be allowed to violate fundamental rights and moral principles to make new discovery*; conversely, 29 % believe that *researchers should be allowed to do this in some special cases*. In addition, 84 % of respondents believe that all *researchers should receive mandatory trainings on scientific research ethics* (like privacy, animal welfare, etc.) and 81 % agree that *scientists should be obliged to declare possible conflicts of interest, such as sources of funding, when advising for public authorities* (European Commission 2013). In the United Kingdom, respondents are mostly convinced that they can *trust university scientists and researchers from university to follow the rules and regulations of their profession* (90 % agreement); again, respondents agreed with this the most for university scientists and researchers compared to all other groups. For example, only 60 % of respondents agree that scientists working for private companies follow the rules and regulations of their professions. Furthermore, *scientists are* regarded to be *honest* by 71 % of British respondents. However, when asked if *scientists adjust their findings to get the answers they want*, 35 % of British respondents agree, while 34 % disagree (Castell et al. 2014).

By large, the public seems to be very positive about the benefits that Science has to offer society, and, related to these expectations, the public mostly trust scientists to produce reliable knowledge of good quality, not biased and adhering to scientific principles. But this is not blind trust, as answers also reflect a kind of suspicion about vested interests when research is funded by private companies [these findings are in line with earlier work by Critchley (2008)]. Furthermore, relevant proportions of the public take into account that scientists might not adhere to the standards of objectivity.

Trust in Science in the Context of Specific Topics In contrast to its generally fairly trustful view of Science, when specific topics are considered, the public varies widely in its amount of trust in Science: The National Science Board's *Science and*

Engineering Indicators show that 25 % of respondents consider *genetically modified foods* to be very or extremely dangerous, and 57 % are in favor or strongly in favor of nuclear energy. In the U.S., *nanotechnology* is not very controversial, as only 11 % of respondents think the *harms outweigh positive benefits*, while 43 % hold no opinion (Besley 2014). The Pew Research Center's survey also shows that U.S. adults are skeptical towards some scientific topics. For example, only 37 % of respondents agree it is *safe to eat genetically modified foods*, and only 28 % think it is *safe to eat food grown with pesticides*. Also in this survey, 50 % of U.S. adults agree that *climate change is due to human activity*, 68 % favor the use of *bioengineered fuel* and 45 % favor *nuclear power plants*. In spite of this, 79 % of U.S. adults agree that *science has a positive impact on the quality of health care*, 62 % *believe in science's positive effect on food* (Pew Research Center 2015). While the Eurobarometer holds no data on specific scientific topics, other data from Europe can provide some insights. In the United Kingdom's *Ipsos Mori* survey, again it is reported that for specific scientific topics, the public's trust is inconsistent. Asked, if the *benefits outweigh the risks*, 84 % agree regarded benefits to be dominant for *vaccination* and 66 % of respondents agreed the same thing for *renewable energy*. Also, 57 % of the questioned British adults agree that benefits outweigh the harms regarding *stem cell research* while only 38 % agree to this for *nanotechnology*. For only a few topics, more than 10 % agree that the harms actually outweigh the benefits. For example, regarding *nuclear power*, 28 % agree that the harms outweigh the benefits, while 48 % agree that the benefits outweigh the harms. For *genetically modified crops*, 28 % see the harms to be dominant, while 36 % believe the benefits outweigh the harms (Castell et al. 2014). In the German *Wissenschaftsbarometer*, respondents were asked how much they trust scientists' statements regarding specific scientific topics. For statements *regarding renewable energies*, 44 % of participants have trustful attitudes, and for statements *regarding the genesis of the universe*, 40 % have trustful attitudes. Statements *regarding climate change* are trusted by 37 % of Germans, but for *genetically modified crops*, only 16 % of participants regard such scientific statements as trustworthy (Wissenschaft im Dialog [WiD] 2014).

Mingling Trust in Science and Personal Stances About Specific Topics The above-mentioned survey questions exemplify that the public seems to trust Science less when considering specific topics (nuclear energy, genetically modified food) then when asked about Science in general. This might be due to the following reasons:

Firstly, many of the survey questions confound the personal stance about a certain Science-based issue or development with the issue of trust in Science. For example, an item like: *"Do you think it is generally safe or unsafe to eat genetically modified foods?"* (Pew Research Center 2015, p. 92) is primarily an item on personal beliefs and positions about this kind of food. It does not distinctly measure the trust in the underlying Science, albeit this could also influence a participants' response. For teasing out both aspects, it is necessary to reflect on the difference between a personal position about a topic and personal trust in the Science that produces knowledge about that topic. For example, the recent German *Wissenschaftsbarometer* asked: *"How much do you trust statements of scientists regarding the topic renewable energies* [author's translation]" (Wissenschaft im Dialog [WiD] 2014, p. 14). The only way to view participants' responses as a statement about their trust or distrust in the scientific knowledge on this topic would be if Science has provided a clear answer about this topic.

Secondly, typically surveys only focus on science- or technology-related topics that are of public interest, and, as a result, these topics are controversially discussed in the mass media. Participants' responses might then reflect their degree of awareness about the very fact *that* a topic is controversial, and this might be confounded with their personal stance on the topic and the underlying Science. We have doubts that this kind of confounding can be prevented by using the following type of statement: *"From what you know or have heard about renewable energy, which of these statements, if any, most closely reflects your own opinion?— saying benefits outweigh the risks/saying risks outweigh the benefits"* (Castell et al. 2014, p. 35).

Both of the above reasons for why the public's has a high general level of 'default' trust in Science yet displays much more varied trust when considering specific topics (including clear distrust by some subsamples) not only point to methodological challenges of survey research, they also imply that trust in Science is inherently 'confounded' with people's perspectives on the topic of interest: When a science-related topic is of interest for segments of the public, then these sub-populations develop personal stances related to this topic. These stances thereby modify their 'default' trust in Science. In other words, trust in Science develops and changes in light of the public's views about specific scientific topics.

4   From Trust to Epistemic Trust

Science (and science-based technology) is essential for life in modern societies, and trust is an essential component of how the public copes with Science; consequently, many recent representative surveys have tackled this topic. However, we have also described that there is some tension between trust and the core idea that Science is a means for freeing people from only relying on authorities to understand the world. In the beginning of this chapter, we had already emphasized that, when it comes to Science, the goods that are provided by the trustee to the trustor is 'knowledge', and the risk to the trustor is that he/she is vulnerable to a *lack of truth* or *validity* of that knowledge. In the following section, we will aim for a theoretical elaboration of what we will call 'epistemic trust', starting with the influential Integrative Model of Organizational Trust (Mayer et al. 1995), which is also discussed in most of the other chapters of this volume. From this, we will develop a definition of epistemic trust, which draws on the work of Origgi (2004, 2014) and Sperber et al. (2010).

Trust: A Rough Approximation Trust is defined by a dependence of a trusting actor on the trusted person or entity (Tseng and Fogg 1999) combined with a vulnerability to risk (Mayer et al. 1995). In consequence, the question of what makes a person (the *trustee*) trustworthy to an interlocutor (the *trustor*) arises. Aristotle defined the following three major character properties a person should possess to be persuasive: "(1) practical intelligence [. . .], (2) a virtuous character, and (3) good will" (Rapp 2010). Later, Mayer et al. (1995) summarized the literature on constituents of interpersonal trust and the extensive work on the credibility of sources (e.g., Hovland et al. 1953) and also arrived at three components that are believed to make up the trustworthiness of a trustee: A trustee should possess (1) ability, the domain-specific skills and competencies that enable the trustee to have influence within the same domain, (2) benevolence, which describes her acting independently from an egocentric profit motive and in a beneficial interest for the trustor, and (3) integrity, i.e., she should act according to a set of rules or principles acceptable to the trustor. According to the seminal model (Mayer et al. 1995), the three dimensions are related but separable. Furthermore, the trustee isn't the only one who must possess certain characteristics; in order to give trust, the trustor must hold an attitude of a general willingness to trust others, a propensity to trust.

Epistemic Trust In the following section, we will use the term 'epistemic trust' to describe the trust in knowledge that has been produced or provided by scientists. Such epistemic trust is unavoidably needed to gain knowledge (Resnik 2011; Sperber et al. 2010). If someone doesn't have the chance to sense or learn something first-hand, she must defer to the testimony of first-hand sources (Hardwig 1991; Harris 2012; Schwab 2008).

Along these lines, researchers in developmental psychology have proposed that children are very good at identifying whom to trust for gathering knowledge (Harris 2012; Keil et al. 2008; Mills 2013). We have the best evidence for the characteristic of knowledgeability (or expertise) being a main constituent of how young children's trust in sources of knowledge. For example, when learning new object names, 3-year-olds prefer informants who have previously displayed accuracy in naming objects (Koenig and Harris 2008). By the age of four, children remember previously accurate informants and prefer to trust them over inaccurate, but familiar, informants (Corriveau and Harris 2009). Children are also sensitive to a source's benevolence: At the age of four, children can infer the intent of an informant either from behavior of informants or from being told of their moral character (Mascaro and Sperber 2009), and they place selective trust in the most benevolent sources. Thus, young children use informant expertise as well as helpfulness to make trustworthiness judgments (Shafto et al. 2012), and sometimes the benevolence of an informant even supersedes her expertise (Landrum et al. 2013). Furthermore, when deciding whom to trust, kindergarteners take into consideration an informant's self-interest (Mills and Keil 2005). In addition, recent studies show that children as young as four take informant honesty (referring to a source's integrity) into consideration when deciding to trust an information source (Lane et al. 2013; Vanderbilt et al. 2012).

In the same vein, when it comes to adults and their trust in Science, placing epistemic trust in someone means trusting her as a provider of information (Wilholt 2013). To minimize the risk of receiving wrong information, epistemic trust relies on evidence that an interlocutor is trustworthy (Resnik 2011) and on some vigilance to avoid the risk of being misinformed or cheated (Sperber et al. 2010). Hence, the notion of epistemic trust is not built on receivers who uncritically accept the authority of experts. In her work on the relations between epistemology and trust, Origgi (2004, 2012) argued that epistemic trust entails (1) a *default trust*, meaning that people are generally trustful to others as a predisposition for communication and cooperation, laying the groundwork for people to defer to the knowledge of others, and (2) *vigilant trust,* which includes cognitive mechanisms that allow people to make rather fine-grained ascriptions of trustworthiness before accepting what others say. From Mayer et al. (1995) as well as from the children's trust in sources of knowledge, we can identify which features of a trustee (the source of science-related information) might be processed within such cognitive mechanisms, leading to the ascription of trustworthiness. But the Mayer et al. (1995) model only roughly specifies these features. Thus, for a conceptual and an empirical analysis of the emergence of trust in Science and its communication, we must reconsider and specify these features. As has been argued before, laypeople might take into account an expert's expertise, benevolence and integrity while deciding if to believe his/her statements on a science-related issue.

Thus, these components describe the features of experts that determine whether recipients will depend on and defer to them when the recipients' own resources are limited: First, a layperson should trust someone who is an expert because she is knowledgeable (Lane et al. 2014); she possesses *expertise*. Expertise refers to someone's amount of knowledge and skill, but more than just the sheer quantities of knowledge and skill is important: the person must also have the relevant expertise. In other words, the dimension of expertise also encompasses the aspect of pertinence (Bromme and Thomm 2015). Second, an expert should be trusted when a layperson believes her to have a reliable belief-forming process (Schwab 2008; Wilholt 2013) and to follow the rules of her profession (Barber 1987; Cummings 2014). These factors make up her perceived *integrity*. Third, an expert is considered trustworthy if she offers advice or positive applications for the trustor or (more generally) for the good of society (Resnik 2011; Whyte and Crease 2010); that is, she must act with *benevolence*. Furthermore, when a layperson considers trusting an expert, a person's propensity to trust can be equally assumed. One may assume that people who display a high trust in Science may be more prone to rely on experts when finding out about a science-related issue (Anderson et al. 2011).

It is quite important for recipients not only to be able to identify speakers that actually possess relevant expertise, but also to critically judge the intentions of such speakers. In other words, recipients must be able to vigilantly identify sources whose intentions might lead to a loss of benevolence or of integrity. For example, due to vested interests, scientific evidence might be distorted by pseudo-evidence produced by industry or policy stakeholders (e.g., evidence about smoking and climate change, Lewandowsky et al. 2012). From this, we can conclude that trust in scientists is not only based on features that are indicative of the epistemic quality of their work (in a narrow sense with regard to the use of reliable processes of knowledge acquisition), but also their moral integrity (Barber 1987; Hardwig 1991) as well as the usefulness of their work for the benefit of society (Resnik 2011).

Some empirical evidence supports that these three dimensions—expertise, integrity, and benevolence—also come into play for adults' trust in knowledge that has been produced or provided by scientists. In three studies, we have shown with factor-analysis (exploratory and confirmatory) that when laypeople judge the epistemic trustworthiness of scientists that are providing science-based information, they indeed assess the scientists' expertise, integrity, and benevolence (Hendriks et al. 2015a). Furthermore, in an experimental study where we varied (fictitious) scientists' characteristics relating to those three dimensions, we showed that when making these epistemic trustworthiness judgements, laypeople consider all three of these dimensions in a differentiated way, again indicating that the dimensions are, albeit interrelated, clearly distinct from each other (Hendriks et al. 2015a).

Also, qualitative data show that when laypeople are asked to make trust evaluations about a scientific expert, they spontaneously report the scientist's expertise, objectivity or work ethic, and potential interests that stand in conflict with the public (Cummings 2014). Furthermore, Peters et al. (1997) showed that when risks are communicated to the public, laypeople again consider an organizations expertise, integrity and benevolence. They also found that laypeople's trustworthiness judgments about the industry (which is believed to care only about profits, but not about public welfare) improves the most when the industry gives off an impression of concern and care about society; the same is true for citizen organizations that give off an impression of competence and knowledgeability. Thus, laypeople seem to be especially vigilant when the trustee defies the trustor's expectations (in this special case, the negative stereotypes). This study shows that giving epistemic trust is not only based on the characteristics of the trustee (the source of the science-related information), but that these features are also weighed against the more general expectations a trustee has about a specific trustor. This is only one example of further conditions that constrain how source characteristics (expertise, integrity, and benevolence) affect judgments of epistemic trust. Expectations about a trustors' intentions are also highly relevant in Science communication.

There is some evidence that the way in which scientific results are communicated may matter for laypeople's assessment of a scientist's communicative intentions. In an experimental study, we investigated if trustworthiness perceptions were affected (a) if a flaw (in this case, an overestimation of a study's generalizability) was disclosed, and (b) who disclosed it (Hendriks et al. 2015b). We found that on the one hand, the participants discarded a scientists' expertise if a flaw was mentioned in a comment by an unaffiliated scientist (in contrast to no mention of the flaw). But on the other hand, the scientist's integrity and benevolence were rated higher when the scientist himself disclosed the flaw (in contrast to when it was disclosed by the unaffiliated scientist). With these results, we showed that a scientist's trustworthiness is judged in close relation to what evidence is known that speaks to the characteristics expertise, integrity and benevolence. By actively putting out such evidence (e.g., disclosing possible flaws themselves), scientists can improve the public's judgments of their trustworthiness. Related results have been found when scientists themselves (in contrast to scientists not affiliated with the research) seem to be responsible for the communication of caveats or uncertainties of their results (Jensen 2008).

Because the above-mentioned characteristics apply to judgments about an individual scientist as well as whole scientific organizations (for example, research institutes, universities or companies who do research; Peters et al. 1997), it may well be assumed that the perception of expertise, integrity and benevolence influences trust in Science in general.

Interestingly, Science is a social as well as a cognitive entity. Science as a social entity refers to the people who produce scientific insights (i.e., who do Science) and to the organizations they work for, while Science as a cognitive entity refers to the continuously developing body of knowledge that evolves from doing Science. As an immediate consequence of its dual entity, it is inevitable that the assumed trustworthiness *of* Science also depends on the public's appreciation of the knowledge claims that are produced *by* Science. In other words, the assumed trustworthiness of scientists depends on assumptions people already possess about what is true knowledge and the new knowledge scientists provide. While discussing the result from surveys that the public seems to be rather skeptical when it comes to trust in Science about specific topics, we have already pointed to the inherent confounding between people's personal stance against the topics which are researched and people's trust into the Science which provides new scientific insights about these topics.

This close entanglement between what is said (the content of Science) and who has said it (the producers of Science) requires us to suspend the categorical distinction between judgments about believability (of the knowledge claims provided by scientists) and trustworthiness (of the providing scientists). Of course, when researching public trust in Science it is possible to scrutinize what laypeople think about scientists, as well as what they think about the content of science-based assertions. However, it is very likely that the provided answers will mostly mingle both aspects, being determined by both. Given that modern sociology of Science also conceives the truth of scientific knowledge as being dependent on its underlying evidence as well as on the regulated discourse about this evidence (Longino 2002), the *public* might be on right track by considering both *what is said* with *who said it* when they place trust in Science.

Appendix

Table 1 Details about the surveys used for data on the public's trust in science and scientists

Region	Title of report	Sponsoring organization	Years of data collection	Respondents (n)	Representative
USA	In: Science and Engineering Indicators 2014, Besley 2014. *Science and Technology: Public Understanding of Science*	National Science Board	This overview presents data from numerous surveys. Unless otherwise stated, we use data from the General Social Survey's *Science and Technology Module* in 2012	1864–2256	Yes
USA	*Public and Scientist's Views on Science and Society*	Pew Research Center	2014	2002	Yes
Europe	Special Eurobarometer 401. *Responsible Research and Innovation (RRI), Science and Technology*	European Commission	2013	27,563 from 27 member states of the European Union (EU)	Yes
UK	*Public Attitudes to Science*	Ipsos MORI	2013	1749 adults and 315 young adults	Yes, weighted
UK	Wellcome Trust Monitor, *Engaging with science*	Ipsos MORI	2012	1396 adults (aged 18+) and 460 young people (aged 14–18)	Yes
Germany	*Wissenschaftsbarometer 2014*	Wissenschaft im Dialog (WiD)	2014	1004	Yes, weighted
Sweden	VA Barometer, *VA Report 2014:4*	Vetenskap and Allmänhet	2015	1000	Yes, weighted

References

Anderson, A. A., Brossard, D., & Scheufele, D. A. (2010). The changing information environment for nanotechnology: Online audiences and content. *Journal of Nanoparticle Research, 12*(4), 1083–1094. doi:10.1007/s11051-010-9860-2.

Anderson, A. A., Scheufele, D. A., Brossard, D., & Corley, E. A. (2011). The role of media and deference to scientific authority in cultivating trust in sources of information about emerging technologies. *International Journal of Public Opinion Research, 24*(2), 225–237. doi:10.1093/ijpor/edr032.

Barber, B. (1987). Trust in science. *Minerva, 25*(1–2), 123–134. doi:10.1007/s11999-014-3488-y.

Besley, J. (2014). Science and technology: Public attitudes and understanding. In National Science Board (Ed.), *Science and engineering indicators 2014* (pp. 1–53). Arlington, VA: National Science Foundation (NSB 14–01).

Blöbaum, B. (2016). Key factors in the process of trust. On the analysis of trust under digital conditions. In B. Bloebaum (Ed.), *Trust and communication in a digitalized world. Models and concepts of trust research.* Berlin: Springer.

Bromme, R., & Goldman, S. R. (2014). The public's bounded understanding of science. *Educational Psychologist, 49*(2), 59–69. doi:10.1080/00461520.2014.921572.

Bromme, R., Kienhues, D., & Porsch, T. (2010). Who knows what and who can we believe? Epistemological beliefs are beliefs about knowledge (mostly) to be attained from others. In L. D. Bendixen & F. C. Feucht (Eds.), *Personal epistemology in the classroom: Theory, research, and implications for practice* (pp. 163–193). Cambrigde: Cambridge University Press.

Bromme, R., & Thomm, E. (2015). Knowing who knows: Laypersons' capabilities to judge experts' pertinence for science topics. *Cognitive Science,* 1–12. doi:10.1111/cogs.12252.

Bromme, R., Thomm, E., & Wolf, V. (2015). From understanding to deference: Laypersons' and medical students' views on conflicts within medicine. *International Journal of Science Education, Part B: Communication and Public Engagement.* doi:10.1080/21548455.2013.849017.

Castell, S., Charlton, A., Clemence, M., Pettigrew, N., Pope, S., Quigley, A., et al. (2014). *Public attitudes to science 2014. Ipsos Mori.* London. Retrieved from https://www.ipsos-mori.com/Assets/Docs/Polls/pas-2014-main-report.pdf

Chinn, C. A., Buckland, L. A., & Samarapungavan, A. (2011). Expanding the dimensions of epistemic cognition: Arguments from philosophy and psychology. *Educational Psychologist, 46*(3), 141–167. doi:10.1080/00461520.2011.587722.

Corriveau, K., & Harris, P. L. (2009). Choosing your informant: Weighing familiarity and recent accuracy. *Developmental Science, 12*(3), 426–37. doi:10.1111/j.1467-7687.2008.00792.x.

Critchley, C. R. (2008). Public opinion and trust in scientists: The role of the research context, and the perceived motivation of stem cell researchers. *Public Understanding of Science, 17*(3), 309–327. doi:10.1177/0963662506070162.

Cummings, L. (2014). The "trust" heuristic: Arguments from authority in public health. *Health Communication, 34*(1), 1–14. doi:10.1080/10410236.2013.831685.

Daston, L., & Galison, P. (2007). *Objectivity.* New York: Zone Books.

European Commission. (2013). *Eurobarometer.* Brussels. doi:10.4232/1.11873.

Eysenbach, G. (2008). Credibility of health information and digital media: New perspectives and implications for youth. In M. J. Metzger & A. J. Flanagin (Eds.), *Digital media, youth, and credibility* (The John D, pp. 123–154). Cambridge, MA: The MIT Press.

Feinstein, N. (2011). Salvaging science literacy. *Science Education, 95*(1), 168–185. doi:10.1002/sce.20414.

Hardwig, J. (1991). The role of trust in knowledge. *The Journal of Philosophy, 88*(12), 693–708.

Harris, P. L. (2012). *Trusting what you're told.* Cambridge, MA: Belknap of Harvard UP.

Hendriks, F., Kienhues, D., & Bromme, R. (2015a). Measuring laypeople's trust in experts in a digital age: The Muenster Epistemic Trustworthiness Inventory (METI). *PLoS ONE, 10*(10), e0139309. doi:10.1371/journal.pone.0139309.

Hendriks, F., Kienhues, D., & Bromme, R. (2015b). Disclose your flaws! Admission enhances perceptions of trustworthiness of an expert blogger. *Manuscript Submitted for Publication.*

Hovland, C. I., Janis, I. L., & Kelley, H. H. (1953). *Communication and persuasion. Psychological issues of opinion change.* New Haven: Yale University Press.

Jensen, J. D. (2008). Scientific uncertainty in news coverage of cancer research: Effects of hedging on scientists and journalists credibility. *Human Communication Research, 34*(3), 347–369. doi:10.1111/j.1468-2958.2008.00324.x.

Keil, F. C. (2010). The feasibility of folk science. *Cognitive Science, 34*(5), 826–862. doi:10.1111/j.1551-6709.2010.01108.x.

Keil, F. C., Stein, C., Webb, L., Billings, V. D., Rozenblit, L., & Sciences, B. (2008). Discerning the division of cognitive labor: An emerging understanding of how knowledge is clustered in other minds. *Cognitive Science, 32*(2), 259–300. doi:10.1080/03640210701863339.

Koenig, M. A., & Harris, P. L. (2008). The basis of epistemic trust: Reliable testimony or reliable sources? *Episteme, 4,* 264–284. doi:10.3366/E1742360008000087.

Landrum, A. R., Mills, C. M., & Johnston, A. M. (2013). When do children trust the expert? Benevolence information influences children's trust more than expertise. *Developmental Science, 16*(4), 622–638. doi:10.1111/desc.12059.

Lane, J. D., Harris, P. L., Gelman, S. A., & Wellman, H. M. (2014). More than meets the eye: Young children's trust in claims that defy their perceptions. *Developmental Psychology, 50*(3), 865–871. doi:10.1037/a0034291.

Lane, J. D., Wellman, H. M., & Gelman, S. A. (2013). Informants' traits weigh heavily in young children's trust in testimony and in their epistemic inferences. *Child Development, 84*(4), 1253–68. doi:10.1111/cdev.12029.

Lewandowsky, S., Ecker, U. K. H., Seifert, C. M., Schwarz, N., & Cook, J. (2012). Misinformation and its correction: Continued influence and successful debiasing. *Psychological Science in the Public Interest, 13*(3), 106–131. doi:10.1177/1529100612451018.

Longino, H. E. (2002). *The fate of knowledge.* Princeton, NJ: Princeton University Press.

Mascaro, O., & Sperber, D. (2009). The moral, epistemic, and mindreading components of children's vigilance towards deception. *Cognition, 112,* 367–380.

Mayer, R. C., Davis, J. H., & Schoorman, F. D. (1995). An integrative model of organizational trust. *The Academy of Management Review, 20*(3), 709–734.

Mills, C. M. (2013). Knowing when to doubt: Developing a critical stance when learning from others. *Developmental Psychology, 49*(3), 1–26. doi:10.1037/a0029500.Knowing.

Mills, C. M., & Keil, F. C. (2005). The development of cynicism. *Psychological Science, 16*(5), 385–390. doi:10.1111/j.0956-7976.2005.01545.x.

Origgi, G. (2004). Is trust an epistemological notion? *Episteme, 1*(1), 61–72. doi:10.3366/epi.2004.1.1.61.

Origgi, G. (2010). Epistemic vigilance and epistemic responsibility in the liquid world of scientific publications. *Social Epistemology, 24*(3), 149–159.

Origgi, G. (2012). Epistemic injustice and epistemic trust. *Social Epistemology, 26*(2), 221–235.

Origgi, G. (2014). Epistemic trust. In P. Capet & T. Delavallade (Eds.), *Information evaluation* (1st ed., pp. 35–54). London: Wiley-ISTE.

Peters, R. G., Covello, V. T., & McCallum, D. B. (1997). The determinants of trust and credibility in environmental risk communication: An empirical study. *Risk Analysis, 17*(1), 43–54. doi:10.1111/j.1539-6924.1997.tb00842.x.

Pew Research Center. (2015). *Public and scientists' views on science and society.*

Rapp, C. (2010). *Aristotle's rhetoric.* Retrieved from http://plato.stanford.edu/entries/aristotle-rhetoric/

Resnik, D. B. (2011). Scientific research and the public trust. *Science and Engineering Ethics, 17*(3), 399–409. doi:10.1007/s11948-010-9210-x.

Rolin, K. (2002). Gender and trust in science. *Hypathia, 17*(4).

Schwab, A. P. (2008). Epistemic trust, epistemic responsibility, and medical practice. *The Journal of Medicine and Philosophy, 33*(4), 302–20. doi:10.1093/jmp/jhn013.

Shafto, P., Eaves, B., Navarro, D. J., & Perfors, A. (2012). Epistemic trust: Modeling children's reasoning about others' knowledge and intent. *Developmental Science, 15*(3), 436–47. doi:10.1111/j.1467-7687.2012.01135.x.

Sperber, D., Clément, F., Heintz, C., Mascaro, O., Mercier, H., Origgi, G., et al. (2010). Epistemic vigilance. *Mind & Language, 25*(4), 359–393. doi:10.1111/j.1468-0017.2010.01394.x.

Stapel, D. (2012). *Ontsporing*. Amsterdam: Prometheus.

Tseng, S., & Fogg, B. (1999). Credibility and computing technology. *Communications of the ACM, 42*(5), 39–44.

Vetenskap and Allmanhet. (2015). *VA Barometer 2014/15*. Stockholm.

Vanderbilt, K. E., Liu, D., & Heyman, G. D. (2012). The development of distrust. *Child Development, 82*(5), 1372–1380. doi:10.1111/j.1467-8624.2011.01629.x.

Wellcome Trust. (2013). *Engaging with science. The Wellcome Trust Monitor*. Retrieved from http://www.wellcome.ac.uk/stellent/groups/corporatesite/@msh_grants/documents/web_docu ment/wtp052590.pdf

Whyte, K. P., & Crease, R. P. (2010). Trust, expertise, and the philosophy of science. *Synthese, 177*(3), 411–425. doi:10.1007/s11229-010-9786-3.

Wilholt, T. (2013). Epistemic trust in science. *The British Journal for the Philosophy of Science, 64*, 233–253. doi:10.1093/bjps/axs007.

Wissenschaft im Dialog. (WiD). (2014). *Wissenschaftsbarometer 2014*. Berlin.

Wolpert, L. (1992). *The unnatural nature of science*. Cambridge, MA: Harvard University Press. doi:10.1016/0140-6736(93)92665-G.

New Ways of Working: Chances and Challenges for Trust-Enhancing Leadership

Philipp Romeike, Christina Wohlers, Guido Hertel, and Gerhard Schewe

Abstract The continued rise of digitalization allows employees to be highly flexible regarding when and where to work, both inside and outside the traditional office, a trend captured in the term new ways of working (NWW). With NWW, increased employee flexibility changes the relationship between supervisor and employees, thereby posing both benefits and new challenges for leadership. For supervisors, NWW particularly complicate the nevertheless necessary task of exercising control over employees. In NWW supervisors often rely on electronic performance monitoring techniques as an alternative to traditional forms of supervisory control. Yet, since employees often perceive electronic monitoring as a signal of their supervisors' distrust, these new monitoring systems can harm the employee–supervisor relationship. At the same time, by accepting the control and monitoring behavior of their supervisors, employees can form high-quality relationships with supervisors, which can in turn translate into greater productivity and mutual trust. By more closely tracing this process, the present chapter investigates how supervisors in NWW can effectively supervise employees by maintaining control while still expressing trust.

Keywords New ways of working • Trust • Control • Electronic performance monitoring • Effective leadership

1 Introduction

During the past two decades, innovations in information and communication technology have severely altered and impacted working life. Today's organizations rely heavily on electronic communication technologies—for example, email, videoconferencing, and mobile devices—to enable more flexible work designs, thereby allowing employees to perform tasks independent of time and place while staying in touch with colleagues and supervisors. Such flexible work designs, which provide employees the autonomy to decide when and where to work, both

P. Romeike (✉) • C. Wohlers • G. Hertel • G. Schewe
University of Münster, Münster, Germany
e-mail: p.d.romeike@uni-muenster.de; christina.wohlers@uni-muenster.de; ghertel@uni-muenster.de; Gerhard.Schewe@wiwi.uni-muenster.de

© Springer International Publishing Switzerland 2016   161
B. Blöbaum (ed.), *Trust and Communication in a Digitized World*, Progress in IS,
DOI 10.1007/978-3-319-28059-2_9

outside and inside the office, all while connected via information and communication technology, can be encapsulated in the term new ways of working (NWW; Demerouti et al. 2014). In essence, any type of teleworking or activity-based flexible office exemplifies NWW (Appel-Meulenbroek et al. 2011; Demerouti et al. 2014). In a recent survey by the German Fraunhofer Institute for Industrial Engineering (IAO), the majority of office workers polled reported working autonomously, and about every fifth office worker indicated having no fixed workstation (i.e., no permanent assigned place for each individual) which has emerged as a central feature of activity-based flexible offices (Bauer 2014). By extension, more than half of the office workers surveyed claimed that they perceived temporal flexibility in their workplaces—that is, employees' capacity to decide when to work—while more than 80 % reported having individual autonomy in choosing how to pursue occupational goals and more than 40 % claimed having spatial autonomy, or the capacity to choose where to work.

For employees, NWW are thus clearly associated with a range of advantages, including increased autonomy. More autonomy can increase employees' job satisfaction (e.g., Baltes et al. 1999) and engagement in their work (e.g., Brummelhuis et al. 2012), as well as diminish work–family conflict (e.g., Byron 2005). Yet, NWW also pose new challenges for leadership. Giving employees autonomy to choose where and when they work impedes supervisors' exercise of control, traditionally viewed to be a core dimension of leadership (Fayol 1930; Scott 1987; Sitkin et al. 2010). Since supervisors depend on high-performing employees in order to ensure organizational success, exercising effective control over employees remains especially crucial in NWW. To maintain control despite spatial and temporal distance, supervisors in NWW primarily have to rely on electronic performance monitoring (EPM) techniques. However, employees may often perceive EPM as a sign of their supervisors' distrust (Stanton 2000a) and thus seek ways to evade such forms of control, which can in turn lessen their supervisors' trust in them. In time, a vicious circle of declining trust and increased reliance on EPM could therefore result. Yet, since trust is a prerequisite for the exchange of knowledge and ideas (Golden and Raghuram 2010; Levin and Cross 2004), its absence in knowledge-intensive settings such as NWW significantly threatens work performance. The question therefore becomes how supervisors can effectively monitor employees in ways that allow them to maintain control over employees without sacrificing their trust.

In response, in this chapter we begin by explaining the concept of NWW and focusing on activity-based flexible offices as one of its most important manifestations. We next discuss factors that drive the implementation of NWW by outlining the associated benefits of NWW for both organizations and employees. We then turn to address a major challenge in NWW—namely, the design and execution of effective methods of control that can at once cultivate mutual trust between supervisors and employees. After detailing factors that can enhance employees' acceptance of EPM as a primary manifestation of control in NWW, we conclude by offering implications for trust-enhancing leadership in NWW.

2   New Ways of Working

Introduced by Baarne et al. (2010), the concept of NWW describes the efforts of organizations to remodel overly rigid work designs into more flexible ones (cf. Brummelhuis et al. 2012). NWW exhibit three general characteristics. First, they lack the fixed time schedules typical of traditional work designs involving 9–to–5 jobs. In NWW, employees are free to decide for themselves when they will work. Second, employees in NWW have more autonomy in deciding where to work, and in response, organizations have begun to abandon fixed, individually assigned workstations to instead allow employees to flexibly choose a workstation from several functional work areas, a practice also known as desk-sharing or hot-desking (e.g., Hirst 2011; Kelliher and Anderson 2008). These functional work areas are designed to promote different kinds of work activities, which at base either require concentration or require communication. Examples of functional work zones that support concentration are so-called silent zones, in which oral communication among employees is prohibited (De Been and Beijer 2014). Office types that provide both desk-sharing and functional work areas have been referred to as activity-based flexible offices (Appel-Meulenbroek et al. 2011; Bodin Danielsson and Bodin 2008; Bodin Danielsson et al. 2014) and non-territorial offices (Elsbach 2003). As part of employees' increased spatial autonomy, NWW also offer employees the possibility of working outside the main office building— for example, at home or while commuting (e.g., on trains). Third, in NWW, information and communication technologies facilitate employees' temporal and spatial flexibility. Employees can thereby collaborate while working in different places or even at different times, largely by relying on information and communication media such as email, mobile devices, and videoconferencing tools, which allow access to work systems and servers from all workstations within and outside the office. As a result, with NWW employees no longer need to go to the office for certain periods or to complete certain tasks, which has generally increased collaboration across scattered locations in today's organizations. In fact, the Global Workforce Study 2012 revealed that 47 % of employees worldwide use teleworking arrangements to at least some extent (Towers Watson 2012).

3   Drivers of New Ways of Working

Three major drivers for the increasing reliance on NWW can be identified. First, changes in the nature of office work impose new demands upon office design. Second, organizations seek to reduce costs through the more effective use of office space. Third, the changed work values of tomorrow's workforce (e.g., Ryan and Kossek 2008) account for the shift toward NWW.

Regarding the first driver, a vast increase in knowledge work has occurred during the last two decades. Knowledge work is characterized by the knowledge worker's need to concentrate on tasks while simultaneously sharing information with other organizational members (Davenport 2013). As a result, the transformation has created new requirements for office design. For one, when tasks require a high level of concentration instead of exchange and communication among colleagues, employees need enclosed office spaces that minimize distraction and disruption by colleagues. By contrast, if tasks require employees to share knowledge and ideas with each other, then enclosed office spaces hinder the flow of communication (Allen and Gerstberger 1973; Bouttelier et al. 2008; Davis 1984). To support knowledge work, work designs should facilitate concentrated work as well as interaction and communication among employees (Hua et al. 2011). Traditional office designs with fixed, individually assigned workstations—for instance, cellular offices[1] and open-plan offices[2]—can only support one of these demands: either concentration without distraction or interactive communication (e.g., Oldham and Brass 1979; Sundstrom et al. 1980; Zahn 1991). These office designs are therefore less suited to the requirements of contemporary knowledge work. To address this challenge, NWW such as in activity-based flexible offices give employees the freedom to choose work environments that fit their current work activities best, either at home or within the office environment (Bodin Danielsson et al. 2014).

Regarding the second driver of NWW, the desk-sharing principle is a way for organizations to offer fewer workstations than the number of current employees. Activity-based flexible offices are usually dimensioned for less than 70 % of the workforce (Bodin Danielsson and Bodin 2008), which reflects the fact that workstations often go unused due to employees' working on client premises or being on vacation or sick leave. By adjusting their office designs accordingly, organizations can cut the costs of office space and operations (Rennecker and Godwin 2005; van der Voordt 2004).

The third driver of NWW is a shift in work values. The ideals underlying NWW—namely, spatial and temporal autonomy for employees—are consistent with the work values of Generation X (born between 1962 and 1979) and Generation Y (born after 1980)[3]. Whereas previous generations such as the Baby Boomers (born 1946–1961) valued status and extrinsic rewards as recognition of their loyalty and commitment (Collins 1998), Generation X more strongly values independence and autonomy (Jurkiewicz 2000). Moreover, members of Generation X prefer organizations that emphasize skill development, productivity, and work-life balance instead of status and tenure (Smola and Sutton 2002). Since Generation Y has experienced similar life events as Generation X, researchers have assumed similar work values for Generation Y—among them, work-life balance and career

---

[1] *Cellular offices are those* with walls up to the ceiling and an office door.

[2] Open-plan offices are commonly used workspaces without interior walls or enclosures that are shared by larger groups of employees with individual workstations often arranged in groups within the office environment (e.g., Brennan et al. 2002; Brookes and Kaplan 1972).

[3] We refer to the classification proposed by Lyons (2004).

development (Zemke et al. 2000). As such, especially autonomy-related values such as work-life balance and discretion over working hours (Lyons 2004) are becoming increasingly important (Cennamo and Gardner 2008; Zemke et al. 2000). By offering work designs such as NWW that accommodate the preference for autonomy of younger generations, organizations can become more attractive to the current and upcoming workforces, which can better allow them to recruit promising talents and retain committed employees.

4 How New Ways of Working Impact Working Life

Besides benefits for organizations such as reduced costs for office space and improved adaptability to organizational turnover (e.g., Baarne et al. 2010; Rennecker and Godwin 2005), NWW can also be expected to improve employees' work experiences, thereby resulting in a healthier and more satisfied, committed, and productive workforce. By offering temporal and spatial autonomy to employees, organizations allow their workers to schedule tasks in ways that suit their current needs, thereby saving both time and energy (Kelliher and Anderson 2008). Furthermore, in being allowed to work while commuting, employees can use time more efficiently, and can better balance work with family (e.g., Parasuraman and Greenhaus 2002). Early studies of how NWW impacts working life underlined these positive effects by demonstrating that NWW foster increased feelings of autonomy that are positively related to job satisfaction (e.g., Baltes et al. 1999), work engagement (e.g., ten Brummelhuis et al. 2012) and reduced levels of work–family conflict (e.g., Byron 2005).

However, despite these positive effects for employees and organizations, NWW also pose challenges for leadership. Giving employees the freedom to choose where and when to work impedes the exercise of traditional control usually seen as a core dimension of leadership (Fayol 1930; Scott 1987; Sitkin et al. 2010). In traditional work designs, in which employees have fixed, individually assigned workstations in close proximity to their colleagues and supervisors, supervisors can easily observe employees as they work. In NWW, by contrast, employees do not necessarily work in close proximity to their supervisors or have any fixed address in the office. This can make it difficult for supervisors to find employees, let alone monitor them. The spatial distance between supervisors and employees becomes even greater if the latter work remotely. In such cases, it can be challenging for supervisors to recognize whether employees at any given moment are in the office building or working remotely. In effect, NWW involve less face-to-face contact between supervisors and employees than in traditional work designs.

5   Effective Supervision in NWW

Given these changes that transform traditional workplaces into those involving NWW, the question arises how supervisors in NWW can ideally supervise employees. Since employees often work on complex tasks of great importance to the success of their organizations, their failure to achieve expected results or counterproductive work behavior can be costly. As such, effective supervision that maintains the supervisor's control over the workflow is essential (Sitkin et al. 2010), though the reduced face-to-face interaction in NWW can render traditional in-person supervision impossible. In that regard, Bijlsma-Frankema and Koopman (2004) have referred to the "oxymoron" of control in today's globalized and digitalized workplaces, namely that the need for trust between supervisors and employees has increased in spite of, as well as because of, the fact that supervisors can no longer observe their employees at every step. At the same time, new ways to exercise control can threaten the mutual trust between supervisors and employees. It is therefore essential to design control systems in NWW that can support the development of trust. In response, we turn to review some traditional control taxonomies to reveal which control modes appear most applicable in NWW, and discuss their potential effects on trust between supervisors and employees.

Theoretically, there are numerous ways in which supervisors in NWW can exercise control over employees. Broadly defined, control encompasses all processes by which supervisors direct attention, motivate, and encourage their subordinates to act in expected ways (Cardinal 2001). Control theory (Ouchi 1979) traditionally distinguishes behavior, output, and clan control. While behavior control refers to the measurement and evaluation of the work process, output control occurs with the measurement and evaluation of results, whereas clan control emerges in the attitudes, values, and beliefs shared among the workforce. Ouchi has argued that two variables in particular determine the selection of the appropriate control mechanism. If both the ability to measure outputs and the supervisor's knowledge of the processes necessary to produce the output are high, then either output or behavior control is appropriate. Meanwhile, if the ability to measure outputs is high, but the knowledge of the so-called transformation process is low, then output control is optimal. Conversely, in the case of difficulties with measuring outputs despite sound knowledge of the transformation process, behavior control becomes mandatory. Lastly, if both measurability and knowledge of the transformation process are low, then organizations should focus on clan control. Kirsch (1996) investigated the modes of control that organizations actually use in practice and confirmed that outcome measurability significantly predicted outcome control, whereas the interaction between behavior observability and the controller's knowledge of the transformation process significantly predicted behavior control. In her work on control choices, Eisenhardt (1985) built upon Ouchi's (1979) research to argue that the level of uncertainty also influences decisions to prioritize output or behavior control. Rustagi et al. (2008) have confirmed that this circumstance also applies to actual organizational practice by showing that the level of uncertainty increases the use of formal controls. Additional antecedents of control decisions include the strategic importance of the task and its complexity, both of which increase reliance upon formal controls (Remus and Wiener 2012).

In NWW, though employees often perform tasks of great importance to the success of their organizations, the reliance upon virtual communication between supervisors and employees involves a great deal of uncertainty (Tangirala and Alge 2006). Though this circumstance seems to suggest that the use of formal controls will be considerable, Kirsch (1997) has noted that, in practice, supervisors implement a range of controls that consists of mixtures of formal (i.e., output and behavior) and informal (i.e., clan-based) modes. In that sense, the specific decision between output and behavior control depends upon the degree to which either the task or the task process can be measured and evaluated. Since NWW increase the distance between supervisors and employees and reduce their level of face-to-face interactions, supervisors must primarily rely upon EPM, which given the technological advancements in recent decades offer supervisors a variety of monitoring techniques. Sophisticated EPM systems can be used to evaluate the output of employees in NWW based on a host of performance indicators, while software that monitors employees' keystrokes, emails, and time spent on websites, as well as location-sensing technologies, can be used to monitor employees' behavior. In effect, today's EPM systems thus encompass techniques for both output and behavior control, and accordingly, in the remainder of this chapter, the terms control and monitoring refer to both output and behavior control techniques. In investigating the predictors of electronic monitoring usage and secrecy, Alge et al. (2004) have demonstrated that supervisors, who depend strongly upon their employees and tend to expect the future performance of their employees to be low, rely heavily upon electronic monitoring. At the same time, supervisors with a low propensity to trust have a tendency to keep these monitoring efforts secret.

6   The Bright and Dark Sides of Electronic Performance Monitoring

Regarding the effects of output and behavior control, an empirical study (Oliver and Anderson 1994) of sales employees revealed that the respective modes of control have distinct effects upon employees' levels of organizational commitment, their acceptance of authority and performance reviews, and their preference for risk. While behavior control noticeably increased organizational commitment and acceptance of authority, output control increased employees' risk preference. Since the publication of these findings, numerous scholars have investigated how control and monitoring affects employees' attributes and behaviors. Apparently, these studies have produced contradictory results: On the one hand, some studies have emphasized the *negative* effects of monitoring and control, for both the people exercising control and those subject to control. Regarding controllers, Strickland (1958) has shown that intensive face-to-face monitoring of outputs can diminish their trust towards the monitored employees. In particular, the level of trust supervisors held in consistently monitored employees tended to be less than that held in employees seldom monitored, while the level of prior monitoring was significantly and positively related to that of subsequent monitoring. These findings have suggested that monitoring can initiate a vicious circle consisting of declining levels of trust followed by even more intense monitoring. Later, Kruglanski (1970) replicated Strickland's results to show that supervisors tend to perceive less-monitored employees to be more trustworthy than more frequently monitored ones. Similarly, McAllister (1995) found that managers' use of control-based monitoring and defensive behavior could not be empirically distinguished from their level of negative cognition-based trust in their peers. In the context of virtual teams, Piccoli and Ives (2003) reached a comparable conclusion, as team members who exercised more behavior control demonstrated less trust in their team than team members who did not exercise such control. These authors argued that the exercise of control increased the vigilance of team members, who in response actively sought out and detected deviant behavior by other team members. This finding is in line with results reported by Dennis et al. (2012), who found that the use of behavior control drove supervisors to perceive the behavior of their employees in a way consistent with their predispositions. In general, it is important to bear in mind that the exercise of control and monitoring always poses added costs (Jensen and Meckling 1976), meaning that for supervisors and organizations alike, it is crucial to gauge whether the exercise of control is actually worth the information it could reveal.

In terms of how monitoring and control affect the people being controlled, numerous studies have underscored similarly negative consequences. Enzle and Anderson (1993) showed that electronic surveillance with video cameras combined with perceived distrust on the side of the person exercising this kind of control diminishes the intrinsic motivation of the people monitored. Later, in conceptualizing trust as the absence of harassment, monitoring, and surveillance, Cunningham and MacGregor (2000) indicated that such trust is significantly and positively related to job satisfaction after controlling for job design factors, yet negatively related to quitting and absence from work. In a recent study of similarly detrimental effects, Crowley (2012) found that supervisors' use of coercive control erodes employees' level of pride and effort via mechanisms of dehumanization and the facilitation of abuse.

On the other hand, empirical evidence also supports the *positive* effects of monitoring and control—again, for both people exercising control and people being controlled. Concerning controllers, McAllister (1995) identified a positive relationship between managers' level of affect-based trust and the degree to which they exercise need-based monitoring—that is, keeping track of others' personal and work-related needs. These results followed those of Komaki (1986), who demonstrated that performance monitoring in the form of work sampling was the critical difference between effective and ineffective managers in terms of their potential to motivate employees. In fact, effective managers invested considerably more time gathering performance information than their ineffective peers.

By the same token, regarding the employees being controlled, Bijlisma and van de Bunt (2003) found a strong, positive correlation between monitoring and employees' level of trust in the monitoring supervisor. In their study, monitoring was operationalized as the supervisors' awareness of whether their employees performed in line with their expectations. Notably, this effect remained significant even after controlling for related variables, including support, guidance, and openness.

7 Employee Perceptions of Monitoring Matters

To reconcile these diverse and apparently contradictory findings, distinguishing both personality-based and situation-based factors appears to be relevant. In terms of personal predispositions, Schoel et al. (2011) showed that employees with low, unstable levels of self-esteem exhibit a preference for autocratic supervisors who exercise a high level of control over them. On a similar note, Rietzschel et al. (2014) found that close monitoring significantly increased intrinsic motivation for employees with high need for structure, yet significantly decreased the job satisfaction of employees with low need for structure.

Stanton's (2000a) framework can provide an overview of a range of potentially influential situation-based factors. Stanton has argued that certain monitoring characteristics influence the cognition of monitoring by the employee (e.g., perceived fairness of monitoring), which translates into immediate reactions (e.g., acceptance or rejection of monitoring) and long-term consequences (e.g., job satisfaction). Among these characteristics are the target of monitoring (i.e., who and what is monitored?), the frequency of monitoring (i.e., how often does monitoring occur?), the source of monitoring (i.e., who exercises monitoring?), the controllability of monitoring (i.e., to which degree can employees control onset and timing of monitoring?), and the consistency of monitoring. Recently, a growing body of research has offered support for the proposition that monitoring, when applied consistently across a group of employees, can deliver accurate information and give employees a feeling of control over monitoring processes, which enhances their perceived fairness of both electronic and traditional monitoring systems (Stanton 2000b). Also regarding control over the monitoring process, Stanton and Barnes-Farrell (1996) earlier found that the ability of employees to delay or prevent electronic monitoring enhances their feelings of personal control and, in turn, their task performance, whereas exact knowledge that monitoring occurred decreased these same feelings. A more recent study by McNall and Stanton (2011) underlined the importance of employees' perceptions of control over the monitoring process by showing that, in the use of location-tracking devices, it is crucial to grant employees "protected spaces" where such monitoring is not exercised. Yet, the degree of perceived personal control over the monitoring process is similarly important in another regard, as Spitzmüller and Stanton (2006) have revealed. Their findings indicated that personal control moderated the relationships among organizational commitment, identification, and employees' intentions to comply with or resist monitoring. In particular, employees with high levels of commitment to and identification with their organizations, coupled with a high degree of perceived control over the monitoring process, are most likely to comply with the monitoring process. At the same time, the use of information produced by monitoring is essential for predicting employees' attitudes toward electronic monitoring (Stanton and Weiss 2000); for example, if employees perceive that such information will be used for punitive instead of supportive purposes, they are more likely to resist monitoring. In the same vein, McNall and Roch (2009) used a social exchange framework to show that employees' perceptions of the purposes of electronic monitoring in terms of whether it supported their professional development or was used for coercion impacts their perceived level of interpersonal justice. These authors also showed that detailed explanations of the use of electronic monitoring actually enhance monitored employees' perceptions of informational justice and that such interpersonal and informational justice can increase their trust in their supervisors, which ultimately translates into greater job satisfaction and performance. Altogether, this line of research suggests that how controlled employees perceive control is crucial when evaluating how control affects outcomes (Bijlsma-Frankema and Costa 2010).

In distinguishing the effects of EPM and traditional monitoring upon fairness, McNall and Roch (2007) revealed that computer monitoring is perceived to be the most procedurally just, whereas conventional face-to-face monitoring is deemed the most interpersonally just and least invasive of employees' privacy. Stanton and Sarkar-Barney (2003) compared the effects of EPM and face-to-face monitoring and found that electronically monitored groups exhibited higher-quality performance than the traditionally monitored group.

To summarize what we have discussed so far, supervisors in NWW are particularly apt to rely on electronic monitoring techniques because NWW increase the distance between supervisors and their employees and decrease their face-to-face interaction. Supervisors who heavily depend on their employees and whose employees have demonstrated weak performance in the past can particularly be expected to rely heavily on electronic monitoring (Alge et al. 2004). At the same time, whether electronic monitoring focuses on employees' output or their behavior depends on the respective measurability of processes versus results. Currently, a body of encouraging empirical results suggests positive effects of electronic monitoring, which if enacted properly, is acceptable to employees and can enhance their job-related attitudes and behavior at work. Electronic monitoring may even pose advantages over traditional face-to-face monitoring if it can deliver more accurate information on employees' performance for use in the reward and evaluation processes and if it gives employees feelings of control over the EMP systems used. In effect, these characteristics enhance employees' perceptions of monitoring transparency and fairness. However, if the design and execution of control is implemented poorly, then adverse consequences are likely to surface, and in particular, employees' trust towards their supervisors may decline.

8 Practical Implications for Supervisors in NWW

Having concluded that NWW are characterized by the need for both effective control and mutual trust, we here highlight the practical implications of the above-discussed dynamics as advice for supervisors in NWW. A growing body of largely conceptual work (Bijlsma-Frankema and Costa 2005; Costa and Bijlsma-Frankema 2007) suggests that under specific circumstances, control and trust can complement and support each other. In that regard, it is essential that the control exercised by supervisors is accepted among employees. Bijlsma-Frankema and Costa (2010) have proposed four factors for determining the acceptance or rejection of any given control technique that readily accommodate the diverse empirical findings concerning drivers of monitoring acceptance summarized above. These authors first argue that to be perceived as legitimate and hence accepted, a control technique must be perceived by employees as a tool for enhancing their competence. This factor parallels McNall and Roch's finding (2009) of the necessity for employees to perceive a developmental purpose in the use of electronic monitoring. For supervisors in NWW, this circumstance implies the need for supervisors using any form of electronic monitoring to give their employees timely, constructive feedback. Such practice can also demonstrate to them how their supervisors actually use electronic monitoring systems, which should in turn boost their acceptance of those systems (Stanton and Weiss 2000). Second, Bijlsma-Frankema and Costa (2010) suggest that employees should be involved in the design and execution of control systems, since such participation promises to increase their level of identification with and thus acceptance of these systems. Third, supervisors should grant their employees some level of autonomy despite the control systems' being in place (Bijlsma-Frankema and Costa 2010). In response to this factor, supervisors should articulate to employees in which ways they exercise control over them, yet at once make clear the ways in which they do not. Notably, the second and third factors of Bijlsma-Frankema and Costa's (2010) framework parallels all of the empirical findings highlighting the importance of employees' perception of personal control over the systems used to monitor them (e.g., McNall and Stanton 2011; Spitzmüller and Stanton 2006). For supervisors in NWW, this implies that the use of electronic monitoring should be restricted to situations in which it is vital and abandoned in all others, a practice that supervisors should articulate to employees to make them aware of their autonomy. Ideally, supervisors should involve their employees when deciding upon which situations will be monitored and which will not. As their fourth and last factor, Bijlsma-Frankema and Costa (2010) have argued that control systems must also enhance employees' perceptions of justice in order to be perceived as legitimate and thus accepted. This factor takes support from Stanton's work (2000a, b), which highlighted the importance of monitoring consistency. For supervisors in NWW, this factor implies the need to use electronic monitoring systems in ways comparable both across employees and across time. Beyond that, they need to ensure that their employees are actually aware of such consistency.

9 Conclusion

In conclusion, NWW pose benefits for both organizations (e.g., reduced costs) and employees (e.g., improved work life balance) that justify NWW as a dominant trend in today's workplaces and support their likely increase in the coming years. However, NWW also pose challenges for leadership in terms of how supervisors can maintain mutual trust with their employees yet still exercise effective control over them. In this chapter, we developed specific suggestions on how this issue can be addressed. In particular, we emphasized that employees' subjective perceptions of monitoring and control systems matter, together with their perceived fairness and transparency. From this idea, we have outlined a clear agenda for supervisors in NWW toward ensuring widespread acceptance for control and monitoring systems. By working toward such acceptance, the benefits that NWW offer for organizations and employees alike can be more fully realized.

References

Alge, B. J., Ballinger, G. A., & Green, S. G. (2004). Remote control: Predictors of electronic monitoring intensity and secrecy. *Personnel Psychology, 57*(2), 377–410. doi:10.1111/j.1744-6570.2004.tb02495.x.

Allen, T. J., & Gerstberger, P. G. (1973). A field experiment to improve communications in a product engineering department: The nonterritorial office. *Human Factors: The Journal of the Human Factors and Ergonomics Society, 15*(5), 487–498. doi:10.1177/001872087301500505.

Appel-Meulenbroek, R., Groenen, P., & Janssen, I. (2011). An end-user's perspective on activity-based office concepts. *Journal of Corporate Real Estate, 13*, 122–135. doi:10.1108/14630011111136830.

Baarne, R., Houtkamp, P., & Knotter, M. (2010). *Unraveling new ways of working*. Assen: Koninklijke van Gorcum/Stichting Management Studies.

Baltes, B. B., Briggs, T. E., Huff, J. W., Wright, J. A., & Neuman, G. A. (1999). Flexible and compressed workweek schedules: A meta-analysis of their effects on work-related criteria. *Journal of Applied Psychology, 84*(4), 496–513. doi:10.1037//0021-9010.84.4.496.

Bauer, W. (2014). *Kurzbericht zur Studie "Office Settings": Die Rolle der Arbeitsumgebung in einer hyperflexiblen Welt.*

Bijlsma, K. M., & van de Bunt, G. (2003). Antecedents of trust in managers: A "bottom up" approach. *Personnel Review, 32*(5), 638–664. doi:10.1108/00483480310488388.

Bijlsma-Frankema, K., & Costa, A. C. (2005). Understanding the trust–control nexus. *International Sociology, 20*(3), 259–282. doi:10.1177/0268580905055477.

Bijlsma-Frankema, K., & Costa, A. C. (2010). Consequences and antecedents of managerial and employee legitimacy interpretations of control: A natural open system approach. In S. B. Sitkin, L. B. Cardinal, & K. Bijlsma-Frankema (Eds.), *Organizational control* (pp. 396–433). Cambridge: Cambridge University Press.

Bijlsma-Frankema, K., & Koopman, P. (2004). The oxymoron of control in an era of globalisation: Vulnerabilities of a mega myth. *Journal of Managerial Psychology, 19*(3), 204–217. doi:10.1108/02683940410527711.

Bodin Danielsson, C. B., & Bodin, L. (2008). Office type in relation to health, well-being, and job satisfaction among employees. *Environment and Behavior, 40*(5), 636–668. doi:10.1177/0013916507307459.

Bodin Danielsson, C., Chungkham, H. S., Wulff, C., & Westerlund, H. (2014). Office design's impact on sick leave rates. *Ergonomics, 57*(2), 139–47. doi:10.1080/00140139.2013.871064.

Bouttelier, R., Ullman, F., Schreiber, J., & Nael, R. (2008). Impact of office layout on communication in a science-driven business. *R & D Management, 38*(4), 372–391.

Brennan, A., Chugh, J. S., & Kline, T. (2002). Traditional versus open office design: A longitudinal field study. *Environment and Behavior, 34*(3), 279–299. doi:10.1177/0013916502034003001.

Brookes, M. J., & Kaplan, A. (1972). The office environment: Space planning and affective behavior. *Human Factors: The Journal of the Human Factors and Ergonomics Society, 14* (5), 373–391. doi:10.1177/001872087201400502.

Byron, K. (2005). A meta-analytic review of work–family conflict and its antecedents. *Journal of Vocational Behavior, 67*(2), 169–198. doi:10.1016/j.jvb.2004.08.009.

Cardinal, L. B. (2001). Technological innovation in the pharmaceutical industry: The use of organizational control in managing research and development. *Organization Science, 12*, 19–36. doi:10.2307/2640394.

Cennamo, L., & Gardner, D. (2008). Generational differences in work values, outcomes and person-organisation values fit. *Journal of Managerial Psychology, 23*(8), 891–906. doi:10.1108/02683940810904385.

Collins, J. (1998). Why we must keep Baby Boomers working. *New Zealand Buisness, 12*(8), 53.

Costa, A. C., & Bijlsma-Frankema, K. (2007). Trust and control interrelations: New perspectives on the trust–control nexus. *Group & Organization Management, 32*(4), 392–406. doi:10.1177/1059601106293871.

Crowley, M. (2012). Control and dignity in professional, manual and service-sector employment. *Organization Studies, 33*(10), 1383–1406. doi:10.1177/0170840612453529.

Cunningham, J. B., & MacGregor, J. (2000). Trust and the design of work: Complementary constructs in satisfaction and performance. *Human Relations, 53*(12), 1575–1591. doi:10.1177/00187267005312003.

Davenport, T. H. (2013). *Thinking for a living: How to get better performances and results from knowledge workers*. Boston, MA: Harvard Business School Publishing.

Davis, T. R. V. (1984). The influence of the physical environment in offices. *Academy of Management Review, 9*(2), 271–283. doi:10.5465/AMR.1984.4277654.

De Been, I., & Beijer, M. (2014). The influence of office type on satisfaction and perceived productivity support. *Journal of Facilities Management, 12*, 142–157. doi:10.1108/JFM-02-2013-0011.

Demerouti, E., Derks, D., ten Brummelhuis, L. L., & Bakker, A. B. (2014). New ways of working: Impact on working conditions, work-family balance, and well-being. In C. Korunka & P. Hoonakker (Eds.), *The impact of ICT on quality of working life* (pp. 123–142). New York: Springer.

Dennis, A. R., Robert, L. P., Curtis, A. M., Kowalczyk, S. T., & Hasty, B. K. (2012). Trust is in the eye of the beholder: A vignette study of postevent behavioral controls' effects on individual trust in virtual teams. *Information Systems Research, 23*(2), 546–558. doi:10.1287/isre.1110.0364.

Eisenhardt, K. M. (1985). Control: Organizational and economic approaches. *Management Science, 31*(2), 134–149. doi:10.1287/mnsc.31.2.134.

Elsbach, K. D. (2003). Relating physical environment to self-categorizations: Identity threat and affirmation in a non-territorial office space. *Administrative Science Quarterly, 48*(4), 622–654.

Enzle, M. E., & Anderson, S. C. (1993). Surveillant intentions and intrinsic motivation. *Journal of Personality and Social Psychology, 64*(2), 257–266. doi:10.1037/0022-3514.64.2.257.

Fayol, H. (1930). *Industrial and general administration*. London: Sir Isaac Pitman & Sons.

Golden, T. D., & Raghuram, S. (2010). Teleworker knowledge sharing and the role of altered relational and technological interactions. *Journal of Organizational Behavior, 31*(8), 1061–1085.

Hirst, A. (2011). Settlers, vagrants and mutual indifference: Unintended consequences of hot-desking. *Journal of Organizational Change Management, 24*(6), 767–788. doi:10.1108/09534811111175742.

Hua, Y., Loftness, V., Heerwagen, J. H., & Powell, K. M. (2011). Relationship between workplace spatial settings and occupant-perceived support for collaboration. *Environment and Behavior, 43*, 807–826. doi:10.1177/0013916510364465.

Jensen, M. C., & Meckling, W. H. (1976). Theory of the firm: Managerial behavior, agency costs and ownership structure. *Journal of Financial Economics, 3*(4), 305–360.

Jurkiewicz, C. L. (2000). Generation X and the public employee. *Public Personnel Management, 29*(1), 55–74.

Kelliher, C., & Anderson, D. (2008). For better or for worse? An analysis of how flexible working practices influence employees' perceptions of job quality. *The International Journal of Human Resource Management, 19*(3), 419–431. doi:10.1080/09585190801895502.

Kirsch, L. J. (1996). The management of complex tasks in organizations: Controlling the systems development process. *Organization Science, 7*(1), 1–21.

Kirsch, L. S. (1997). Portfolios of control modes and IS project management. *Information Systems Research, 8*(3), 215–239. doi:10.1287/isre.8.3.215.

Komaki, J. L. (1986). Toward effective supervision—An operant analysis and comparison of managers at work. *Journal of Applied Psychology, 71*(2), 270–279. doi:10.1037//0021-9010.71.2.270.

Kruglanski, A. W. (1970). Attributing trustworthiness in supervisor-worker relations. *Journal of Experimental Social Psychology, 6*(2), 214–232. doi:10.1016/0022-1031(70)90088-0.

Levin, D. Z., & Cross, R. (2004). The strength of weak ties you can trust: The mediating role of trust in effective knowledge transfer. *Management Science, 50*(11), 1477–1490.

Lyons, S. (2004). *An exploration of generational values in life and at work*. Dissertation Abstracts International, 3462A.

McAllister, D. J. (1995). Affect- and cognition-based trust as foundations for interpersonal cooperation in organizations. *Academy of Management Journal, 38*(1), 24–59. doi:10.2307/256727.

McNall, L. A., & Roch, S. G. (2007). Effects of electronic monitoring types on perceptions of procedural justice, interpersonal justice, and privacy. *Journal of Applied Social Psychology, 37*(3), 658–682. doi:10.1111/j.1559-1816.2007.00179.x.

McNall, L. A., & Roch, S. G. (2009). A social exchange model of employee reactions to electronic performance monitoring. *Human Performance, 22*(3), 204–224. doi:10.1080/08959280902970385.

McNall, L. A., & Stanton, J. M. (2011). Private eyes are watching you: Reactions to location sensing technologies. *Journal of Business and Psychology, 26*(3), 299–309. doi:10.1007/s10869-010-9189-y.

Oldham, G. R., & Brass, D. J. (1979). Employee reactions to an open plan office : A naturally occurring quasi-experiment. *Administrative Science Quarterly, 24*(2), 267–284.

Oliver, R. L., & Anderson, E. (1994). An empirical test of the consequences of behavior- and outcome-based sales control systems. *Journal of Marketing, 58*(4), 53–67. doi:10.2307/1251916.

Ouchi, W. G. (1979). A conceptual framework for the design of organizational control mechanisms. *Management Science, 25*(9), 833–848.

Parasuraman, S., & Greenhaus, J. H. (2002). Toward reducing some critical gaps in work–family research. *Human Resource Management Review, 12*(3), 299–312.

Piccoli, G., & Ives, B. (2003). Trust and the unintended effects of behavior control in virtual teams. *MIS Quarterly, 27*(3), 365–395.

Remus, U., & Wiener, M. (2012). The amount of control in offshore software development projects. *Journal of Global Information Management, 20*(4), 1–26. doi:10.4018/jgim.2012100101.

Rennecker, J., & Godwin, L. (2005). Delays and interruptions: A self-perpetuating paradox of communication technology use. *Information and Organization, 15*(3), 247–266. doi:10.1016/j.infoandorg.2005.02.004.

Rietzschel, E. F., Slijkhuis, M., & Van Yperen, N. W. (2014). Close monitoring as a contextual stimulator: How need for structure affects the relation between close monitoring and work outcomes. *European Journal of Work and Organizational Psychology, 23*(3), 394–404. doi:10.1080/1359432X.2012.752897.

Rustagi, S., King, W. R., & Kirsch, L. J. (2008). Predictors of formal control usage in IT outsourcing partnerships. *Information Systems Research, 19*(2), 126–143. doi:10.1287/isre.1080.0169.

Ryan, A. M., & Kossek, E. E. (2008). Worklife policy implementation: Breaking down or creating barriers to inclusiveness? *Human Resource Management, 47*(2), 295–310.

Schoel, C., Bluemke, M., Mueller, P., & Stahlberg, D. (2011). When autocratic leaders become an option-uncertainty and self-esteem predict implicit leadership preferences. *Journal of Personality and Social Psychology, 101*(3), 521–540. doi:10.1037/a0023393.

Scott, W. R. (1987). *Organizations: Rational, natural, and open systems* (2nd ed.). Englewood Cliffs, NJ: Prentice-Hall.

Sitkin, S. B., Cardinal, L. B., & Bijisma-Frankema, K. (2010). Control is fundamental. In S. B. Sitkin, L. B. Cardinal, & K. Bijlsma-Frankema (Eds.), *Organizational control* (pp. 3–15). Cambridge: Cambridge University Press.

Smola, K., & Sutton, C. D. (2002). Generational differences: Revisiting generational work values for the new millennium. *Journal of Organizational Behavior, 23*(4), 363–382. doi:10.1002/job.147.

Spitzmüller, C., & Stanton, J. M. (2006). Examining employee compliance with organizational surveillance and monitoring. *Journal of Occupational and Organizational Psychology, 79*(2), 245–272. doi:10.1348/096317905X52607.

Stanton, J. M. (2000a). Reactions to employee performance monitoring: Framework, review, and research directions. *Human Performance, 13*(1), 85–113. doi:10.1207/S15327043HUP1301_4.

Stanton, J. M. (2000b). Traditional and electronic monitoring from an organizational justice perspective. *Journal of Business and Psychology, 15*(1), 129–147. doi:10.1023/A:1007775020214.

Stanton, J. M., & Barnes-Farrell, J. L. (1996). Effects of electronic performance monitoring on personal control, task satisfaction, and task performance. *Journal of Applied Psychology, 81*(6), 738–745. doi:10.1037/0021-9010.81.6.738.

Stanton, J. M., & Sarkar-Barney, S. T. M. (2003). A detailed analysis of task performance with and without computer monitoring. *International Journal of Human-Computer Interaction, 16*(2), 345–366. doi:10.1207/S15327590IJHC1602_11.

Stanton, J., & Weiss, E. (2000). Electronic monitoring in their own words: An exploratory study of employees' experiences with new types of surveillance. *Computers in Human Behavior, 16*(4), 423–440. doi:10.1016/S0747-5632(00)00018-2.

Strickland, L. H. (1958). Surveillance and trust. *Journal of Personality, 26*(2), 200–215. doi:10.1111/j.1467-6494.1958.tb01580.x.

Sundstrom, E., Burt, R. E., & Kamp, D. (1980). Privacy at work: Architectural correlates of job satisfaction and job performance. *Academy of Management Journal, 23*(1), 101–117. doi:10.2307/255498.

Tangirala, S., & Alge, B. J. (2006). Reactions to unfair events in computer-mediated groups: A test of uncertainty management theory. *Organizational Behavior and Human Decision Processes, 100*(1), 1–20.

Ten Brummelhuis, L. L., Bakker, A. B., Hetland, J., & Keulemans, L. (2012). Do new ways of working foster work engagement? *Psicothema, 24*(1), 113–120.

Towers, W. (2012). *Global workforce study 2012: Engagement at risk: Driving strong performance in a volatile global environment.* http://www.towerswatson.com/assets/pdf/2012-Towers-Watson-Global-Workforce-Study.pdf. Accessed 6 Oct 2015.

Van der Voordt, T. J. (2004). Productivity and employee satisfaction in flexible workplaces. *Journal of Corporate Real Estate, 6*, 133–148. doi:10.1108/14630010410812306.

Zahn, G. L. (1991). Face-to-face communication in an office setting: The effects of position, proximity, and exposure. *Communication Research, 18*(6), 737–754. doi:10.1177/009365091018006002.

Zemke, R., Raines, C., & Filipczak, B. (2000). *Generations at work: Managing the clash of Veterans, Boomers, Xers, and Nexters in your workplace.* New York: Amacom.

Trust Fostering Competencies in Asynchronous Digital Communication

Jens Kanthak and Guido Hertel

Abstract The development of digital communication media fosters the employment of geographically dispersed teams by companies around the globe. Although virtual teams are widely employed today, only little is known about the required competencies of team members that arise from the challenges of digital communication and geographical dispersion. Especially, teams working across several time zones face several demands. According to Media Synchronicity Theory, the two main challenges that rise from asynchronous communication are coordination problems and low (perceived) interactivity. These challenges might negatively influence trust and performance of virtual teams. In this chapter, we develop a competency model for asynchronous communication in working teams. According to this model, central competencies to overcome the negative effects of asynchronous communication are extraversion, conscientiousness, proactivity, computer-mediated communication skills, self-management skills, and prospective memory. At the end of this chapter we discuss different research approaches in the field of virtual team competencies.

Keywords Asynchronous communication • Competency model • Trust • Virtual teams

1 Virtual Teams

The rapid development of digital media and the possibility to digitalize data have significantly influenced the way people live and work together. While in 2000, about 75 % of the data we used were in analogous form such as print media, by 2007 about 90 % of the data were digitalized (Hilbert and López 2011). The advantages of digitalized data are manifold. Digitalized data are easy to store. The data of a whole library can be fit on one modern hard drive. Digitalized data are quite easy to manage as one can use search programs to immediately find the required information. But probably the most important feature of digitalized data is the possibility to copy and share your data with other people around the globe within seconds. For

J. Kanthak (✉) • G. Hertel
University of Münster, Münster, Germany
e-mail: jens.kanthak@uni-muenster.de; ghertel@uni-muenster.de

© Springer International Publishing Switzerland 2016   177
B. Blöbaum (ed.), *Trust and Communication in a Digitized World*, Progress in IS,
DOI 10.1007/978-3-319-28059-2_10

business companies this has several implications. Companies are able to quickly share information between their various company sites, which significantly facilitates the central coordination of the company. Therefore, digitalization can be viewed as an important driver of the globalization and the development of globally acting companies. The requirements of a geographically dispersed company and the possibilities granted by digital data sharing and digital communication media brought forth a variety of new cooperation forms that can be subsumed as "virtual teams." In contrast to classical, co-located face-to-face teams "(v)irtual teams are groups of geographically and/or organizationally dispersed coworkers that are assembled using a combination of telecommunications and information technologies to accomplish an organizational task" (Townsend et al. 1998). Virtual teams are not a homogeneous group of teams but may vary widely on several dimensions. Therefore, it is more precise to consider the degree of these dimensions of virtuality than to make a clear distinction between virtual and non-virtual teams (Hertel et al. 2005). For example, the research department of Microsoft Corporation has 11 research labs around the globe (Microsoft Research 2015). Within such a lab, team members can meet face-to-face to quickly clarify questions and coordinate their work by just walking down the hall. They are likely to meet on informal occasions like lunch breaks and become easily acquainted with each other. In contrast, when team members reside in different research labs, chances to meet face-to-face are reduced significantly. If the two research labs are in the same city or time zone, team members might conference via telephone and arrange weekly face-to-face meetings. However, if the research labs are in different time zones, face-to-face meetings are rather difficult, and even telephone use might be reduced. For instance, if a team member in Redmond, WA works together with a team member in Cambridge, UK, the time delay amounts to 7 h. When a team member in Redmond starts her computer in the morning, her colleague in England is almost on his way home. Thus, spontaneous communication is limited and team members have to arrange for a phone call or a video conference. In the meantime, they have to rely on asynchronous media such as e-mail or voice message.

The extent of communication media reliance in comparison to face-to-face interaction can be considered as a dimension of virtuality. According to Kirkman and Mathieu (2005), asynchronicity has two implications for the virtuality of the cooperation. The first implication is the time delay of the communication. Team members working together across time zones are mostly restricted to using asynchronous communication media. Thus, there is a time lag in the communication that can negatively influence the communication and team coordination as arising questions might have to wait until the next work day. However, Dennis et al. (2008) argue that asynchronous communication is not always inferior to synchronous communication. Instead, the match between communication task and synchronicity is of importance. A synchronous medium is advantageous when a task requires fast feedback and exchange of arguments. If, however, a task requires the reliable conveyance of specific and detailed information, asynchronous media might be the better choice as the sender can take her time to craft the message, and the receiver can save and reprocess the message. Teams within the

same time zone can choose between synchronous and asynchronous communication media depending on the current goals and communication tasks. Teams
working across time zones more often have to rely on asynchronous media regardless of their goals and communication tasks. It is therefore important to ask how
coordination can be improved in asynchronously working teams.

From the limited choice of communication media that accompanies asynchronous cooperation arises the second implication for team virtuality. According to
Kirkman and Mathieu (2005), asynchronous teams often have to rely on communication media low in information value. Information value is a concept that
describes the ability of a communication medium to convey information that is
needed for a certain task. For example, when the discussion of controversial issues
is the task, face-to-face conversations have a higher information value than e-mails
as they are able to convey nonverbal information via intonation and gestures that
aid in resolving ambiguity. But, when writing software is the task, an e-mail with an
attached program code might be of higher information value than the face-to-face
conversation as a written code is easier to process than verbal instructions. Thus,
geographical dispersion is not always a disadvantage for asynchronous teams with
respect to information value of communication as long as the available communication media fit the task. As teamwork often includes a variety of different tasks,
different communication media might provide the best information value. Again,
while co-located teams or teams within a single time zone can choose from a wide
variety of communication media, asynchronous working teams are limited to
asynchronous media, which are sometimes a suboptimal choice regarding the
informational value.

In this chapter we will discuss how virtual cooperation influences trust as an
important driver for cooperative behavior in virtual teams. We will particularly
examine the effect of asynchronous cooperation as it brings special challenges to
the cooperation. After describing a model of asynchronous communication, we will
deduce its implications for the building of trust in virtual teams. Based on these
considerations we will develop a competency model for virtual teams that should
help to overcome the main challenges of asynchronous communication. At the end
of this chapter, we will depict a research agenda that might help to get empirical
access to the field of virtual teamwork competencies.

2 Trust in Virtual Teams

In this section, we will give a short overview of the importance of trust in both face-
to-face and virtual teams. We will further discuss how the virtuality of cooperation
can negatively influence the formation of trust in virtual teams.

Within the literature on traditional face-to-face teams, trust is regarded as a
central emergent state (e.g., Costa 2003). Mayer et al. define trust as the willingness
of a trustor to be vulnerable to the actions of a trustee, expecting the trustee to
perform a particular action. This is an important precondition for cooperation and

coordination in teams. Especially, when the tasks performed by individual team members are highly interdependent, team members are vulnerable to the actions of their fellow team members. If one team member misses a deadline and does not deliver results that are needed by other team members, the whole team process is slowed down. With low levels of trust, team members would not voluntarily engage in task sharing, and cooperation benefits would be difficult to achieve. Even if team members engage in cooperation, they will probably use additional time to monitor their colleagues' progress. The positive relation between trust and team performance has been shown in various studies (for a meta-analytical review see Breuer et al. 2015). It is important to note that the relation between trust and performance is not unidirectional. High team performance might also have positive effects on team trust and the appraisal of one's fellow team members. Besides the influence of trust on team performance, trust is related to various other positive outcomes in team contexts such as team cohesiveness, affective commitment, extra-role behavior, and a lower rate of counterproductive behavior (Mach et al. 2010; Colquitt et al. 2007). While there is quite a substantial amount of literature on the importance of trust in face-to-face teams, the importance of trust in virtual teams has been given less attention. Initial studies suggest that trust is an important driver for team cohesiveness (Jarvenpaa et al. 2004) and performance in virtual teams (Breuer et al. 2015). However, the structures of virtual teams often lead to a slowed development of trust. Due to the reduced contact in virtual teams it is more difficult for a team member to assess features of their colleagues that refer to trustworthiness (ability, benevolence, integrity; cf. Mayer et al. 1995). Members of face-to-face teams often share their coffee breaks and have the chance to learn about each other's interests and values in an informal way. Therefore, they should be able to estimate their colleagues' integrity and benevolence. In addition, they are more likely to know about the success or failure of their colleagues' tasks, and should therefore be able to estimate their colleagues' task-related abilities. Within virtual teams, informal communication is usually reduced and it takes team members longer to get to know each other. Hence, team members have less information about the trustworthiness of their colleagues and it should take longer to develop the same levels of trust as in face-to-face teams.

3   Asynchronous Communication

Asynchronous communication brings additional challenges to virtual teams, especially regarding the formation of trust. Therefore, we include the description of a theory of asynchronous communication and its implications for virtual cooperation in this section.

As mentioned earlier, working in different time zones constrains the choice of communication media a team can use and therefore negatively influences the performance on certain tasks. Daft and Lengel (1984) introduced the concept of "media richness" to rank communication media regarding their ability to convey a certain amount of information in a certain time. The crucial factors of media richness are a communication medium's ability to handle multiple information cues, enable rapid feedback, build a personal focus, and use natural language. In this logic, face-to-face communication is the richest medium while written documents are the leanest media. The intention of media richness theory was to evaluate communication media within organizations regarding their appropriateness for a specific communication task. While unambiguous information can be either conveyed via a lean or a rich medium, equivocal messages require a high amount of media richness. It is important to note that the richness of a medium is a constant in media richness theory. Only the requirements of a communication task may change while the richness of a medium has to match or exceed the requirements of a message's equivocality. Therefore, regarding the success of a communication task it would always be an appropriate choice to use rich media such as face-to-face communication. But as rich media often only reach a few addressees, it is sometimes more efficient to use a leaner communication medium, as long as it is able to resolve the equivocality of the message. In asynchronous cooperation, team members are restricted to relatively lean communication media. Thus, media richness theory would predict a suboptimal fit for the conveyance of messages high in equivocality. The consequences of this mismatch could be prolonged time costs for additional explanations or, in the worst case, misunderstandings as a result of unresolved equivocality.

Dennis and Valacich (1999) and Dennis et al. (2008) advanced the idea of media richness and introduced the concept of media synchronicity. The premise of this theory is that media vary in their support of synchronicity in communication, which is defined as shared focus. Further, there are two basic categories of communication tasks that require different levels of synchronicity. Thus, for effective communication the level of synchronicity a medium supports has to match the requirements of the communication task. Media synchronicity theory identifies five characteristics of communication media that define their support of synchronicity: transmission velocity (time delay between sending and receiving a message), symbol sets (number and richness of media channels), parallelism (possibility to have several conversations at a time), rehearsability (possibility to take some time to craft a message), and reprocessability (possibility to reread or rehear a message). A high transmission velocity and the conveyance of several symbol sets enhance the synchronicity of a medium. Parallelism, rehearsability, and reprocessability are features of rather asynchronous media. A high transmission velocity enables team members to rapidly exchange ideas and arguments and equivocality can be resolved quickly. The more symbol sets such as language, gestures, and voice a medium transmits, the easier it is to avoid misunderstandings because messages can be sent on multiple channels. For example, in face-to-face interaction, an ironic statement can be marked by a change in voice or a hand sign for quotation marks. Even if the recipient does not understand the irony, the sender has the chance to explain the situation if recognizing a puzzled look of the conversation partner. Using a text based medium such as e-mail, an ironic statement might be misinterpreted more easily and it is less likely that the misunderstanding will be resolved.

Parallelism describes the number of conversations that can be held simultaneously via a medium. When using synchronous media such as telephone or face-to-face interaction, people can only have one conversation at a time. Even though the number of participants is theoretically not limited, only one participant at a time can effectively convey his/her message because the channel for the other participants is blocked during that time. In contrast, with e-mails people can engage in multiple conversations at a time, using the time delay in a specific single conversation for other conversations. Also, more than one person at a time can produce a message and send it via the medium without blocking it for the other users.

Rehearsability is the possibility for a sender to fine tune or to craft a message before sending it. In synchronous communication, a sender does not have much time to think about the exact wording of a message as recipients are waiting for a quick response whereas in asynchronous communication a sender can take his time to rewrite a message or to adjust the wording to the recipient. Research has shown that this additional time is particularly valued by introverted (as compared to extraverted) persons and by persons high in social anxiety, suggesting that asynchronous communications provide additional leeway and protection for the communicating parties (Hertel et al. 2008). On the side of the recipient, asynchronous communication offers the advantage that a message is saved for reprocessing. Whether it is a voice memo or an e-mail the recipient can rehear or review the message several times until he has fully decoded and understood the message. Additionally, while the content of a synchronous conversation is often prone to memory errors, the content of an asynchronous conversation is protocolled for later review.

Concerning conversation tasks, Media Synchronicity Theory discriminates between conveyance processes and convergence processes. Conveyance describes the one-way communication of new information from a sender to one or more recipients. Conveyance of information enables the recipients to create or revise their mental models of a situation. Convergence is the discussion of preprocessed information and the matching of individual mental models of all participants of the conversation. As convergence processes involve the discussion of information, they require a high transmission velocity. Hence, synchronous communication media are better suited for a communication task including a high level of convergence than asynchronous communication media. On the other hand, conveyance processes afford exact information processing on the side of the receivers. The possibility to craft a message to enhance its comprehensibleness and the possibility for the receivers to reprocess a message and take their time to decode it are beneficial for conveyance processes. Hence, asynchronous as compared to synchronous communication media might be better suited for communication tasks including high levels of conveyance.

As mentioned earlier, members of virtual teams often do not have the choice to use synchronous media, especially when they are dispersed over different time zones. Thus, communication media cannot always be matched perfectly to their communication tasks, making the coordination within the team more difficult. For instance, it is more difficult for members of asynchronously communicating teams to discuss and build a shared schedule as it is harder to keep track of each member's progress. Especially, when the team task is highly interdependent, asynchronous teams might experience loss of efficiency if they cannot manage to coordinate their work. Poor coordination will not only directly affect the team's performance but will also negatively influence the trust within the team. If coordination problems occur, team members are likely to attribute them to stable internal factors of their colleagues (Weiner 2001). They will assume that their colleagues either lack the ability to perform their task in time or that they are not willing to do so and therefore lack integrity.

Another challenge for the development of trust in asynchronously communicating teams is the low perceived interactivity between the team members (Burgoon et al. 2010). As most people only rarely engage in informal chatting in asynchronous communication, team members are less likely to get to know each other and experience similarities between them and their colleagues. Thus, they are less likely to assume that their colleagues are benevolent toward them.

Taken together, coordination difficulties and low experienced interactivity as the two main challenges of asynchronous communication should complicate the development of trust in asynchronously communicating teams.

4   Competencies in Virtual Teams

In this section, we will discuss competencies that help to overcome the challenges of virtual cooperation. We will start by giving a short review of the literature on competencies in virtual teams. Based on this review, we propose a set of competencies that should be particularly crucial for building and maintaining trust in asynchronous virtual cooperation.

4.1   Literature on Virtual Team Competencies

The growing prevalence of virtual teams has triggered a great deal of research on the preconditions of effective collaboration in geographically dispersed groups. However, this research so far has focused on communication technologies, task fit, and interpersonal processes while the required competencies at the person level have been rather neglected (Krumm and Hertel 2013). This is quite surprising as knowledge of competency requirements is a necessary condition for efficient staffing and development of virtual teams.

Arguably, considering competencies for virtual teamwork might start with skills that are necessary for face-to-face teamwork (Hertel et al. 2006). Stevens and Campion (1994) proposed a taxonomy for traditional teamwork competencies, including taskwork and teamwork related skills. Taskwork skills are similar to skills required when persons work alone. They include the technical skills that are necessary to perform a given task. For example, a software engineer needs to know the programming language and an accountant needs to know business sciences, regardless of working alone or within a team. More specifically for working in groups, teamwork skills include interpersonal skills such as conflict resolution skills, collaborative problem solving skills, and communication skills, as well as self-management skills such as goal setting and performance management skills, and planning and task coordination skills.

However, in addition to taskwork and teamwork skills, virtual teamwork might also require competencies as a consequence of the specific working conditions (Hertel et al. 2006). Research on such telecooperation related skills is relatively rare. The existing literature on competencies in virtual teams mainly comprises case studies that derive competency requirements based on the comparison of successful and unsuccessful virtual teams, or of theoretical analyses that derive competencies from the additional demands in virtual as compared to face-to-face teams. For instance, Shin (2004) argues that media literacy and virtual communication skills are important because members of virtual teams often depend on digitized and asynchronous communication for their team coordination. Moreover, as trust is harder to establish in virtual teams, a high trustworthiness on the one hand and a high propensity to trust on the other hand should foster the formation of trust. Since it is often difficult for a virtual team to track the progress of each team member (Harvey et al. 2004) in order to adjust the allocations of responsibilities within the team, it seems important that team members are capable of organizing and managing their own work. Hence, self-management skills and a high degree of conscientiousness should be advantageous. Members of virtual teams are often confronted with different cultural backgrounds (Ellingson and Wiethoff 2002). Even if a team does not work across geographical borders, team members can be confronted with different norms and rules based on the different sites of their organization. Therefore, openness for new experience, the ability to adapt to new circumstances, and tolerance toward ambiguity should be helpful in virtual cooperation. Although plausible assumptions about relevant competencies can be derived from the demands of virtual teamwork, empirical studies to test these assumptions are needed.

As perhaps the first quantitative study, Hertel et al. (2006) developed and tested a model of virtual teamwork competencies comprising the three factors of taskwork related competencies, teamwork related competencies, and telecooperation related competencies. The latter included competencies such as persistence, willingness to learn, creativity, independence, interpersonal trust, and intercultural skills. Based on this model the authors developed a web based selection tool for members of virtual teams (Virtual Teamwork Competency Inventory, VTCI), and validated this instrument using a sample of 258 members of organizational virtual teams. Participants completed the VTCI, and both individual and team performance were rated by the team managers. The results for the individual performance ratings confirmed only taskwork and teamwork related competencies as significant predictors. However, at the team level the selected telecooperation related competencies explained significant parts of the team performance, in particular cooperativeness and creativity.

Conscientiousness and independence had at least a marginally significant influence on performance.

In addition to the lack of empirical work, the current literature on virtual team competencies is rather unsystematic so far. Krumm and Hertel (2013) suggested linking the research on virtual team competencies to established general work competency taxonomies. In an empirical study Krumm et al. (2015) fitted 60 competencies from literature research on virtual teams to the eight dimensions of the Great Eight Model (Bartram 2005). This theoretical model was validated with 175 members of virtual teams and 205 members of traditional face-to-face teams, respectively, who were asked to assess the importance of each competency for the success of their team (either traditional or virtual). The results showed that the Great Eight dimensions of Leading & Deciding and Analyzing & Interpreting were considered to be more important in virtual than in traditional team contexts. Thus, this study provides an initial framework for structuring competencies relevant for virtual team members.

The research on competencies so far mainly focuses on performance as the primary outcome measure, neglecting socio-emotional outcomes such as trust. However, socio-emotional outcomes, and trust in particular, might provide more process-oriented information, enabling both a more thorough understanding of team processes as well as a more timely intervention (e.g., by team managers) when things go wrong. An initial study on competencies in virtual teams that also incorporates trust has been conducted by Cogliser et al. (2012). They examined the Big Five personality dimensions as potential predictors of performance, emergent leadership, and perception of trustworthiness in virtual teams. The results showed positive effects for the Big Five dimensions of Agreeableness, Extraversion, and Stability as predictors of perceived trustworthiness of team leaders. Although the authors did not include a direct measure for trust, trustworthiness can be regarded as an important antecedent of trust. Therefore, this study shows that personality can have a significant influence on the development of trust in virtual teams.

4.2 A Model of Competencies in Asynchronous Virtual Teams

Research on competencies in virtual teams is still in its early stages and empirical studies to test theoretical claims are scarce. This is even more the case for specific dimensions of virtuality, such as asynchronicity that have a strong impact on the demands of the teamwork. Despite the importance of trust for team processes like cohesion, satisfaction and performance, trust has so far been neglected as an outcome measure in empirical research. Therefore, we developed a model of competencies that should foster trust in teams that have to mainly rely on asynchronous communication media. We will describe this model in this section.

The two main challenges that asynchronous communication brings to virtual teams are hindered coordination and the feeling of reduced interactivity. Hindered coordination leads to negative attribution regarding colleagues' abilities and integrity. The reduced interactivity hinders the team members from getting to know each other. Hence, it is less likely that team members perceive their colleagues to be benevolent. Taken together, we assume that the evaluation of trustworthiness is lower in asynchronous contexts, which in turn reduces trust.

For our model we tried to identify competencies that help members of asynchronous virtual teams increase the interactivity of the teamwork and to improve the coordination of the team. When the perceived interactivity in a team is low, the probability that team members engage in conversations is also low. An extraverted team member would be most likely to start a conversation, engage in informal chats, and share private information. This action could trigger the colleagues to also engage in conversations and thus increase the level of interactivity within the team. Additionally, when the exchange between team members is relatively low, it is necessary for team members to be proactive, in order to share and ask for information. Team members who are familiar with the use of asynchronous media perceive them as richer than team members unfamiliar with these media. Therefore, team members who are familiar with asynchronous media should perceive more interactivity in their team and be more likely to engage in conversations. Further, they know how to adapt their message to a particular receiver and hence foster mutual understanding. Thus, the competencies of extraversion, proactivity and knowledge in computer mediated communication (CMC) should help team members to actively engage in conversations and increase the perceived interactivity.

Hindered coordination in asynchronous teams prevents teams from frequently attuning the responsibilities and tasks assigned to each team member according to the actual necessities of the team. Therefore, it is important that team members fulfill their allocated tasks within the deadlines, as the delay of one team member could block the whole team if their tasks are strongly interdependent. For this purpose, team members need self-managing skills that help them to estimate their workload when task allocation is discussed and to plan and execute their tasks within the deadlines. In addition to the ability to organize their own workload and to perform within agreed upon time limits, team members also need to be willing to do so. Conscientious team members work thoroughly on allocated tasks and try hard to fulfill them on time. In order to directly improve the coordination within the team, it would be essential to improve team members' knowledge about their colleagues' progress. Thus, proactive gathering and sharing of information would be productive. Asynchronous communication features the possibility to have more than one conversation at once. Some of these conversations are more important at a given time than other conversations. When a team member fails to deliver information that is needed by a colleague to fulfill a task, coordination losses occur. It is therefore crucial that team members keep track of their conversations and answer at the right time. The knowledge about the used medium helps to organize one's conversations and to address the right recipients. Additionally, team members need to remember when they have to answer a message or deliver a certain piece of

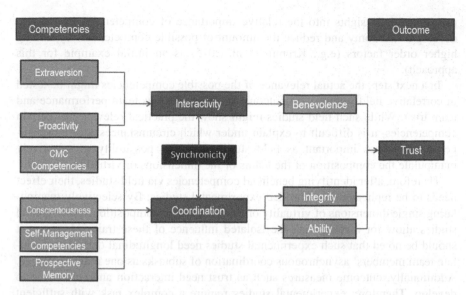

Fig. 1 A model of competencies in asynchronous virtual teams

information. In summary, self-management competencies, conscientiousness, proactivity, CMC competencies, and prospective memory can help to make up for coordination difficulties in asynchronous cooperation. A graphical overview of the model is provided in Fig. 1.

5 Research Approaches on Competencies in Virtual Teams

Virtual teams are widely established despite a lack of empirical knowledge about competency requirements. In order to develop a substantial basis for personnel selection and development of virtual teams, empirical research is necessary. In this section we will discuss some research approaches that could help to test theoretical claims and further develop competency models for virtual teams.

The goal of research should be the development of a taxonomy of competencies that are important for members of virtual teams. As Hertel et al. (2006) have argued, there might be a substantial overlap between competencies necessary for virtual and for face-to-face teamwork. In order to identify the competencies that are specific for virtual teamwork, it is necessary to include face-to-face teams as baseline measures into research designs (Krumm and Hertel 2013). Moreover, as virtual teams are not a homogeneous group of teams but might vary in group composition and dimensions of virtuality, it is necessary to further investigate the isolated influence of these traits on competency requirements.

Since a profound database from systematic empirical research is still lacking, pilot studies with experienced members and managers of virtual teams might provide initial insights into the relative importance of competencies in order to develop a taxonomy and reduce the amount of possible competencies by finding higher order factors (e.g., Krumm et al. 2015, as an initial example for this approach).

In a next step, the actual relevance of the possible competencies might be tested in correlative field studies with outcome measures such as team performance and team trust. While such field studies might show the practical relevance of certain competencies, it is difficult to explain under which circumstances a certain competency becomes important as field studies lack the possibility to selectively manipulate the composition of the teams or the dimensions of virtuality.

Therefore, after identifying beneficial competencies via field studies, their effect needs to be replicated in controlled experimental studies. By selectively manipulating single dimensions of virtuality or aspects of team composition, experimental studies allow for investigating the isolated influence of these traits. However, it should be noted that such experimental studies need longitudinal designs to simulate team members' asynchronous coordination of subtasks as one main challenge. Additionally, outcome measures such as trust need interaction and some time to develop. Therefore, experimental studies require a complex task with sufficient interdependency of the team members to simulate a virtual team setting.

The overarching question, "Which competencies are needed in virtual teams?" is quite complex. The answer is dependent on team composition and the communication media the team uses. Additionally, some competencies that are needed for face-to-face teamwork might also be beneficial. In this chapter, we have given an example of a model development and discussed a possible research agenda that can help to add another piece to this puzzle. In order to achieve a final answer to the question, more theoretical framework that considers the dimensions of virtuality and, most of all, more empirical research is needed. This will lead to practical implementations that might help to improve the success of virtual teams via more efficient team staffing and development.

References

Bartram, D. (2005). The great eight competencies: A criterion-centric approach to validation. *Journal of Applied Psychology, 90*(6), 1185.

Breuer, C., Hüffmeier, J., & Hertel, G. (2015). Does trust matter more in virtual teams? A meta-analysis on virtuality and documentation as moderators of the relationship between trust and team effectiveness. Manuscript submitted for publication.

Burgoon, J. K., Chen, F., & Twitchell, D. P. (2010). Deception and its detection under synchronous and asynchronous computer-mediated communication. *Group Decision and Negotiation, 19* (4), 345–366.

Cogliser, C. C., Gardner, W. L., Gavin, M. B., & Broberg, J. C. (2012). Big five personality factors and leader emergence in virtual teams relationships with team trustworthiness, member performance contributions, and team performance. *Group & Organization Management, 37* (6), 752–784.

Colquitt, J. A., Scott, B. A., & LePine, J. A. (2007). Trust, trustworthiness, and trust propensity: A meta-analytic test of their unique relationships with risk taking and job performance. *Journal of Applied Psychology, 92*(4), 909.

Costa, A. C. (2003). Work team trust and effectiveness. *Personnel Review, 32*, 605–622.

Daft, R. L., & Lengel, R. H. (1984). Information richness: A new approach to managerial behavior and organization design. In B. M. Staw & L. L. Cummings (Eds.), *Research in organizational behavior* (Vol. 6, pp. 191–233). Greenwich, CT: JAI Press.

Dennis, A. R., Fuller, R. M., & Valacich, J. S. (2008). Media, tasks, and communication processes: A theory of media synchronicity. *MIS quarterly, 32*(3), 575–600.

Dennis, A. R., & Valacich, J. S. (1999, January). Rethinking media richness: Towards a theory of media synchronicity. In *Proceedings of the 32nd Annual Hawaii International Conference on Systems Sciences, 1999, HICSS-32* (10pp). IEEE.

Ellingson, J. E., & Wiethoff, C. (2002). From traditional to virtual: Staffing the organization of the future today. In R. L. Heneman & D. B. Greenberger (Eds.), *Human resource management in virtual organizations* (pp. 141–177). Greenwich, CT: Information Age.

Harvey, M., Novicevic, M. M., & Garrison, G. (2004). Challenges to staffing global virtual teams. *Human Resource Management Review, 14*(3), 275–294.

Hertel, G., Geister, S., & Konradt, U. (2005). Managing virtual teams: A review of current empirical research. *Human Resource Management Review, 15*(1), 69–95.

Hertel, G., Konradt, U., & Voss, K. (2006). Competencies for virtual teamwork: Development and validation of a web-based selection tool for members of distributed teams. *European Journal of Work and Organizational Psychology, 15*(4), 477–505.

Hertel, G., Schroer, J., Batinic, B., & Naumann, S. (2008). Do shy people prefer to send e-mail? Personality effects on communication media preferences in threatening and non-threatening situations. *Social Psychology, 39*(4), 231–243.

Hilbert, M., & López, P. (2011). The world's technological capacity to store, communicate, and compute information. *Science, 332*(6025), 60–65.

Jarvenpaa, S. L., Shaw, T. R., & Staples, D. S. (2004). Toward contextualized theories of trust: The role of trust in global virtual teams. *Information systems research, 15*(3), 250–267.

Kirkman, B. L., & Mathieu, J. E. (2005). The dimensions and antecedents of team virtuality. *Journal of Management, 31*(5), 700–718.

Krumm, S., & Hertel, G. (2013). Knowledge, skills, abilities and other characteristics (KSAOs) for virtual teamwork. In A. Bakker & D. Derks (Eds.), *The psychology of digital media and work* (pp. 80–100). East Sussex: Psychology Press.

Krumm, S., Kanthak, J, & Hertel, G. (2015). What does it take to be a virtual team player? The knowledge, skills, abilities, and other characteristics required in virtual teams. *Human Performance* (in press)

Mach, M., Dolan, S., & Tzafrir, S. (2010). The differential effect of team members' trust on team performance: The mediation role of team cohesion. *Journal of Occupational and Organizational Psychology, 83*, 771–794.

Mayer, R. C., Davis, J. H., & Schoorman, F. D. (1995). An integrative model of organizational trust. *Academy of management review, 20*, 709–734.

Microsoft Research. (2015). *Research labs worldwide—Microsoft Research.* http://research.microsoft.com/en-us/labs/

Shin, Y. (2004). A person-environment fit model for virtual organizations. *Journal of Management, 30*(5), 725–743.

Stevens, M. J., & Campion, M. A. (1994). The knowledge, skill, and ability requirements for teamwork: Implications for human resource management. *Journal of management, 20*(2), 503–530.

Townsend, A. M., DeMarie, S. M., & Hendrickson, A. R. (1998). Virtual teams: Technology and the workplace of the future. *The Academy of Management Executive, 12*(3), 17–29.

Weiner, B. (2001). Intrapersonal and interpersonal theories of motivation from an attribution perspective. In *Student motivation* (pp. 17–30). New York: Springer.

Trust in Electronically Mediated Negotiations

Jens Mazei and Guido Hertel

Abstract Interpersonal negotiations can be critically important. For instance, individuals negotiate central personal issues such as salaries or the division of labor, organizations negotiate consequential business deals, and political parties negotiate peace agreements. Notably, such negotiations are increasingly realized and supported by electronic communication media—for example by e-mail, telephone, or video-conferencing systems. Besides potential advantages such as decreased travel and opportunity costs, however, such electronically mediated negotiations are often characterized by low levels of trust among negotiators, which in turn might hamper the achievement of mutually beneficial (i.e., "Win–Win") agreements in negotiations. This paper illuminates both the antecedents and consequences of trust in negotiations. While it is conducive to exchange information about one's interests related to a negotiation to achieve mutually beneficial agreements, providing such information can render negotiators vulnerable to exploitation by their counterparts. Therefore, beneficial negotiation outcomes are facilitated by trust. First, we discuss whether and how trust is in fact helpful to achieving mutually satisfactory negotiation agreements. We then focus on the potential effects of electronic communication on trust at the bargaining table. We conclude with psychological strategies that might support trust in (electronically mediated) negotiations, helping people to gauge the potential of negotiations as consequential form of social interaction.

Keywords Negotiation • Trust • Electronic media • Virtual • Integrative potential

1 Introduction

> Mutual trust is an essential ingredient in effective [...] negotiations
> Thompson et al. (2010, p. 501)

J. Mazei (✉)
TU Dortmund University, Dortmund, Germany
e-mail: jens.mazei@tu-dortmund.de

G. Hertel (✉)
University of Münster, Münster, Germany
e-mail: ghertel@uni-muenster.de

© Springer International Publishing Switzerland 2016   191
B. Blöbaum (ed.), *Trust and Communication in a Digitized World*, Progress in IS,
DOI 10.1007/978-3-319-28059-2_11

Communicating over electronic media has increasingly become an integral part of our society (Hilbert and López 2011). Across domains and countries, people use electronic devices to connect, communicate, and pursue their objectives. Reflecting this current trend, interpersonal negotiations are also increasingly conducted using electronic communication media (Kurtzberg et al. 2009; Stuhlmacher and Citera 2005). Negotiation, in turn, can be central to success in a variety of domains of life. Resources such as salaries or promotions, business deals or joint ventures, as well as political conflicts are frequently negotiated. In general, negotiation often takes place when people are unable to realize their goals on their own (Thompson 2009; Thompson et al. 2010). Whether and how electronic communication affects negotiations is therefore important for researchers and practitioners alike (Moore et al. 1999; Thompson and Nadler 2002). On the one hand, electronic media provide many benefits: people located in different countries and time zones can directly negotiate with each other while saving travel costs (Morris et al. 2002). Moreover, negotiators are enabled to thoroughly adapt their plans during the course of negotiating, or to reprocess previously exchanged offers, which can be more difficult during a face-to-face meeting. On the other hand, however, electronically mediated negotiations may come with specific challenges: when negotiating over electronic media, people can experience lowered trust and less desire to interact again with each other as compared to face-to-face negotiations (Naquin and Paulson 2003). How, then, can trust be supported to mitigate this drawback?

The current paper discusses the role of trust in electronically mediated negotiations. Following a description of central concepts in the domain of negotiations to provide a conceptual basis for our analysis (Sect. 2), we first outline whether trust generally helps negotiators to achieve beneficial negotiation agreements (Sect. 3). Afterwards, we describe the theoretical and practical relevance of trust in *electronically mediated* negotiations, and portray how such negotiations differ from face-to-face negotiations with respect to trust (Sect. 4). Finally, we discuss how trust can be supported in electronically mediated negotiations (Sect. 5). Examples of psychological strategies that should help e-negotiators to develop trust at the table are provided.

2 Negotiation: Terms and Concepts

Negotiation is defined as communication among two or more parties to resolve differences in interests (Pruitt 1998). As can be inferred from this definition, one remarkable characteristic of negotiation is its omnipresence (Thompson et al. 2010). People frequently engage in negotiations, including those that take place in formal (e.g., about employment terms) and also informal contexts (e.g., when discussing which movie to see, or when to meet at a bar). However, negotiations can differ with respect to their underlying structural characteristics. Negotiation research typically distinguishes between two broad types of negotiation situations (Thompson 2009). In the first type—*distributive* negotiation—usually a single negotiation issue is discussed. In this situation, one party's gain equals the other party's loss (fixed-sum situation). For example, a new employee at a large organization may negotiate a better salary as the sole issue: the more money the employee receives, the less the supervisor has left for other purposes.

While distributive negotiations usually include only a single issue, *integrative* negotiations (the second general type of negotiation situations) include multiple issues. Most importantly, the relevant issues may be valued differently by the negotiating parties, reflecting a variable-sum situation (Thompson et al. 2010). Given the different valuation of negotiation issues, integrative negotiations enable negotiators to obtain *joint gains* (i.e., achieve "Win–Win" agreements). Suppose, for example, a new employee negotiates not only salary (issue #1) but also the total number of work hours (issue #2). The employee may be especially interested in obtaining a high salary to purchase a new car, while being relatively flexible in working a couple of more hours every week. Conversely, the supervisor may be relatively more interested in having the employee work extra hours, perhaps because a new time-consuming project is pending, and less concerned about granting a higher salary (as the work done by the employee may be worth it or be needed). This negotiation includes *integrative potential* since the two negotiators appear to value the included issues (salary and number of work hours) differently, making it possible for both sides to trade-off the issues to better reconcile their underlying interests. Furthermore, integrative negotiations may also contain issues for which negotiators even have identical preferences (Thompson and Hastie 1990). For example, both the supervisor and the employee may want the work location (issue #3) to be Chicago instead of a smaller city nearby in the Midwest, although the negotiators need not be aware of this fact. Such a *compatible* issue also enables negotiators to obtain joint gains if they, in fact, recognize their converging preferences. Notably, however, such a situation theoretically allows for exploitation, which we describe below in our discussion of trust.

Interestingly, it is assumed that "integrative potential exists in just about every negotiation situation" (Thompson 2009, p. 75). Therefore, a central outcome of negotiations is the extent to which the negotiators are actually able to integrate their interests. In other words, do negotiators realize a negotiation's integrative potential and obtain high *integrative negotiation outcomes*, or do they unnecessarily leave value on the table? In fact, research has shown that negotiators often fail at fully realizing the integrative potential (Thompson and Hastie 1990). Much negotiation research thus has investigated when and how negotiators can obtain better integrative outcomes. In this respect, task-relevant information exchange about the interests related to a negotiation has been shown to be very conducive to attaining high integrative outcomes (Thompson 1991). De Dreu and his colleagues (2006, p. 927), for example, asserted that

> to develop agreement, people need to get a good understanding of their own preferences and priorities, to communicate those to their counterpart, and to integrate information about other's preferences and priorities into their own understanding of the problem at hand.

By exchanging information about their interests, negotiators may realize that they value several issues differently, or even have identical preferences regarding a negotiation issue. This may allow them to come up with ideas about how to settle for a deal that integrates their needs (Thompson 1991). However, despite the potential effectiveness of this strategy, negotiators may be reluctant to simply share information and reveal what they want in a negotiation because they may think that providing such information will disadvantage them. One critical facilitator of the process of information sharing—and therefore potential precursor of integrative negotiation outcomes—should be trust (Gunia et al. 2011; Kong et al. 2014).

3   Trust in Negotiations

Negotiation scholars often acknowledge the critical importance of trust for successful negotiations (Thompson et al. 2010). Trust can be defined as "a psychological state comprising the intention to accept vulnerability based upon positive expectations of the intentions or behavior of another" (Rousseau et al. 1998, p. 395; Mayer et al. 1995). While our previous discussion focused on the tangible *economic outcomes* of a negotiation (i.e., the specific terms of a negotiation agreement; e.g., whether to let the employee work in Chicago or in a smaller town nearby), trust can be conceptualized as a *socioemotional outcome* (also known as the social psychological outcome or subjective value) of a negotiation (Curhan et al. 2006; Thompson 1990). More specifically, trust reflects a central component of the relationship among negotiators (Curhan et al. 2006) and may play an important role at the negotiation table.

As previously mentioned, cooperative behaviors such as information exchange are often helpful in negotiations because negotiators can discover differences and similarities in their interests, which allows them to generate mutually beneficial solutions (Thompson 1991). Exchanging such information, however, also entails risks, which negotiators may recognize: a negotiating counterpart may strategically use the received information to deceive a negotiator, or simply may not reciprocate the received information (Kong et al. 2014). For example, when learning that the employee wishes to work in Chicago instead of a smaller town in the Midwest, the supervisor may pretend that it is important for the employee to work in the smaller town, although this may not be true. Following this line of thought, the supervisor may allegedly "concede" on the work location issue and agree on Chicago as location but insist on concessions regarding the salary from the employee. In this situation, providing information clearly backfired for the employee. Taken together, although sharing information about one's interests can be a helpful means to find mutually beneficial agreements (Thompson 1991), this strategy makes negotiators vulnerable (Gunia et al. 2011). Vulnerability, in turn, is especially relevant for the context of negotiations, as people often negotiate objectives of high importance (e.g., peace agreements or consequential business deals). As trust reflects the willingness to *accept* vulnerability based on positive expectations regarding another person's behaviors and intentions (Rousseau et al. 1998), it should enable negotiators to engage in cooperative but risky behaviors such as information sharing (Thompson et al. 2010). Therefore, the level of trust among negotiators should eventually relate to the joint success of negotiations.

To examine trust effects at the negotiation table, recent research has meta-analyzed the extant literature on trust in negotiation (Kong et al. 2014). The authors were able to include 38 independent studies on the relationship between trust and process as well as outcome variables in negotiation. In line with the theoretical reasoning, the results showed that trust was indeed positively related to joint outcomes in negotiations (the average corrected correlation was estimated at $r = .26$). In other words, mutual trust helped negotiators find an agreement that satisfied their underlying interests. Furthermore, this main effect was mediated by integrative behaviors such as information sharing. The data also revealed several critical contingencies of the main effect. One major moderator was a negotiation's integrative potential: as expected, trust is increasingly positively related to integrative behaviors like information sharing as well as to joint outcomes in negotiations with relatively more integrative potential. However, many practitioners and scholars may ask whether the mutual success at the bargaining table comes at the cost of individual outcomes. In other words, does trusting others in negotiation impair one's own profit? By definition, trusting leads to vulnerability, thereby allowing others to take advantage of this vulnerability (Gunia et al. 2011; Kong et al. 2014). The meta-analysis by Kong and colleagues (2014) also examined this question and revealed that trust was also positively related to a trustor's individual outcome, although to a somewhat lesser degree (overall corrected $r = .10$).

In conclusion, trust appears to be an influential factor in negotiations. Most notably, trust increases joint success at the negotiation table by facilitating conducive negotiation behaviors such as information sharing. In this respect, trust fulfills an important *indirect* function in negotiations because it works as a process variable to achieve mutually beneficial negotiation agreements. Moreover, trust can also be an important outcome on its own: trust, as an integral part of the relationship among negotiators, reflects a relevant socioemotional negotiation outcome. Negotiators, in turn, appear to care a lot about such subjective results of a negotiation, and trust at the bargaining table can provide a valuable basis for a potential future (working) relationship (Curhan et al. 2006). Trust, therefore, can be important beyond a single current negotiation situation.

Given the rise of electronic forms of communication that enable negotiation, the question arises whether and how negotiating over electronic media affects trust (Naquin and Paulson 2003). This issue is discussed in the following section.

4 Trust in Electronically Mediated Negotiations

Many modern work processes are already performed via information technologies due to a multitude of changes in the environment, including the pervasive general usage of electronic communication media and the globalization (Gilson et al. 2015; Hertel et al. 2005; Thompson and Nadler 2002). As a result, people also increasingly negotiate over electronic media nowadays (Moore et al. 1999; Morris et al. 2002). Electronically mediated negotiations are those that are conducted "using media other than face-to-face communication" (Stuhlmacher and Citera 2005, p. 70). The specific media by which people negotiate can be manifold: e-mail, phone, video-conferencing systems and text messaging applications all provide opportunities to negotiate, although these different media, of course, also differ in many respects (Purdy et al. 2000; Thompson 2009). Of special relevance to the current section, we focus on consequences of negotiating over electronic media for trust at the bargaining table. How do electronically mediated negotiations differ from face-to-face negotiations, and how does this impact trust?

Negotiation research has accumulated substantial knowledge about the psychology of negotiating over information technology (Thompson and Nadler 2002). One remarkable difference between e-mail negotiations and face-to-face negotiations, for instance, is the reduced amount of informal conversation—talking about issues not directly relevant to a negotiation itself (Morris et al. 2002). In e-mail negotiations, negotiators "schmooze" much less than in face-to-face negotiations as they disclose less personal information and also ask their counterpart fewer questions about issues unrelated to the negotiation (Morris et al. 2002; Thompson and Nadler 2002). While this difference between electronic and face-to-face negotiations pertains to the *verbal* aspects of communication, it is important to acknowledge that the communication medium itself also often limits the available personal cues about one's counterpart, or complicates the (verbal) provision of such cues. In e-mail negotiations, for instance, visual information or paraverbal characteristics such as looks, tone of voice, and so on are absent. However, paraverbal or non-verbal gestures such as nodding or briefly exchanging personal information (e.g., "how did you get here today?"; "how was the flight?") are elements that often naturally occur in face-to-face interactions and that facilitate the establishment of rapport among negotiators (Morris et al. 2002; Thompson and Nadler 2002). Furthermore, compensating for the genuine lack of social cues by writing in a pronounced relational style, for example, may be inappropriate in certain (business) contexts, which additionally makes it difficult to exchange relational information and to build a foundation for a working relationship (Naquin and Paulson 2003).

Further dynamics are engendered in electronically mediated negotiations beyond this lack of informal or relational conversation. In an initial meta-analysis on the topic, Stuhlmacher and Citera (2005) found that electronically mediated negotiations are characterized by more hostility than traditional face-to-face negotiations. Relatedly, Purdy and colleagues (2000) showed that people collaborate more (and compete less) in face-to-face negotiations as compared to negotiators interacting via phone or computer chat. And finally, it seems that using competitive behaviors is especially detrimental to e-negotiations. The use of threats or ultimatums impair reaching integrative agreements more in e-mail negotiations than in face-to-face negotiations (Morris et al. 2002). Negotiators interacting over electronic media thus appear to be very sensitive with respect to such behaviors. Summarizing these manifold influences that appear to reduce, or even deteriorate, the perceived interpersonal connection between negotiators, it is likely that negotiating over electronic media may strongly impact trust as a central part of the negotiator's relationship at the bargaining table (Morris et al. 2002; Thompson and Nadler 2002).

In a seminal study on this question, Naquin and Paulson (2003) specifically focused on the impact of negotiating over electronic media on trust by comparing face-to-face negotiations with negotiations conducted via e-mail. Their findings revealed several important insights. First, negotiators indeed appeared to trust each other less following e-mail negotiations as compared to negotiations conducted face-to-face (however, see also Wilson et al. 2006). Given the potentially important influence of trust in negotiations, this finding reveals a central pitfall of e-mail negotiations. A second and almost more important finding emerged in their study: negotiating over e-mail even reduced the experienced trust *prior* to the negotiation—an effect that was extraordinarily large (Cohen's $d = 3.55$)—which suggests that people's expectations regarding trust in electronically mediated negotiation are rather negative. Furthermore, the results also revealed that e-mail negotiators desired a future relationship with their counterpart to a lesser degree than face-to-face negotiators (Naquin and Paulson 2003). This finding is especially unfortunate as negotiation often plays a role in establishing a working relationship (e.g., many business contacts are initiated through negotiating).

In conclusion, although trust is an important precursor to success in negotiation, trust appears to be relatively low in e-negotiations compared to face-to-face negotiations. Given the fact, however, that many modern negotiations are or must be conducted over electronic media, advice on how to support trust appears helpful. Indeed, the reported findings of Naquin and Paulson (2003) suggested that at least part of the negative effects of electronically mediated negotiations might result from mere assumptions and negative expectations that need not necessarily be valid, but can still limit the outcome of electronic negotiations in advance. In what follows, we thus report relevant research to the question of how trust can be strengthened in electronically mediated negotiations.

5   Antecedents: How to Support Trust in Electronically Mediated Negotiations?

At first glance, the preceding insights on the lack of trust may promote a pronounced negative view of negotiations conducted over electronic media. However, evidence not only suggests that strategies can be applied to mitigate adverse effects occurring in electronically mediated negotiations (Moore et al. 1999), but that they may also provide several distinct advantages (e.g., reduced travel expenses; see below). Furthermore, as noted by Morris and his colleagues (2002, p. 89), "because uses of technologies evolve over time, it would be a mistake to assume that the social dynamics associated with e-mail are inevitable byproducts of inherent properties of the technology." In the following, we therefore report research on four strategies aimed at supporting trust development in electronically mediated negotiations by compensating for the detrimental effects of electronic communication: (a) exchanging personal information (schmoozing), (b) using humor, (c) having or establishing a shared group membership, and (d) heightening the salience of group memberships whose related norms support or value trust. Afterwards, we also outline three potential strengths of electronic negotiation that are often neglected: (e) (asynchronous) forms of electronic communication provide opportunities for drafting offers "safely" without immediate confrontation with counterparts, which can be particularly important for non-native speakers or people with social anxieties or uncertainties (Hertel et al. 2008); (f) asynchronous written communication might help deescalate emotionally "hot" negotiations under certain circumstances; and (g) automatic documentation (e.g., of offers, commitments, and so on) as the default in some electronic communication environments such as e-mail might build trust or compensate for lack of trust in virtual negotiations (Breuer et al. 2015; Naquin and Paulson 2003). These strategies might be interrelated or work in concert in certain contexts. For example, without exchanging any personal information in an electronic negotiation, the negotiators may not even realize that they share meaningful group memberships, which precludes the application of other strategies. Therefore, the suggested strategies should be most effective when applied in concert rather than as purely disjunctive strategies.

5.1   Exchanging Personal Information

As previously discussed, electronically mediated and face-to-face negotiations often differ from each other with respect to the amount of personal and task-irrelevant information exchanged (Morris et al. 2002). Such informal conversation, however, helps to establish rapport and trust at the bargaining table (Thompson and Nadler 2002). Therefore, inducing negotiators to exchange personal information should be a helpful means of mitigating the related disadvantages of electronically mediated negotiations. Indeed, empirical investigations of this strategy revealed promising findings. Among the many positive effects, inducing e-negotiators to exchange personal information led to more rapport prior to and after a negotiation, more positive perceptions of one's counterpart, more positive expectations regarding a working relationship, and eventually fewer negotiation impasses (Moore et al. 1999; Morris et al. 2002). It is important to note that, in this research tapping into the effects of schmoozing, the intervention to schmooze did not demand much from the participants: schmoozers "only" received some additional information about their counterpart (e.g., a small photo and some biographical information) and were instructed to have a brief phone call about personal issues prior to the negotiation, for instance (Morris et al. 2002). This research shows that even little things can make a dramatic change in electronically mediated negotiations (Thompson and Nadler 2002).

5.2 Using Humor

Beyond exchanging any information unrelated to a negotiation itself prior to (or as part of) a digitized communication, the exchange of *specific* content might also be helpful. A recent study suggests that using humor may be a valuable strategy for e-negotiations (Kurtzberg et al. 2009). The authors reasoned that sharing a humorous anecdote may generate positive feelings in interactions and create a shared positive experience, which may allow for trust to develop. In fact, using humor has been shown to be effective in electronically mediated negotiations. In two studies, some participants were induced to share a humorous cartoon (on the topic of negotiation) at the beginning of their actual negotiation while others were not, and the effects were very promising. Sharing the humorous cartoon not only led to more trust, but also to greater joint outcomes (Study 1; Kurtzberg et al. 2009). The results further revealed that the joint outcomes were higher because the negotiators more often realized that they had identical preferences regarding some negotiation issues (compatible issues), which underscores the heightened trust at the table (see above). Moreover, sharing the humorous cartoon led to more balanced, or fair, relative outcomes in the negotiations (Study 2). Taken together, humor can be very helpful in electronically mediated negotiations. As a final note of caution, however, it must be acknowledged that negotiators should aim to ensure that the humor does not invite misunderstandings or offensive interpretations (e.g., due to intercultural differences in social norms) to best gauge the potential of humor as a trust-supporting means (cf. Kurtzberg et al. 2009).

5.3 Shared Group Membership

Ample social psychological research suggests that group membership can provide a basis for the attribution of positive characteristics. According to social identity theory (Tajfel 1982; Tajfel and Turner 1979), people aim at generating self-esteem from being members of particular groups (cf. Smith and Mackie 2007). This can motivate people to generally evaluate members of one's ingroup (or the group as a whole) relative to outgroup members in more positive terms—a tendency called intergroup bias (Hewstone et al. 2002). Moore et al. (1999, p. 25) noted that in an "e-mail communication, individuals have fewer cues to interpret the actions, behaviors, and motivations of their partner, and may rely even more readily on the assumptions provided by common group membership." Consider the example of two professors negotiating the terms of a shared research project (e.g., who writes up which studies as first author). When they negotiate via e-mail, an especially salient characteristic might be their university affiliation (i.e., their respective group membership), as this information is provided as part of the e-mail address and also the signature at the end of each e-mail, whereas other personal characteristics like height or pronunciation normally available are less salient in the digital encounter. If the professors' affiliations are the same, they would be expected to engage in more positive mutual attributions—which may include trustworthiness—than when their affiliations differ (e.g., Harvard University and Yale University—two universities with a history of athletic rivalry). To sum up, if a common ingroup is available, e-negotiators may capitalize on the resulting tendency to mutually afford relatively more positive evaluations.

But what happens when a shared group membership is not yet available? In this situation, negotiators may attempt to generate a common ingroup or to recategorize the involved negotiators. According to the common ingroup identity model developed by Gaertner and colleagues (1993), creating a superordinate ingroup encompassing both subgroups allows for (previous) outgroup members to be seen as members of a common ingroup. As a result, they may be evaluated in a similar positive fashion, which can include trustworthiness (Gaertner and Dovidio 2012). Considering our example, the professors may reframe the negotiation as an interaction between two social psychologists with a shared interest in the topic of trust, which may be regarded as a meaningful common social group by the protagonists.

5.4 Groups Whose Norms Support Trust

Social norms—a group's accepted and endorsed ways to behave, think, or feel (Smith and Mackie 2007)—can exert a powerful influence on people. Do group norms also guide people's behavior when interacting rather anonymously as in certain forms of electronically mediated interaction? Interestingly, while some research has suggested that being anonymous leads people to depart from social norms, the social identity model of deindividuation effects (SIDE) suggests that people may actually increase their adherence to the currently available shared group norms (Postmes et al. 1998). The idea is that when individuating information is missing, people tend to see themselves more in terms of the available group memberships and thereby more strongly behave consistent with a group's norms or stereotypes (Postmes and Spears 2002; Postmes et al. 1998). This suggests an interesting avenue to support trust in electronically mediated negotiations. If the situation does not allow for meaningful individuating information, it would be wise to make salient those shared group memberships whose norms support trustworthy behavior. For instance, negotiators may emphasize that they are all paramedics or firefighters—occupations that are often perceived as trustworthy. If such an option is available, people may thus capitalize on the helpful consequences.

So far, we have outlined potential compensation strategies for the difficulties arising in electronically mediated negotiations. On the other hand, however, electronic media may also provide distinct strengths for negotiation (Galin et al. 2007), which are—of course—important to consider as well. Three potential advantages of electronically mediated negotiations are therefore delineated in the following sections.

5.5 Drafting and Intermediate Planning

An interesting advantage resulting from certain forms of electronic communication is that they naturally allow for thorough drafting and adapting of offers, strategies or plans while negotiating. When negotiating via e-mail, for instance, negotiators can take their time, evaluate what happened before, and adapt their plans to the current status of a negotiation. This can be especially relevant for people not negotiating in their first language, or for people who feel insecure in social situations (Hertel et al. 2008). Being able to engage in intermediate planning instead of responding immediately can thus provide a valuable opportunity for negotiators.

5.6 Potential for Deescalating Negotiations

Negotiations can include a multitude of emotions such as happiness or anger, which may strongly influence negotiation processes and outcomes (van Kleef et al. 2004). Although electronically mediated negotiations often seem to hinder a trusting or friendly course of interaction (Naquin and Paulson 2003; Stuhlmacher and Citera 2005), supporting negotiations with electronic media may also allow for emotions to calm down in certain circumstances. Introducing a pause in a heated debate among negotiators and deciding to continue negotiating over electronic devices may help negotiators to refocus on the negotiation issues themselves. In this respect, electronically-mediated negotiations may help negotiators separate the issues from the people involved (cf. Galin et al. 2007). Therefore, negotiations supported by electronic media may sometimes provide a potential for deescalating "hot" negotiations if the involved negotiators agree to interact more amiably when continuing negotiations via a more impersonal form of communication.

5.7   *Documentation of Course of Interaction*

A central feature of several electronic media is that they automatically document the course of interaction. In e-mail negotiations, for instance, automatic storage reflects the default option. Interestingly, such environments might reduce the perceived risks at the negotiation table because competitive tactics such as deceptions might be perceived as more easily revealed—even long after the completion of a negotiation (Naquin and Paulson 2003; see also Breuer et al. 2015). Therefore, the need for trust might be reduced when negotiators think of their counterparts as engaging in rather cooperative behaviors, since otherwise this might eventually backfire. Another advantage of the automatic documentation is that it allows negotiators to reprocess the previously exchanged offers and counteroffers, thereby potentially facilitating the generation of more complex offers. Indeed, research has shown that negotiating via e-mail increased the number of offers including multiple issues (Morris et al. 2002). Certain electronic media may thus also facilitate aspects of the course of negotiating.

6   Conclusion

Electronically mediated negotiations are increasingly becoming a pervasive part of modern life. In many contexts, people now rely on information technology to negotiate, which brings about many benefits (e.g., reduced travel and opportunity costs). Negotiating over electronic media, however, often comes at the cost of reduced trust. Given that trust can be a central facilitator of conducive negotiation behaviors such as information sharing, and simultaneously an important outcome on its own, we outlined strategies to overcome this drawback of e-negotiations. When people negotiate over electronic media, they are well advised to include an informal personal conversation as part of the beginning of an interaction, to use humor (if appropriate), to stress or generate shared group memberships where possible, and to heighten the salience of specific common groups whose norms support trust. Moreover, the genuine strengths of electronic communication media, such as intermediate planning and drafting opportunities regarding one's own interests (e.g., in asynchronous text-based communication forms such as e-mail) or the automatic documentation and reprocessability of the interaction can provide additional opportunities for trust maintenance in negotiations that are only initially understood.

References

Breuer, C., Hüffmeier, J., & Hertel, G. (2015). *Does trust matter more in virtual teams? A meta-analysis on virtuality as a moderator of the relationship between trust and team effectiveness.* Manuscript under review.

Curhan, J. R., Elfenbein, H. A., & Xu, H. (2006). What do people value when they negotiate? Mapping the domain of subjective value in negotiation. *Journal of Personality and Social Psychology, 91,* 493–512. doi:10.1037/0022-3514.91.3.493.

De Dreu, C. K. W., Beersma, B., Stroebe, K., & Euwema, M. C. (2006). Motivated information processing, strategic choice, and the quality of negotiated agreement. *Journal of Personality and Social Psychology, 90,* 927–943. doi:10.1037/0022-3514.90.6.927.

Gaertner, S. L., & Dovidio, J. F. (2012). The common ingroup identity model. In P. A. M. Van Lange, A. W. Kruglanski, & E. T. Higgins (Eds.), *Handbook of theories of social psychology* (pp. 439–457). Thousand Oaks, CA: Sage.

Gaertner, S. L., Dovidio, J. F., Anastasio, P. A., Bachman, B. A., & Rust, M. C. (1993). The common ingroup identity model: Recategorization and the reduction of intergroup bias. *European Review of Social Psychology, 4,* 1–26. doi:10.1080/14792779343000004.

Galin, A., Gross, M., & Gosalker, G. (2007). E-negotiation versus face-to-face negotiation what has changed–if anything? *Computers in Human Behavior, 23,* 787–797. doi:10.1016/j.chb.2004.11.009.

Gilson, L. L., Maynard, M. T., Young, N. C. J., Vartiainen, M., & Hakonen, M. (2015). Virtual teams research: 10 years, 10 themes, and 10 opportunities. *Journal of Management, 41,* 1313–1337. doi:10.1177/0149206314559946.

Gunia, B. C., Brett, J. M., Nandkeolyar, A. K., & Kamdar, D. (2011). Paying a price: Culture, trust, and negotiation consequences. *Journal of Applied Psychology, 96,* 774–789. doi:10.1037/a0021986.

Hertel, G., Geister, S., & Konradt, U. (2005). Managing virtual teams: A review of current empirical research. *Human Resource Management Review, 15,* 69–95. doi:10.1016/j.hrmr.2005.01.002.

Hertel, G., Schroer, J., Batinic, B., & Naumann, S. (2008). Do shy people prefer to send e-mail?: Personality effects on communication media preferences in threatening and nonthreatening situations. *Social Psychology, 39,* 231–243. doi:10.1027/1864-9335.39.4.231.

Hewstone, M., Rubin, M., & Willis, H. (2002). Intergroup bias. *Annual Review of Psychology, 53,* 575–604. doi:10.1146/annurev.psych.53.100901.135109.

Hilbert, M., & López, P. (2011). The world's technological capacity to store, communicate, and compute information. *Science, 332,* 60–65. doi:10.1126/science.1200970.

Kong, D. T., Dirks, K. T., & Ferrin, D. L. (2014). Interpersonal trust within negotiations: Meta-analytic evidence, critical contingencies, and directions for future research. *Academy of Management Journal, 57,* 1235–1255. doi:10.5465/amj.2012.0461.

Kurtzberg, T. R., Naquin, C. E., & Belkin, L. Y. (2009). Humor as a relationship-building tool in online negotiations. *International Journal of Conflict Management, 20,* 377–397.

Mayer, R. C., Davis, J. H., & Schoorman, F. D. (1995). An integrative model of organizational trust. *Academy of Management Review, 20,* 709–734. doi:10.5465/AMR.1995.9508080335.

Moore, D. A., Kurtzberg, T. R., & Thompson, L. L. (1999). Long and short routes to success in electronically mediated negotiations: Group affiliations and good vibrations. *Organizational Behavior and Human Decision Processes, 77,* 22–43. doi:10.1006/obhd.1998.2814.

Morris, M., Nadler, J., Kurtzberg, T. R., & Thompson, L. L. (2002). Schmooze or lose: Social friction and lubrication in e-mail negotiations. *Group Dynamics: Theory, Research, and Practice, 6,* 89–100. doi:10.1037//1089-2699.6.1.89.

Naquin, C. E., & Paulson, G. D. (2003). Online bargaining and interpersonal trust. *Journal of Applied Psychology, 88,* 113–120. doi:10.1037/0021-9010.88.1.113.

Postmes, T., & Spears, R. (2002). Behavior online: Does anonymous computer communication reduce gender inequality? *Personality and Social Psychology Bulletin, 28*, 1073–1083. doi:10. 1177/01461672022811006.

Postmes, T., Spears, R., & Lea, M. (1998). Breaching or building social boundaries? SIDE effects of computer-mediated communication. *Communication Research, 25*, 689–715. doi:10.1177/ 009365098025006006.

Pruitt, D. G. (1998). Social conflict. In D. T. Gilbert, S. T. Fiske, & G. Lindzey (Eds.), *The handbook of social psychology* (pp. 470–503). Boston, MA: McGraw-Hill.

Purdy, J. M., Nye, P., & Balakrishnan, P. V. (2000). The impact of communication media on negotiation outcomes. *International Journal of Conflict Management, 11*, 162–187.

Rousseau, D. M., Sitkin, S. B., Burt, R. S., & Camerer, C. (1998). Not so different after all: A cross-discipline view of trust. *Academy of Management Review, 23*, 393–404. doi:10.5465/ AMR.1998.926617.

Smith, E. R., & Mackie, D. M. (2007). *Social psychology*. New York, NY: Psychology Press.

Stuhlmacher, A. F., & Citera, M. (2005). Hostile behavior and profit in virtual negotiation: A meta-analysis. *Journal of Business and Psychology, 20*, 69–93. doi:10.1007/s10869-005-6984-y.

Tajfel, H. (1982). Social psychology of intergroup relations. *Annual Review of Psychology, 33*, 1–39. doi:10.1146/annurev.ps.33.020182.000245.

Tajfel, H., & Turner, J. C. (1979). An integrative theory of intergroup conflict. In W. Austin & S. Worchel (Eds.), *The social psychology of intergroup relations* (pp. 33–47). Pacific Grove, CA: Brooks/Cole.

Thompson, L. L. (1990). Negotiation behavior and outcomes: Empirical evidence and theoretical issues. *Psychological Bulletin, 108*, 515–532.

Thompson, L. L. (1991). Information exchange in negotiation. *Journal of Experimental Social Psychology, 27*, 161–179. doi:10.1016/0022-1031(91)90020-7.

Thompson, L. L. (2009). *The mind and heart of the negotiator*. Upper Saddle River, NJ: Prentice Hall.

Thompson, L. L., & Hastie, R. (1990). Social perception in negotiation. *Organizational Behavior and Human Decision Processes, 47*, 98–123. doi:10.1016/0749-5978(90)90048-E.

Thompson, L. L., & Nadler, J. (2002). Negotiating via information technology: Theory and application. *Journal of Social Issues, 58*, 109–124. doi:10.1111/1540-4560.00251.

Thompson, L. L., Wang, J., & Gunia, B. C. (2010). Negotiation. *Annual Review of Psychology, 61*, 491–515. doi:10.1146/annurev.psych.093008.100458.

Van Kleef, G. A., De Dreu, C. K. W., & Manstead, A. S. (2004). The interpersonal effects of anger and happiness in negotiations. *Journal of Personality and Social Psychology, 86*, 57–76. doi:10.1037/0022-3514.86.1.57.

Wilson, J. M., Straus, S. G., & McEvily, B. (2006). All in due time: The development of trust in computer-mediated and face-to-face teams. *Organizational Behavior and Human Decision Processes, 99*, 16–33. doi:10.1016/j.obhdp.2005.08.001.

Trust in the Information Systems Discipline

Ayten Öksüz, Nicolai Walter, Bettina Distel, Michael Räckers, and Jörg Becker

Abstract The digitalization of today's world has greatly advanced during the last few years and affects nearly all areas of life. The research discipline Information Systems (IS) views digitalization from multiple perspectives. On the one hand, IS is concerned with the development and functionality of technological artifacts. On the other hand, researchers in this field also investigate questions of how users perceive and actually use technological innovations. This last point brings about the question of how users deal with perceptions of risks that are inevitably connected to the use of technology (e.g., data theft, abuse of personal data). Thereby, trust research found its way into IS research since trust is widely considered to be a key factor in dealing with risk perceptions. Trust relations are commonly described as the relation between two parties: the trustor (who trusts) and the trustee (who is trusted). So far, technology has mainly been viewed as a medium through which trust can be transmitted or developed. With the emergence of quasi humans (e.g., recommendation agents), this ascription becomes more and more difficult and raises the question of whether or not a technology can be trusted. This article gives an overview of perspectives on the relations between users' perceptions of risk, trust through and in technologies, and trust towards technology providers. We furthermore provide insights into the state of the art of trust research in the IS discipline.

Keywords Trust • Risk • Technology • Quasi humans • Digitization • Information Systems

1 Introduction

In the digitized world of today, more and more services are carried out online and people are more strongly connected to technology than ever before (van Eimeren and Frees 2014). While shopping for books on Amazon is an example of early times

A. Öksüz • N. Walter • B. Distel • M. Räckers • J. Becker (✉)
University of Münster - ERCIS, Münster, Germany
e-mail: ayten.oeksuez@ercis.uni-muenster.de; nicolai.walter@ercis.uni-muenster.de; bettina.
distel@ercis.uni-muenster.de; michael.raeckers@ercis.uni-muenster.de; joerg.becker@ercis.
uni-muenster.de

© Springer International Publishing Switzerland 2016
B. Blöbaum (ed.), *Trust and Communication in a Digitized World*, Progress in IS,
DOI 10.1007/978-3-319-28059-2_12

of the World Wide Web, consumers and businesses currently think about online services such as mobile applications, the Internet of things, and cloud computing (Gartner 2013). Moreover, while computers originate from the domain of business, and it took a while for personal computers to succeed, nowadays many people own a smartphone and, thus, carry a supercomputer in their pocket. The use of technology offers several opportunities, such as mobile apps that enable fast access to online services like traffic information, or cloud computing, which is considered to increase the comfort of file management, flexibility of computing resources, and overall lower costs (Armbrust et al. 2010).

What all these trends have in common is that they include some aspect of information technology (IT). The Information Systems (IS) discipline follows two lines of research on IT (Hevner et al. 2004). On the one hand, the internet is an IT infrastructure accessed via software programs like 'apps' on hardware devices like smartphones. This entails many questions of how information systems and devices should be designed in order to function as intended. This perspective originates from the designers' view of information systems. On the other hand, the users and their behaviors highly influence how technology is used and what services are actually adopted (Benbasat 2010). This brings about the question of how users perceive information systems, for example, as useful and easy to use. While the focus of IS was originally limited to organizations, the discipline has evolved. Current research also deals with trust and IT in the context of e-government, as well as the personal sphere (social media).

However, the presence of IT does not offer only opportunities. On the downside of technology usage, many individuals and organizations have heightened perceptions of risk. When individuals carry out transactions on the internet, (personal) data may be recorded on servers that could be located anywhere. Individuals may, for example, post personal information on Facebook, buy on eBay, or take out an insurance policy on a web portal. Furthermore, the relationship between online providers and their (potential) customers is characterized by information asymmetry and social distance between the parties (Ba and Pavlou 2002; Gefen and Straub 2003; Pavlou et al. 2007). This means that individuals interacting with an online provider often do not exactly know how their personal data is used and processed by the provider (McKnight et al. 2002a). Third parties also pose a threat to individuals and organizations by gaining unauthorized access to sensitive data stored on the servers of a provider (Bélanger et al. 2002). Furthermore, online environments or interactions are considered to be more anonymous and impersonal than offline interactions (Wang and Emurian 2005) and, thus, lack human contact and warmth (Gefen and Straub 2003). Risk perceptions associated with the threats in online environments and the related lack of trust in online providers and e-commerce shops often lead to individuals' and organizations' reluctance to use certain new technologies or online services (Garrison et al. 2012; Hoffman et al. 1999). As a consequence, trust is suggested to be a key factor for the diffusion of innovations and adoption of new technologies or online services (e.g., Gefen et al. 2003). Research on how to improve IT security is fundamental for trust building in the digitized world.

As a first reaction, the development and implementation of new security measures shall contribute to an improved security of online transactions. However, besides the technical safety, dealing with individuals' and organizations' risk perceptions and trust building is also a question of communication (Khan and Malluhi 2010; Öksüz 2014). Trust can be built only when providers adequately communicate the implemented measures to ensure the security of data (Khan and Malluhi 2010; Öksüz 2014).

The omnipresence of technology in our daily lives has raised a high need for trust. While in computer science trust is understood as security in terms of technical safety, IS emphasizes the socio-emotional perspective (Recker 2013). In this sense, the IS discipline considers trust as an individual's perception of another party as being competent, benevolent, and as having integrity (Li et al. 2008; Mayer et al. 1995). As the nature of the IS discipline always involves an IT artifact, not only the IT artifacts themselves are diverse, but so are the relationships between trust and the IT artifacts. Trust research in IS ranges from dealing with the question of trusting another party interacted with in a computer-mediated setting (e.g., collaboration between virtual team members carried out via technology-mediated communication), to the question of trusting the IT artifact itself (McKnight et al. 2011). With regard to trust in IT, one of the most prominent examples is the area of e-commerce. When dealing with online providers, the provider's website is the primary and often sole source of information (Wang and Emurian 2005). Online providers mainly depend on their websites to represent themselves to consumers (Wang and Emurian 2005). As a result, many consumers tend to focus on the website design when assessing its or the online provider's trustworthiness (such as easy navigation and use of the website) (Karimov et al. 2011). This also shows that it is not always clear who the trustee is in a specific online trust relationship: the e-commerce website or the online provider the website represents. In this context, the question of whether or not the website can be trusted at all arises. Furthermore, websites sometimes include some contact opportunities, such as live chats. However, these chats may fully or partly be operated by software scripts, such as chat bots. There are even virtual agents that are software programs embedded into the website with which the user can interact (e.g., Qiu and Benbasat 2009). This leads to the question of whether or not algorithms, software, and technology can be trusted from a socio-emotional perspective.

Thus, the IS discipline distinguishes between three notions of trust: trust in individuals through technology, trust in quasi-humans (such as recommendation agents), and trust in a technology itself (cf. Fig. 1). This discussion paper includes all of these trust issues and presents approaches that try to structure the different streams of trust, as well as insights into studies that show the role and effects of trust in the IS discipline. The remainder of this article is structured as follows. First, we deal with trust when IT or an IT artifact is a mediator among humans or between humans and organizations. Second, we elaborate on the role of quasi-humans, such as virtual agents, for trust building. Third, the technology itself comes into focus and we discuss the role of trust in IT. Finally, we conclude with an outlook on trust research in the Information Systems discipline.

Fig. 1 Different trustees in the digitized world (images are kindly provided for commercial use by www.icons-land.com, www.creativefreedom.co.uk, and www.designcontest.com)

2 Trust in Individuals Through Technology

Trust research in the IS discipline can either focus on trust in the IT artifact itself or on trust in a service provider or another human (Söllner et al. 2012). In the latter case, the IT artifact functions as a mediator between two or more users. Based on an IT-artifact, such as websites, users may interact with individuals (e.g., on social network sites (SNS) or through social media (SM)), an organization (e.g., on e-commerce websites), or an administration. Each of these relationships is characterized by the fact that the website or the social media profile often becomes the sole source of information about the transaction or communication partner (Wakefield et al. 2004; Wang and Emurian 2005). Commonly, researchers in the IS discipline describe communication or interactions through websites or, more generally, communication based on IT as asymmetric (Wang and Benbasat 2007); that is, the user cannot, to a certain degree, predict or control the actions and outcomes of the service provider's behavior (i.e., seller, communication partner, administration, etc.) (Glover and Benbasat 2011). While in interpersonal relationships the communication partner's character traits and trustworthiness as well as potential risks of an interaction can be assessed directly, in a technology-based communication, this comes about only indirectly (Verhagen et al. 2006). As a consequence, since the user has to rely on the veracity of the information given on the website, interactions through websites always include risks for the user, not only in matters of technical security (e.g., risk of privacy breaches), but also referring to the providers' trustworthiness (e.g., Pavlou 2003). When, for example, shopping for a new camera, the customer in a shop can estimate the weight, design, or functionality of the camera directly. He can also ask a vendor for more technical details and advice on alternatives. When shopping for a camera online, the customer cannot try the different functionalities or get advice from the vendor, but has to rely on photographs and written descriptions. He also has to disclose private data to perform the transactions (e.g., bank data, address) and often has to pay in advance. Therefore, the user has to rely on information given on the website to estimate the provider's trustworthiness. Hence, trust is understood as a necessity to bridge the perceived uncertainties (Verhagen et al. 2006).

The IS discipline adopted this view from business science where trust is mainly understood as one's (the trustor's) "...willingness ... to be vulnerable to the actions of another party [trustee] based on the expectation that the other will perform a particular action important to the trustor, irrespective of the ability to monitor or control that other party" (Mayer et al. 1995, p. 712). In this view, the trustworthiness of the trustee consists of his or her *ability* (skills, expertise, capability, etc.), *benevolence* (willingness to perform an action on behalf of the trustor without any profit motives), and *integrity* (a common or at least similar set of beliefs and principles) to perform a certain action. These so-called factors of perceived trustworthiness are not bipolar, but rather understood as a continuum with situation-specific degrees of each belief (Mayer et al. 1995). For example, one might think the plumber apprentice is willing to repair a broken water pipe and wants to do his job the best possible way. The client believes him to be benevolent and to have the needed integrity to fulfill the task. Even though the client might also think the apprentice has the needed abilities, he might, in comparison to the apprentice's foreman, believe the latter to be *more* able to fix the water pipe. Accordingly, although both of them might be perceived as being benevolent and having integrity, the client would perhaps put more trust towards the foreman due to his long lasting experience and resulting expertise. Still, the same client would not trust either of them to take care of his or her child, since the client does not know what experiences both have in child care or whether or not they are willing to do the best for the wellbeing of the child.

Trust research in the IS discipline mainly focused on e-commerce for a long time. Since the digitalization of the world proceeds quite fast, more and more parts of daily life are digitized and a lot of services are carried out online (van Eimeren and Frees 2014). Today, the World Wide Web enables more than online shopping: organizations, for example, carry out their business online and collaborate with other organizations in the form of virtual teams or use new technologies like cloud computing, and bank customers can transfer their money via online banking services from home. SNS, like Facebook or Twitter, facilitate interpersonal communication across long distances. In contrast, they not only but mainly relate to the personal sphere. Since SNS also facilitate the self-presentation of organizations and communication between businesses and their potential customers, some features of SM also relate to the business sector. More recently, governments and administrations started to enlarge their online services and some countries, such as Estonia, have, for example, initiated pilot schemes of online voting (e.g., Estonia 2015). In order to structure the different fields of online interactions, we adapt the distinction between personal sphere as well as the public and business sector as known from social and political sciences. Here, the public sphere is understood as an arena where a speaker and an audience come together to communicate (Neidhardt 1994). This public sphere is commonly defined as open and accessible to everyone and forms a contrast to the private sphere (Marschall 1998). Since businesses do not negotiate public or political issues and are, in contrast to the public sphere, not open to everyone, they are viewed as a separate construct in this paper. The personal sphere, which only comprises private communication and interactions, is also viewed as a separate construct.

Although the described services relate to different spheres, they all have one thing in common: the user of these services has to share private and sensitive information. Aside from security or technology related concerns, foremost the user has to trust the provider, that he or she will not take advantage of this data and will take suitable measures to ensure data security and the protection of privacy. This also entails trust in the assurance of the service's frictionless operation (e.g., Corritore et al. 2003). At the same time, the users' willingness to adopt an online service is highly influenced by the perceived trustworthiness of the communication or transaction partner, meaning that the more trustworthy one is perceived, the more probable an interaction will occur (e.g., Becker et al. 2014). All online service providers therefore need to build trust through their websites (e.g., Karimov et al. 2011); trust towards an IT artifact as a mediator is therefore not only important in the business sector, but also applies to the personal sphere and the public sector. The following section presents examples of each field, business and public sectors and the personal sphere, as well as insights into some studies and research results.

2.1 Business Sector

One of the earliest and well researched services in the IS discipline is e-commerce (e.g., Li et al. 2008; Wang and Benbasat 2008; Wang and Emurian 2005). E-commerce is not an object of scientific interest only because it is widespread, but also because it creates a typical situation of trusting behavior on the internet (e.g., Hoffman et al. 1999). The offered products cannot be assessed physically concerning quality or the price-performance ratio, and (potential) buyers have to rely on the information provided on the online merchants' websites (Verhagen et al. 2006). This entails certain risks since consumers often have to pay in advance, not knowing whether or not the product will be delivered as expected or will be delivered at all (Kim et al. 2008). Despite transaction related concerns, a lot of potential users are concerned with identity theft or abuse of private data (McKnight et al. 2002b). Thus, trust is a core constituent of successful e-commerce (e.g., Wang and Benbasat 2008; Wang and Emurian 2005). Researchers and practitioners are interested in explaining the role of trust in interactions on the internet (e.g., Lowry et al. 2008; Pavlou and Fygenson 2006; Colquitt et al. 2007; Bundesministerium des Inneren 2015).

Mayer et al. (1995) state that, besides perceptions of the trustee's ability, benevolence, and integrity, a trustor's general disposition to trust influences his or her perceptions regarding the trustee's trustworthiness. Additionally, McKnight et al. (2002b) propose the concept of *institution-based trust* what one could call security in terms of technical safety: Users are convinced that "structures like guarantees, regulations, promises, legal recourse, or other procedures are in place to promote success [. . .and] that the environment [the Internet] is in proper order and success is likely because the situation is normal or favorable" (McKnight et al. 2002b, p. 339). Institution based trust is not necessarily vendor specific. In contrast, the factors of perceived trustworthiness describe "perceptions of specific web vendor attributes" (McKnight et al. 2002b, p. 337), which are communicated through the vendor's website. Based on the Theory of Reasoned Action (TRA), a frequently cited framework for technology adoption, the authors argue that factors of perceived trustworthiness form trusting intentions, meaning the personal intention to interact with the web-vendor (McKnight et al. 2002b). Trust in an online shop will likely lead to the intention to buy from the shop, which in turn will likely lead to an actual purchase.

Although the work of McKnight et al. (2002b) is a good framework to explain how internet-users adopt e-commerce services, the model does not explain what specific elements of a website constitute the factors of perceived trustworthiness. Karimov et al. (2011) developed a classification of trust-inducing elements a website can or should include in order to appear trustworthy. As the website functions as mediator between two unknown parties, it should be designed in a way that creates trust in the supplier, respectively trustworthiness of the supplier (Söllner et al. 2012). Following Karimov et al. (2011), this includes not only design or layout, but also content and information, technical aspects, and usability. Based on the cue-signaling theory the authors develop a classification with three categories relating to each form of trust. The authors conduct a literature analysis to classify antecedents of trust and distinguish three categories of trust-inducing website elements: the *visual design*, including all graphical and structural elements; the *social cue design*, including the availability of social media, human-like features, and assistive interfaces; and the *content design*, which comprises the informativeness of the website, brand alliances, and e-assurances (Karimov et al. 2011). In summary, the willingness of a user to depend on an online-provider and the offered online-service highly relies on the provider's website and its capability to create trust.

In addition to Karmiov et al.'s (2011) model, there are conceptualizations that also take, besides design dimensions, cultural conditions into account (Cyr 2013). In this context, Cyr (2013) shows with a cross-national study of "user perceptions of B2C Web pages" (Cyr 2013, p. 377) that perceptions of the website design are influenced by "overall cultural values" (Cyr 2013, p. 381) and that these design perceptions do influence users' trust. This shows that the development of a trust-inducing website design also depends on the context of the business as well as on cultural conditions. Although the classification of Karimov et al. (2011) is not applied by Cyr (2013), the study of Cyr includes similar perceptions of visual and content design and leads to the assumption that a careful website design can create trust. Cyr (2013) states that, especially in countries with lower uncertainty avoidance, the presentation, accuracy, and accessibility of information, as well as an appealing visual design and high usability, can create higher levels of trust in an e-vendor (Cyr 2013). Hence, a well-designed trust-inducing website is a core factor to successful e-commerce.

2.2 Personal Sphere

In the past few years another web-based technology has attracted much attention: SNS and SM like Facebook or Twitter. Since the usage of these services has rapidly increased over the past few years and still grows, scholars have started to investigate why users trust services like Facebook, and not only transmit but also disclose private data (e.g., Bryce and Fraser 2014; Taddei and Contena 2013). The use of SNS or SM forms a situation to users that is similar to e-commerce, although the risks involved are different. When using a social network website, users disclose very personal information not only through their own profiles but also through interpersonal communication with other users (Canfora and Visaggio 2012). In contrast to e-commerce, users do not necessarily risk a material loss, like paying for a product, which is not delivered. SM users rather risk the theft or abuse of their private data (Sherchan et al. 2013). In contrast to the e-commerce context, trust in the provider, its website, and the underlying technology, as well as trust in other users might be relevant (Lankton and McKnight 2011). Lankton and McKnight (2011) differentiate between interpersonal trust and technological trust (trust in the IT-artifact itself). Although this distinction can be made and the two types exist, the authors state that SNS "represent a technology in which the distinction between human and technology characteristics is less clear" (Lankton and McKnight 2011, p. 34). Their survey consequently shows "that [Facebook] users blend human demonstrations of trust with technology demonstrations of trust. This could be because users think of the Facebook website both as a technology and a quasi-person, even though it is a technical artifact" (Lankton and McKnight 2011, p. 47).

Besides the fact that users of SNS view these services as technology as well as an organization led by humans, other difficulties arise in studies of trust in social networks. While the usage of guarantees or (official) seals (e.g., http://www.trustedshops.de/) is steadily disseminating in the field of e-commerce or e-businesses in particular, most SNS cannot control the actions of their users. A user may trust Facebook to not abuse personal or private data because Facebook, as a company, has general terms and conditions to which it is legally bound. But users should not necessarily trust (unknown) other users to be benevolent or have integrity since other companies or users can create fake profiles to contact other users to come into possession of personal data (Canfora and Visaggio 2012). Therefore, a user may trust the website (the technology as well as the provider), but at the same time distrust other users. Currently, in addition to questions of interpersonal vs. technological trust (e.g., Lankton and McKnight 2011), mechanisms to manage *trust in other users* in the context of SM are under research (e.g., Canfora and Visaggio 2012).

The steady dissemination of SM also leads to a growing embedding of SM applications into other websites. Karimov et al. (2011) states that customer reviews belong to the group of social media that can enhance the feeling of humaneness on a website and thus influence users' trust. For instance, a study conducted by Kumar and Benbasat (2006) shows that recommendations and consumer reviews embedded in online shops can influence perceptions of human warmth, which in turn can be seen as a strong predictor of trust (Walter et al. 2013). SM (components) like consumer reviews and user-to-user support platforms are considered to lead to more trust, since they are seen to raise feelings of human contact and sociability and consequently partly compensate for the lack of closeness as known from face-to-face interactions (Kumar and Benbasat 2006; Ortbach et al. 2014).

2.3 Public Sector

The public sector (administrations and governments) has also made use of IT-artifacts, mainly websites, to deliver services to citizens. In the beginning, authorities mainly used the internet as a mere digital brochure to inform about opening hours or contact persons. Today, most administrations sophisticatedly use web services and offer numerous services online (e.g., Horst et al. 2007; Hofmann et al. 2012). Besides a lacking supply of online-services in some countries or districts, currently, the adoption behavior of citizens is occupying the scientific interest of researchers around the globe (e.g., Bélanger and Carter 2008; Akkaya et al. 2011; Belanche et al. 2012; Hofmann et al. 2012; Hofmann and Heierhoff 2012). There is broad agreement that, similar to e-commerce adoption, trust and risk perceptions are of great importance to the success or failure of e-government services (Akkaya et al. 2011). Therefore, theoretical frameworks popular in the IS discipline, like the Technology Acceptance Model (TAM) (e.g., Belanche et al. 2012) or the TRA (e.g., Bélanger and Carter 2008), are also used in the research of e-government service adoption (e.g., Hofmann et al. 2012).

The usage of e-government services comprises similar risks to those in e-commerce services: citizens face security breaches and the potential abuse of private and personal data as users do not have control over how public administrations use transmitted data (Akkaya et al. 2011). Furthermore, as with any other service, administrations are not immune to data theft by hackers. Here, again, users' trust can either relate to the technology as the trustee or the mediator of trust. In the latter case, the trustees are service providing administrations. Bélanger and Carter (2008) distinguish these forms of trust into *trust of the internet* (IT) and *trust of the government* (organization). Besides concerns about the handling of private data (which relates to trust of the government), Akkaya et al. (2011) show that trust in respective public authorities is a key differentiator in the acceptance and adoption of e-government services. This emphasizes the need of administrations to build trust through their websites. As Bélanger and Carter (2008) state, governments should "take advantage of trust-building mechanisms used by e-commerce vendors, such as posting security and privacy seals, to encourage adoption of e-government services" (Bélanger and Carter 2008, p. 172). Studies like this show that similar mechanisms apply to e-government adoption as to e-commerce, but that there are also great differences. While e-vendors are either completely unknown or can build on an ongoing trust relationship, governments face the problem that they are already known to the potential users and only offer a new form of their services. They have to deal with their already existing reputation and perceptions among the population. Hence, Horsburgh et al. (2011) state that "it is possible that those [citizens] with low trust in politicians may mistrust government information, including that provided via e-government channels." (Horsburgh et al. 2011, p. 233). As Beldad et al. (2010) further point out in their literature review, the offline presence of a provider may influence perceptions of this provider's online presence. This could be especially true for e-government services since most citizens presumably hold strong beliefs about the government, which in turn influence perceptions about its benevolence, integrity, and ability to provide helpful and secure online services.

3   Trust in Quasi-Humans

Besides visual and content cue design, social cue design is also important when designing websites to be more trustworthy (Karimov et al. 2011). This dimension is important as the digitized world is usually characterized by a high social distance between interacting parties such as buyers and sellers or consumers and online service providers (Gefen and Straub 2003; Pavlou 2003). There are a multitude of options for how social cues can be embedded into websites; for example, human images may be used (Cyr et al. 2009). However, besides non-interactive social cues, human or non-human interaction website features also exist. Regarding human features, these may, for example, be contact forms that forward website visitor messages to user support employees. More sophisticated are live-chats embedded into a website. While the common notion may be that these applications are operated by humans, in some live-chats users may actually be paired with chat-bots; i.e., software programs that are trained to adequately respond to user input. Moreover, while in some cases, at first, a chat-bot deals with user requests, this chat-bot may switch roles with a human as soon as conversations take courses that a chat-bot cannot handle. In addition to a shared service provision of humans and computers, there are also software applications that complement human support staff to an even greater extent. These so-called quasi-humans are virtual agents referred to as "animated embodiments [i.e., visual, often human-looking represen-tations] that respond to users through verbal and nonverbal communication" (Chattaraman et al. 2012, p. 2055). Many companies make use of them on their websites. In terms of trust, a kind of virtual agent who is not only capable of holding conversations but can also give recommendations about products and services is especially relevant (Hess et al. 2009). As a consequence, these agents, so-called social recommendation agents, are the object of many studies of trust in the field of Information Systems (Walter 2014). While they have primarily been tested in e-commerce and real estate (Qiu and Benbasat 2009; Richards and Bransky 2014), current studies also validate their influence in the context of cloud computing services (Walter et al. 2014).

Academic research in the Information Systems discipline has dealt with the question of how to make these agents more trustworthy (e.g., Hess et al. 2009; Qiu and Benbasat 2005, 2009). There are different approaches that lead to this goal. The basic notion is that the design of social recommendation agents can be influenced. The design of a social recommendation agent refers to its appearance; i.e., the type of embodiment, output signals like voice or text-to-speech, and even an agent's personality, use of gestures, and options to interact with users (Walter 2014). One study shows, for example, that an extroverted social recommendation agent that is designed with respect to more outgoing statements, a voice with faster pace and volume, and more extensive use of gestures leads to more trust than an introverted agent (Hess et al. 2009). Other studies suggest that the facial expressions of an agent are important in raising users' trust (Lisetti et al. 2013).

In the digitized world, relationships between interacting parties are not only characterized by a higher social distance than face-to-face interactions, but also by information asymmetry (e.g., Xiao and Benbasat 2007). Sellers, for example, usually know more about their delivery reliability or product quality. When it comes to social recommendation agents, the issue of information asymmetry also exists (Xiao and Benbasat 2007). Does a social recommendation agent really provide the best recommendation in the users' interest (i.e., regarding the users' (previously stated) preferences), or does the agent perhaps optimize the recommendation with respect to the online shop's profit margin? Why does a specific provider embed a social recommendation agent anyway? The main reason may be because the provider has learned this would instill more trust because there is a real interest for the users' needs, i.e., the provider really wants users to be better educated about product and service information. The human interface of virtual agents may obscure the fundament that is 'behind' those agents, namely algorithms. Thus, it does not matter whether or not there is a simple chat-bot without an embodiment or a social recommendation agent with sophisticated 3D animation. Both systems are solely based on algorithms. The additional humanness may not, from a rational and pragmatic standpoint, count as more trustworthy as it may be open to influence from providers like most other information systems. This brings us to the question of how far information systems and the underlying operations (i.e., algorithms) can be trusted at all.

4 Trust in Technology

The advent of new technologies and the rapid pace of technological change in the digital world present new challenges with regard to trust. With the increasing use of digital services and the resulting increasing amounts of data, data security and privacy become more and more important social issues. The widespread concerns about data security and privacy and the lack of trust leads to the fact that many individuals and organizations make only limited use of some of these new technologies or do not use them at all (Deutsche Telekom/T-Systems 2014). The role of trust and risk perceptions in the acceptance and adoption of technologies has been the object of scientific research in the IS discipline for quite some time. For example, recent research has shown that beyond the perceived ease of use (PEOU) and perceived usefulness (PU), the intention to use a new IT highly depends on trust (Gefen et al. 2003). The fact that trust is an important factor influencing the acceptance and usage intention of (new) technologies led to the extension of the technology acceptance model (TAM) by the factor trust (Gefen et al. 2003). Consequently, trust can be seen as a key factor influencing the acceptance and use of emerging technologies, especially whenever risk perceptions (such as concerns about data security and privacy) are in place.

One of the most discussed technology trends in the last few years is cloud computing. The use of cloud computing promises considerable advantages, such as cost savings, but also poses several data protection risks for potential users (Armbrust et al. 2010; Kerschbaum 2011; Takabi et al. 2010; Zissis and Lekkas 2012). Third parties, for example, could gain unauthorized access to sensitive user data stored in the cloud (Kerschbaum 2011). Furthermore, users of cloud services are often not able to completely control the data handling practices of cloud computing providers (Takabi et al. 2010). They do not always know whether their data is handled in a lawful manner (Takabi et al. 2010). Since the emergence of cloud computing, issues relating to data privacy and the security of personal and sensitive data became even more the focus of public attention. Consequently, cloud computing providers face the challenge of gaining the trust of potential users with the objective to motivate them to use their services (Öksüz 2014; Walter et al. 2014). From the perspective of computer science, the trust problem can be solved by developing new security technologies and solutions (e.g., new encryption methods to prevent unauthorized access to sensitive data) in order to make the cloud safer and more secure (Kerschbaum 2011). In this sense, computer scientists understand trust as security and aim to enable cloud computing providers to protect customer data more securely. Research in this area might have significantly contributed to the fact that improvements in cloud security have been achieved over time and that data security will keep getting better (Allouche 2014). However, the mere development and implementation of new security measures is not enough to gain potential users' trust (Öksüz 2014). This is because trust is based on perceptions regarding a cloud provider's ability and willingness to protect (potential) users' data and ensure privacy (Chellappa and Pavlou 2002). This in turn depends on (potential) users' perceived security level (Chellappa and Pavlou 2002). The perceived security level determines the subjective probability with which users believe that their data will be protected against loss, abuse, and unauthorized access or hacker attacks at any time (Chellappa and Pavlou 2002). Potential users' perceived security level might differ from the actual security offered by the cloud provider (Chellappa and Pavlou 2002). It could be, for example, that users do not perceive a high security level even though a provider is able and willing to protect users' (personal) data by using the latest security and privacy measures (Öksüz 2014). One of the reasons for this is often a lack of communication or transparency (Khan and Malluhi 2010; Öksüz 2014). Communication is a key element in the formation of perceptions (Rogers 2003). Cloud providers have to provide information on their data handling practices and their implemented security measures in order to gain users' trust (Khan and Malluhi 2010; Öksüz 2014). They have to adequately communicate which security and privacy measures they have implemented in order to protect users' data and to ensure privacy (Khan and Malluhi 2010; Öksüz 2014). Thus, for trust building it is important that cloud providers first implement appropriate security measures and take responsibility for their clients' data, and second, adequately communicate the implemented security measures and data handling practices.

Beyond that, potential users also have to trust in the mechanisms (security and privacy measures) implemented by the provider to protect user data (Zissis and Lekkas 2012). In this context, some researchers state that trust in IT or trust in the technology also plays an important role in the acceptance and adoption of new technologies (Li et al. 2008; McKnight et al. 2011). However, very few research directly deals with trust in certain technology (McKnight et al. 2011). To some extent, research on trust in social recommendation agents focuses on trust in an IT artifact (McKnight et al. 2011; Orlikowski and Iacono 2001). This is because (social) recommendation agents are automated online assistants helping users to decide among various product alternatives (Wang and Benbasat 2007). In this sense, social recommendation agents are IT artifacts (McKnight et al. 2011). However, social recommendation agents act like humans and interact with users in human-like ways (Hess et al. 2009). As a result, studies on trust in social recommendation agents have measured trust in the social recommendation agent by using trust-in-people scales (McKnight et al. 2011). Thus, trust in social recommendation agents has not actually been studied in terms of trust in IT, but rather in terms of trust in humans (McKnight et al. 2011).

McKnight et al. (2011) have developed a conceptual definition and operationalization of trust in technology. In doing so, they explain how trust in technology differs from trust in people. Similar to trust in people, users' assessments of attributes reflect their beliefs about a technology's ability to deliver on the promise of its objective characteristics (McKnight et al. 2011). The researchers suggest that, with respect to the characteristics or attributes of a technology, the counterpart to competence is functionality, to benevolence is helpfulness, and to integrity is reliability (McKnight et al. 2011). *Functionality* refers to the question of whether or not the technology functions as promised by providing features that are required to fulfill a task (McKnight 2005). *Helpfulness* represents "users' beliefs that the technology provides adequate, effective, and responsive help" (McKnight et al. 2011, p. 5). *Reliability* means that the technology or IT artifact operates continually (i.e., with little or no downtime) or responds predictably to inputs (e.g., printing on command) (McKnight et al. 2011). However, from other researchers' point of view "people trust people, not technology" (Friedman et al. 2000, p. 36). They assume that trust can only exist if the trustee has his or her own will and a freedom of choice and thus, can consciously decide between right and wrong at his or her own discretion (Friedman et al. 2000). Since technology has no moral principles, users perceive no caring emotions when interacting with technologies (McKnight et al. 2011; Friedman et al. 2000). These two contrary views show that there is no broad consensus on "trust in IT" yet. Nevertheless, for trust building in providers of IT-based services—where data security and privacy is of high importance—it is important that potential users believe in the functionality of the implemented security and privacy measures.

5 Conclusion and Outlook

Trust in information systems and IT offers two sides of a coin. Looking from a more computer science driven perspective, it is a question of security—and trust in IT. Lots of research was and still is invested in the question of how to make information systems and their underlying technology more secure in terms of privacy, data protection, and further issues. In fact, this is comparable to the rabbit and the hedgehog phenomenon. Once the 'rabbits' developed a new, secure algorithm or data protection concept, the 'hedgehogs' are already there and have found a new way to bypass the protection. In the end, there is no absolute security. Therefore, we need a second concept of trust. We have to believe in the technology and, even more, in the providers of technology, that they provide us with the best possible security; we also have to believe in their honesty about boundaries of security and what we additionally have to do or consider when using their technology. A good example of this is the new aspect of trustworthiness Google implemented in their search engine. The 'Knowledge Vault' database consists of assured facts, which are found first when using Google as a search engine. Even if other aspects (or 'wrong facts') are searched more often, if they are not accepted as 'true' they will not occur in the upper search results (cf. e.g., Hodson 2014).

We face an era of digitalization. In fact, we are transforming into a world permeated by IT and will be digitized. In this article, we argue that IT is becoming normal, not only in the business sector but also in the personal sphere. Our complete lives, in every aspect, are depending more and more on digital goods and digital support.

Our society is changing completely. Amazon, for example, is working on a new way to deliver their goods to customers, faster than before: Amazon Prime Air will be a service that delivers customer orders with drones—minutes after the receiving the order (Amazon 2015). With this, technology is becoming more and more complex and we will more and more not understand aspects of security. Therefore, trust in IT, trust in quasi-humans, and trust in individuals, but being contacted through IT, becomes increasingly important.

For future research on trust and IT and in its facets and characteristics, this implies that the discussion of trust and trustworthiness of IT will become more and more important in the coming years. We have to trust that the information we have is correct and trustworthy without having the possibility to prove this on our own. Research in disciplines such as Psychology, Communication Science, and IS— together—have to investigate this phenomenon and the impact on our society and personal lives. Not only does trust in IT have influence on our personal decisions of usage or non-usage of IT, which is a single and, more or less, private decision (Ortbach et al. 2015), but it also has influence on our business decisions and thus on the growth of our economy. Information technology has become the undisputable engine and key success factor of our economic growth. Companies and sectors dealing with these aspects of trust will be more effective in the position to use this key factor for their success.

References

Akkaya, C., Obermeier, M., Wolf, P., & Krcmar, H. (2011). Components of trust influencing eGovernment adoption in Germany. In M. Janssen, H. J. Scholl, M. A. Wimmer, & Y.-H. Tan (Eds.), *Electronic government. 10th IFIP WG 8.5 International Conference, EGOV 2011 Delft, The Netherlands, August/September 2011. Proceedings* (pp. 88–98). Heidelberg: Springer.

Allouche, G. (2014). The future of cloud computing. *CMS Report*. http://cmsreport.com/articles/the-future-of-cloud-computing-8210. Accessed 6 April 2015.

Amazon. (2015). *Amazon Prime Air*. http://www.amazon.com/b?node=8037720011. Accessed 9 April 2015.

Armbrust, M., Fox, A., Griffith, R., Joseph, A. D., Katz, R. H., Konwinski, A., et al. (2010). A view of cloud computing. *Communications of the ACM, 53*(4), 50–58.

Ba, S., & Pavlou, P. A. (2002). Evidence of the effect of trust building technology in electronic markets: Price premiums and buyer behavior. *MIS Quarterly, 26*(3), 243–268.

Becker, J., Heddier, M., Öksüz, A., & Knackstedt, R. (2014). The effect of providing visualizations in privacy policies on trust in data privacy and security. In *47th Hawaii International Conference on System Sciences (HICSS)* (pp. 3224–3233).

Belanche, D., Casaló, L. V., & Flavián, C. (2012). Integrating trust and personal values into the technology acceptance model: The case of e-government services adoption. *Cuadernos de Economía y Dirección de la Empresa, 15*(4), 192–204. doi:10.1016/j.cede.2012.04.004.

Bélanger, F., & Carter, L. (2008). Trust and risk in e-government adoption. *Journal of Strategic Information Systems, 17*, 165–176. doi:10.1016/j.jsis.2007.12.002.

Bélanger, F., Hiller, J. S., & Smith, W. J. (2002). Trustworthiness in electronic commerce: The role of privacy, security, and site attributes. *The Journal of Strategic Information Systems, 11*(3), 245–270.

Beldad, A., De Jong, M., & Steehouder, M. (2010). How shall I trust the faceless and the intangible? A literature review on the antecedents of online trust. *Computers in Human Behavior, 26*(5), 857–869.

Benbasat, I. (2010). HCI research: Future challenges and directions. *AIS Transactions on Human-Computer Interaction, 2*(2), 16–21.

Bryce, J., & Fraser, J. (2014). The role of disclosure of personal information in the evaluation of risk and trust in young peoples' online interactions. *Computers in Human Behavior, 30,* 299–306.

Bundesministerium des Inneren. (2015). *Digital Trust is a location factor of fundamental importance.* http://www.bmi.bund.de/SharedDocs/Kurzmeldungen/EN/2015/02/security-congress-rogall.html. Accessed 6 April 2015.

Canfora, G., & Visaggio, C. a. (2012). Managing trust in social networks. *Information Security Journal: A Global Perspective, 21*(4), 206–215. doi:10.1080/19393555.2012.660677.

Chattaraman, V., Kwon, W.-S., & Gilbert, J. E. (2012). Virtual agents in retail web sites: Benefits of simulated social interaction for older users. *Computers in Human Behavior, 28*(6), 2055–2066. doi:10.1016/j.chb.2012.06.009.

Chellappa, R. K., & Pavlou, P. A. (2002). Perceived information security, financial liability and consumer trust in electronic commerce transactions. *Logistic Information Management, 15* (5/6), 358–368.

Colquitt, J. A., Scott, B. A., & LePine, J. A. (2007). Trust, trustworthiness, and trust propensity: A meta-analytic test of their unique relationships with risk taking and job performance. *The Journal of Applied Psychology, 92*(4), 909–927.

Corritore, C. L., Kracher, B., & Wiedenbeck, S. (2003). On-line trust: Concepts, evolving themes, a model. *International Journal of Human-Computer Studies, 58*(6), 737–758.

Cyr, D. (2013). Website design, trust and culture: An eight country investigation. *Electronic Commerce Research and Applications, 12*(6), 373–385.

Cyr, D., Head, M., Larios, H., & Pan, B. (2009). Exploring human images in website design: A multi-method approach. *MIS Quarterly, 33*(3), 539–566.

Deutsche Telekom/T-Systems. (2014). *Sicherheitsreport 2014: Ergebnisse einer repräsentativen Bevölkerungsumfrage.* https://www.telekom.com/static/-/244706/5/140801-sicherheitsreport2014-s. Accessed 6 April 2015.

Estonia. (2015). *i-Voting.* https://e-estonia.com/component/i-voting/. Accessed 6 April 2015.

Friedman, B., Khan, P. H., & Howe, D. C. (2000). Trust online. *Communications of the ACM, 43* (12), 34–40.

Garrison, G., Kim, S., & Wakefield, R. L. (2012). Success factors for deploying cloud computing. *Communications of the ACM, 55*(9), 62–68.

Gartner. (2013). Gartner identifies the top 10 strategic technology trends for 2014. *Press release.* http://www.gartner.com/newsroom/id/2603623. Accessed 6 April 2015.

Gefen, D., Karahanna, E., & Straub, D. W. (2003). Trust and TAM in online shopping: An integrated model. *MIS Quarterly, 27*(1), 51–90.

Gefen, D., & Straub, D. W. (2003). Managing user trust in B2C e-services. *e-Service, 2*(2), 7–24.

Glover, S., & Benbasat, I. (2011). A comprehensive model of perceived risk of e-commerce transactions. *International Journal of Electronic Commerce, 15*(2), 47–78. doi:10.2753/JEC1086-4415150202.

Hess, T. J., Fuller, M., & Campbell, D. (2009). Designing interfaces with social presence: Using vividness and extraversion to create social recommendation agents. *Journal of the Association for Information Systems, 10*(12), 889–919.

Hevner, A. R., March, S. T., Park, J., & Ram, S. (2004). Design science in information systems research. *MIS Quarterly, 28*(1), 75–105.

Hodson, H. (2014). Google's fact-checking bots build vast knowledge bank. *NewScientist.* http://www.newscientist.com/article/mg22329832.700-googles-factchecking-bots-build-vast-knowledge-bank.html#.VSVJGuG2KHR. Accessed 9 April 2015.

Hoffman, D. L., Novak, T. P., & Peralta, M. (1999). Building consumer trust online. *Communications of the ACM, 42*(4), 80–85.

Hofmann, S., & Heierhoff, L. (2012). Adoption of municipal e-Government services – A communication problem? *18th Americas Conference on Information Systems (AMCIS 2012)* (pp. 1–10).

Hofmann, S., Räckers, M., & Becker, J. (2012). Identifying factors of e-Government acceptance - A literature review. *Thirty Third International Conference on Information Systems, Orlando* (pp. 1–19).

Horsburgh, S., Goldfinch, S., & Gauld, R. (2011). Is public trust in government associated with trust in e-Government? *Social Science Computer Review, 29*(2), 232–241. doi:10.1177/0894439310368130.

Horst, M., Kuttschreuter, M., & Gutteling, J. M. (2007). Perceived usefulness, personal experiences, risk perception and trust as determinants of adoption of e-government services in The Netherlands. *Computers in Human Behavior, 23*, 1838–1852. doi:10.1016/j.chb.2005.11.003.

Karimov, F. P., Brengman, M., & Van Hove, L. (2011). The effect of website design dimensions on initial trust: A synthesis of the empirical literature. *Journal of Electronic Commerce Research, 12*(4), 272–301.

Kerschbaum, F. (2011). Secure and sustainable benchmarking in clouds. *Business & Information Systems Engineering, 3*(3), 135–143.

Khan, K. M., & Malluhi, Q. (2010). Establishing trust in cloud computing. *IT Professional, 12*(5), 20–26.

Kim, D. J., Ferrin, D. L., & Rao, H. R. (2008). A trust-based consumer decision-making model in electronic commerce: The role of trust, perceived risk, and their antecedents. *Decision Support Systems, 44*, 544–564.

Kumar, N., & Benbasat, I. (2006). The influence of recommendations and consumer reviews on evaluations of websites. *Information Systems Research, 17*(4), 425–439. doi:10.1287/isre.1060.0107.

Lankton, N. K., & McKnight, D. H. (2011). What does it mean to trust facebook? Examining technology and interpersonal beliefs. *ACM SIGMIS Database, 42*(2), 32–54. doi:10.1145/1989098.1989101.

Li, X., Hess, T. J., & Valacich, J. S. (2008). Why do we trust new technology? A study of initial trust formation with organizational information systems. *The Journal of Strategic Information Systems, 17*(1), 39–71.

Lisetti, C., Amini, R., Yasavur, U., & Rishe, N. (2013). I can help you change! An empathic virtual agent delivers behavior change health interventions. *ACM Transactions on Management Information Systems, 4*(4), 1–28. doi:10.1145/2544103.

Lowry, P. B., Vance, A., Mood, G., Beckman, B., & Read, A. (2008). Explaining and predicting the impact of branding alliances and web site quality on initial consumer trust of e-commerce web sites. *Journal of Management Information Systems, 24*(4), 199–224.

Marschall, S. (1998). Netzöffentlichkeit - eine demokratische Alternative? In W. Gellner & F. von Korff (Eds.), *Demokratie und Internet* (pp. 43–54). Baden-Baden: Nomos Verlag.

Mayer, R. C., Davis, J. H., & Schoorman, F. D. (1995). An integrative model of organizational trust. *The Academy of Management Review, 20*(3), 709–734.

McKnight, D. H. (2005). Trust in information technology. In G. Davis (Ed.), *The Blackwell encyclopedia of management* (Management Information Systems, Vol. 7, pp. 329–331). Oxford: Blackwell.

McKnight, D. H., Carter, M., Thatcher, J. B., & Clay, P. (2011). Trust in a specific technology: An investigation of its components and measures. *ACM Transactions on Management Information Systems, 2*(2), 1–15.

McKnight, D. H., Choudhury, V., & Kacmar, C. (2002a). The impact of initial consumer trust on intentions to transact with a web site: A trust building model. *The Journal of Strategic Information Systems, 11*(3), 297–323.

McKnight, D. H., Choudhury, V., & Kacmar, C. (2002b). Developing and validating trust measures for e-commerce: An integrative typology. *Information Systems Research, 13*(3), 334–359.

Neidhardt, F. (1994). *Öffentlichkeit, öffentliche Meinung, soziale Bewegungen. Kölner Zeitschrift für Soziologie und Sozialpsychologie.* Opladen: Westdeutscher Verlag.

Öksüz, A. (2014). Turning dark into white clouds – A framework on trust building in cloud providers via websites. In *Proceedings of the 20th Americas Conference on Information Systems (AMCIS 2014)*, Savannah, Georgia.

Orlikowski, W. J., & Iacono, C. (2001). Desperately seeking the "IT" in IT research: A call to theorizing the IT artifact. *Information Systems Research, 12*(2), 121–134.

Ortbach, K., Gaß, O., Köffer, S., Schacht, S., Walter, N., Maedche, A., et al. (2014). Design principles for a social question and answers site: Enabling user-to-user support in organizations. In *Proceedings of the Advancing the Impact of Design Science: Moving from Theory to Practice* (Lecture Notes in Computer Science, Vol. 8463, pp. 54–68). doi:10.1007/978-3-319-06701-8_4.

Ortbach, K., Walter, N., & Öksüz, A. (2015). Are you ready to lose control? A theory on the role of trust and risk perception on bring-your-own-device policy and information system service quality. In *Proceedings of the 23rd European Conference on Information Systems (ECIS 2015)*.

Pavlou, P. A. (2003). Consumer acceptance of electronic commerce: Integrating trust and risk with the technology acceptance model. *International Journal of Electronic Commerce, 7*(3), 101–134.

Pavlou, P. A., & Fygenson, M. (2006). Understanding and predicting electronic commerce adoption: An extension of the theory of planned behaviour. *MIS Quarterly, 30*(1), 115–143.

Pavlou, P. A., Liang, H., & Xue, Y. (2007). Understanding and mitigating uncertainty in online exchange relationships: A principal-agent perspective. *MIS Quarterly, 31*(1), 105–136.

Qiu, L., & Benbasat, I. (2005). Online consumer trust and live help interfaces: The effects of text-to-speech voice and three-dimensional avatars. *International Journal of Human-Computer Interaction, 19*(1), 75–94.

Qiu, L., & Benbasat, I. (2009). Evaluating anthropomorphic product recommendation agents: A social relationship perspective to designing information systems. *Journal of Management Information Systems, 25*(4), 145–182.

Recker, J. (2013). *Scientific research in information systems: A beginner's guide.* Heidelberg: Springer.

Richards, D., & Bransky, K. (2014). ForgetMeNot: What and how users expect intelligent virtual agents to recall and forget personal conversational content. *International Journal of Human-Computer Studies, 72*(5), 460–476.

Rogers, E. M. (2003). *Diffusion of innovations.* New York: Free Press.

Sherchan, W., Nepal, S., & Paris, C. (2013). A survey of trust in social networks. *ACM Computing Surveys, 45*(4), 1–33.

Söllner, M., Hoffmann, A., Hoffmann, H., Wacker, A., & Leimeister, J.M. (2012). Understanding the formation of trust in IT artifacts. In *Thirty Third International Conference on Information Systems* (pp. 1–18), Orlando.

Taddei, S., & Contena, B. (2013). Privacy, trust and control: Which relationships with online self-disclosure? *Computers in Human Behavior, 29*(3), 821–826.

Takabi, H., Joshi, J. B. D., & Ahn, G. J. (2010). Security and privacy challenges in cloud computing environments. *IEEE Security & Privacy, 8*(6), 24–31.

van Eimeren, B., & Frees, B. (2014). Ergebnisse der ARD/ZDF-Onlinestudie 2014: 79 Prozent der Deutschen online – Zuwachs bei mobiler Internetnutzung und Bewegtbild. *Media Perspektiven, 7–8*, 378–396.

Verhagen, T., Meents, S., & Tan, Y.-H. (2006). Perceived risk and trust associated with purchasing at electronic marketplaces. *European Journal of Information Systems, 15*(6), 542–555.

Wakefield, R. L., Stocks, M. H., & Wilder, W. M. (2004). The role of web site characteristics in initial trust formation. *Journal of Computer Information Systems, 45*(1), 94–103.

Walter, N. (2014). "Do you trust me?" – A structured evaluation of trust and social recommendation agents. In *SIGHCI 2014 Proceedings*.

Walter, N., Öksüz, A., Walterbusch, M., Teuteberg, F., & Becker, J. (2014). "May I help you?" Increasing trust in cloud computing providers through social presence and the reduction of information overload. In *Proceedings of the 35th International Conference on Information Systems (ICIS 2014)*.

Walter, N., Ortbach, K., Niehaves, B., & Becker, J. (2013). Trust needs touch: understanding the building of trust through social presence. In *Proceedings of the 19th Americas Conference on Information Systems (AMCIS 2013)*. Chicago, IL.

Wang, W., & Benbasat, I. (2007). Recommendation agents for electronic commerce: Effects of explanation facilities on trusting beliefs. *Journal of Management Information Systems, 23*(4), 217–246.

Wang, W., & Benbasat, I. (2008). Attributions of trust in decision support technologies: A study of recommendation agents for e-commerce. *Journal of Management Information Systems, 24*(4), 249–273.

Wang, Y. D., & Emurian, H. H. (2005). An overview of online trust: Concepts, elements, and implications. *Computers in Human Behavior, 21*(1), 105–125.

Xiao, B., & Benbasat, I. (2007). E-commerce product recommendation agents: Use, characteristics, and impact. *MIS Quarterly, 31*(1), 137–209.

Zissis, D., & Lekkas, D. (2012). Addressing cloud computing security issues. *Future Generation Computer Systems, 28*(3), 583–592.

Trust the Words: Insights into the Role of Language in Trust Building in a Digitalized World

Regina Jucks, Gesa A. Linnemann, Franziska M. Thon, and Maria Zimmermann

Abstract There is more to words than just the meanings they convey. Especially in online settings in which information about others is limited, the words employed play an important role in assessing an interlocutor's trustworthiness. Therefore, based on ability, benevolence, and integrity as the components of trustworthiness, we investigated word usage in three exemplary digitalized settings. The first scenario is a peer-to-peer discussion in online forums (e.g., when students need support in overcoming their procrastination). The second scenario is searching for online health advice (e.g., retrieving health information from other users with varying medical expertise). The third is online communication with spoken dialogue systems (e.g., asking Apple's® Siri® how to find one's way in an unknown town). Referring to the word usage in the respective communication setting, we address central language-related trust issues: (a) self-disclosure and the communication of empathy, (b) technical language and cues regarding the fragility of evidence, and (c) perceiving a shared view through lexical overlaps. The contribution ends with an outline of future research on the interplay between these three issues and trust.

Keywords Trust • Communication • Self-disclosure • Spoken dialogue systems • Technical language

1 How Language Influences Trust Building

Words are not just used to transport a certain message. They also indicate our emotional states, our deeply grounded attitudes, and our relation to the given communication partner. Hence, words communicate not only with but also beyond their content. When it comes to trust building with words, one might well ask for trust directly (e.g., "Please trust me, I know what I'm talking about"). However, language offers further ways to indicate that one's message is trustworthy. When

R. Jucks (✉) • G.A. Linnemann • F.M. Thon • M. Zimmermann
University of Münster, Münster, Germany
e-mail: jucks@uni-muenster.de; gesa.linnemann@uni-muenster.de; f.thon@uni-muenster.de; maria.zimmermann@uni-muenster.de

© Springer International Publishing Switzerland 2016   225
B. Blöbaum (ed.), *Trust and Communication in a Digitized World*, Progress in IS,
DOI 10.1007/978-3-319-28059-2_13

deciding whether or not to trust somebody, people have to perform an elaborate analysis of the language of the message. If the message givers talk in a very eloquent and structured way, recipients may assess their words as being more trustworthy than the same information presented in an unelaborated way (Lev-Ari and Keysar 2010). Recipients seem to be well aware of the mechanisms guiding how and when we attribute trustworthiness (Thon and Jucks submitted). In general, trustworthiness is not an all-or-nothing issue, but might best be conceptualized as a continuum. Finally, but just as importantly, trustworthiness is also built up by using certain wordings (e.g., using words such as "mostly" to emphasize the tentativeness of a scientific finding).

Many settings provide no more information than the actual words. In these cases, the mere words have to serve as an indicator of whom to trust. Following the model of organizational trust (Mayer et al. 1995), trustworthiness is then assessed by interpreting these words in terms of the ability, benevolence, and integrity they indicate in the provider of the information. Ability thereby refers to the speakers' competence; benevolence, their willingness to help; and integrity, their orientation toward a set of values similar to that of the trust provider. In the following, we shall outline what certain words contribute to the attribution of trustworthiness. We shall illustrate this with three different scenarios that are relevant in online communication: giving peer-to-peer advice, retrieving information from other users of varying expertise, and interacting with a spoken dialogue system. In each of these scenarios, we shall focus on the specific way that words contribute to trust building through: (a) self-disclosure and the communication of empathy, (b) technical language and cues regarding the fragility of evidence, and (c) perceiving a shared view through lexical overlaps. Finally, we outline future research perspectives on the role of language in online trust-building processes.

2   Self-Disclosure and Empathy in Online Peer-to-Peer Interactions

The Internet has become a social environment that people use to exchange personal information. Various social platforms offer space for public discussions in which people may post their specific questions to unknown others. This often takes place in a peer-to-peer context, for instance, students exchanging knowledge and advice on procrastination in online forums (Thon and Jucks 2014). Procrastination is the behavior of postponing intended actions despite possible negative consequences, and is a phenomenon with which most students are familiar (cf. Steel 1991). Imagine a typical forum post from a student starting with a description of the context of her problem: For example, she wants to pass several exams in the following weeks, but instead of learning she often finds herself browsing the Internet. Another forum user then responds by making suggestions on how to overcome her procrastination (e.g., by setting an incentive for successful learning sessions). When giving advice, people often take their own personal experience into account (e.g., "I always reward myself after having worked through one chapter"). This "process of making the self known to others" (Jourard and Lasakow 1958, p. 91) is referred to as self-disclosure. The extent of information shared is influenced by the discloser, the recipient, and the specific context of the conversation (see Ignatius and Kokkonen 2007, for a review) and is determined on three different dimensions: duration, breadth, and depth (cf. Cozby 1973). Duration refers to the length of the self-disclosure and can be measured by the number of utterances starting with a first-person personal pronoun (e.g., "I procrastinate"). Breadth describes the range of different contents addressed (cf. Barak and Gluck-Ofri 2007), that is, (a) personal information or facts (e.g., one's academic year), (b) a thought or an opinion (e.g., hoping to pass an exam), and (c) feelings (e.g., being sad). However, self-disclosure also differs in its depth, that is, the intimacy of disclosed content. Sharing personal information with one person but not another permits the establishment of trust and intimacy in relationships. However, providing personal information poses a risk by exposing one's vulnerability to the recipient of the information. Therefore, sharing information demonstrates a willingness to be vulnerable and can be interpreted as an offer of trust. An offer of trust is often reciprocated (cf. Jourard 1971), leading to increased self-disclosure in the communication (e.g., Barak and Gluck-Ofri 2007; McAllister and Bregman 1985). Hence, the disclosure of personal experiences does not just provide information on, for example, possible strategies to prevent procrastination, but also functions as a communication strategy supporting trust-building processes. However, boundaries for the ownership of the disclosed information need to be negotiated and managed (cf. Petronio 2002). "If one trusts the recipient of the personal information, then one can act with relative freedom" (Joinson and Paine 2007, p. 242). Nonetheless, compared to talking to a fellow student in the student hall, information in online communication is transmitted on fewer dimensions (cf. Clark and Brennan 1991). Information about the specific audience of a conversation (e.g., bystanders, eavesdroppers, and side participants; cf. Clark 1996) is not as overt as in face-to-face settings, and this makes the question regarding whom we are talking to more difficult to answer. Online media play a crucial role in these communication settings because they address different audiences and thereby provide different levels of privacy. Interlocutors in e-mail communication actively determine who takes part in the conversation. Compared to other online communication media, people thereby feel private (Frye and Dornisch 2010). In contrast, online forums have multiple actors and audiences, and the extent of privacy is determined by features of the specific forum. Although there is a high variability between different online platforms, most forums are public and privacy is therefore low. Thus, the one-to-one interactions between interlocutors in online forums are only pseudo-private: The boundary between private and public communication is blurred. When the two students exchange their personal experiences on procrastination in an online forum thread, millions of people could be lurking. And because self-disclosure can also lead to negative experiences when establishing a relationship and seeking advice, such as being rejected, it can be risky even under anonymous conditions.

As outlined above, revealing and concealing private information are both of interest when seeking advice from others on procrastination behavior. However, they are also dialectical, that is, opposing processes. Multiple models in different disciplines often attempt to explain how people can deal with this dialectic by proposing some form of calculation between the benefits and risks of self-disclosure (e.g., Afifi and Steuber 2009; Omarzu 2000). Nonetheless, whereas social interactions require some kind of self-disclosure in order to establish a trusting relationship, the extent of this self-disclosure can be regulated to satisfy privacy needs. Addressing this interplay between self-disclosure and privacy in different media, Thon and Jucks (2014) investigated how sensitively users assess and react to their specific audience in online communication. A predominantly student sample answered a written inquiry from a student seeking advice on procrastination behavior. Thon and Jucks varied whether the inquiry contained high emotion-based self-disclosure or not and whether the communication situation was public or private. Results showed that participants sensitively detected the interlocutor's self-disclosure and were aware of the degree of privacy in the context. Surprisingly, high emotion-based self-disclosure impacted negatively on the perception of benevolence. It may well be that the problem-focused content of the inquiry contributed to the perception that the interlocutor in the low self-disclosure condition was more concerned about the well-being of others. In addition, participants self-disclosed personal information when responding to the inquiry independently of whether they had received an offer of trust in the first place as well as independently of the privacy context. Interestingly, although participants did not react specifically to the offer of trust, they did respond by using more positive emotion words when the inquiry contained emotional self-disclosure. Engaging in and connecting to the interlocutor's emotional state can be interpreted as a form of empathy possibly facilitating the formation of trust. Although trust and empathy are closely related (e.g., Ickes et al. 1990), in face-to-face interactions, empathy is transferred strongly through nonverbal cues (Ickes 1997; Ickes et al. 1990). Communicating empathy through emotion words might therefore be another communication strategy with which to establish trust in text-based online communication. Similarly, Feng et al. (2004) found that people who not only inferred other people's feelings correctly but also gave supportive responses increased interpersonal trust in an online textual environment. Overall, these findings indicate that both self-disclosure and communicating empathy are important mechanisms for establishing trust in online peer-to-peer communication, and that they might even be privileged over other important needs in online environments such as privacy (Moll and Pieschl 2015; Thon and Jucks 2014).

3 Technical Language and Cues Regarding the Fragility of Evidence as Indicators of an Interlocutor's Trustworthiness

People seek health information from others in order to make health-related decisions. Although access to online information can empower health information seekers (cf. Bromme and Jucks 2014; Hu and Sundar 2009), the availability of information per se does not necessarily contribute to patients' actual understanding of a medical issue. Online communication thereby is not restricted to peer-to-peer communication—as in the previous scenario of this chapter—but also extends to expert–layperson communication. Many "ask the expert" sites provide a communication platform between someone who is an expert and a less knowledgeable person, with online health advice being a very prominent topic (Jucks and Bromme 2007). The joint goal in such communication settings is to empower patients to make well-informed health-related decisions. However, the patients' limited understanding of medical issues creates a dependence on the advice givers. Tseng and Fogg (1999) argue that one cannot depend on information but only on a person. Hence, trust in information always involves credibility. Overall, while searching for information on the Internet, patients have to identify aspects indicating the trustworthiness of the authors and the credibility of the advice. Asking themselves whom to trust involves questions such as whether experts are trustworthy because of their academic status, because of their social role, or because they talk knowledgeably. Should they have more trust in an advice giver who uses medical terminology or should they believe someone who provides comprehensive information?

According to Mayer et al. (1995), the question whom to trust is a question of who is able to give credible advice, is benevolent, and is integer. Persons with high levels of ability are termed experts on the specific area of expertise. With regard to health-related issues, a medical expert should be expected to be more credible than someone without medical expertise (e.g., a lawyer). Medical expertise can be characterized by features such as status, long-term training, certificates, and membership of an organization. Nonetheless, in an online environment, there are no doctoral assistants and status-indicating features such as lab coats or expensive medical equipment. Hence, experts giving health advice are identified primarily by their professional knowledge. Because the vast majority of online communication refers to written characteristics, word use thereby becomes crucial. As one example of a specific language use of experts, technical language could enhance perceived trustworthiness by indicating expertise. Features indicating the comprehensibility of technical language are the use of technical terms, the frequency of words, and the complexity of sentences (Pickering and Garrod 2004). Focusing on word choice, technical terms can be defined as "meaningful entities needed to perform a task in the area of expertise" (Bromme 1996, p. 184, translated). Hence, technical terms are used in particular contexts (e.g., when doctors discuss a medical case), but may not be well understood outside these areas (e.g., when doctors communicate with patients). Therefore, assumptions regarding the effect of technical terms on credibility are twofold: On the one hand, technical terms are perceived as more complex and difficult to understand (Jucks and Paus 2011) and can therefore serve as an indicator of a person's expertise. On the other hand, translating information containing technical language into comprehensive information when giving health advice to laypersons can also be understood as a function of expertise (DeVito 1995; Stehr and Grundmann 2015; Windshuttle and Elliot 1999). That is, experts need to adapt their language to a nonexpert audience (Jucks et al. 2016). Hence, online health advice might be perceived as being more credible when it is comprehensive and easy to understand. Previous studies on the effect of technical language on credibility have delivered mixed findings. On one side, Thomm and Bromme (2012) found that scientific texts including relativizations and citations are perceived as being more scientific and credible. These findings suggest that people have assumptions about the use of scientific language. When investigating the influence of tentativeness cues on the credibility of scientific arguments, Thiebach et al. (2015) demonstrated that arguments including cues on the fragility of evidence were judged to be more scientific and more credible. These results indicate that more complicated language might increase credibility. On the other side, when examining the credibility of written assertions, Scharrer et al. (2012) showed that people judged assertions to be less plausible when the presented texts included complicated terminology. Moreover, Thon and Jucks (submitted) varied cues on the profession (medical vs. nonmedical) and the word choice (technical vs. everyday terminology) of people providing online health advice. Note that this experiment was carried out in German, a language in which technical terms used by doctors (e.g., myocardial infarction) often have an everyday equivalent used by laypersons (e.g., heart attack). Participants were asked to judge the credibility of the medical information given (e.g., "A myocardial infarction is one of the most common causes of death in the industrial states") and, subsequently, the trustworthiness of the advice givers (e.g., "Mr. Peters, doctor of medicine"). Results demonstrated that authors with a medical profession were perceived not only to have a higher expertise but also to be more benevolent and integer. Hence, health advice givers with a medical profession were judged to be more trustworthy than those with a nonmedical profession. In addition, messages from authors with a medical profession were more often accepted as true than messages from authors with a nonmedical profession. The word choice used by the advice givers thereby interacted with the background information about their professions: Statements including everyday language terms were judged to be more credible when used by nonmedical authors, whereas technical terms were judged to be more credible when used by medical authors. Overall, medical authors were judged to be the most credible independent of their word choice, whereas nonmedical authors were credible only when using everyday terminology. These findings indicate complex relations between aspects of technical language and their impact on the attribution of trustworthiness in experts. Even though difficulty of specialist terminology could signal expertise, findings also indicate that comprehensive everyday terminology leads to more credibility when the interlocutor's medical expertise is low. Hence, simply talking big will not increase the credibility of one's information in online communication, but might actually decrease it—unless one can further demonstrate that one is qualified to use the language. Future research should focus more strongly on the interplay between directly provided information (e.g., "trust me, I am a doctor") and implicitly conveyed expertise through language, such as the use of medical terms when giving health advice. It would also be interesting to take into account the complex nature of interpersonal interactions by examining, for example, multiple turns between interlocutors.

4 Repetition of Words as an Indicator of Trustworthiness in a Spoken Dialogue System

Having examined written communication in the last two sections, in the third scenario, we move on to spoken communication. Furthermore, we explore communication with an artificial communication partner.

Language reflects the relationship we maintain with other people. We react to the way people talk to us. For example, we can adjust the choice of our words to those employed by our conversational partner (so-called *lexical alignment*, e.g., Branigan and Pearson 2006) and we can express either convergence or divergence with the conversational partner and the topic (Communication Accommodation Theory; Giles et al. 1991). In a discussion on abortion, for example, using the term "unborn child" instead of the previously used term "fetus" supports the position of an anti-abortionist and the wish to distance oneself from the presented point of view (cf. Danet 1980; see also *lexical differentiation*, Van der Wege 2009). Furthermore, linguistic adjustment can serve as a marker for the social quality of a relationship (Giles et al. 1991; Ireland and Pennebaker 2010). In addition, the adoption of the communication partner's words reflects politeness (Branigan et al. 2010, p. 2358; Torrey et al. 2006) and evokes positive feelings in the other person (Bradac et al. 1988; Branigan et al. 2010; van Baaren et al. 2003).

Nowadays, we communicate not only with other humans but also computers. As early as 1966, the chatter-bot "Eliza" was able to have quite natural written conversations with people, and the latter entrusted Eliza with lots of information (Weizenbaum 1966). Linguistic patterns such as the adjustment described above are likewise observable in human–computer interaction. As Brennan (1996) has described, people react politely when the system is polite although this may cause miscommunication. Nonetheless, the type of conversational partner also influences linguistic behavior. In a series of experiments, Branigan et al. (2011) got subjects to perform a word reference task in a Wizard-of-Oz setting. That is, they made people believe they were communicating with either a human or a computer. In reality, they always collaborated with a computer. Branigan and her colleagues found a greater number of adopted words when people thought they were communicating with computers compared to when they were convinced they were communicating with humans. Furthermore, subjects adopted a higher amount of terms used by computers when they considered them to be less capable (although, in fact, their capacity remained the same). In an experiment with a more natural setting, we examined how convergence on the lexical level depends on the conversational partner and language style (Linnemann and Jucks 2016). We varied whether the communication partner was a human or a computer system (realized as a Wizard-of-Oz experiment) and whether the employed language style was elaborated or rather restricted. The number of adopted words turned out to be higher when the conversational partner employed a restricted language style. Moreover, an elaborated language style led subjects to prefer the human partner in terms of likeability and cognitive demand.

However, computer systems have become more and more powerful and they are now approaching natural communication abilities and are capable of affective interaction, multiple speech acts, and multilevel learning (López-Cózar et al. 2015).

Almost natural human–computer interactions find their way into everyday life through spoken dialogue systems (SDS; Edlund et al. 2008). These are computer systems that are able to understand and produce spoken language in various applied fields. For example, López-Cózar et al. (2015) list intelligent environments, in-car applications, personal assistants, smart homes, and interaction with robots and assistants for disabled and elderly people. In particular, the use of personal assistants—well-known and common representatives are, for instance, Siri from Apple® and Google Now® installed on mobile devices—affects many people's communicative routines and personal data. With each question and answer, users reveal sensitive data without knowing exactly where it will be saved and how it will be processed and connected. SDS have become increasingly powerful (Allen et al. 2001). When SDS are capable of maintaining natural conversations, people can perceive them as effective communication partners and social actors (Nass and Lee 2000). From then on, trust comes into play (cf. Tseng and Fogg 1999). Users can draw on personal components of an SDS such as the ability, benevolence, and integrity found in Mayer et al.'s (1995) model. Furthermore, research and development aim to construct SDS that are able to maintain long-term relationships with particular users (López-Cózar et al. 2015). For that purpose, SDS have to be enabled to recognize individual users through their voice, preferences, interests, and social relationships. Not only should SDS always be ready to answer requests and perform tasks (*human initiative*, Mavridis 2015), but they must be proactive and, on occasion and when appropriate, start a conversation by themselves or contribute helpful information without being asked explicitly (*mixed initiative dialogue*, Mavridis 2015). Thus, SDS can represent attentive, caring, and close assistants that are always ready to talk. Therefore, if people are to accept their daily use, they need to perceive SDS as benevolent and integer (Mayer et al. 1995). To benefit from these tempting possibilities, users need to trust their human-like communication partner. Prior research has shown that even SDS that are not as far developed can get people to disclose intimate information about themselves and may even be preferred to human beings (Petrie and Abell 1995; Weisband and Kiesler 1996). Today, permanent connection to the Internet dramatically enhances the knowledge and communication abilities of computer systems (Mavridis 2015). Admittedly, this involves the storage of personal data and usage of information on distal servers beyond the control of users. That is, users depend on the goodness and morality of their artificial communication partner—they have to trust them (Tseng and Fogg 1999).

What does this mean in detail? Consider the example of a student in her first term: Beginning one's studies represents an important step in life, requiring much organization and finding solutions to personal issues such as familiarizing oneself with a new environment, making new friends, or coping with loneliness. A personal assistant, on the one hand, can support the student by delivering information, and, on the other hand, by listening actively and showing sympathy. On a linguistic level, the latter is strengthened by lexical adjustment as depicted above, and this simultaneously increases the student's willingness to trust (see Linnemann and Jucks 2016). The student can activate the SDS by either pressing a button on her device or talking directly to the system by calling its name. Likewise, the common systems Siri and Google Now can be addressed, saying "Siri!" or "Okay Google!" respectively, followed by a request. No physical contact with a technical device is necessary. In addition, the user can employ a normal, natural voice. The activation is the first trust-based decision directed toward the SDS. Imagine this student activating her personal SDS after a long day of studying, having lots of questions and new experiences in mind:

Student: "I attended my first lecture today."
   SDS: "You attended your first lecture? How did it go?"
   Student: "Whew, it was really exciting, but also very difficult to listen. The topic was quite complicated and it was a bit noisy. Is that normal?"
   SDS: "It is quite normal that it is really exciting and difficult to listen in the first lecture. A survey revealed that 80 % of freshmen reported feelings of excitement and 70 % felt overwhelmed by the new situation."

The SDS actively shows interest in the student's activities. The repetition of the statement in the form of an enquiry underlines its attentiveness and intention to care. Hence, it elicits a more detailed answer from the student; she entrusts a personal experience. The SDS comments on the utterance and enriches it with information retrieved from the Internet. This strengthens the relationship and enhances the perceived trustworthiness of the SDS. The duration of the relationship makes it easier for the student to assess the SDS's capabilities and leads to a very low amount of conscious monitoring of the wording of own utterances. As a consequence of this, the adjustment of words by the SDS is usually also not even noted consciously.

Moreover, the SDS is able to handle a wide range of requests such as writing e-mails, managing incomes, calculating taxes, translating, checking something up in the Internet, and so forth. Once again, this involves very personal information. Trust is indispensable for a smooth and natural communication between humans and SDS. We (Linnemann and Jucks 2016) have started to identify how language— and especially lexical adjustment—serves as a mediating parameter. Many more aspects of language—phonological, syntactic, pragmatic, et cetera—have to be taken into account and investigated further. From a psychological perspective, it will be interesting to compare trust building in interpersonal communication (e.g., Thon and Jucks 2014) with trust building in human–computer interaction (e.g., Linnemann and Jucks 2016). This could contribute to the acceptance and development of SDS. The economic relevance of SDS is very high: In 2012, the market for global intelligent virtual assistants was calculated at over 350 million US dollars, and the annual growth rate from 2013 to 2020 is expected to exceed 30 per cent (Grand View Research 2014). Furthermore, the combination of technology and language seems to offer a very promising way to gain insights into what accounts for trustworthiness. When technology comes into play, we gain a comparison point for human behavior.

5   Future Perspectives on the Issue of Trust in Words and Words of Trust

In this chapter, we have outlined three scenarios related to the wording of messages that contribute to trust-building: (a) self-disclosure and the communication of empathy, (b) technical language and cues regarding the fragility of evidence, and (c) perceiving a shared view through lexical overlaps. What they all have in common is that the choice of words is a vehicle for establishing trust in interpersonal online communication—regardless of whether it is written or spoken and whether the interaction is with another human or an artificial interlocutor. We have pointed out that there are multiple and complex reactions to the wording. This chapter has provided an overview of the literature on typical online communication settings. We could show that Mayer et al.'s (1995) model of organizational trust offers a helpful framework with which to investigate the influence of language on trust. The components of the model—ability, benevolence, and integrity—can be applied to a broad range of settings as presented in the present chapter. In the first setting of a peer-to-peer forum discussion, we outlined the role of self-disclosure for building trust. Because sharing information indicates a willingness to be vulnerable, we assumed that self-disclosure is interpreted as an offer of trust and therefore increases trustworthiness. However, in Thon and Jucks' (2014) problem-based advice setting, emotion-based self-disclosure even had detrimental effects on the perception of a student's benevolence. The second setting addressed the retrieval of medical information from other online users with varying medical expertise. Thon and Jucks' (submitted) findings indicate complex relations in the attribution of trustworthiness between background information on users' expertise and the technicality of their messages. The third setting, communication with a SDS, shows that the model's components can also be used to investigate human-computer interaction. Linnemann and Jucks' (2016) results demonstrated that an elaborated computer system was the precondition for perceived ability. Complex SDS that serve as personal assistants and present themselves as human interlocutors can be perceived as benevolent or integer. The application of Mayer et al.'s components of trust-worthiness in the context of artificial intelligence offers insights into the human trust-building process in general, because programmed features can be manipulated systematically or held constant. Overall, experimental psychology has enhanced our understanding of the effects of word usage on trust-building processes, demonstrating that there are multiple reactions to different words used to communicate online. Nonetheless, we do not have the necessary statistical data to study the impact of the combination of and interaction between these words. Hence, one big challenge for future research is to engage in the empirical study of the interplay between different word usages that have been shown to impact on trust.

References

Afifi, T., & Steuber, K. (2009). The Revelation Risk Model (RRM): Factors that predict the revelation of secrets and the strategies used to reveal them. *Communication Monographs, 76* (2), 144–176. doi:10.1080/03637750902828412.

Allen, J. F., Byron, D. K., Dzikovska, M., Ferguson, G., Galescu, L., & Stent, A. (2001). Toward conversational human–computer interaction. *AI Magazine, 22*(4), 1–9. doi:10.1609/aimag. v22i4.1590.

Barak, A., & Gluck-Ofri, O. (2007). Degree and reciprocity of self-disclosure in online forums. *CyberPsychology & Behavior, 10*, 407–417. doi:10.1089/cpb.2006.9938.

Bradac, J. J., Mulac, A., & House, A. (1988). Lexical diversity and magnitude of convergent versus divergent style shifting: Perceptual and evaluative consequences. *Language & Communication, 8*(3–4), 213–228. doi:10.1016/0271-5309(88)90019-5.

Branigan, H., & Pearson, J. (2006). Alignment in human-computer interaction. In K. Fischer (Ed.). *How people talk to computers, robots, and other artificial communication partners. Proceedings of the Workshop Hansewissenschaftskolleg* (pp. 140–156). http://www.sfbtr8.uni-bremen. de/papers/SFB_TR_8_Rep_010-09_2006.pdf. Accessed 9 September 2015.

Branigan, H. P., Pickering, M. J., Pearson, J., & McLean, J. F. (2010). Linguistic alignment between people and computers. *Journal of Pragmatics, 42*(9), 2355–2368. doi:10.1016/j. pragma.2009.12.012.

Branigan, H. P., Pickering, M. J., Pearson, J., McLean, J. F., & Brown, A. (2011). The role of beliefs in lexical alignment: Evidence from dialogs with humans and computers. *Cognition, 121*(1), 41–57. doi:10.1016/j.cognition.2011.05.011.

Brennan, S. E. (1996). Lexical entrainment in spontaneous dialog. *Proceedings of ISSD, 96*, 41–44.

Bromme, R. (1996). Fachbegriffe. In G. Strube, B. Becker, C. Freska, U. Hahn, G. Palm, & K. Opwis (Eds.), *Wörterbuch der Kognitionswissenschaft* (p. 184). Stuttgart: Klett-Cotta.

Bromme, R., & Jucks, R. (2014). Fragen Sie Ihren Arzt oder Apotheker: Die Psychologie der Experten-Laien-Kommunikation. In M. Blanz, A. Florack, & U. Piontkowski (Eds.), *Kommunikation. Eine interdisziplinäre Einführung* (pp. 237–249). Stuttgart: Kohlhammer.

Clark, H. H. (1996). *Using language.* Cambridge, England: Cambridge University Press.

Clark, H. H., & Brennan, S. E. (1991). Grounding in communication. In L. B. Resnick, J. Levine, & S. D. Behrend (Eds.), *Perspectives on socially shared cognition* (pp. 127–149). Washington, DC: American Psychological Association.

Cozby, P. (1973). Self-disclosure: A literature review. *Psychological Bulletin, 79*, 73–91. doi:10. 1037/h0033950.

Danet, B. (1980). "Baby" or "fetus"? Language and the construction of reality in a manslaughter trial. *Semiotica, 32*(3-4), 187–220.

DeVito, J. A. (1995). *Human communication.* New York, NY: Addison Wesley Longman.

Edlund, J., Gustafson, J., Heldner, M., & Hjalmarsson, A. (2008). Towards human-like spoken dialogue systems. *Speech Communication, 50*(8-9), 630–645. doi:10.1016/j.specom.2008.04. 002.

Feng, J., Lazar, J., & Preece, J. (2004). Empathy and online interpersonal trust: A fragile relationship. *Behaviour & Information Technology, 23*(2), 97–106.

Frye, N. E., & Dornisch, M. M. (2010). When is trust not enough? The role of perceived privacy of communication tools in comfort with self-disclosure. *Computers in Human Behavior, 26,* 1120–1127. doi:10.1016/j.chb.2010.03.016

Giles, H., Coupland, N., & Coupland, J. (1991). Accommodation theory: Communication, context, and consequence. In H. Giles, J. Coupland, & N. Coupland (Eds.), *Contexts of accommodation* (pp. 1–68). New York, NY: Cambridge University Press.

Grand View Research. (2014). *Intelligent virtual assistant market analysis and segment forecasts to 2020.* http://www.grandviewresearch.com/industry-analysis/intelligent-virtual-assistant-industry. Accessed 15 April 2015.

Hu, Y., & Sundar, S. S. (2009). Effects of online health sources on credibility and behavioral intentions. *Communication Research, 37*(1), 105–132. doi:10.1177/0093650209351512.

Ickes, W. (1997). *Empathic accuracy.* New York, NY: Guildford Press.

Ickes, W., Stinson, L., Bissonnette, V., & Garcia, S. (1990). Naturalistic social cognition: Empathic accuracy in mixed-sex dyads. *Journal of Personality and Social Psychology, 59,* 730–742.

Ignatius, E., & Kokkonen, M. (2007). Factors contributing to verbal self-disclosure. *Nordic Psychology, 59,* 362–391. doi:10.1027/1901-2276.59.4.362.

Ireland, M. E., & Pennebaker, J. W. (2010). Language style matching in writing: Synchrony in essays, correspondence, and poetry. *Journal of Personality and Social Psychology, 99*(3), 549–571. doi:10.1177/0956797610392928.

Joinson, A. N., & Paine, C. B. (2007). Self-disclosure, privacy and the Internet. In A. N. Joinson, K. Y. A. McKenna, T. Postmes, & U.-D. Reips (Eds.), *Oxford handbook of Internet psychology* (pp. 237–252). Oxford, England: Oxford University Press.

Jourard, S. M. (1971). *Self-disclosure: An experimental analysis of the transparent self.* New York, NY: Wiley.

Jourard, S. M., & Lasakow, P. (1958). Some factors in self-disclosure. *Journal of Abnormal and Social Psychology, 56*(1), 91–98. doi:10.1037/h0043357.

Jucks, R., & Bromme, R. (2007). Choice of words in doctor–patient communication: An analysis of health-related Internet sites. *Health Communication, 21,* 267–277. doi:10.1080/10410230701307865

Jucks, R., Päuler, L., & Brummernhenrich, B. (2016). "I need to be explicit: You're wrong:" Impact of face threats on social evaluations in online instructional communication. *Interacting with Computers, 28*(1), 73–84. doi:10.1093/iwc/iwu032.

Jucks, R., & Paus, E. (2011). What makes a word difficult? Insights into the mental representation of technical terms. *Metacognition Learning, 7*(2), 91–111. doi:10.1007/s11409-011-9084-6.

Lev-Ari, S., & Keysar, B. (2010). Why don't we believe non-native speakers? The influence of accent on credibility. *Journal of Experimental Social Psychology, 46,* 1093–1096. doi:10.1016/j.jesp.2010.05.025

Linnemann, G. A., & Jucks, R. (2016). "As in the question, so in the answer?" Language style of human and machine speakers affects interlocutors' convergence on wordings. *Journal of Language and Social Psychology.* doi:10.1177/0261927X15625444

López-Cózar, R., Callejas, Z., Griol, D., & Quesada, J. F. (2015). Review of spoken dialogue systems. *Loquens, 1*(2), e012.

Mavridis, N. (2015). A review of verbal and non-verbal human–robot interactive communication. *Robotics and Autonomous Systems, 63,* 22–35.

Mayer, R. C., Davis, J. H., & Schoorman, F. D. (1995). An integrative model of organizational trust. *Academy of Management Review, 20*(3), 709–734.

McAllister, H. A., & Bregman, N. J. (1985). Reciprocity effects with intimate and nonintimate self-disclosure: The importance of establishing baseline. *Journal of Social Psychology, 125*, 775–776. doi:10.1080/00224545.1985.9713552.

Moll, R., & Pieschl, S. (2015). Expecting collective privacy – A new perspective on trust in online communication. In B. Bloebaum (Ed.), *Trust and communication in a digitalized world. Models and concepts of trust research.* Heidelberg: Springer.

Nass, C., & Lee, K. M. (2000, April). Does computer-generated speech manifest personality? An experimental test of similarity-attraction. In *Proceedings of the CHI 2000 Conference on Human factors in computing systems*, The Hague, Netherlands. doi:10.1145/332040.332452.

Omarzu, J. (2000). A self-disclosure decision model: Determining how and when individuals will self-disclose. *Personality and Social Psychology Review, 4*, 174–185. doi:10.1207/S15327957PSPR040205.

Petrie, K., & Abell, W. (1995). Responses of parasuicides to a computerized interview. *Computers in Human Behavior, 10*(4), 415–418.

Petronio, S. S. (2002). *Boundaries of privacy: Dialectics of disclosure.* Albany, NY: SUNY Press.

Pickering, S., & Garrod, S. (2004). Towards a mechanistic psychology of dialogue. *Behavioral and Brain Sciences, 27*, 169–226.

Scharrer, L., Bromme, R., Britt, M. A., & Stadtler, M. (2012). The seduction of easiness: How science depictions influence laypeople's reliance on their own evaluation of scientific information. *Learning and Instruction, 22*(3), 231–243. doi:10.1016/j.learninstruc.2011.11.004.

Steel, J. L. (1991). Interpersonal correlates of trust and self-disclosure. *Psychological Reports, 68*, 1319–1320. doi:10.2466/PR0.68.4.

Stehr, N., & Grundmann, R. (2015). *Expertenwissen - Die Kultur und die Macht von Experten, Beratern und Ratgebern.* Weilerswist: Velbrück Wissenschaft.

Thiebach, M., Mayweg-Paus, E., & Jucks, R. (2015). "Probably true" says the expert: How two types of lexical hedges influence students' evaluation of scientificness. *European Journal of Psychology of Education, 30*(3), 369–384. doi:10.1007/s10212-014-0243-4.

Thomm, E., & Bromme, R. (2012). It should at least seem scientific! Textual features of "scientificness" and their impact on lay assessments of online information. *Science Education, 96*(2), 187–211.

Thon, F. M., & Jucks, R. (submitted). *Believing in expertise: How authors' credentials and language use influence the credibility of online health information.*

Thon, F. M., & Jucks, R. (2014). Regulating privacy in interpersonal online communication: The role of self-disclosure. *Studies in Communication Sciences, 2014*, 3–11. doi:10.1016/j.scoms.2014.03.012.

Torrey, C., Powers, A., Marge, M., Fussell, S. R., & Kiesler, S. (2006, March). Effects of adaptive robot dialogue on information exchange and social relations. In *Proceedings of the 1st ACM SIGCHI/SIGART conference on Human-robot interaction* (pp. 126–133). ACM.

Tseng, S., & Fogg, B. J. (1999). Credibility and computing technology. *Communications of the ACM, 42*(5), 39–44.

van Baaren, R. B., Holland, R. W., Steenaert, B., & van Knippenberg, A. (2003). Mimicry for money: Behavioral consequences of imitation. *Journal of Experimental Social Psychology, 39* (4), 393–398. doi:10.1016/S0022-1031(03)00014-3.

Van Der Wege, M. M. (2009). Lexical entrainment and lexical differentiation in reference phrase choice. *Journal of Memory and Language, 60*(4), 448–463. doi:10.1016/j.jml.2008.12.003.

Weisband, S., & Kiesler, S. (1996, April). Self disclosure on computer forms: Meta-analysis and implications. In *Proceedings of the SIGCHI conference on human factors in computing systems* (pp. 3–10). ACM.

Weizenbaum, J. (1966). ELIZA – a computer program for the study of natural language communication between man and machine. *Communications of the ACM, 9*(1), 36–45.

Windshuttle, K., & Elliot, E. (1999). *Writing, researching, communicating. Communication skills for the information age* (3rd ed.). Sydney: Irwin/McGraw-Hill.

Expecting Collective Privacy: A New Perspective on Trust in Online Communication

Ricarda Moll and Stephanie Pieschl

Abstract Digitization has opened unprecedented opportunities for online communication. In contrast to face-to-face communication, online communication often involves large audiences that consist of other social media users (network audience) but also of governmental and private institutions (institutional audiences). Consequently, how users manage their privacy is a key component of digital literacy. Interestingly, users' privacy-management behaviors may largely be influenced by trust. Here, we argue that traditional conceptualizations of dyadic trust cannot adequately explain this aspect of online communication and therefore need to be extended. Thus, we suggest that when communicating online, users act in a default trust mode based on their trust in collective privacy: users experience a common online phenomenon, such as information overload, and might project this experience onto other users. As such, they might assume that other users also have limited capacities to process all incoming content. As a consequence, users may expect collective privacy; namely, that their disclosed information is not actively processed by large audiences because it is surrounded by so much other "noise". Moreover, this expectation may take the shape of a stable subjective theory, thereby shaping all privacy-related perceptions and behaviors. We discuss theoretical and empirical evidence for these arguments, as well as their implications for digital privacy regulation.

Keywords Collective privacy • Default trust • Online communication • Audience expectations • Self-disclosure

1 Introduction

The digitization of modern societies affects many areas of people's everyday lives; for example, much of our daily communication takes place online, via E-Mail or social media. In particular, communicating on social networking sites (SNS) allows people to stay in touch with their offline contacts, thereby strengthening their social capital (Ellison et al. 2007), present themselves in an authentic way (Davis 2012),

R. Moll (✉) • S. Pieschl
University of Münster, Münster, Germany
e-mail: r.moll@uni-muenster.de; pieschl@uni-muenster.de

© Springer International Publishing Switzerland 2016
B. Blöbaum (ed.), *Trust and Communication in a Digitized World*, Progress in IS,
DOI 10.1007/978-3-319-28059-2_14

and obtain information about current news and events from different online communities. Inherent in using SNS systems, though, is that users must reveal information about themselves (self-disclosure). Such disclosed information is often public by default and thus accessible by many other users (*network audience*). This information also persists on the providers' servers (Boyd 2008), which are also potentially accessible by private and governmental institutions (*institutional audience*). Thus, self-disclosing information online is inherently tied to a loss of informational privacy; namely, the loss of control over access to one's personal information (Burgoon et al. 1989).

Self-disclosing personal information opens users up to various risks tied to the receiving audiences (see Moll 2015). For example, while risks related to the *network audience* include harsh judgments and even cyberbullying (e.g., Pieschl et al. 2015; Slonje et al. 2013), the mere existence of an *institutional audience* puts users at risk of having their data easily manipulated for financial gain or used for systematic surveillance (Greenwald 2014; Schaar 2009; Solove 2007). This implies that it is important but challenging for users to actively regulate their digital privacy (Altman 1975; Petronio 2002).

Privacy regulation can be seen as an example of self-regulation that is based on comparing a *current state* of privacy to a corresponding goal or *target state* (e.g., Miller et al. 1960; Pintrich et al. 2000)—an idea that is present in most theories on privacy regulation (Altman 1975; Petronio 2002; Trepte and Dienlin 2014). Importantly, to regulate their privacy according to their goals, users first require an accurate representation of the current state of their privacy. Without this, users are unlikely to detect potential discrepancies between the current and target states. However, users' knowledge of the current state of their privacy seems to be limited (see Moll 2015 for an overview). First, users seem to have limited knowledge about their *potential audience*—namely, what information they have disclosed to which network audience—and they also do not seem to be aware that they lack this knowledge (Moll et al. 2014a, 2015a; Pieschl and Moll 2015; see also Junco 2013). Second, users do not know who and how many people actually access their disclosed information. Clearly, users cannot know such *actual audiences* because SNS privacy settings only restrain the network audience to a partially restricted public; they do not reveal who actually reads the disclosed information (Bernstein et al. 2013) and they cannot prevent access by institutional audiences.

Consequently, while users' digital literacy partly hinges on how well they regulate their privacy regarding online audiences, they have limited knowledge and inherent uncertainties about these audiences.

At the same time, users need to feel confident about communicating online, since for most users refraining from such communication altogether is not a viable option. Scholarly discussions therefore circle around the idea of the so-called privacy paradox; namely, that people seem to be concerned about their privacy but nonetheless keep self-disclosing information (e.g., Acquisti and Gross 2006; Barnes 2006; Norberg et al. 2007). Oftentimes, the key concept used to explain people's (absence of or seemingly irrational) privacy regulating behaviors, is *trust* (see section "Traditional Conceptualizations of Trust").

We will argue that trust is a fundamentally important concept to explain users' privacy-related behaviors, but that traditional conceptualizations of trust within dyadic-like relationships need to be extended. Previously, we have elaborated on the idea of trust in collective privacy (Moll et al. 2014b), and we will now discuss the theoretical and empirical arguments as well as implications for this in the context of digital privacy regulation.

2 Traditional Conceptualizations of Trust

Many psychological theories and empirical studies show that people tend to compensate for their lack of knowledge in different areas with subjective *beliefs*, which allow people to continue to act in the presence of risk and uncertainty (e.g., Ames 2004; Giddens 1996). When such beliefs are associated with other *people*, they can be seen as the cognitive process underlying the genesis of trust. However, it is an open question as to *what kinds* of beliefs users build with regard to their audiences in order to trust that their privacy will be preserved.

Traditional conceptualizations of trust often focus on *dyadic* relationships, whereby a trusting person (trustor) makes her/himself vulnerable to another agent (trustee), whose trustworthiness is judged based on cues about her expertise, benevolence, and integrity (see Mayer et al. 1995; Joinson et al. 2010). In other words, users are assumed to build beliefs about the *intent of the trustee*. Moreover, the trustee is likely to be *aware* of the fact that s/he is trusted with the trustor's goal (*strong delegation of responsibility*; Castelfranchi and Falcone 2001).

These traditional conceptualizations are often applied to the context of online communications (see Moll 2015). Thus, studies have argued that users trust in the provider, in other network users, or sometimes in a diffuse mixture of both (e.g., Beldad et al. 2010; Dwyer et al. 2007; Fogel and Nehmad 2009; Krasnova et al. 2010; Taddei and Contena 2013). However, the extent to which this traditional understanding of trust adequately explains how people regulate their privacy online is limited.

For example, when users trust in the benevolence of their network audience, they might believe that other network users will not judge their contents harshly or even engage in cyberbullying (Pieschl and Porsch 2014). However, network audiences are often quite large and usually contain multiple and potentially conflicting social spheres whose members may judge the self-disclosed contents very differently (e.g., Binder et al. 2009; Brandtzæg et al. 2010). Therefore, users likely do not trust in the benevolent intent of all these members. Moreover, as mentioned earlier, users often do not even know to whom they make their content accessible, so they probably do not apply dyadic trust in the benevolent intent of this unknown audience.

To give another example, if users were to trust in the provider, they would have to believe, for example, that their providers will protect their disclosed data from access by third parties (e.g., Frye and Dornisch 2010). However, this seems simply unrealistic, especially because users acknowledge that the trade with their data is part of the providers' business model. Thus, users probably know that the "trustee" will not act in their own interest, and that even the opposite might be true. For example, Facebook has been widely criticized for several changes in their privacy policies (Van Alsenoy et al. 2015), making it unlikely that people actually trust Facebook to protect their privacy.

We argue that the relevance of trust in online communication takes a different form than the described conceptualizations of trust within dyadic relationships. Importantly, we do not rule out the possibility that dyadic forms of trust exist and might be relevant for self-disclosing behaviors, but we argue that limiting the concept of trust to dyadic relationships will not suffice to explain people's privacy-regulating behaviors in online environments.

Other traditional conceptualizations of trust may capture selected aspects of trust in online communication more adequately. For example, Castelfranchi and Falcone (2001) argued that trust may also occur as *weak delegation* of responsibility. This sort of trust presumes that the trustor knows that the trustee does not have a specific intent directed at her/him and therefore is not aware that s/he is trusted. Nonetheless, the trustor may *expect* certain behaviors of the trustee, which s/he believes to be part of the trustees behaviors anyway. The authors exemplify this as follows:

> ... consider a hunter who is waiting and is ready to shoot an arrow at a bird flying towards its nest. In his plan the hunter includes an action of the bird: to fly in a specific direction; in fact, this is why he is not pointing at the bird but at where the bird will be in a second. He is delegating to the bird an action in his plan; and the bird is unconsciously and unintentionally collaborating with the hunter's plan." (p. 57)

This very simple form of social delegation may be transferred to users' beliefs about their audience's behavior: when users reason about their audience, they might expect them to behave in a certain way that is—unintentionally—beneficial to the users' goal of preserving their own privacy. In the following sections we will elaborate several consecutive ideas related to this argument. More specifically, we elaborate what exactly trustors may expect of their trustee audiences in online communication, leading to their expectation of collective privacy.

3 Trust in Collective Privacy

The premise for our following points is an argument put forward by Lundblad (2004) (see Moll 2015; Moll et al. 2014b). He proposed that we live in a so-called *noise society*, in which members produce a constant flow of information (noise). In this pool of information, agents can only attend to few pieces due to their limited cognitive capacities. Importantly, members of the *noise society* understand these conditions and thus expect that although others potentially have access to their content, it is unlikely that they would make a resource-intense effort to actually retrieve it (see Lundblad 2004; Moll 2015; Moll et al. 2014b).

Trust, in this sense, would contain the expectation that unauthorized access to one's data is possible yet unlikely. Referring directly to Lundblad (2004), we will call this *trust in collective privacy*. Trust in collective privacy resembles (but is not restricted to) trust as *weak delegation* of responsibility: users know that members of the audience have no specific intent to fulfill their own privacy-related goals. However, audience members may unintentionally do so nonetheless by not attending the trustor's disclosed information because of their limited information processing capacities.

In order to infer the audience's behaviors, users are likely to engage in so-called mindreading processes; that is, they might build beliefs from which they infer, explain, and predict others' mental states and behaviors (e.g., Grainger et al. 2014). The genesis of these beliefs and their meaning for trust in collective privacy can be structured into three core assumptions, which we will explain in detail subsequently.

1. Online users have very characteristic *everyday experiences* when communicating online.
2. Users project these experiences onto other people and draw *inferences about others' minds and behaviors*.
3. These inferences build up to a subjective theory resulting in *default trust*.

3.1   Everyday Experiences

We assume that people have at least three important experiences when being online (Moll 2015; Moll et al. 2014b). The first is that users may experience a latent *helplessness* about regulating their own privacy, which may arise because users know that institutional audiences partake in privacy-intruding practices, yet most users do not know how to adequately protect their privacy (Trepte et al. 2015). Second, people may experience *diffuse audience reactions*, such that not everyone who has access to their uploaded content ultimately responds to it; users likely build hypotheses to explain why not everyone responds. Third—and we expect that this is all users' core experience—people in modern information societies are likely to experience *information overload* (Klapp 1986; Toffler 1970); namely, users receive more information than they can process (Eppler and Mengis 2004). Social Media users in particular experience this sort of overload as stress with potential consequences for their health (Beaudoin 2008; Bontcheva et al. 2013; Jones et al. 2004; LaRose et al. 2014; Reinecke et al. 2015; Rodriguez et al. 2014).

As a consequence, people learn that they have to somehow protect themselves from the incoming flood of information—for example in being selective in their own information consumption, as they cannot read and understand every piece of information they see or can potentially access (see also Franck 1998). Thus, people seem to develop strategies to cope with this overload, such as "engaging a sophisticated mix of attention and inattention" (Hargittai et al. 2012, p. 163). For example, results from an exemplary eye-tracking study showed that Twitter users cope with information overload by attending to each tweet only for a few seconds and remembering <70 % of what they saw (Counts and Fisher 2011). Empirical studies further support this idea (see Moll 2015).

3.2 Inferences About Others

Castelfranchi and Falcone (2001) argued that trust requires people to represent the minds of their counterparts, because only through this modeling can the trustee become predictable in some way. Extending the concept of trust as weak delegation, we assume that people have specific expectations towards the collective and unintentional behavior of their audience and how this might secure their perceived (collective) privacy (see below).

Modeling the minds of others is studied in different psychological subfields, such as in social psychology regarding social (meta-) cognition (Jost et al. 1998; Michaelian 2012; see Moll 2015 for an overview) and in developmental psychology regarding a so-called theory of mind, which describes how far children and adults represent others' mental states and acknowledge that others' mental states may be different from their own (Gopnik and Wellman 1992). However, Keysar et al. (2003) showed that although a theory of mind is attained during early childhood, the mere capability to represent others' mental states does not mean that people actually make use of this competence. Rather, people are known to systematically use themselves as default models to infer the mental states and behaviors of others (Ames 2004; Bromme et al. 2001; Nickerson et al. 1987; Nickerson 1999).

When people do this with regard to their online experiences, this might lead to the assumption that others have information overload as well, and therefore others must select what information to actually attend to. Users may furthermore assume that others primarily select information they find interesting, and might then reason about *how many* people will find their information interesting enough to invest their limited processing capacity. As a consequence, users might expect that only few people actually retrieve the disclosed information, although many of them potentially have access to it (*collective privacy expectation*, see Lundblad 2004; Moll et al. 2014b).

Evidence for such an inferential structure comes from a series of experiments in which participants predicted the reading behavior of their audiences. Results showed that in the presence of specific noise cues—namely, high information density or a large audience—participants expected a smaller percentage of the potential audience to read a specific piece of information compared to when less "noise" was present (Moll et al. 2015b).

3.3   Default Trust

In the sections "Everyday Experiences" and "Inferences About Others", we described the experiences and inferences that might form the basis of trust in collective privacy. However, we argued that the resulting trust is not a swift reaction to these inferences arising in a given situation, but it has developed into something more enduring and profound (Moll 2015; Moll et al. 2014b). We propose that the described inferences may be strongly tied to each other and form a "hierarchy of statements of varying degree of abstraction and thus of explanatory power" (Bromme 2003, p. 287). In that way, the structure of the described complex of related premises and conclusions may resemble a formal *theory*. Such knowledge structures are called *subjective theories* (similar concepts are referred to as implicit, intuitive, lay, naïve, or folk theories). In contrast to formal scientific theories, subjective theories lack systematic evidence, coherence, and scientific rationality (Gelman and Noles 2011; Furnham and Elmsford 1988). Thus, "trust in collective privacy" may function as a subjective theory, which may be applied by default (*default trust;* see Sperber et al. 2010). This *default trust* would therefore operate as a stable mental framework on whose basis all further perceptions may be grounded (Dweck et al. 1995; Molden and Dweck 2006). As a consequence, people might eventually stop questioning the premise of this trust, and might even neglect other information relevant to their privacy. For example, people—when applying default trust—might process information about their self-disclosures and their potential audience in a more superficial way, which would further rob them of the opportunity to adjust to situational risks (Moll et al. 2014b).

Ultimately, such a stable mental framework might not be restricted to trusting that others will behave as expected; it might also be related to a subjective belief about the nature of privacy itself. Thus, when people believe that privacy can (only) be achieved through the behavior of the collective, this might even resemble a form of systemic trust (for a traditional conceptualization of systemic trust see Giddens 1996). For this (mentalized) system to work, the individual trustor assumes that many different agents with similar reading behaviors unknowingly operate together in a way that seemingly secures the confidentiality of a potentially public piece of information (Moll 2015).

4   General Discussion

In summary, we have argued that when people self-disclose information in online environments, their limited knowledge and uncertainty about their audience may be counterbalanced by what we call trust in collective privacy (see Lundblad 2004; Moll et al. 2014b). This trust is assumed to be based on the projection of one's own online experiences—for example, of information overload—onto one's potential audience, leading to inferences about the behaviors of other users. These inferences consist of several premises and conclusions that may build up to a more stable subjective theory, constituting the default trust that one's online information is protected by the "noise" generated by all other users.

However, although we have some anecdotal evidence for our arguments (e.g., Hoadley et al. 2010; Solove 2007), there is little scientific evidence that trust in collective privacy exists (see above; see Moll et al. 2014b). Thus, future research needs to systematically assess the existence of knowledge and trust structures with regard to online privacy. For example, future research might assess if users actually behave differently and disclose more in the presence of higher noise, and which other psychological mechanisms play a role in this context.

Throughout our discussion, we have been deliberately quiet about one potentially obvious question: is it even *rational* to have trust in collective privacy? To answer this question, we must consider a few different dimensions.

First, one might consider the perspective of the individual. From this view, trust in collective privacy seems rational because it is,—to some extent,—*functional* to the individual. For example, Luhmann (1968) argued that trust is never rational when looking at it from the outside, but that it creates for individuals an inner certainty about the future, thus making it possible for them to act. More specifically, regardless if collective privacy objectively "works" or not, it provides a framework against which users can overcome their privacy concerns (Frye and Dornisch 2010) and thus reap the benefits of online communication with their *network audience*. Additionally, it might even be true that strangers have too little time and motivation to retrieve information they simply have no reason to be interested in, possibly rendering common citizens the "needle in the haystack" they hope to be. However, while trust in collective privacy may help individuals secure their social capital, it may also inherently bias their perceptions of privacy and how they regulate it.

For example, trust in collective privacy is based on a mere probability assessment, but it does not give the user any actual control over their personal information in terms of informational privacy (see above; Burgoon et al. 1989). Furthermore, the *institutional audience* is likely to overcome the problem of information overload because they can process large amounts of stored user data through algorithm-driven analyses. This type of activity undermines the very foundation of trust in collective privacy. In that way, recent scandals about systematic surveillance by intelligence services make it difficult to overstate the long-term risks of cumulative online self-disclosures (see Beckedahl and Meister 2013).

This also implies a second perspective that needs to be considered when evaluating trust in collective privacy: the risks and benefits of individual online communication are mirrored on a societal level. Thus while our increasingly complex society relies on networks of trusted communities in which online communication and transactions are fundamentally important to secure its functioning (see Quandt 2012), the information shared in such networks is stored and accessible by outsiders, putting at risk our basic democratic rights (such as informational self-determination).

Ultimately, the arguments put forth in this chapter do not necessarily imply that people should stop self-disclosing altogether. However, it seems worthwhile to consider how we can encourage users to regulate their privacy according to their actual needs instead of a perception derived from trust in collective privacy. For example, we might encourage users to question the *validity* of collective privacy, and to thereby become aware of their own lack of knowledge and potentially biased beliefs (e.g., Moll et al. 2014b). Although research on conceptual change shows that it is very difficult to alter a stable and seemingly coherent subjective theory (Anderson and Lindsay 1998), we see potential for such conceptual change if we can deliberately raise awareness about the problems with trust in collective privacy. Because anecdotal evidence indicates that this topic is a subliminal constant in many common attitudes, defining the problem can be seen as a first step toward tackling it.

References

Acquisti, A., & Gross, R. (2006). Imagined communities: Awareness, information sharing, and privacy on the Facebook. In *Proceedings of the 6th International Conference on Privacy Enhancing Technologies* (pp. 36–58). Berlin, Heidelberg: Springer. doi:10.1007/11957454_3.

Altman, I. (1975). *The environment and social behavior*. Belmont, CA: Wadsworth.

Ames, D. R. (2004). Inside the mind reader's tool kit: Projection and stereotyping in mental state inference. *Journal of Personality and Social Psychology, 87*(3), 340–353. doi:10.1037/0022-3514.87.3.340.

Anderson, C. A., & Lindsay, J. J. (1998). The development, perseverance, and change of naive theories. *Social Cognition, 16,* 8–30. doi:10.1521/soco.1998.16.1.8.

Barnes, S. (2006). A privacy paradox: Social networking in the Unites States. *First Monday, 11*(9). Accessed September 30, 2015, from http://firstmonday.org/ojs/index.php/fm/article/view/1394/1312

Beaudoin, C. E. (2008). Explaining the relationship between internet use and interpersonal trust: Taking into account motivation and information overload. *Journal of Computer-Mediated Communication, 13,* 550–468. doi:10.1111/j.1083-6101.2008.00410.x.

Beckedahl, M., & Meister, A. (2013). *Überwachtes Netz: Edward Snowden und der größte Überwachungsskandal der Geschichte* [Surveillance of the Internet: Edward Snowden and the largest surveillance Scandal in History]. Berlin: epubli GmbH.

Beldad, A., de Jong, M., & Steehouder, M. (2010). How shall I trust the faceless and the intangible? A literature review on the antecedents of online trust. *Computers in Human Behavior, 26,* 857–869. doi:10.1016/j.chb.2010.03.013.

Bernstein, M. S., Bakshy, E., Burke, M., Karrer, B., & Park, M. (2013). Quantifying the invisible audience in social networks. In: *Proceedings of the SIGCHI Conference on Human Factors in Computing Systems* (pp. 21–30). doi:10.1145/2470654.2470658.

Binder, J., Howes, A., & Sutcliffe, A. (2009). The problem of conflicting social spheres: Effects of network structure on experienced tension in social network sites. In: *Proceeding of Chi 2009* (pp. 965–974). doi:10.1145/1518701.1518849.

Bontcheva, K., Gorrell, G., & Wessels, B. (2013). Social Media and information overload: Survey results. *CoRR*. http://arxiv.org/abs/1306.0813

Boyd, D. (2008). *Taken out of context: American teen sociality in networked publics*. Doctoral Dissertation, School of Information, University of California-Berkeley. http://www.danah.org/papers/TakenOutOfContext.pdf

Brandtzæg, P. B., Lüders, M., & Skjetne, J. H. (2010). Too many Facebook "friends"? Content sharing and sociability versus the need for privacy in Social Network Sites. *International*

Journal of Human-Computer Interaction, 26, 1006–1030. doi:10.1080/10447318.2010. 516719.

Bromme, R. (2003). On the limitations of the theory metaphor for the study of teachers' expert knowledge. In M. Kompf & P. Denicolo (Eds.), *Teacher thinking twenty years on: Revisiting persisting problems and advances in education* (pp. 283–294). Lisse: Swets and Zeitlinger.

Bromme, R., Rambow, R., & Nückles, M. (2001). Expertise and estimating what other people know: The influence of professional experience and type of knowledge. *Journal of Experimental Psychology: Applied, 7*(4), 317–330.

Burgoon, J. K., Parrott, R., Le Poire, B. A., Kelley, D. L., Walther, J. B., & Perry, D. (1989). Maintaining and restoring privacy through communication in different types of relationships. *Journal of Social and Personal Relationships, 33*, 131–158. doi:0803973233.

Castelfranchi, C., & Falcone, R. (2001). Social trust: A cognitive approach. In C. Castelfranchi & Y. H. Tan (Eds.), *Trust and deception in virtual societies* (pp. 55–90). Dordrecht: Kluwer. doi:10.1007/978-94-017-3614-5_3.

Counts, S., & Fisher, K. (2011). Taking it all in? Visual attention in microblog consumption. In: *Proceedings of the Fifth International AAAI Conference on Weblogs and Social Media* (pp. 97–104). Menlo Park, CA: The AAAI Press.

Davis, J. L. (2012). Accomplishing authenticity in a labor-exposing space. *Computers in Human Behavior, 28*, 1966–1973. doi:10.1016/j.chb.2012.05.017.

Dweck, C. S., Chiu, C., & Hong, Y. (1995). Implicit theories elaboration and extension of the model. *Psychological Inquiry, 6*(4), 322–333. doi:10.1207/s15327965pli0604_12.

Dwyer, C., Hiltz, S. R., & Passerini, K. (2007). Trust and privacy concern within social networking sites: A comparison of Facebook and MySpace. In: *Proceedings of the Thirteenth Americas Conference on Information Systems (AMCIS)*, August 9–12. Keystone, Colorado. http://csis.pace.edu/~dwyer/research/DwyerAMCIS2007.pdf

Ellison, N. B., Steinfield, C., & Lampe, C. (2007). The benefits of Facebook 'friends': Social capital and college students' use of online social network sites. *Journal of Computer-Mediated Communication, 12*(4), 1143–1168. doi:10.1111/j.1083-6101.2007.00367.x.

Eppler, M. J., & Mengis, J. (2004). The concept of information overload: A review of literature from organization science, accounting, marketing, MIS, and related disciplines. *The Information Society, 20*, 325–344. doi:10.1080/01972240490507974.

Fogel, J., & Nehmad, E. (2009). Internet social network communities: Risk taking, trust, and privacy concerns. *Computers in Human Behavior, 25*, 153–160. doi:10.1016/j.chb.2008.08. 006.

Franck, G. (1998). *Ökonomie der Aufmerksamkeit—Ein Entwurf* [Economy of attention—A blueprint]. München: Hanser.

Frye, N. E., & Dornisch, M. M. (2010). When is trust not enough? The role of perceived privacy of communication tools in comfort with self-disclosure. *Computers in Human Behavior, 26*(5), 1120–1127. doi:10.1016/j.chb.2010.03.016.

Furnham, A., & Elmsford. (1988). *Lay theories: Everyday understanding of problems in the social sciences.* New York: Pergamon Press.

Gelman, S. A., & Noles, N. S. (2011). Domains and naïve theories. *Wiley Interdisciplinary Reviews: Cognitive Science, 2*(5), 490–502. doi:10.1002/wcs.124.

Giddens, A. (1996). *Konsequenzen der Moderne* [Consequences of modernity]. Frankfurt am Main: Suhrkamp.

Gopnik, A., & Wellman, H. M. (1992). Why the child's theory of mind really is a theory. *Mind and Language, 7*(1–2), 145–171. doi:10.1111/j.1468-0017.1992.tb00202.x.

Grainger, C., Williams, D. M., & Lind, S. E. (2014). Metacognition, metamemory, and mindreading in high-functioning adults with autism spectrum disorder. *Journal of Abnormal Psychology, 123*(3), 650–659. doi:10.1037/a0036531.

Greenwald, G. (2014). *No place to hide.* New York, NY: Metropolitan Books/Henry Holt.

Hargittai, E., Neumann, W. R., & Curry, O. (2012). Taming the information tide: Perceptions of information overload in the American home. *The Information Society, 28*, 161–173. doi:10. 1080/01972243.2012.669450.

Hoadley, C. M., Xu, H., Lee, J. J., & Rosson, M. B. (2010). Privacy as information access and illusory control: The case of the Facebook News Feed privacy outcry. *Electronic Commerce Research and Applications, 9*, 50–60. doi:10.1016/j.elerap.2009.05.001.

Joinson, A. N., Reips, U. D., Buchanan, T., & Paine Schofield, C. B. (2010). Privacy, trust, and self-disclosure online. *Human–Computer Interaction, 25*(1), 1–24. doi:10.1080/ 07370020903586662.

Jones, Q., Ravid, G., & Rafaeli, S. (2004). Information overload and the message dynamics of online interaction spaces: A theoretical model and empirical exploration. *Information Systems Research, 15*(2), 194–210. doi:10.1287/isre.1040.0023.

Jost, J. T., Kruglanski, A. W., & Nelson, T. O. (1998). Social metacognition: An expansionist review. *Personality and Social Psychology Review, 2*(2), 137–154. doi:10.1207/ s15327957pspr0202_6.

Junco, R. (2013). Comparing actual and self-reported measures of Facebook use. *Computers in Human Behavior, 29*(3), 626–631. doi:10.1016/j.chb.2012.11.007.

Keysar, B., Lin, S., & Barr, D. J. (2003). Limits on theory of mind use in adults. *Cognition, 89*, 25–41. doi:10.1016/s0010-0277(03)00064-7.

Klapp, O. E. (1986). *Overload and boredom: Essays on the quality of life in the information society*. New York: Greenwood Press.

Krasnova, H., Spiekermann, S., Koroleva, K., & Hildebrand, T. (2010). Online social networks: Why we disclose. *Journal of Information Technology, 25*, 109–125. doi:10.1057/jit.2010.6.

LaRose, R., Connolly, R., Lee, H., Li, K., & Hales, K. D. (2014). Connection overload? A cross cultural study of the consequences of social media connection. *Information Systems Management, 31*(1), 59–73. doi:10.1080/10580530.2014.854097.

Luhmann, N. (1968). *Vertrauen. Ein Mechanismus der Reduktion sozialer Komplexität* [Trust. A mechanism to reduce social complexity]. Stuttgart: Ferdinand Enke Verlag.

Lundblad, N. (2004). Privacy in the noise society. *Scandinavian Studies in Law, 47*, 349–371. http://www.scandinavianlaw.se/pdf/47-16.pdf

Mayer, R. C., Davis, J. H., & Schoorman, F. D. (1995). An integrative model of organizational trust. *The Academy of Management Review, 20*(3), 709–734. doi:10.2307/258792.

Michaelian, K. (2012). (Social) metacognition and (self-)trust. *Review of Philosophy and Psychology, 3*(4), 481–514. doi:10.1007/s13164-012-0099-y.

Miller, G. A., Galanter, E., & Pribram, K. H. (1960). *Plans and the structure of behavior*. New York, NY: Henry Holt and Co. doi:10.1037/10039-000.

Molden, D. C., & Dweck, C. S. (2006). Finding 'meaning' in psychology: A lay theories approach to self-regulation, social perception, and social development. *American Psychologist, 61*, 192–203. doi:10.1037/0003-066X.61.3.192.

Moll, R. (2015). *(Meta-) cognitive parameters of privacy regulation on social networking sites*. Dissertation Thesis, Westfälische Wilhelms-Universität Münster, Germany.

Moll, R., Pieschl, S., & Bromme, R. (2014a). Competent or clueless? Users' knowledge and misconceptions about their online privacy management. *Computers in Human Behavior, 41*, 212–219. doi:10.1016/j.chb.2014.09.033.

Moll, R., Pieschl, S., & Bromme, R. (2014b). Trust into collective privacy? The role of subjective theories for self-disclosure in online social networks. *Societies, 4*, 770–784. doi:10.3390/ soc4040770.

Moll, R., Pieschl, S., & Bromme, R. (2015a). Blessed oblivion? Knowledge and metacognitive accuracy in online social networks. *International Journal of Developmental Science, 9*(2), 57–60. doi:10.3233/DEV-14155.

Moll, R., Pieschl, S., & Bromme, R. (2015b). *Achieving collective privacy—The impact of noise cues onto online users' audience expectations*. Manuscript submitted for publication.

Nickerson, R. S. (1999). How we know—and sometimes misjudge—what others know: Imputing one's own knowledge to others. *Psychological Bulletin, 125*(6), 737–759. doi:10.1037/0033-2909.125.6.737.

Nickerson, R. S., Baddeley, A., & Freeman, B. (1987). Are people's estimates of what other people know influenced by what they themselves know? *Acta Psychologica, 64*, 245–259. doi:10.1016/0001-6918(87)90010-2.

Norberg, P. A., Horne, D. R., & Horne, D. A. (2007). The privacy paradox: Personal information disclosure intentions versus behaviors. *The Journal of Consumer Affairs, 41*(1), 100–126. doi:10.1111/j.1083-6101.2009.01494.x.

Petronio, S. (2002). *Boundaries of privacy: Dialectics of disclosure*. Albany, NY: State University of New York Press.

Pieschl, S., Kuhlmann, C., & Porsch, T. (2015). Beware of publicity! Perceived distress of negative cyber incidents and implications for defining cyberbullying. *Journal of School Violence, 14*(1), 111–132. doi:10.1080/15388220.2014.971363.

Pieschl, S., & Moll, R. (2015). *For they know not what they do? Target memory and metacognitive monitoring of self-disclosures on online social networks*. Unpublished manuscript, Westfälische Wilhelms-Universität Münster, Germany.

Pieschl, S., & Porsch, T. (2014). Cybermobbing—mehr als "Ärgern im Internet" [Cyberbullying—More than "teasing on the Internet"]. In T. Porsch & S. Pieschl (Eds.), *Neue Medien und deren Schatten. Mediennutzung, Medienwirkung und Medienkompetenz* [New media and their shadows. Media use, media effects, and media literacy] (pp. 133–158). Göttingen: Hogrefe.

Pintrich, P. R., Wolters, C. A., & Baxter, G. P. (2000). Assessing metacognition and self-regulated learning. In G. Schraw & J. Impara (Eds.), *Issues in the measurement of metacognition* (pp. 43–97). Lincoln, NE: The University of Nebraska Press.

Quandt, T. (2012). What's left of trust in a network society? An evolutionary model and critical discussion of trust and societal communication. *European Journal of Communication, 27*(1), 7–21. doi:10.1177/0267323111434452.

Reinecke, L., Aufenanger, S., Beutel, M. E., Dreier, M., Quiring, O., Wölfling, K., et al. (2015). Digital stress over the life span: The effects of communication load and internet multitasking on perceived stress and psychological health impairments in a German probability sample. In: *Proceedings of the 65th Annual Conference of the International Communication Association (ICA)*. San Juan, Puerto Rico.

Rodriguez, M. G., Gummadi, K., & Schoelkopf, B. (2014). Quantifying information overload in social media and its impact on social contagions. In: *Proceedings of the 8th International AAAI Conference on Weblogs and Social Media (ICWSM)*, June 2014. Ann Arbor, MI. http://arxiv.org/abs/1403.6838

Schaar, P. (2009). *Das Ende der Privatssphäre – Der Weg in die Überwachungsgesellschaft* [The end of privacy—Living in the surveillance society]. München: Bertelsmann Verlag.

Slonje, R., Smith, P. K., & Frisén, A. (2013). The nature of cyberbullying, and strategies for prevention. *Computers in Human Behavior, 29*, 26–32. doi:10.1016/j.chb.2012.05.024.

Solove, D. J. (2007). 'I've got nothing to hide' and other misunderstandings of privacy. *San Diego Law Review, 44*, 745–772.

Sperber, D., Clément, F., Heintz, C., Mascaro, O., Mercier, H., Origgi, G., et al. (2010). Epistemic vigilance. *Mind and Language, 25*, 359–393. doi:10.1111/j.1468-0017.2010.01394.x.

Taddei, S., & Contena, B. (2013). Privacy, trust and control: Which relationships with online self-disclosure? *Computers in Human Behavior, 29*(3), 821–826. doi:10.1016/j.chb.2012.11.022.

Toffler, A. (1970). *Future shock*. New York: Random House.

Trepte, S., & Dienlin, T. (2014). Privatsphäre im Internet [Privacy on the internet]. In T. Porsch & S. Pieschl (Eds.), *Neue Medien und deren Schatten. Mediennutzung, Medienwirkung und Medienkompetenz* [New media and their shadows. Media use, media effects, and media literacy] (pp. 53–80). Göttingen: Hogrefe.

Trepte, S., Teutsch, D., Masur, P. K., Eicher, C., Fischer, M., Hennhöfer, A., et al. (2015). Do people know about privacy and data protection strategies? Towards the "Online Privacy Literacy Scale" (OPLIS). In S. Gutwirth, R. Leenes, & P. de Hert (Eds.), *Reforming European data protection law* (pp. 333–365). Heidelberg: Springer Netherlands. doi:10. 1007/978-94-017-9385-8.

Van Alsenoy, B., Verdoodt, V., Heyman, R., Ausloos, J., & Wauters, E. (2015). *From social media service to advertising network—A critical analysis of Facebook's revised policies and terms*. Accessed September 30, 2015, from http://www.law.kuleuven.be/icri/en/news/item/ facebooks-revised-policies-and-terms-v1-1.pdf

Printed in the United States
By Bookmasters

Printed in the United States
By Bookmasters